Solutions for the World's Biggest Problems

The world has many pressing problems. Thanks to the efforts of governments, NGOs, and individual activists there is no shortage of ideas for resolving them. However, even if all governments were willing to spend more money on solving the problems, we cannot do it all at once. We have to prioritize; and in order to do this we need a better sense of the costs and benefits of each "solution."

Solutions for the World's Biggest Problems offers a rigorous overview of twenty-three of the world's biggest problems relating to the environment, governance, economics, and health and population. Leading economists provide a short survey of the state-of-the-art analysis and sketch out some promising policy solutions for which they provide cost–benefit ratios.

The book is aimed not just at policy makers, but also at the many thousands of concerned citizens who want to see progress in the fight against poverty, disease, armed conflict and environmental degradation. Finding the best solutions requires as wide and as informed a debate as possible. To this end, a unique feature of the book is the provision of freely downloadable software which allows individual readers to make their own prioritizations of their preferred options for spending money to make the world a better place.

Bjørn Lomborg is Director of the Copenhagen Consensus Center and Adjunct Professor at Copenhagen Business School. He is the author of the controversial bestseller, *The Skeptical Environmentalist* (Cambridge, 2001), and was named as one of the most globally influential people by *Time* magazine in 2004.

Contributors:

Harold Alderman, Kym Anderson, Jere R. Behrman, Dan Biller, Paul Collier, Ian Coxhead, J. Paul Dunne, Henk Folmer, Michael J. Greenwood, Peter Blair Henry, John Hoddinott, Guy Hutton, Dean T. Jamison, Daniel Linotte, Katerina Lisenkova, Bjørn Lomborg, Donato Masciandaro, Keith E. Maskus, Jeffrey A. Miron, Peter F. Orazem, Ragnar Øygard, Harry Anthony Patrinos, Roger A. Pielke, Jr., Susan Rose-Ackerman, G. Cornelis van Kooten, Brinda Viswanathan, Robert E. Wright, Gary Yohe

Solutions for the World's Biggest Problems

Costs and Benefits

Edited by

BJØRN LOMBORG

CAMBRIDGE UNIVERSITY PRESS

CAMBRIDGE UNIVERSITY PRESS
Cambridge, New York, Melbourne, Madrid, Cape Town, Singapore, São Paulo

Cambridge University Press
The Edinburgh Building, Cambridge CB2 8RU, UK

Published in the United States of America by Cambridge University Press, New York

www.cambridge.org
Information on this title: www.cambridge.org/9780521715973

© Copenhagen Consensus Center 2007

This publication is in copyright. Subject to statutory exception
and to the provisions of relevant collective licensing agreements,
no reproduction of any part may take place without
the written permission of Cambridge University Press.

First published 2007

Printed in the United Kingdom at the University Press, Cambridge

A catalogue record for this publication is available from the British Library

This book was made possible by generous donation from The Tuborg Foundation.

ISBN   978-0-521-88772-4   hardback
ISBN   978-0-521-71597-3   paperback

Because of the unusual speed of publication of this book, it has not
proved possible to provide complete details for some of the references
cited in the text. The publisher will continue to attempt to provide this
information, and it will be displayed on the Cambridge University Press
website at http://www.cambridge.org/9780521715973

Cambridge University Press has no responsibility for
the persistence or accuracy of URLs for external or
third-party internet websites referred to in this book,
and does not guarantee that any content on such
websites is, or will remain, accurate or appropriate.

Contents

Figures

Tables

Contributors

HAROLD ALDERMAN is Social Protection Advisor in the Africa Region of the World Bank.

KYM ANDERSON is Professor of Economics at the University of Adelaide, Australia, and Lead Economist in the International Trade Unit of the World Bank's Development Research Group.

JERE R. BEHRMAN is the William R. Kenan, Jr. Professor of Economics and Research Associate of the Population Studies Center, University of Pennsylvania.

DAN BILLER is Lead Economist in the World Bank's East Asia and the Pacific Region, Sustainable Development Department.

PAUL COLLIER is Professor of Economics, Director for the Centre for the Study of African Economies, and Professorial Fellow of St Antony's College, Oxford University.

IAN COXHEAD is Professor of Agricultural and Applied Economics, University of Wisconsin-Madison.

J. PAUL DUNNE is Professor of Economics at the School of Economics, Bristol Business School, University of the West of England, Bristol.

HENK FOLMER is Professor of Research Methodology, Department of Spatial Sciences and Professor of Environmental and Resource Economics, Department of Economics, University of Groningen, The Netherlands.

MICHAEL J. GREENWOOD is Professor of Economics, University of Colorado at Boulder.

PETER BLAIR HENRY is Professor of Economics, Stanford University Graduate School of Business, Research Associate of the National Bureau of Economic Research, and a non-resident senior fellow of the Brookings Institution.

JOHN HODDINOTT is Deputy Division Director, FCND, International Food Policy Research Institute.

GUY HUTTON is the Founding Director of DSI, Development Solutions International.

DEAN T. JAMISON is the T. & G. Angelopoulos Visiting Professor of Public Health and International Development at the John F. Kennedy School of Government and the School of Public Health, Harvard University and Professor in the School of Medicine, University of California, San Francisco.

DANIEL LINOTTE is an international consultant in applied economics and security. He was formerly Senior Adviser to the Organization for Security and Co-operation in Europe and governments in the Balkans and Caucasus.

KATERINA LISENKOVA is Research Fellow, University of Strathclyde.

DONATO MASCIANDARO is Professor and Chair of Economics of Financial Regulation, Bocconi University, Milan.

KEITH E. MASKUS is Stanford Calderwood Professor of Economics at the University of Colorado, Boulder.

JEFFREY A. MIRON is Senior Lecturer, Department of Economics, Harvard University.

PETER F. ORAZEM is University Professor of Economics, Department of Economics, Iowa State University.

RAGNAR ØYGARD is Associate Professor, Department of Economics and Resource Management, Norwegian University of Life Sciences, Ås, Norway.

HARRY ANTHONY PATRINOS is Lead Education Economist at the World Bank.

ROGER A. PIELKE JR. is Professor in the Environmental Studies Program and a fellow of the Cooperative Institute for Research in Environmental Sciences, University of Colorado at Boulder.

SUSAN ROSE-ACKERMAN is Henry R. Luce Professor of Jurisprudence, Law School and Department of Political Science, Yale University.

G. CORNELIS VAN KOOTEN is Professor and Canada Research Chair in Environmental Studies, Department of Economics, University of Victoria, Canada and Professor of Agricultural Economics, Wageningen University, The Netherlands.

BRINDA VISWANATHAN is Associate Professor, Madras School of Economics.

ROBERT E. WRIGHT is Professor of Economics in the Strathclyde Business School, Department of Economics, University of Strathclyde.

GARY YOHE is Woodhouse/Sysco Professor of Economics, Economics Department, Wesleyan University.

Acknowledgements

It has been possible to compile this important and comprehensive publication of global challenges and their solutions only through the dedicated effort of a large number of people. We wish to offer special thanks to The Tuborg Foundation and its former Deputy Director Finn Terkelsen, who has financed the chapters of this book and shown great interest in the project. Many thanks should also be given to all the chapter contributors for taking part in the project and for the interesting analyses and results they have brought about. The contribution of authors is the very core of the Copenhagen Consensus process and it is remarkable to bring so many important topics and economic experts together in one publication. The Copenhagen Consensus team and especially Sonja Thomsen and Elsebeth Søndergaard deserve acknowledgement for their commitment and assistance in editing the chapters. We also thank David Young and Martin Livermore for providing valuable comments on the book. Finally, we are indebted to the team at Cambridge University Press for wanting to publish the work of the many contributors and for helping put it all together under severe time constraints. This book is dedicated to all these people who put their insights and effort into this project.

Bjørn Lomborg
Copenhagen, June 2007

Introduction

BJØRN LOMBORG

The simple idea

A mayor has a million dollar surplus which he wants to allocate to a good cause. Dozens of groups clamor for the cash. One wants to buy computers for an inner-city high school. Another hopes to beautify a local park. A third would promote energy efficiency. Each group makes a persuasive case outlining the benefits they could achieve. What should the politician do?

The straightforward answer is to divide the cash into equal amounts. Intuitively, the idea seems fair: nobody will walk away empty-handed. But the obvious answer is probably wrong.

With more information, it is possible to quantify the spin-offs from each alternative. Some options will always be better than others. Shouldn't any extra money go first to the cause with the greatest social value? The idea is simple: with scarce resources it is necessary to prioritize.

On a larger scale, this is what underpins the Copenhagen Consensus. Imagine you had $75bn to donate to worthwhile causes. You could do a tremendous amount of good. What would you do?

The world has many pressing problems. Governments and the United Nations have massive – but limited – budgets to reduce suffering. Even they tend to distribute any extra money thinly across different causes, often following the media's roving attention. A little extra is spent battling HIV/AIDS, malaria and malnutrition. Some more is devoted to stamping out corruption and conflict. Other cash is set aside for holding back climate change and warding off avian flu.

If politicians give everyone something, nobody complains. It's politically astute. But it may not be the best use of our resources.

The Copenhagen Consensus in 2004 was the first attempt to put this simple idea into action in a transparent way. A short list of ten major problems was devised and priorities agreed. The results – published

1

as *Global Crises, Global Solutions* – were thought-provoking. In turn this led to more focused Copenhagen Consensus events designed to assist the United Nations and Latin America. In 2008 a new global Copenhagen Consensus will take place, once again stocktaking the world's biggest problems.

Why should we prioritize?

Tremendous progress has been made in our lifetimes. People in most countries live longer, healthier lives; air and water quality in the developed world is generally getting better; and a much larger population is being adequately fed.

But there are still many problems to tackle. The minority of us lucky enough to have been born in the developed world take for granted universal education, an assured food supply and clean, piped water. Hundreds of millions of people are not so lucky. And although the world's problems fall disproportionately heavily on the developing world, rich countries also have their own problems, including drugs, conflicts and corruption.

When it comes to the globe's toughest issues, policy-makers have a huge list of spending possibilities akin to a gigantic menu at a restaurant. But this menu comes without prices or serving sizes. If an international agency spends $10m on one project instead of another, how much more good will it do? Global leaders can rarely answer that question. They need better information and so do ordinary citizens. Economics gives us the tools to look at the costs of taking effective action and measure the expected benefits. When we know the costs and benefits, it will be a lot easier to choose the best projects – the projects which do the most good with the money available.

National governments prioritize all the time. Government revenues are finite and there are many competing demands for expenditure. Responsible economic management means balancing priorities between defense, education, healthcare and welfare. This prioritization is straightforward enough in a democratic nation state: although the debate may be vigorous and high-pitched, the result is an explicitly acknowledged trade-off between different segments of society and different problem areas for a share of a finite pot of money. There is widespread recognition that governments do not have infinite resources and that they must satisfy important social needs without running unsustainable deficits.

But when we come to global welfare projects, the situation gets murky. We seem to believe that we can achieve anything, that the pool of money is infinite, and that everything should be tackled at once.

In effect, the majority of the big decisions are made by international agencies that receive money from rich nations and use it for the benefit of the world, especially developing countries. Each such organization has its own remit, scope of work and funding base. But most operate as independent silos. There is little incentive for cross-agency comparison. After all, there's little to be gained and much to lose if one organization's work turns out to be costlier or less effective than that of another. As a result, there are few attempts to contrast the work of, say, the United Nations Environment Program (UNEP) with that of the United Nations Educational, Scientific and Cultural Organization (UNESCO), and almost no overt efforts at comparing the outcomes achieved by development charities such as Oxfam and Médecins Sans Frontières.

Of course, in principle we ought to deal with all the world's woes. We should win the war against hunger, end conflicts, stop communicable diseases, provide clean drinking water, step up education and halt climate change. But we don't. We live in a world with limited resources and even more limited attention for our biggest problems.

This means we have to start asking the crucial question: if we don't do it all, what should we do first?

An explicit economic prioritization between the world's many different problem areas hasn't effectively been attempted outside the Copenhagen Consensus. In fact, the very idea of prioritization sparks considerable resentment. I think it's disliked because prioritization means we don't just work out where we should do more (which is seen as benevolent) but we also identify challenges that we should put aside for later (which is seen as cynical).

This view puzzles me; not talking about prioritization does not make it go away. We can only spend each dollar once, so we are actually prioritizing with every dollar we spend doing good. If we don't discuss our priorities then they just become murkier, less democratic and less efficient. Refusing to decide for ourselves explicitly what deserves our immediate attention means letting somebody else make that call. Often, the media sets decision-makers' priorities. That's wrong. Imagine doctors at a perpetually overrun hospital refusing to perform triage on casualties, instead attending all patients as they arrive and fast-tracking those whose families made the most fuss. A failure to prioritize explicitly wastes resources and costs lives.

Choosing between alternative solutions to global challenges does not mean we should ignore the lower-priority ones. It is just that more people will benefit more quickly if the higher-priority items are tackled first. This will then free up resources to tackle the issues originally given a lower priority. Trying to deal with every challenge at once simply reduces the level of effective help.

Where should we prioritize?

Copenhagen Consensus focuses on the funding that the developed world spends on improving the world in general. Of course, most nations spend the vast bulk of their cash on themselves – perhaps 99 percent of developed nations' GDP. In a well-functioning political system, this internal spending already gets prioritized. Moreover, the relevant players are typically well represented – both donors (taxpayers) and a wide range of recipients – which allows for a clearly delineated debate about trade-offs.

However, the last 1 percent of spending – the portion that goes outside a nation's borders – is less well developed. This spending ranges from Official Development Assistance (ODA) to peacekeeping forces, research into tropical diseases and some attempts to alleviate crossboundary environmental pollution and the like.

Here, the donors participate in a debate but the recipients typically do not, meaning their interests are instead represented by pictures and stories in the press. That only donors are present goes some way to explain why total spending is rather low. That the recipients are only represented in the media means that there is a tendency for resources to go to the places with the best and most accessible stories and the cutest pictures tugging at our heartstrings. One massive tsunami might get global attention and prompt millions of dollars of aid (and hundreds of foreign journalists) to pour in, while another tragic earthquake in a more remote region of the world will be all but forgotten, particularly if it happens when news bulletins are already crowded. Needless to say, this form of prioritization is not likely to achieve the most good.

Often, explicit prioritization is ignored altogether by policymakers. The United Nations Millennium Development Goals (MDGs) consist of a long list of laudable things to achieve by 2015 (including halving the proportion of people living on less than a dollar a day, halving the proportion of people who suffer from hunger, ensuring that all boys and girls complete a full course of primary schooling, and reducing by two-thirds the mortality rate among children under five and the maternal mortality ratio). Achieving these important goals is estimated to cost around US$40–70bn extra per year. That kind of funding isn't forthcoming. Because the goals aren't prioritized, the world is not attempting to knock off the most important one first – in fact, nobody's having a discussion about what the most pressing goal might be.

The MDGs are also not the only commitments the world has signed up to. Countries at the United Nations have signed major treaties including sustainable development (in Rio), climate change (in the Climate Convention Framework), the Convention against Transnational Organized Crime (Palermo), the International Convention for the Suppression of the Financing of Terrorism (New York) and biological diversity (Cartagena Protocol on Biosafety).

What should we prioritize?

This is the main topic of this book, and takes up the rest of the chapters. In the 2004 Copenhagen Consensus we tried to identify all the world's major challenges by scanning every major United Nations publication between 2000 and 2003: if an issue was sufficiently important to merit consideration at the Copenhagen Consensus, it was unlikely to have gone unmentioned in any UN publication, given that organization's commitment to tackle global problems. This scan resulted in a multitude of challenges being identified.

We narrowed this unwieldy list by considering only major issues with a global scope, capable of being defined, evaluated and addressed in a reasonably rigorous fashion. Of course, not all challenges were at the same level, and to some extent there is an overlap. This we considered unavoidable and harmless, since the goal of the list was didactic and meant only to inform the eventual list of opportunities. Moreover, some overarching "challenges" like poverty are not considered in their entirety, since they consist of many different subcategory problems that are more easily addressable like a lack of access to healthcare, education, water and free access to markets.

One very plausible approach would be to identify the problem affecting the most people, and then try to solve that first.

However, tackling the "biggest" problems first doesn't work. A challenge might be vast, but if we don't have a good way of mitigating it, then we shouldn't focus on it first. At the end of the day, the biggest personal problem each of us faces is that we will all die. Yet we don't have good technology or knowledge to solve that problem, so therefore we don't devote every waking second of our lives to warding off every conceivable form of the Grim Reaper.

Thus, instead of dwelling on the biggest *problems*, we should focus on identifying the best *solutions*. This is why all the chapters on individual challenges don't just say "this is a big problem" but instead, "here are some of the smartest and most feasible solutions and this is what they would cost and what they would achieve."

How do we prioritize?

It's tempting to base our decisions on a utopian vision of an entirely different and much better world where all major challenges can be entirely wiped out. But embracing a solution to its fullest extent is often unrealistic and ultimately unhelpful. Providing drinking water to everyone in the world would probably be prohibitively expensive (getting piped water to the last family living on a mountain-top would be infeasible), but getting water to half of those without it might be a great idea.

That is why the Copenhagen Consensus process suggests we look at *partial* (or marginal) change – how we might make the world a somewhat better place, starting from where we are right now. This recognizes that most solutions do not completely solve a problem, but somewhat ameliorate it. The advantage of this reality-based approach is that partial solutions are achievable and our models are much better at predicting how much they could improve a problem.

At the heart of the Copenhagen Consensus, we ask ourselves a question that drives everything else: if we had an extra $75bn to do good for the world over the coming four years, where could that money do the most good? The resulting prioritized list of solutions identifies where we could do the most good, the second-most good, etc.

This does not imply that we should only spend money on the top solution. While it is the best investment, all the solutions towards the top of the list are very good solutions, where we can achieve a lot with our money. What it does mean is that we should not spend money on, say, solution number 40, while we still haven't tackled 1, 2 and 3.

The Copenhagen Consensus does not make any decision on what would be an appropriate level of extra investment. If we only invested another $10bn, the list would still make sense except we could not do as much. Likewise, if the world were to invest $150bn, we could go even further down the list.

To rank these partial solutions, the Copenhagen Consensus process utilizes a cost-benefit analysis.

To some this sounds heartless. But in reality, it's just a way of trying to measure the expense and advantages of any suggested partial solution. While it is typically easy to find the cost of each approach (providing clean drinking water means spending money on piping, drilling, maintenance, etc.), it is often harder to measure the benefits in monetary terms (less sickness, more comfort, better hygiene, better productivity, societal consequences from less sickness, etc.). However, economists have worked hard to put prices on many of these outcomes, based on individual behavior (our own implicit valuation) or social behavior (society's implicit valuation). If we are to make meaningful comparisons between the vast array of different solutions to the world's many woes, measuring costs *and* benefits seems to be an efficient and transparent way to convey crucial information about these issues.

Problems of prioritization

The four biggest concerns expressed about economic cost-benefit analysis are simply put.

- How can you put a value on human life?
- How do you balance current and future needs?
- What about the interaction between different problems and their solutions?
- Should you really focus on economics when choosing?

These are questions which arise because of humans' natural compassion, and they deserve a proper answer.

We cannot wave a magic wand and make the world's problems disappear. Generally, there are no silver bullets. We have to focus resources on an achievable number of clear, realistic objectives if we are to make progress. The best tool to handle this prioritization is economic cost–benefit analysis.

This does mean that we have to put a value on costs and benefits to compare them. Refusing to put a value on human life does not help to save lives. In practice, prioritization occurs in healthcare and aid programs all the time. That's how we know, for example, that it makes much more sense to have a program of mass vaccination than to invest in clinics to treat people who are ill. Prevention is nearly always better and more cost-effective than curing.

One tool that helps us compare the burden of major challenges is the measure of the "Disability Adjusted Life Year" or DALY. The DALY adds up the years of life that are lost and the impact of disability.

Some people will still find this approach clinical and even distasteful, but difficult decisions need to be underpinned by the best possible framework, and this is the best we have at present.

How do we balance our own needs against those of future generations? In essence, there must always be some discounting: if not, we could eventually starve now to do better for our grandchildren. The problem comes in setting the actual discount rate. For commercial projects, it is considered normal to discount at the level of current or expected market interest rates. Economists often recommend a rate of 6 percent for discounting development projects, and we have also taken this as a baseline for our evaluation.

However, we have also asked our authors to use a rate of 3 percent for comparison. This lower rate means that projects which take longer to produce significant benefits still look attractive. Comparing the results for the two discount rates shows the sensitivity of the analysis to different assumptions and also gives us more information on which to base decisions. Which rate is more appropriate is a matter for debate, but the important thing is to have a consistent basis for comparison.

The issue of the discount rate becomes particularly important in the case of climate change. Proposed solutions to climate change show no benefits for several decades, but their ultimate value could be enormous. Conventional discounting, even at the lower rate we use, makes any intervention – which would have very high up-front costs – unattractive in cost–benefit terms. Some economists (including Sir Nicholas Stern in his 2006 report, *The Economics of Climate Change*) argue that it is wrong to value our needs above those of our grand-children, and that we should effectively have a zero rate of pure time preference. Clearly, embracing this suggestion would mean we must make huge investments to tackle all future problems. Compare this to a problem like malaria where small immediate costs can lead to large benefits which begin to accrue quite quickly. In this case, normal economic discounting still makes the benefit–cost ratio attractive.

Although delineating twenty-three separate global challenges makes sense – because only in this way do we have a chance to make a proper analysis and prioritization – in practice, boundaries are not clearly defined. In particular, action in one area will have indirect positive effects in others. For example, supplying clean water to rural farmers can free women and children from the task of fetching water from far away, allowing more time for children to attend school. However, in principle all of these issues should be dealt with in the analysis of clean drinking water.

Clearly, any attempt to define and analyze the world's largest problem areas is open to criticism, but we believe that the Copenhagen Consensus has the merits of clarity, rigor and transparency and forms a good basis for decision-making. There are those who argue that the whole process is skewed against environmental issues because of their longer time horizons, but this is clearly not the case. At the end of the day, all the partial solutions tackled here will have short- and long-term costs and short- and long-term benefits. Dealing with malaria will not only help present generations but also improve the lives of future generations, as they stand on the shoulders of their healthier parents.

High-profile figures in the global debate – Jeffrey Sachs included – argue that only including economists in the Copenhagen Consensus is inappropriate, and that the prioritization should only be made by natural science experts in each of the different issues. The problem is that these experts lack a common denominator for setting priorities. If you ask a climatologist, you're likely to be told that climate change is the biggest issue facing the planet. If you ask a malaria expert, she will probably say malaria is the biggest issue. If we ask them jointly to make a decision where to allocate extra resources, we shouldn't be surprised if they choose the intuitive solution of the fictional mayor in the opening paragraph – spending half on each problem, neglecting the reality that one investment might do much more good than the other.

I believe, along with all the members of the Copenhagen Consensus team, that there is a moral imperative to do global good in ways which will bring lasting benefits to as many people as possible, as quickly as possible. Because of the wide variety of projects which could be funded, economic cost–benefit analysis provides the best and most rational tool for comparison and decision-making. By bringing together expert economists who do not have specific interests in any one project, we hope that we can make progress towards a rational and transparent choice of which of the world's problems to tackle first.

Your part

We asked many international economists to tell us about each of the biggest challenges for humanity and what can be done. This book is the result.

The expert panel for the Copenhagen Consensus in 2008 will make their pick of the ten issues that will be studied in more detail. But we invite you to read all the chapters and make your own individual prioritization. You will find guidance on how to do this in the last chapter of the book.

We believe the Copenhagen Consensus process has much to offer policy-makers, philanthropic organizations and generous individuals. But it becomes much more powerful if more people get involved, not just by reading the results in the media, but by making their own judgments. There are no absolutely right answers. New studies will be done on challenges, new solutions will be identified, and fresh analysis will enable us to see things in a different light. It is the discipline of the process which is important. There are critical decisions to be taken, and these must be underpinned with a rational framework.

We believe this book is the broadest published look at the major challenges facing the world today. Even so, it is not entirely comprehensive: some of the problems we identified turn out to have received very little or no economic research. Surprisingly, these include the area of infrastructure, the lack of which can be a major barrier to development in many countries: there are simply too few economists working in this area. While the research for this book is therefore not complete, it at least gives us the ability to tackle the highest-priority challenges from an extremely wide range of areas, and it can thus make a significant contribution towards improving the lot of people round the world.

For the rest of this chapter, we summarize the key points from the problem papers which you can read in full in later chapters. The chapters are written by economists in each field and are based on the existing literature plus the authors' own analysis. They aim to show clearly the assumptions used and the way calculations are done. Inevitably, hard data is more difficult to identify for certain challenges, and in no case are the figures to be taken as complete and accurate. These are the experts' estimates, sufficient in most cases to make meaningful comparisons and set priorities.

Economic challenges

It may seem as though purely economic issues should rate low on any prioritization which has human welfare at its heart, but in fact these challenges can present significant barriers for development at a personal level. They deserve full consideration.

"Financial Instability" is a recurrent problem for many developing countries. Peter Blair Henry (Stanford University) argues that this problem may wipe out much more than the 1 percent of emerging nations' GDP *growth* which has previously been estimated. He points out that although nations may statistically suffer a financial crisis only every twelve years, the impact is a set-back of around 9 percent of economic output when it does occur. The economic devastation reduces the ability of poor nations to care for their most vulnerable citizens.

Weak market institutions prevent developing nations from issuing debt in their own currencies, so Henry sees a crucial need to reform market institutions. Sound institutions give governments credibility and create confidence that they will not default on loans.

Henry proposes building developing nations' capacity to design and implement institutional reforms that will be suited to their own circumstances. For an estimated annual cost of $0.5bn, the annual gross benefits could be over $150bn. On the face of it, economic considerations alone would make this proposition very attractive. It addresses the root of the problem of financial instability and could even lead to better overall governance and faith in public institutions.

The second chapter in this section addresses "Lack of Intellectual Property Rights." According to Keith Maskus (University of Colorado), this problem doesn't just hold back economic progress, but also claims lives. That's because weak intellectual property rights allow producers of potentially dangerous counterfeit drugs and other products to prosper.

If we can protect and foster intellectual property rights in developing nations, we can encourage more local innovation and foreign investment. However, improved protection will only work when it's backed up by good general governance, and that's much more complicated to achieve.

Maskus comes up with two proposals. The first is to improve intellectual property regulations and their enforcement. The cost on a per-country basis would be quite modest – $4–5m for set-up, with annual costs of several million dollars after that. Although this might seem cheap, it certainly won't be easy: there are around 150 countries that could benefit from this treatment, and it could take twenty years before many become self-sufficient. That means that total costs for the project would reach between $3.5bn and $4.1bn (depending whether we use a 6 percent or 3 percent discount rate).

The benefits would come from better healthcare (because of a reduction in counterfeiting of medicines), more innovation and job creation. Although the ongoing costs would come to $1.9bn annually over the course of the project, benefits would be between 2.4 and 5.2 times greater.

Secondly, Maskus believes companies in developing countries should be encouraged to protect their intellectual property, perhaps most controversially by providing more opportunities for students to study and work in industrialized countries. The important issue is to raise awareness about intellectual property rights and spread information about techniques and marketing strategies. In this case, for a total (discounted) outlay of around $6bn, benefits are estimated to be about 9 times greater.

The author himself counsels caution in estimating real direct benefits of the two solutions which, combined with fairly modest benefit–cost ratios, might make this seem a low priority. We should not forget that such basic groundwork might pay handsome indirect dividends as part of a package of measures which could enable strong and sustained economic development.

The problem of "Money Laundering" is discussed by Donato Masciandaro (Bocconi University, Milan). Cutting the money flow to terror and crime would save money, lives and heartbreak.

While it's easy to see why terrorism finance must be stopped, money laundering is sometimes seen as a victimless crime. It's helpful to remember that a proportion of the cash being "recycled" will be used to finance more criminal ventures.

Handlers of crime and terror money may be corrupt or honest but insecure. The easy use of offshore financial centers poses a significant concern.

Because of its very nature, the extent of money laundering is difficult to estimate, although there's general agreement it adds up to several percent of world GDP. The direct economic impact might be relatively small, but the indirect effect on the victims of crime is certainly significant. Masciandaro estimates the net value of money laundering to come to an astonishing $3.8tn, equivalent to 9 percent of world GDP.

His proposed solution is to set up a regulatory system to deter institutions from getting involved in money laundering, whether deliberately or inadvertently. The benefit to the global economy could be $1.7tn. The regulation would come at considerable cost, because it would reduce the efficiency of the banking sector. But even taking this into account, the benefits outweigh the costs by 3 to 1.

Limiting the scope for criminal activity would greatly reduce the misery and financial loss for victims of crime and terror.

Kym Anderson (University of Adelaide and World Bank) builds on his contribution to the 2004 Copenhagen Consensus in his chapter on "Subsidies and Trade Barriers". Anderson focuses on the harm caused by government intervention in markets. Much of this burden is carried by the poor.

Completely removing all trade barriers and agricultural barriers would have benefits estimated to reach $287bn a year. Put services on the trade liberalization table and those benefits would skyrocket to $2,400bn. This would provide a massive boost to the global economy, and developing nations would receive many of the benefits.

While global trade liberalization would boost GDP growth rates significantly, the benefits of regional free-trade areas are much smaller.

There are costs, of course. Cushioning those who lose their jobs would prove a short-term headache, although studies indicate that the boost to economic growth would soon create many new jobs.

The benefits would be somewhere between 67 and 260 times the costs, depending on the assumptions and discount rate we use. These figures make a compelling argument for trade liberalization to receive a high priority from decision-makers, particularly given the longer-term benefits which such widely distributed additional prosperity could bring.

Environmental challenges

For many, the environment has become the world's greatest cause of concern. The 2004 Copenhagen Consensus was criticized because of the low priority it gave to environmental matters. This book includes six major challenges in this category.

Guy Hutton (Development Solutions International) contributes with a chapter on "Air Pollution." He identifies two main problem areas: *indoor* pollution from wood and other fires made from plant matter (known as biomass). This is mainly an issue in rural areas, while *outdoor* pollution from industry and transport is primarily urban.

Smoke from indoor cooking fires is estimated to kill more than 1.5 million people annually. In economic terms, it has a total disease burden of 38.5 million DALYs, hurting developing countries the most. Outdoor air pollution may cause around half this number of deaths, with most lives lost in the developing countries of Asia.

Indoor air pollution can be reduced by moving away from solid fuel to alternatives like liquefied petroleum gas (LPG) or ethanol, and by using more efficient stoves. The world already has technical solutions to reduce outdoor air pollution, but cost puts these solutions out-of-reach for much of the developing world.

Hutton estimates it would cost around $23.6bn a year to switch half the users of solid fuel stoves to LPG. This would knock around $10bn off the cost of fuels and provide further health, time-saving and environmental benefits. Depending on the assumptions used, the benefits are between 3 and 4.7 times the costs.

Providing more efficient stoves for half the current solid fuel users would cost $2.3bn and save $36.7bn in fuel costs along with other major health benefits. This means the benefits outweigh the costs by 55:1.

Studies of outdoor air pollution abatement have generally been restricted to single cities or regions, whereas the Copenhagen Consensus aims to take a global approach. Typically though, the studies show that every dollar spent will produce $3 of benefit, and that is before we take into account indirect benefits for agricultural production and the broader environment.

Tackling air pollution – both indoors and outdoors – has a less impressive cost-benefit ratio than tackling some other issues, but the human welfare gains would be significant, and many see this as an essential component of sustainable development.

"Climate Change" has attracted enormous attention, and is the subject of a contribution from Gary Yohe (Wesleyan University). There is now well-established agreement that climate change is man-caused, but estimates of its projected impact continue to be revised and refined. Developing nations are most vulnerable, but the industrialized world is certainly not immune. The consensus view is that full solutions are not available but partial amelioration is an option.

It's possible to use economic analysis to work out the net cost of emitting each tonne of carbon into the air. However, the resulting estimates vary enormously, with a median of $13 per tonne, a mean of $43 and an upper range of more than $350. These differences reflect a range of assumptions on factors such as climate sensitivity, discount rate and equity rating.

Yohe advocates the introduction of a $50 per tonne carbon tax that would, in his view, have a positive benefit-cost ratio. The tax would need to increase by 2–3 percent each year. Although higher tax levels might be needed to make technologies such as carbon sequestration economically viable, an initial level of $50 or less (increasing annually) would certainly influence investment decisions in new generating capacity, for example. It would also produce a significant revenue stream which could be used to offset the inevitably regressive nature of the tax.

Because of uncertainties in the assumptions, the net benefits are difficult to quantify, but Yohe argues that not tackling climate change would undermine efforts to tackle other high-profile challenges.

"Deforestation," reviewed here by Henk Folmer (Universities of Groningen and Wageningen) and Cornelis van Kooten (Universities of Victoria and Wageningen), is today primarily a problem in the tropics; temperate forests have actually increased in area.

During the 1990s, there was a continuing steady loss of tropical forests: the decline was about 0.5 percent annually. The current rate of loss means that forests overall are not in immediate danger and, of course, regeneration is possible in time.

Tropical forests perform many useful services for humanity, including their role in carbon storage (in the face of climate change) and biodiversity maintenance.

While their economic value is largely derived from their destruction in the form of logging, it's important to note that commercial logging hardly ever employs clear felling any more.

There is no one cause for deforestation around the world. While commercial logging is largely to blame in Asia, agriculture is the major driver of deforestation in the Amazon. Agriculture and forests can coexist when sustainable farming practices are used (such as shifting farming areas to allow the forest to regenerate).

There is uncertainty about the role that increasing population plays in deforestation. The effect of deforestation on net incomes is also unknown. However, the ultimate driver of deforestation is government policy. This occurs in the form of incentives for citizens to clear forests to create agriculture, through indirect subsidies to loggers, and in policies that shift population growth from overcrowded cities to more remote forest regions.

The lack of vital information is a problem when it comes to this challenge. Government policy designed to reduce clear cutting could end up limiting the growth of agriculture and hampering the economic development of poor countries. On the other hand, some will argue that the role of forests in carbon sequestration may ultimately be too important to ignore.

"Land Degradation" is covered by Ian Coxhead (University of Wisconsin-Madison) and Ragnar Øygard (Norwegian University of Life Sciences). They focus on farmland and the deterioration that's caused by poor practice.

Major types of degradation include soil erosion, nutrient depletion and salinization. Some problems, such as loss of nutrients, are easily reversible, but it has been estimated that 0.3–0.5 percent of the world's arable land is permanently lost each year. This will not necessarily continue indefinitely: it is estimated that three-quarters of farmland has had fairly stable soil quality for half a century. But there has been substantial loss of productivity in developing countries, particularly in Africa and Central America. The bitter blow is that the degradation is occurring mainly in areas which are already marginal for agriculture.

Reducing pernicious subsidies would help, as would the elimination of tariff barriers which encourage the use of marginal local land, especially for food crops that compete with imports. Improving property rights would lead to better land management. Investment in agricultural technologies shows good rates of return and is likely to conserve land quality without compromising crop yields.

Benefit-cost ratios for the various approaches are difficult to estimate. However, some interventions that involve removing existing policy distortions would cost little or nothing and produce significant benefits. It is important to note that a growing, more prosperous world population will require a significant expansion of food production, and that solutions such as the removal of trade barriers and strengthening property rights are likely to be part of a general reform package to assist development in the world's poorest countries.

Dan Biller (World Bank) tackles problems caused by "The Economics of Biodiversity Loss" in his chapter. He uses biodiversity as shorthand for all our biological resources – whether we currently use them or not – and explains that putting a value on concepts such as altruism and our bequest to future generations means we can frame this challenge in terms of economic analysis.

Nevertheless, it is challenging to come up with a rigorous cost-benefit analysis that will be generally accepted.

In many cases, biological resources are compromised by perverse incentives introduced to support particular industries such as agriculture and fishing. The removal of these incentives may be politically difficult but the costs would not be particularly high.

Biller also recommends privatizing elements of biodiversity so that owners have a clear incentive to conserve (as, for example, in private game parks). Two other options are the bundling of certain aspects of biodiversity and the creation of a regulated market (e.g. fishing quotas) and using policy to secure a minimum level of biodiversity as a public good.

While many of us believe that biodiversity should be protected, some will question how this particular solution could be given a high priority, given this challenge seems less urgent than many others. The counter-argument is that extinction is irreversible; since we may not know the true value of a species until it is too late, precaution should prevail.

Roger Pielke Jr. (University of Colorado) writes about "Vulnerability to Natural Disasters." Natural disasters may claim proportionately fewer lives today, but economic loss from natural disasters – primarily earthquakes, floods and storms – has escalated rapidly in the developed world, and remains a major challenge to developing nations.

The case for reducing the vulnerability of societies to natural disasters is irrefutable. Reducing the vulnerability of a nation is much more effective, according to Pielke, than energy policies designed to reduce carbon dioxide emissions and mitigate the weather disasters of climate change.

In the context of the Copenhagen Consensus, this challenge poses a problem because there is a lack of proper cost-benefit analysis of proposed solutions. An odd cycle takes place: cost-benefit analysis is needed to justify spending money on vulnerability reduction, but an initial willingness to give such projects higher priority is needed to justify the cost-benefit analysis. It seems it's easier to access disaster relief funding after the worst has already happened. This may change along with attitudes as – for example – reinsurance contracts are introduced to share risks and hedge against uncertainties.

Nonetheless, there are many examples of successful, usually non-costed, mitigation policies, including changes to building codes (in earthquake zones) and evacuation plans coupled with accurate tracking of storm paths. Consider what happened to the Dominican Republic and Haiti (the two states on the island of Hispaniola) during the 2004 hurricane season: 2,000 people died in poor, unprepared Haiti, while fewer than 10 people passed away in the Dominican Republic which has emergency evacuation plans and a network of hurricane shelters.

Without a proper cost-benefit analysis, the strongest case for this challenge is made by the impressive benefits to be gained by adaptation to changing weather patterns (or, indeed, to current ones).

Governance challenges

The next set of challenges to be addressed comes under the general heading of "governance," and covers a diverse set of issues.

First up is "Arms Proliferation," covered by Paul Dunne of the University of the West of England. Although the genocide in Rwanda taught us horrifically that arms are not essential for widespread tragedy to unfold, proliferation can raise the probability of conflict and worsen its consequences. This is true whether we're talking about a build-up in more and more lethal technology or simply an increase in the supply of small arms.

Proliferation control can be expected to increase security and allow people to live more secure, prosperous lives.

It costs a fortune and much effort for a nation to get nuclear weapons, but once it has them there is the potential for international catastrophe.

Nuclear disarmament would be very expensive: safe dismantlement would cost the United States of America up to $31bn while clean-up costs could be ten times greater. Recent figures show that the total cost for the USA in financial year 2004 was around $2bn. But to a large extent these are costs which would have been incurred in any case as nuclear weapons aged, and the costs of maintaining nuclear weapons are still greater than those of dismantling. Overall, global costs could be $3–6bn a year, but these are dwarfed by the benefits of avoiding a nuclear war which could easily cost 5 percent of global GDP or over $1,500bn.

While the build-up of sophisticated conventional weapons systems can change the balance of power in a region and lead to wasteful expenditure, trade in small arms is most difficult to control and causes the most agony: it is estimated that half a million people are killed by "light" weapons annually.

Global military spending is reckoned to be about $1tn, or 2.6 percent of GDP, but the (legitimate) international arms trade represents only 0.5–0.6 percent of world trade. Anti-proliferation measures are unlikely to have major negative economic drawbacks overall, although a few countries (Russia in particular) would be hit harder. In any case, reduction in arms manufacture gives an opportunity for industrial growth in other sectors.

An effective United Nations intervention force could prevent potential conflicts taking hold. Developing such an agency would cost up to $50bn, but the benefits are massive. Relying on diplomatic pressure or sanctions is cheaper but once a war takes place (as in Iraq), costs escalate enormously.

An arms trade treaty would have significant enforcement costs, but benefits would be much higher than costs. The final option Dunne presents is a tax on arms transfers with the proceeds earmarked for international development. Even allowing for the benefits that the aid would bring, the positive spin-offs would be lower than for the other options.

War devastates lives, societies and countries and any effective intervention would seem to be well worth the price.

"Conflicts" is a closely related challenge explored by Paul Collier from Oxford University (co-author of a challenge chapter on civil wars for the

2004 Copenhagen Consensus). Security threats to developed countries are often the main focus of our attention, but poor countries are subject to the scourges of civil war, coups and high military spending.

Developing countries are more prone to civil wars, which carry enormous costs in both human and economic terms. There have been over 200 attempted or successful coups in Africa alone in the last 30 years, at a direct cost of about 3 percent of GDP in the year each coup occurred. Each action spurs additional indirect costs because military spending increases to avert or reinforce a coup. Intriguingly, military spending itself does nothing to reduce the threat of civil war.

Among the possible solutions is increased aid. This can be very helpful if properly applied in post-conflict situations, but there is a danger that money will just go straight into military spending. Conditional aid is estimated to have positive spin-offs that are worth double the amount spent.

Another option is the expansion of the role of peacekeeping forces. Although they are often seen as ineffective, an analysis of UN data suggests they have a significant benefit–cost ratio. Such intervention need not always be direct, but its existence "over the horizon" can be very helpful. A case in point is France's security policy towards Francophone Africa until the late 1990s. This is believed to have reduced the incidence of conflict by three-quarters – a benefit of about $5bn – for a cost of $1bn at most.

The favorable benefit-cost ratios and the seriousness of the challenge make a strong case for this to be a high priority.

"Corruption" is a topic covered by Susan Rose-Ackerman (Yale University), who also contributed to the 2004 Copenhagen Consensus.

Low-level corruption occurs when officials and others take opportunities to benefit personally within an otherwise functional legal framework. Although small-scale, the costs can be large: embezzlement in the Brazilian pharmaceutical sector has been estimated to reach $637m annually, and 42 percent of VAT revenues in Bolivia were lost prior to tax reform.

Higher-level or "grand" corruption has features in common with garden-variety corruption, but the consequences can be even more serious. The economy and faith in the government itself may be undermined. Whole areas of the public sector may be organized to collect bribes. A particularly egregious example is in education, where a study of seven countries estimated $2.5bn was being paid to "teachers" who do not teach. The result is not just economic inefficiency but the tragedy of a vast bulk of the population that is being very poorly educated.

Worldwide, more than $1tn changes hands in bribes each year – that's more than 3 percent of global income. Poorer countries or those with a low growth rate tend to suffer more corruption. This is probably part of a vicious circle, because corruption hikes the cost of doing business and discourages foreign direct investment.

Rose-Ackerman suggests the international community should help vulnerable nations to create appropriate counter-measures to corruption. She also advocates the increased enforcement of international treaties, the creation of agreements between investors and poor but resource-rich countries, and the reduction of money laundering.

Real costs are impossible to estimate but the author suggests that an investment of $5bn might reduce bribes by 10 percent or $100bn. A reduction in corruption would mean that spending on other global challenges would become more effective.

For the challenge of "Lack of Education," Peter Orazem of Iowa State University specifically targets strategies to combat illiteracy. Investment in education pays dividends, but a year's schooling is only worthwhile if it develops basic cognitive skills such as literacy.

Orazem relies on demand-side policies to encourage greater take-up of primary education and better literacy rates. In his view, these provide a cost-effective way of targeting particular populations. Proposals include programs aimed at health (providing food or nutritional supplements or de-worming medicines for primary school-children), lowering the cost of schooling (eliminating public school fees, providing vouchers for spare private school capacity or funding part-qualified after-school tutors) and appropriately targeted conditional cash transfers.

In every case the benefit-cost ratios are large, particularly when the policies are targeted at a child's early years of schooling. However, it's important to note that there are no universal solutions applicable to all countries and both rural and urban areas. Good projects include targeting the high proportion of children with worm infestation in Kenya and poor Indian children without access to tutors.

Investing in effective schooling programs to increase literacy is an important step in the development of a skilled population, which boosts economic growth. Education makes a lasting difference to individuals and societies, which seems a compelling reason to make this challenge a high priority.

Daniel Linotte (former Senior Adviser to the Organization for Security and Co-operation in Europe) writes on the topic of "Terrorism." This has become a global challenge to security and peace and is a daily menace in many countries. There is no overall consensus on how to define "terrorism"; although the 9/11 attacks certainly fit the bill, the present violence in Iraq is seen by some as closer to civil war.

Terrorists do not just cause personal misery; economic losses are huge, but costs are difficult to tie down. We know that the devastation of 9/11 generated many billions in direct and indirect costs, and it has been estimated that world GDP in 2002 would have been an astonishing $3.6tn higher in the complete absence of international terrorism.

Of course, there are no simple measures to eliminate terrorist violence. Nevertheless, there are a number of areas where progress could be made, such as rebuilding economies and societies in some troubled countries, cracking down on money laundering to cut off funding, and increasing shipping security.

As a rough estimate of the costs of fighting terrorism, we can use the global spending on defense post-9/11: about $0.8tn. Eliminating terrorism could result in global GDP growth of $3.6bn: already a very healthy benefit-cost ratio, but one which is probably understated. If the scourge of terrorism could be truly eliminated, the expense seems a bargain. The required investment is well above the nominal 2008 Copenhagen Consensus "budget" of $75bn, but a good case has been made for giving this challenge a high priority.

Health and Population challenges

Unsurprisingly, the list of challenges in this category is the longest.

Jeffrey A. Miron (Harvard University) tackles the controversial issue of "Drugs." We usually focus attention on policies designed to halt or limit the drugs trade, but these are both costly and of limited effectiveness. While there is an obligation to minimize the harmful effects of drug use, the current approach of driving trade underground encourages criminality and violence.

Although it seems logical that prohibition should reduce drug use to some extent, the reduction seems to be relatively modest: countries with weak enforcement regimes tend not to have significantly higher consumption. Legalization could result in a relatively small (25 percent) increase in illicit drug use, but all other effects would be beneficial. The challenge is to reduce the harm caused by the remaining (and increased) drug use.

The global net benefit of legalization is calculated at $130bn annually. There would be no direct costs, and tax revenue would increase significantly: this windfall could be used to minimize some of the inevitable negative impact of drug use through enforcement of regulations against driving or using machinery under the influence of drugs.

At least superficially, this opportunity should be a very high priority, since it is essentially free. However, there are many ethical and cultural barriers to overcome before this initiative could be embraced.

"Disease Control" is the subject covered by Dean Jamison of Harvard and University of California, San Francisco. Tremendous progress has been made in recent decades in improving health in low- and middle-income countries, which gives confidence that continuing gains can be made with appropriately targeted projects. It is also clear that big gains do not need to be preceded by significant income growth.

Improved health has direct economic benefits because workers become more productive and growth is boosted. It also encourages investment as longer life expectancy promotes planning for retirement.

Major health challenges which require continued focus include childhood illnesses (including malaria and infectious diseases), HIV/AIDS (prevention and anti-retroviral treatment), the increasing burden of non-communicable disease (cardio-vascular disease, cancer, psychiatric disorders, etc.) in developing countries, and tobacco addiction.

Many healthcare programs have been evaluated, and seven initiatives are promoted in this chapter, including HIV prevention, TB treatment, management of heart attacks, malaria prevention and treatment and childhood immunization. The benefits from these initiatives significantly outweigh costs, and together they could save millions of lives. Jointly, their expected cost is a little over $9bn, with benefits between 7 and 30 times that figure. The proviso is that an increase in healthcare capacity may be required to deliver the benefits, but the case for doing so seems compelling.

"Lack of People of Working Age," covered by Robert Wright and Katerina Lisenkova (both University of Strathclyde), is unusual in the context of the Copenhagen Consensus because it is essentially a problem facing the developed world. As societies grow richer, fertility declines, the population ages and fewer people of normal working age are available for employment.

It is estimated that there will be 755 million people aged between 20 and 64 in industrialized countries in 2010 – a slight rise from today – but by 2050, 100 million will be lost from this group. As developed nations currently account for 75 percent of world GDP, the implications for the global economy are significant. Wright and Lisenkova refer to models that indicate a net present value of the loss to the world economy from 2010 to 2050 of $19tn (3 percent discount rate) or $8tn (6 percent).

This imbalance of ages will in fact be a transitory problem as societies move to a steadier demographic spread. However, politically, doing nothing does not seem to be a realistic policy option. Since those in work fund the benefits of those not in work, solutions have to be found which do not place undue burdens on workers or compromise the welfare of the retired.

There are a number of ways to tackle this, including raising productivity through a "lifelong learning" approach, increasing participation of women in the labor market, or raising retirement ages. The authors' favored proposal, which results in the lowest costs for taxpayers, is to provide incentives for immigration and use monetary payments to encourage immigrants to remain in developed nations. Benefit–cost ratios are high even allowing for quite substantial payments to immigrants. Developing countries currently suffer from the opposite demographic problem: a bulge of young people with too few jobs.

With so many pressing problems in the developing world, some may ask why this particular challenge deserves to be given a high priority. But because developed countries produce such a high percentage of global GDP, anything that reduces this would compromise development programs elsewhere. Ignoring this challenge could greatly reduce resources available for other initiatives.

"Living Conditions of Children" are addressed in a chapter by Harry Anthony Patrinos of the World Bank. Nearly half the world's population is aged under twenty-five, and 90 percent of this age group live in developing countries. Half a billion children (aged under fourteen) live on less than $1 a day, and a majority of children in parts of Africa and South Asia do not even attend primary school. Child labor is common, and half the world's children do not have access to clean water. For these and other reasons, child mortality remains high, and many are left orphaned by the ravages of civil war and HIV/AIDS.

Education is enormously helpful as a way to build human capital and give children a better future, but spending must be targeted. There is evidence that providing more schools increases attendance and raises attainment levels: demand-side interventions as described by Peter Orazem in the chapter "Lack of Education" can also be highly effective.

Earlier interventions in education also show very favorable rates of return. A pre-school program costing $1,000 per child has positive spin-offs 3.5 times higher in the poorest countries, and returns are still very favorable in wealthier nations. Expanding the program to include the provision of healthcare, nutrition and additional assistance for the first two grades of school gives even better outcomes, although at a higher cost.

Overall, this reinforces the strong case already made for investment in education in poor countries.

Brinda Viswanathan of the Madras School of Economics covers "Living Conditions of Women" in her contribution. In many societies, women continue to be disadvantaged because of their gender rather than their abilities. Raising the status of women creates many benefits for society, but quantifiable costs and benefits are more difficult to establish.

Viswanathan makes two concrete proposals: reducing the educational gender gap, particularly at the primary school age, and increasing labor-force participation by providing childcare facilities.

In the world's poorest countries, the female literacy rate is typically only 70 percent of the often already low level achieved by men. Better education for women has a number of indirect benefits such as making women less vulnerable to sexual abuse and empowering them to make better decisions on health and nutritional matters for their families.

Very good results have been achieved in Bangladesh with the Food for Education program. At a cost of $36 per child per year, this has increased primary education for girls at about twice the rate for boys.

Projected benefits from similar programs across South Asia and sub-Saharan Africa are impressively high: a minimum of twenty times the costs accruing over ten years, at a 6 percent discount rate and an assumed doubling of the cost per child.

Education brings many benefits for women, but not necessarily labor-market participation, even in the developed world. Although cultural differences explain some of this, the provision of good-quality, affordable childcare can increase the female workforce considerably and ensure that those women in work have a lower absentee rate and are more likely to stay employed. Not only does this benefit the economy, but also it enables some women to be lifted out of welfare dependency.

Viswanathan argues that closing the status gap between the genders would have a range of direct and indirect benefits. It could also be argued that such improvements would improve the effectiveness of other projects proposed for the 2008 Copenhagen Consensus.

"Malnutrition and Hunger" is a well-known and obvious problem, covered here by Jere R. Behrman (University of Pennsylvania), Harold Alderman (World Bank) and John Hoddinott (International Food Policy Research Institute). Nearly a billion people are chronically malnourished (160 million of them are pre-school children) and each year 12 million underweight babies are born due to maternal malnourishment. Although acute famines catch our attention, the long-term problem is more serious. Tackling this would not only have enormous human welfare benefits but would also release resources for other challenges. A healthier population would mean a better economic output.

One approach suggested is the reduction of the incidence of low-birth-weight babies, which would greatly reduce infant mortality and result in healthier, more productive adults. Putting a value on human life is always problematic, never more so than in low-wage societies. But even putting a low value on a DALY gives a benefit-cost ratio well above 1.

A range of interventions to improve infant nutrition forms the next opportunity. In this case, benefit–cost ratios are even higher.

The authors' third suggested solution is to reduce micro-nutrient deficiencies (specifically iron, iodine and Vitamin A). Costs are low and benefits are found throughout life, so the benefit-cost ratio is extremely favorable, starting at 67.5 for even the highest discount rate and lowest DALY value.

While the human tragedy of malnutrition and hunger is vast, the economic arguments alone make a strong case for tackling this challenge.

Guy Hutton (Development Solutions International) discusses the problem of "Unsafe Water and Lack of Sanitation." The problem affects even more people than hunger and malnutrition: 1.1 billion have no access to clean water and 2.6 billion do not have decent sanitation facilities. The great majority of those afflicted live in Africa and Asia. The cost is high, and the problem is likely to get worse as pressure on water supplies grows.

Hutton proposes low-cost solutions to provide water alone, water plus improved sanitation, and water/sanitation plus an improvement in water quality.

Water supply itself costs about $17–55 per person; piped supplies to houses costs between $92 and $142 depending on region. Simple improved sanitation such as pit latrines costs $26–91 for each person, while more advanced solutions with septic tanks or connections to a sewer cost up to $160.

Benefits come from improved health and greater productivity. Hutton draws on the relatively few published economic analyses to estimate the annual cost of providing water ($1.75bn) and water plus sanitation ($11.05bn). The figures are based on the expenditure necessary over a fifteen-year period to meet the MDG of halving the number of people without access to water or proper sanitation. Universal access to water, sanitation and household water treatment using chlorine would cost $26.2bn a year.

The costs are large, but benefits outstrip them by 8.8 for water alone and about 11 for the two other options, with a discount rate of 3 percent.

It can be argued that clean water and sanitation are prerequisites for proper development and therefore are an essential part of the mix if decent living standards are to be achieved by all.

The final chapter, "Population: Migration," is written by Michael J. Greenwood (University of Colorado). To a large degree, migrants are economic and move with an expectation of personal gain. In many industrialized countries, immigration is the sole or primary cause of population increase and is generally reckoned to have a positive economic impact. However, uncontrolled immigration puts pressure on healthcare, educational and housing resources and can be a source of social tension. It can also push wages downward and displace some of the native labor force.

The net effects of migration vary significantly from country to country. In all cases, the migrants themselves will benefit, as will their employers if wages are depressed. Some native workers will lose by being displaced or receiving lower wages, but whether the society gains or loses overall depends on many factors.

Migration is seen as a problem to the extent that it is outside the control of the receiving country. Given that the illegal component is largely responsible for this perception (particularly, for example, in the USA), Greenwood proposes to create a market in which the country receiving immigrants will benefit and thereby be able to compensate disadvantaged native workers. In the case of the USA, it is estimated that there are 12 million illegal immigrants unwilling to wait for the possibility of a visa but able to pay several thousand dollars to be brought into the country. Setting a market price of around $1,000 for a visa could therefore benefit both migrants and native workers.

Migration will continue to take place whether or not there is any concerted initiative to manage it more effectively. Greenwood makes the case for a potentially beneficial solution which essentially costs nothing other than the market's administration.

Conclusions

This introduction has attempted to summarize the key issues raised by the twenty-three global problems in the long list for consideration by the Copenhagen Consensus 2008 panel. In doing so, we have not been able to give a truly balanced picture, but hope to have made the case for each being worthy of proper consideration.

Faced with the list of issues, many people will believe it's obvious that the world must spend Copenhagen Consensus' nominal $75bn budget over the next four years on human welfare issues such as hunger and malnutrition or access to water and sanitation. Others, though, will believe that environmental issues – particularly climate change – must top the list.

Obviously, it is difficult to compare such widely differing problems. This is where a rational and objective economic cost-benefit analysis comes into its own. Some will argue that it is impossible to put a value on a human life or environmental goods, but assigning a monetary value is the best way we have of introducing a common frame for comparison. Using economic tools, we can also gauge how outcomes alter when we alter discount rates, the value of life (DALY) or change our assumptions about costs and outcomes. The result is not perfection, but it does focus our efforts on using the best tools we have.

This analysis may produce some surprising insights. Investing in education, for example, not only produces a more highly skilled workforce, but also a population better able to understand the importance of hygiene and nutrition. The result is not just a more literate or numerate society, but also a healthier and more prosperous one. Equally, we may not immediately think that the reduction of corruption or money laundering should be a high priority, but the pernicious effects of such practices breed lawlessness and cause misery for millions. Eliminating corruption in many countries could put populations on course for prosperity.

Other ideas run counter to our understanding of the world. The argument is made in this book for legalization of illicit drugs. We all know that individuals and society suffer great harm from drugs, so it's taken for granted that legalization is exactly the wrong thing to do. A closer look shows that the majority of the problems from drugs come from crime caused by the trade being underground. Legalization would see tax revenues boosted and more money to deter bad behavior. You may not agree with this point of view, but it is certainly an argument worth considering.

Something that becomes very clear from reading this material is the degree to which many of the world's greatest challenges and opportunities are interrelated. There are big overlaps between increasing primary education attendance, improving children's health and nutrition and providing good access to water and sanitation, for example.

Why, then, have we insisted in breaking down all these problems and demanding that they be prioritized? Because at the end of the day, we don't do everything. These problems are difficult ones which the world has had to endure for a long time. Current efforts to solve them seem to be doing too little. Distilling the issues into topics allows us to identify the best, most achievable opportunities. Setting priorities tells us that we are spending the money the best way we can on individual programs. Finding synergies between them is an added bonus.

Now, it is over to you, the reader, to read the contributions from our expert authors and make your own judgment. Our panel of top economists will be making their shortlist and agreeing on priorities in Copenhagen in May 2008. Theirs will be a well-reasoned and expert outlook, but it will only be one perspective. We invite you to ensure your view is informed by reading the book and making your own prioritization as we suggest in the final chapter.

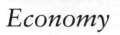

PART I

Economy

1 | Financial Instability

PETER BLAIR HENRY

1. Introduction

The world has not seen a major financial crisis since Argentina's meltdown in 2001, but history tells us that the current period of tranquility is unlikely to last. The world's major central banks continue to raise interest rates in an effort to stave off a resurgence of inflation, and in the past, rising interest rates have often triggered financial difficulties for developing countries. Indeed, the upswing in volatility of emerging market asset prices this past spring provides a stark reminder that the specter of financial instability is never far away. The prospect of more turbulent seas ahead makes now a good time to review the lessons of the Copenhagen Consensus 2004 Challenge Paper on Financial Instability (Eichengreen, 2004).

In that paper, Barry Eichengreen identifies three types of financial instability: banking crises, currency crises, and twin crises (the simultaneous occurrence of a banking crisis and a currency crisis). He demonstrates that the cost of a financial crisis is large – approximately one percentage point of the gross domestic product (GDP) of a country – and proposes four possible policy solutions to the problem: (1) reregulation of domestic financial markets to address the problem of banking crises; (2) reimposition of capital controls to address the problem of currency crises; (3) creation of a single global currency; and (4) pursuit of an international financial engineering solution to the problem. Eichengreen estimates that the costs associated with each of the first two options outweigh the benefits. He rules out the third option on the grounds that it is politically infeasible (although it would have positive net benefits in his estimation). Only the fourth solution is deemed to be both feasible and worth doing.

This "problem" paper provides a brief review of Eichengreen's challenge paper and then critiques it in some detail. My fundamental problem with Eichengreen's proposed solution to the problem of

financial stability is that it assumes financial crises occur in developing countries for reasons that lie almost exclusively beyond their
control. The critique offered over the next few pages casts doubt on
the validity of this assumption. Weak domestic institutions play a
central causal role. Accordingly, I end my critique with a counter-
proposal that would help developing countries build the institutional
capacity they need to solve their own problems.

2. The cost of financial instability

Eichengreen's challenge paper estimates the cost of a financial crisis by
surveying the empirical literature on financial crises and performing
simple back-of-the-envelope calculations. Specifically, he estimates the
cost in two steps. First, he notes that the average output loss associated
with a financial crisis is approximately 9 percent of GDP or 0.09
(Bordo, Eichengreen, Klingebiel, and Martinez Peria, 2001). Next, he
documents that the probability of a randomly selected country experiencing a crisis in a given year is 8 percent or 0.08. Finally, the expected
output loss associated with a financial crisis is the product of the preceding two numbers. The resulting figure is 0.0072, or roughly seven-
tenths of a percentage point of GDP growth per year.

Other authors have reached similar conclusions using different
methodologies, so there is little doubt that the average cost of a financial crisis is large. For example, table 1.11 in Dobson and Huffbauer
(2001: 68) reports that the average annual loss of GDP in emerging
markets due to financial crises in the 1990s was about 0.7 percentage
points of growth per year. After surveying the literature more
broadly, Eichengreen concludes that a reasonable estimate of the
cost of a financial crisis is roughly 1 percentage point of GDP growth
per annum.

The one percentage point number is the cost of all financial crises
lumped together – banking crises, currency crises and twin crises. In
order to compute the cost of a stand-alone banking crisis, the paper
performs another series of calculations. The cost of a typical banking
crisis is 53 percent of the cost of the typical currency crisis and, in any
given year, a banking crisis is 66 percent as likely to occur as a currency
crisis. Multiplying 53 percent by 66 percent gives the fraction of the
financial crisis-induced reduction in output that is attributable to
banking crises alone – roughly 30 percent or 0.3 percentage points of

GDP growth per year. The cost of a currency crisis is taken to be the remainder of the financial crisis-induced reduction in GDP – 0.7 percentage points of growth per year.

3. Are the calculations reasonable?

There are many grounds on which to question the validity of Eichengreen's calculations, but the organizers of the Copenhagen Consensus imposed the discipline of coming up with an answer. Economists who want to be helpful sometimes have to step outside the pristine environs of the university seminar room and carefully feel their way through the murky empirical reality of the policy world (McMillan, 2003). Taken in that spirit, Eichengreen's estimates of the cost of financial stability are surely in the right neighborhood. In fact, they may even be too conservative.

There are two costs of financial instability. The first cost is direct – financial crises induce collapses in actual output. The second is indirect – weak economic institutions that lie at the heart of financial instability may also contribute to poor resource allocation, thereby reducing potential output. Eichengreen's estimates capture the first effect but not the second, so the economic consequences of financial instability may be even greater than the already large effects suggested by Eichengreen's conservative approach.

4. What causes financial instability?

A suitable cure for financial crises must begin with a proper diagnosis of the potential causes. Eichengreen identifies four: (1) unsustainable macroeconomic policy; (2) fragile financial systems; (3) institutional weaknesses; and (4) flaws in the structure of international financial markets. Eichengreen's preferred policy option focuses on the last of these four causes.

One flaw in the structure of international financial markets that plays a central role in Eichengreen's analysis is the idea that financial markets are incomplete. A particularly striking example is the absence of a market in which developing countries are able to raise external financing with debt contracts denominated in their own currency (as opposed to US dollars), a phenomenon that Eichengreen and Hausmann (2003) call original sin.

The problem with a country issuing dollar-denominated debt is that it creates a *currency mismatch*: the country's flow of income is denominated largely in domestic currency while its liabilities are denominated in dollars. Consequently, devaluing the currency, which is sometimes the appropriate policy response to a macroeconomic shock that requires a country to export more and import less, will also increase the country's repayment burden.

5. The financial engineering proposal for curbing financial instability

If currency mismatches cause financial instability, then it would seem that one way to reduce instability is for countries to borrow in local-currency-denominated debt instead of in dollars. Because developing countries have trouble issuing debt in their own currency, Eichengreen proposes that the World Bank and other international financial institutions (IFIs) step in to help. Specifically, this chapter proposes a three-step international solution to the currency mismatch problem.

First, the IFIs would define a synthetic index called the EM, comprising a basket of emerging market currencies. Second, the IFIs would issue debt denominated in EMs and, at the same time, convert their concessional loans into claims denominated in the inflation-indexed currency of the countries comprising the index. Converting their concessional loans in this fashion would allow the IFIs to avoid a currency mismatch. Third, G-10 countries would issue debt in EMs. In order for the G-10 issuers to avoid a currency mismatch, they would swap their EM-denominated liabilities with the countries whose currencies comprise the EM index. By engaging in these swaps, the developing countries would reduce their currency mismatches by passing their dollar-denominated debt obligations to the G-10 countries in exchange for inflation-indexed local currency-denominated liabilities. Eichengreen calculates that the expected net benefit to developing countries of adopting this proposal would be about seven-tenths of a percentage point of GDP growth per year.

6. Would the financial engineering scheme work?

I have several doubts about the ability of Eichengreen's scheme to deliver benefits of the magnitude envisioned. The third step of the proposal assumes that transactions costs are the principal obstacle to developing countries being able to issue debt in their own currency. The transactions-cost argument says that developing countries are "forced" to issue dollar-denominated debt because global financial portfolios are concentrated in the currencies of a few large countries. Outside of these large countries, the transactions costs associated with borrowing and lending in an additional currency exceed the marginal benefit that would accrue to developed country investors. Consequently, they refuse to do so.

But the swaps envisioned in the proposal would involve precisely the kinds of transactions costs that Eichengreen sees as the leading explanation of original sin. The only difference is that under Eichengreen's proposal the transactions costs shift from institutional investors to G-10 governments. To the extent that transactions costs are the obstacle to local currency lending, it is not obvious that G-10 governments have a greater incentive to bear these costs than institutional investors.

Another problem with the transactions-costs argument is that it applies with equal force to the purchase of dollar-denominated debt. Many countries default on their dollar-denominated debt as a matter of course (Reinhart and Rogoff, 2004). When defaults occur, bondholders incur transactions costs in the form of debt negotiations and restructurings. It is not obvious that the transactions costs associated with managing a bond portfolio of multiple domestic currencies are significantly larger than the expected renegotiation costs associated with purchasing dollar-denominated debt from countries prone to default.

Furthermore, currency swaps cannot get around the risk that the counterparty will renege on their obligations. If developing country governments do not uphold their end of the swap, then G-10 governments will be stuck with the legal responsibility for servicing the EM debt. Knowing this up front, the G-10 governments may charge a swap fee that raises the cost of the swap to developing country counterparties. Potential investors in EM bonds are also forward-looking. They realize that after the swaps take place they will effectively be left holding local currency-denominated claims on developing country governments. To the extent that the original sin argument is valid, potential investors might also require a premium for bearing the risk of potential debt servicing disruption in the case of counterparty default.

7. Institutions matter

Swaps are not a free lunch. Successfully addressing the problem of financial instability requires a better answer to the fundamental question: Why can't developing countries issue debt in their own currency? An alternative view to original sin says that developing countries cannot raise financing in their own currency because weak economic institutions – lax fiscal policy, profligate monetary policy, and poor creditor rights, to name a few – make investors reluctant to buy their debt. Requiring countries to borrow in dollar-denominated debt may simply be the way that lenders insure themselves against the possibility that sovereign borrowers will attempt to inflate away the real value of their payment obligations.

If inflation risk is the problem, then why don't countries simply issue inflation-indexed debt? Well, inflation-indexed debt protects lenders against inflation risk, but they still bear the risk that the government will default on its obligations outright. If a government has weak fiscal institutions – a poor tax collection system, for example – then it simply may not have the capacity to raise the real resources needed to service its debt, and the risk of default may be significant. The central issue here is *credibility*. Whether debt contracts are written in dollars or inflation-indexed local currency terms, the question is whether markets believe that the government has the ability to collect, and the will to deliver, the resources necessary to honor its debt obligations. No amount of financial engineering can circumvent this reality.

Broadly speaking, fiscal and monetary policy institutions in developing countries continue to improve. In comparison with the 1970s and 1980s, fiscal deficits today are smaller, central banks more independent, and monetary policies more conservative (Rogoff, 2003). Why, then, do governments still resort to dollar-denominated debt? At least three possible answers come to mind.

First, credibility does not come overnight. In today's low-inflation environment, it is easy to forget that things were not always so. In 1979, Paul Volcker, then Chairman of the US Federal Reserve Board, engineered a recession – the prime rate hit 21 percent at one point during the year – in order to reduce inflation. The Fed's current inflation-fighting credibility is the hard-won prize of two consecutive decades of a vigilant anti-inflationary stance. In contrast, relatively low inflation in Latin America (for example) is a much more recent phenomenon.

Second, although fiscal deficits are smaller, many developing countries still have less efficient tax collection systems than their developed country counterparts. The government must be both able and willing to service its debt, irrespective of the currency in which that debt is denominated.

Third, countries may simply need to try harder to avoid dollar-denominated debt. Politicians in search of the next election victory may find it in their narrow self-interest to issue dollar-denominated debt, ignoring the obvious externalities it imposes on the populace (Rajan, 2004). It makes sense for the World Bank and other IFIs to index the repayment of their concessional loans to the real-local currency value of the countries to which they lend. But instead of having the World Bank serve as an intermediary between developing countries and G-10 lenders, why not let the developing countries issue inflation-indexed debt to them directly? In fact, several developing countries, including Chile and Mexico, have already begun to issue inflation-indexed, local-currency-denominated debt (Del Valle and Ugolini, 2003; Turner, 2003).

8. A counter-proposal

At the time Eichengreen wrote his challenge paper, some observers were openly questioning the wisdom of permitting any free capital movements whatsoever. The first two policy options proposed by Eichengreen are best viewed as demonstrating the obvious downside of putting into practice the illiberal thinking that was gaining currency at the time. Eichengreen was right to demonstrate that policies which promote financial stability by curtailing the movement of capital may also reduce growth and end up being negative net present value endeavors.

But while it is true that policies to restrain financial markets have costs as well as benefits, the tradeoffs need not be so stark as Eichengreen implies. For instance, prudential oversight and supervision of domestic financial markets need not amount to financial repression. Similarly, there is a continuum of reasonable policy options between completely unfettered international capital flows, on the one hand, and the reimposition of strict capital controls, on the other. A more balanced view of domestic and international financial policy – monitoring and surveillance as opposed to reregulation and prohibition – delivers a more sanguine (and accurate) picture of the potential for sensible banking and capital account policies to reduce the frequency and severity of crises. Also domestic and international financial policies are not mutually exclusive. For example, capital account and banking system policies interact with one another. As such, they should be viewed as part of a package of policies that try to reduce financial instability by strengthening domestic institutions.

No single set of institutional changes is right for all countries, but reforms can work when designed in a country-specific context to meet the feasibility constraints of the domestic social and political systems.[1] Because all politics are local, residents of developing countries have a comparative advantage in designing their own such policies. In order to do so, however, many developing countries will require a significant increase in the number of people sufficiently skilled to perform such duties (Krueger, 2000). Therefore, money spent to help countries train and retain such individuals would yield greater long-run benefits than implementing a financial engineering policy that tries to circumvent the currency mismatch problem without addressing the more fundamental institutional causes of financial instability.

Accordingly, Table 1.1 presents the cost–benefit analysis of an alternative proposal that would make funds available to help developing countries design and implement their own proposals for building the institutional structures they need to achieve greater financial stability. As in Eichengreen (2004), I make no pretense about the precision of the estimates. The numbers merely illustrate the point that stronger institutions would produce increase in GDP by (1) raising potential output and (2) reducing the frequency and severity of crises.

The primary argument against the proposal to fund institution building is that it would take too long – after all, the developed countries of the world took centuries to put their functional, if imperfect, institutions in place. But all proposals would take time, and the litany of failed attempts at institution building around the world provides a rich history that could hasten developing countries' transition to financial stability by helping them to avoid the unnecessary missteps made by others in the past.

---

[1] For a more complete enumeration of the institutional issues facing developing countries see Henry (2004).

Table 1.1. *Summary of costs and benefits*

Opportunity	Annual gross benefits, 2006 (bn)	Annual gross costs, 2006 (bn)	Annual initial benefits –costs (bn)	Remarks
Provide funds to help developing countries build better institutions for promoting financial stability	Greater than $153	$0.5	$152	Delivers largest net benefits by reducing crises and increasing potential output
Re-regulate financial markets	$46	$153	−$107 billion	Costs exceed benefits
Re-impose capital controls	$107	$153	−$46	Costs exceed benefits
Create a single world currency	$107	$16	$91	Not politically feasible
Have IFIs borrow and lend in emerging market currencies	$107	$0.5	$ 106	Eichengreen's preferred solution

Notes: With the exception of the first opportunity, which is my suggestion, this table replicates Table 5 in Eichengreen (2004). For purposes of comparability, the cost–benefit estimates for the institution-building opportunity follow the same methodology as Eichengreen's calculations.

References

Bordo, Michael, Barry Eichengreen, Daniela Klingebiel, and Soledad Maria Martinez Peria (2001): Is the Crisis Problem Growing More Severe?, *Economic Policy*, 32: 51–82.

Del Valle, Clemente and Piero Ugolini (2003): The Development of Domestic Markets for Government Bonds, in Robert E. Litan, M. Pomerleano, and V. Sundararajan (eds.), *The Future of Domestic Capital Markets in Developing Countries*, Brookings Press: Washington, DC.

Dobson, Wendy and Gary Clyde Huffbauer (2001): *World Capital Markets: Challenge to the G-10*, Institute for International Economics: Washington, DC.

Eichengreen, Barry (2004): Financial Instability, in B. Lomborg (ed.), *Global Crises, Global Solutions*, Cambridge University Press: Cambridge.

Eichengreen, B. and R. Hausmann (2003): Original Sin: The Road to Redemption, in B. Eichengreen and R. Hausmann (eds.), *Other People's Money: Debt Denomination and Financial Instability in Emerging Market Economies*, University of Chicago Press: Chicago.

Henry, Peter Blair (2004): Perspective Paper on Financial Instability, in B. Lomborg (ed.), *Global Crises, Global Solutions*, Cambridge University Press: Cambridge.

Krueger, Anne O. (2000): Conflicting Demands on the International Monetary Fund, *American Economic Review*, 90(2), 38–42.

McMillan, John (2003): Market Design: The Policy Uses of Theory, *American Economic Review*, 93 (2), 139–144.

Rajan, Raghuram (2004): How Useful are Clever Solutions? *Finance and Development*, 41(1), 56–57.

Reinhart, C. M. and K. S. Rogoff (2004): Serial Default and the "Paradox" of Rich to Poor Capital Flows, *American Economic Review*, 94(2).

Rogoff, Kenneth (2003): Globalization and Global Disinflation, *Federal Reserve Bank of Kansas City Bulletin*, 88(4), 45–81.

Turner, Philip (2003): Bond Market Development: What Are the Policy Issues? in Robert E. Litan, M. Pomerleano, and V. Sundararajan (eds.), *The Future of Domestic Capital Markets in Developing Countries*, Brookings Press: Washington, DC.

2 | Lack of Intellectual Property Rights

KEITH E. MASKUS

1. Describing the problem: weak IPR

Many developing countries, including certainly the poorest economies, do not adequately protect intellectual property rights (IPR). While laws and regulations may offer comprehensive protection on paper, the ability and willingness of governments to enforce patents, copyrights, plant variety rights and trademarks are almost completely absent. In part this situation reflects simple political economy: the vast majority of firms who own IPR in poor countries are foreign. The problem also reflects the strategic view that weak IPR may help governments gain cheap access to, say, patented medicines and assist domestic firms to imitate international technologies without paying license fees.

These are important concerns and a balance needs to be struck in establishing IPR policies that are sensible for development. However, a weak system of IPR raises critical problems. First, poor enforcement invites trademark counterfeiters to sell unsafe goods, which may be damaging to public health. Recent WHO estimates find that counterfeiting of medicines is rising sharply and that globally fake pharmaceuticals amount to perhaps $32 billion, with a portion of this amount being dangerous.[1] Second, weak IPR limit the ability of domestic entrepreneurs and artists to create and sell new products. Survey evidence suggests that this problem makes it difficult for up to 4–5 percent of the population to overcome poverty in such countries as Indonesia (Luthria and Maskus 2004). Third, without some form of exclusive marketing rights international firms are reluctant to sell locally new medicines and vaccines and other critical technologies, such as new agricultural varieties. To my knowledge there are no studies of the costs of such delayed product launches. Fourth, evidence indicates that a weak environment for protecting IPR is a deterrent to the inward flow

[1] Study cited in *International Herald Tribune*, 5 September 2006.

of foreign direct investment (FDI) and licensing. Econometric work suggests this problem may reduce GDP growth by perhaps 0.1–0.25 percentage points per year in larger developing countries (Maskus 2000).[2]

Each of these issues is complex and the application of benefit–cost analysis is extremely difficult. Many of the problems generated by weak IPR are poorly measured (or not measured at all if they are informal or illegal activities). Neither are IPR specific conditions (e.g., diseases or hunger) that call for precise interventions that can be applied on a per-patient basis. IPR are different from inefficient trade restrictions or burdensome taxes, which, if removed or reformed, would expand national income. Rather, IPR are a form of business regulation in imperfect markets, implying that reforms will call forth both benefits and costs.

Perhaps most importantly, the inability to protect IPR is part of a weak regulatory environment that arises from insufficient expertise, poor governance, and corruption. In short, weakly enforced IPR are a part of an overall business climate that tends to discourage domestic innovation and diminish inward flows of FDI and trade. The weak IPR regimes in most developing countries are a drag on growth and should be reformed. At the same time, such reforms are only likely to be meaningful in the context of capacity building and systemic improvements in governance. Therefore, benefit–cost analysis of IPR reforms alone can be highly misleading. For example, simply enforcing patents without improving the competitive environment will not achieve the intended benefits.

2. Solutions, costs and benefits

Why IPR?

Briefly, intellectual property rights are policy interventions that set out the boundaries within which inventors and creators can claim exclusive rights to produce and sell what they have developed. Given the limited space in this chapter, I will assume readers are familiar with the basic devices of intellectual property protection.[3] These

---

[2] Such calculations are heavily dependent on an assumption of "other things equal" and only illustrate an average tendency.
[3] Maskus (2000) provides a review.

are patents (including utility models and industrial designs), plant variety rights, copyrights, trademarks, certification marks, and geographical indications. Regulations for protecting trade secrets are closely related.

IPR are aimed at addressing certain failures in markets for technology and information. The first of these is the inability of markets to exclude free riders from copying and selling new goods so quickly that the inventor cannot earn enough returns to cover the costs of the investment. IPR protect exclusive production and distribution rights for a period of time to encourage investments in new goods. A second objective is to promote disclosure and commercialization of new products. Turning a new idea into a marketable product may be costly and IPR encourage investments in market development. Further, IPR facilitate markets for domestic and international technology transfer. IPR also help allocate rights across participants to share in the profits from creating complex knowledge goods. A final basic purpose arises in trademarks. Consumers benefit from knowing the true origin of the goods they purchase, for it reduces their costs of searching for a reliable mix of price and quality.

While these are important benefits, governments also place limitations on the scope of IPR in order to achieve a social balance. Among these limits are compulsory licensing, exhaustion of rights (permitting parallel imports), research exceptions in patent use, and fair-use provisions in copyrights. Governments also use anti-monopoly policies and price controls (especially in medicines) to limit market power associated with IPR.

There is always a risk that policy can be out of balance. It may be overly strong, making markets rigid and monopolized. It may be too weak, discouraging firms from investing sufficiently in innovation. Either problem will slow down innovation and growth, the former by restricting dynamic competition and the latter by diminishing incentives for invention in the first place.

Finally, even if the laws and regulations are well balanced, IPR are inadequately protected if the enforcement regime is weak. In developing countries, trademark counterfeiting and copyright piracy are endemic. So is patent infringement, especially where local firms can readily adapt patented technologies to domestic market conditions. Thus, IPR policy comes in two categories: setting the balance in the laws and regulations and choosing how strongly to prosecute infringement.

There are virtually no countries in which IPR are "absent" in the sense of having no laws, but there are many countries where IPR are very weak because enforcement is lax.

Solutions

This discussion suggests there are two general problems at which policy could be aimed. The first is to improve the structure of laws and enforcement to reduce infringement. The second is to provide incentives for firms and entrepreneurs in developing countries to make greater use of the opportunities offered by IPR. I organize the discussion accordingly and offer crude estimates of potential costs and benefits, with magnitudes based on limited available evidence. These figures are based on estimates of total activities rather than a per-person cost.

Solution 1: Increase technical and financial assistance for improving IPR regulations and for increasing enforcement against infringement, especially copyright piracy and trademark counterfeiting

Some assistance for this purpose already is provided for developing countries by the World Intellectual Property Organization and the US and European patent offices but it is not nearly enough for the task. The activities that would be covered include: (a) expert advice on legal reforms in IPR and related areas, such as price controls and competition policy; (b) education to increase the number of IP experts and judges; (c) training to increase the number of officials and their productivity in domestic and border enforcement; (d) linkage of enforcement efforts with activities in the public health, industry, and/or labor ministries to offer retraining and relocation assistance for those displaced by reducing infringement.

The costs of such assistance are both one-time setup costs and continuing training costs. There are perhaps 150 countries that could be targeted because they otherwise lack the resources for enforcement. Crude literature estimates suggest that the one-time costs might average $4–$5 million per country (total of $600–$750 million upfront). Some of the larger and more developed countries would be able to "graduate" to an effective enforcement system more rapidly

Table 2.1. *Calculations of costs and benefits of enforcement*
(*$ millions*)

Costs Expend			PDV 3%	PDV 6%
	One-time		750	750
	Ongoing		3397	2799
Consumer			29,115	23,100
Total costs			33,262	26,649

Benefits (at 80% enforcement)	Low DALY	High DALY	Low DALY	High DALY
Health				
Remove danger	15,342	76,711	12,173	60,863
Remove ineffective	7662	38,310	6079	30,395
Innovation				
Income gains	57,464	57,464	45,593	45,593
Total benefits	80,168	172,485	63,845	136,851
B/C ratio	2.42	5.19	2.40	5.14

than others. Thus, a reasonable guess is that average annual operating costs would amount to perhaps $2.5 million per year for 10 years for the 50 faster nations and $1.5 million per year for 20 years for the 100 others.[4] These cost estimates are demonstrated in the first row of Table 2.1, with the ongoing costs discounted at 3 percent and 6 percent, according to Copenhagen Consensus 2008 guidelines. Total project costs would be $4.1 billion over 20 years under low discounting and $3.5 billion under high discounting.

I identify three types of benefits from this policy change. I reiterate that the extent to which these benefits would emerge depends greatly on other factors in each economy, in addition to the responsiveness of prices, innovation, and investment to changes in opportunities. There is little reliable information on these issues. Each requires some initial explanation.

[4] These figures are based on UNCTAD (1996).

Benefit 1. Reducing risks to consumer health

The most immediate problem with absent enforcement in trademarks is that fake medicines, beverages and foodstuffs are placed on the market. Toxic counterfeit products pose a considerable health risk. While there are many examples of such episodes throughout the developing world, it is impossible to compute their overall economic costs in the absence of a consistent database. As noted above, anecdotal (business survey) evidence suggests that the total annual volume of counterfeit drugs in the world is perhaps $32 billion. I parse this figure into an estimate of benefits, making very strong assumptions. For one, I cut all of the figures otherwise estimated by 20 percent because it is generally not feasible to reduce counterfeiting fully.

Assume that of the $32 billion, about 60 percent, or $19.2 billion, exists in our target developing countries. Of that sum, suppose that approximately 1/3, or $6.3 billion, are knockoffs that actually contain effective chemical formulations and may be used to treat diseases. Patent and trademark enforcement would remove these effective drugs from the market and raise their prices. I assume that these drugs would continue to be fully prescribed, at a 30 percent higher price, with a market value of $8.2 billion.[5] Thus, consumers would pay an extra $1.9 billion per year for drugs of equal effectiveness, a pure loss for consumers. In Table 2.1 the PDV of these costs is accumulated over 20 years.

Next, of the remaining $12.9 billion, assume that 1/4, or $3.2 billion, is actively dangerous to health. I am aware of no studies that try to translate such counterfeiting figures into estimated impacts on patient deaths or illness burdens; indeed, it is not clear how one might make such an assignment. On the basis of sporadic news coverage, I assume that there may be up to 10 such deaths per country per year, with another 100,000 per country suffering sickness of one month's duration.[6] In Table 2.1 the benefits for reducing the implied DALYs are listed, using the CC08 convention of $1000 and $5000.

These assumptions leave $9.7 billion in fake drugs that provide no therapeutic benefit but are not harmful either, except to the extent that

---

[5] A careful study by Fink (2001) of the Indian pharmaceutical market suggests markups in this range.

[6] The latter figure may seem high but if the estimate of the volume of counterfeit drugs is sensible then the number of people suffering must be of this general magnitude.

patients remain sicker because they are not truly being treated. With IPR enforcement, these drugs would disappear, replaced by effective drugs at some lower volume with higher prices. Thus, there would be gains in terms of lives saved and lowered illness. Demand for new drugs in poor countries seems fairly elastic, so if we presume a 30 percent price rise and a 60 percent volume cut, the new market value of effective drugs would be $7.9 billion.[7] It seems reasonable to assume that this situation would not save lives but might reduce illnesses by another 50,000 per country. These benefits are again translated at the high and low DALY estimates in Table 2.1.

Benefit 2. Improving the environment for local innovation

Weakly enforced IPR can significantly diminish innovation incentives, even in poor countries. This issue has been studied in various countries.[8] The conclusions reached are based on surveys of enterprise officials and policymakers. While the surveys are not completely comparable, these authors find strong indications that weak IPR is a deterrent to local business development and creativity. For example, a study of the music industry in Senegal found that there are few successful musicians, all of whom record abroad where their copyrights are protected. But there are thousands of local musicians in whom no recording company will invest because popular music is immediately pirated in the region. Moreover, the absence of copyright enforcement blocks the development of an effective copyright collection society. In China domestic firms complained of an inability to undertake interprovincial marketing because of local counterfeiting. This problem also is an impediment to developing scale economies.

Such survey evidence should be treated cautiously. Further, the conclusions should be qualified because some forms of copying (e.g., of software code) can encourage local learning in poor countries. Overall, though, the evidence is that poor enforcement of trademarks, copyrights, and trade secrets is a significant drag on entrepreneurship in poor nations. Transparent enforcement of these rights would be

---

[7] This is likely an overestimate of the additional amounts that could be sold by patent holders.
[8] See Maskus (2004a) for Lebanon, Maskus, *et al.* (2004) for China, Luthria and Maskus (2004) for Indonesia, and the chapters in Finger and Schuler (2004) for numerous other examples.

pro-innovation and encourage growth. In turn, there would be a gain in reduced poverty as creative individuals shift more into the formal sector.

Again, assigning benefits figures to such outcomes relies on strong assumptions about the responsiveness of inventiveness and incomes to greater enforcement. I would offer the following conservative estimate. Within our 150 target economies there is a population of perhaps 5 billion people. If just 3 percent of these are moved into creating and selling new cultural goods and market products, then 150 million people would enjoy higher incomes, with a consequent reduction in poverty. The calculation of welfare benefits in this situation is difficult. As a simple example, suppose that the average income gain is 5 percent on an average per-capita GNP of $500, or around $25 per person. The aggregate income gain would be $3.75 billion per year, discounted in Table 2.1. Over 20 years the income gains would be between $45 and $57 billion in present value. No attempt is made to translate these impacts into DALYs.

Benefit 3. *Reducing a deterrent to technology transfer*

Access to international technology transfer (ITT) is the most important source of innovation and technical change in developing countries. Local firms learn by acquiring and adapting technological information to local uses. Empirically ITT is the most frequently studied aspect of IPR and development.[9] The evidence supports the claim that countries with stronger IPR will attract significantly more inward ITT through imports, FDI and licensing. The primary reason is that stronger IPR reduce the costs of achieving successful ITT contracts. Potential spillover benefits from greater ITT point to a marked productivity gain from strengthening patent rights.[10]

There is little possibility of estimating the potential benefits from this factor, for the welfare gains would come through income growth net of tax payments to foreign firms and also would need to account for sub-stitute impacts on domestic production. Overall the effects should raise

---

[9] See Maskus (2004b) for an extensive review.
[10] Javorcik (2004a, 2004b) provides strong evidence that the technology content of FDI rises with IPR protection and that there are significant backward spillovers from FDI.

the benefits somewhat, making the figures in Table 2.1, conservative on this score.

An important caveat is that simply improving IPR is not likely to attract more ITT to countries with otherwise weak investment climates. Thus, the real priority in the poorest countries is to improve the overall economic environment, meaning reducing corruption, expanding transparency, and improving infrastructure and education in addition to IPR enforcement.

Overall benefit–cost ratio

From the calculations above, it seems that reducing piracy and trademark counterfeiting considerably through stronger enforcement could generate a global benefit–cost ratio of between 2.4 and 5.2.

Solution 2: Provide technical and financial assistance to encourage the use of IPR by firms in developing countries

A second approach is to note that supply responses to stronger IPR may be weak in poor countries for a variety of reasons. There are a number of problems in gaining information about opportunities at home and abroad, while the costs of undertaking patent applications and marketing can deter new and small enterprises. Thus, a companion program to encourage the registration and use of IPR would involve the following: (a) raised awareness on the part of domestic inventors and creators; (b) established registries of traditional knowledge and use of the information in them to expand the definition of prior art and protect traditional technologies through benefit sharing; (c) assistance in registering patents abroad, including help in opposing invalid patents issued abroad; (d) information-sharing programs about effective marketing strategies; and (e) increases in temporary visas for students and technical or management personnel in developing countries to study and work in developed countries.

Of these, the last is both most controversial and, in my view, most important for actually encouraging technology development techniques and the ability to use IPR, though it does extend far beyond the IPR policy realm.

Rather than explain assumptions and figures in detail, I simply summarize my calculations here. Costs for items (a) through (d) might be

Table 2.2. *Calculations of costs and benefits of subsidies ($ millions)*

Costs Expend.		PDV 3%	PDV 6%
	Direct	3616	2994
	study	3065	2432
Total costs		6681	5426
Benefits		61,295	48,632
B/C ratio		9.17	8.96

$3 million per year for each of the 50 larger and more developed economies and $1.5 million per year for each of the other 100. Subsidies to foreign study and training for 10,000 student/workers would add up to $200 million per year. The discounted costs are given in Table 2.2.

The benefits are virtually impossible to estimate, since so much depends on the evolution of markets, product qualities and demands. One enthusiastic observer argues that products developed from traditional knowledge and sold internationally could amount to $50 billion – $100 billion per year if suitable marketing and IP protection channels were found.[11] This range may even be small given the enormous potential for developing new drugs and other goods from biological and genetic resources. Support for international patent and trademark applications and training subsidies through international visas would add as well to potential gains in export revenues.

Of course, some of this increase would happen without such intervention. Suppose we take the high end of this range and assume that 20 percent of it would not emerge without assistance. However, the $20 billion generated is export revenue and should not be counted as an economic benefit except to the extent that it generates value added that would not otherwise exist. One reasonable supposition is that the gain in value added from producing and selling newer products might be 20 percent, implying an income gain of $4 billion per year in poor countries. The benefits calculation in Table 2.2 is discounted again over 20 years.

---

[11] Ron Layton, personal conversation.

In this case the benefit–cost ratio rises to about 9 to 1. It is likely that this is an overestimate of the potential gains, despite my attempt to be conservative.

3. Conclusions and caveats

Figures of this kind must be treated with great caution, based as they are on strong assumptions about market sizes and other parameters. Unfortunately, there are few available studies on which to base such calculations. Still, the economic case for intervention to improve enforcement, on the one hand, and encourage the use of IPR, on the other, seems rather strong.

Many readers will question the selection of items to be analyzed here. In particular, I did not consider the impacts of stronger patents on reducing generic competition (a loss), nor on R&D in the development of new medicines (a gain). Nor does the analysis attempt to link closely the anticipated gains and losses from enforcement to other elements of policy, such as price controls, compulsory licensing, or competition policies.

References

Arora, A., A. Fosfuri and A. Gambardella (2001). *Markets for Technology: The Economics of Innovation and Corporate Strategy* (MIT Press).

Branstetter, L. G., R. Fisman and C. F. Foley (2006). "Do Stronger Intellectual Property Rights Increase International Technology Transfer? Empirical Evidence from U.S. Firm-Level Panel Data," *Quarterly Journal of Economics* 121: 321–49.

Chaudhuri, S., P. K. Goldberg and P. Jia (2003). "The Effects of Extending Intellectual Property Rights Protection to Developing Countries: A Case Study of the Indian Pharmaceutical Market," Yale University, manuscript.

Finger, J. M. and P. Schuler (eds.) (2004). *Poor People's Knowledge: Promoting Intellectual Property in Developing Countries* (Washington, DC and Oxford: World Bank and Oxford University Press).

Fink, C. (2001). "Patent Protection, Transnational Corporations, and Market Structure: A Simulation Study of the Indian Pharmaceutical Industry," *Journal of Industry, Competition and Trade* 1: 101–21.

Javorcik, B. (2004a). "The Composition of Foreign Direct Investment and Protection of Intellectual Property Rights: Evidence from Transition Economies," *European Economic Review* 48: 39–62.

Javorcik, B. (2004b). "Does Foreign Direct Investment Increase the Productivity of Domestic Firms? In Search of Spillovers through Backward Linkages," *American Economic Review* 94: 605–27.

Kremer, M. (2002). "Pharmaceuticals and the Developing World," *Journal of Economic Perspectives* 16: 67–90.

Luthria, M. and K. E. Maskus (2004). "Protecting Industrial Inventions, Authors' Rights and Traditional Knowledge: Relevance, Lessons and Unresolved Issues," in K. Krumm and H. Karas (eds.), *East Asia Integrates: A Trade Policy Agenda for Shared Growth* (World Bank and Oxford University Press).

Maskus, K. E. (2000). *Intellectual Property Rights in the Global Economy* (Washington, DC: Institute for International Economics).

Maskus, K. E. (2004a). "Strengthening Intellectual Property Rights in Lebanon," in C. Fink and K. E. Maskus (eds.), *Intellectual Property and Development: Lessons from Recent Economic Research* (World Bank and Oxford University Press).

Maskus, K. E. (2004b). *Encouraging International Technology Transfer*, UNCTAD/ICTSD Project on Intellectual Property Rights and Sustainable Development, Issue Paper No. 7. Geneva: UNCTAD.

Maskus, K. E., S. M. Dougherty, and A. Mertha (2004). "Intellectual Property Rights and Development in China," in C. Fink and K. E. Maskus (eds.), *Intellectual Property and Development: Lessons from Recent Economic Research* (World Bank and Oxford University Press).

Maskus, K. E. and J. H. Reichman (2004). "The Globalization of Private Knowledge Goods and the Privatization of Global Public Goods," *Journal of International Economic Law*, 7: 279–320.

UNCTAD (1996). *TRIPS and the Developing Countries* (Geneva: UNCTAD).

3 Money Laundering

DONATO MASCIANDARO *

1. Describing the problem: money laundering

To understand how to design possible policies in combating money laundering (ML) all around the world, we must review the economic peculiarities of this criminal phenomenon, with classic demand and supply schedules.

1.1 The demand side

In recent years, particular emphasis has been placed on the study of ML because of its central role in the development of any crime that generates revenues. The conduct of any illegal activity may be subject to a special category of transaction costs, linked to the fact that the use of the relevant revenues increases the probability of discovery of the crime and therefore incrimination. Those transaction costs can be min-imised through an effective laundering action, a means of concealment that separates financial flows from their illegal origin.

Therefore, from a microeconomic point of view, ML performs a *peculiar financial function*, responding to the overall demand for black finance services expressed by individuals or groups that have commit-ted *income-producing crimes*. The microfoundations of ML allow us to shed light on its macroeconomic effects. In fact, if at the micro level the demand should be matched by an effective supply – see below – it is possible to show that ML, in a given economy with legal and illegal sectors, can play the role of multiplier of the volume of the economic endowments that are in the hands of the illegal agents.

From September 2001, the need to increase the fight against the laundering of illicit capital was included in the agenda. But we have

---

* This chapter builds extensively on different articles by the author (see References, pp. 70–2), which provide considerable detail that space precludes presenting here.

to stress that the *financing of terrorism* (money dirtying) is a phenomenon conceptually different from the recycling of capital (money
laundering).

The financing of terrorism resembles ML in some respects and differs
from it in others. The objective of the activity is to channel funds of
any origin to individuals or groups to enable acts of terrorism, and
therefore crimes. Again, in this case, an organisation with such an
objective must contend with potential transaction costs, since the
financial flows may increase the probability that the crime of terrorism
will be discovered, thus leading to incrimination. Therefore, an effective money dirtying action – i.e an activity of concealment designed to
separate financial flows from their destination – can minimise the
transaction costs.

The main difference between ML and financing of terrorism is in the
origin of the financial flows. While in the money laundering process the
concealment regards capitals derived from illegal activity, the terrorist
organisations use both legal and illegal funds for financing their actions.
Money laundering and money dirtying may coexist when terrorism is
financed through the use of funds originating from criminal activities.

In summing up, one is prompted to think that the operational techniques of the two phenomena – the laundering of criminal capital and
financing of terrorism – are at least in part coincident. It is important,
however, that the partial overlapping of money dirtying and ML remain
a hypothesis to be tested from time to time, rather than a thesis. This
caveat is important to remember, given that, at the end of 2001, following the September 11 attack, the international organisations – in
particular the IMF, the World Bank and the Financial Action Task Force
(FATF) – introduced a joint Anti-Money-Laundering and Combating
Financing of Terrorism (AM-FT) programme.

1.2 The supply side

Who satisfies the demand for concealment? It is easy to demonstrate
that in every national context – at a macro level – *banking and financial industry* can perform an important function in the concealment
activity, irrespective of the level of consciousness of the single intermediary or operator at the micro level. At the same time, taking an international perspective, the existence of *offshore financial centres* (OFCs)
raises concerns about potential risks to financial integrity.

1.2.1 National perspective

By reducing the overall transaction costs, financial intermediaries improve the agents' capacity to decide how to allocate their purchasing power in terms of consumption, savings and investment. Intermediaries animate an industry in which the services offered and sold are intangible, with an information content that is high but not uniformly distributed among all the market participants. The characteristics of every agent in the economic system are thus known to the financial firms through the supply and sale of their services, and the individual intermediaries seek to maximise their profit precisely through the management and enhancement of their information assets. As a result, with regard to the purpose of concealment, the financial industry acquires a high value for two crucial attributes: a greater-than-normal degree of 'opacity' (information asymmetry), since the exchanges and flows of purchasing power are filtered, coordinated and administered by specialised operators (the intermediaries); and the privileged position of such operators.

Banking and financial intermediaries are therefore at the centre of attention of both criminal organisations and the law enforcement authorities. For criminal parties, the presence of intermediaries who collude with them (*crooked intermediaries*) and/or are honest but inefficient in protecting their integrity (*lax intermediaries*) increases the possibility of using the financial services system for their concealment objectives. At the same time, for the inquiring and investigative authorities, the information assets in the possession of those companies can serve an essential reporting function in the identification of the presence of criminal organisations.

1.2.2 International perspective

In the international community the existence of OFCs raises concerns about potential risks to financial integrity. The capacity of OFCs to attract foreign capitals depends on their different regulatory design with respect to the onshore jurisdiction. The regulatory gap can make it difficult to monitor and assess the risks that financial conglomerates face in increasingly integrated world markets, as well as the risks of the proceeds of crime gaining access to these markets. In recent years several international fora undertook initiatives to evaluate the compliance of the OFCs with respect to their standards and procedures: the Financial Stability Forum (FSF) from April 2000, the FATF from

June 2000, the OECD in 1998 and then from 2000, and the IMF from 1999.

2. Describing the solution: the design of anti-money-laundering regulation

If ML can act as the multiplier of the illegal revenues, the general consensus is that the only available solution will be a correct *regulatory design*, in order to provide the right incentive alignment for the relevant players, at both national and international levels. Unfortunately it is clear that at present the literature does not provide robust empirical studies on ML activities. Furthermore, no attempt has been made at a cost-benefit analysis of the current state of anti-money-laundering regulations.

However, in order to provide even a rough draft of a possible solution, let me propose first a short review section, then a simple framework for estimating the benefits and costs of designing effective anti-money-laundering regulation.

2.1 The review

As has correctly been pointed out, most literature on ML effects is pure speculation, or is based on figures that are wrongly quoted, or misinterpreted or just invented. And it is evident that the figures for the amount of laundered money identified through investigations underestimate the phenomenon. A systematic review essay (Unger and Rawlings 2005) claims that there are only three potentially useful empirical sources in these respects:

(A) Tanzi (2000) and Quirk (1996, 1997): the IMF estimates ML at 2% to 5% of the world GDP, and Quirk estimated that an increase of 10% in ML produced a 0.1% reduction in annual GDP. The same indication was provided in a 1998 speech by Michel Camdessus, at the time IMF's Managing Director, in which he also claimed that ML transactions are estimated at 2% to 5% of global GDP. Unfortunately the IMF documents never explained how they reached these figures.

(B) Walker (1999): Walker estimated world ML at $2.85 trillion, about 4% of the world GNP (US ML: $1.3 trillion per year). Unger and Rowland (2005) used a revised Walker model to estimate the ML in Netherlands (Walker = $18 billion; Unger and Rawlings = from $8.6 billion to $14.8

billion, only taking into account money from Dutch crime, while $30 billion are laundered in or through The Netherlands every year). Again, the Walker methodology was characterised by low disclosure. Unger and Rawlings (2005) noted that, when they tried to reproduce his estimations, it appears that he used 'tacit knowledge' and 'feeling' to calibrate his model.

My conclusion is that the IMF model and the Walker model – if they can be called models – cannot be reproduced. We share with Schneider and Windischbauer (2006) the opinion that these kinds of results are scientifically dubious, since they are not reproducible and not proven.

Recently three more estimates of money laundering activity have been developed.

(C) Argentieri *et al.* (2006) presented a methodology for constructing a chain of ML in Italy (1980–2001), starting from a theoretical model. In their estimation, ML accounts for approximately 9% of GDP. Unfortunately, the paperwork seems to be inconsistent with the model: in fact the authors basically modelled the underground economy, not ML activity, and – as we will discuss below – the two phenomena are linked, but different.

(D) Schneider and Windischbauer (2006) attempted a quantification of the volume and development of ML activities in twenty highly developed OECD countries. The volume of laundered money was, in the years 1994–95, $554 billion, and increased to $742 billion in 2002–3. On a worldwide base in 2005, $1.038 billion are estimated to have been laundered, from the illegal drugs trade alone. The authors acknowledged that these figures are only provisional.

Schneider and Windischbauer used a DYMIMIC estimation, where the volume of ML is treated as a latent variable. The estimation procedure uses various causes for more laundering (i.e. various criminal activities) and indicators (confiscated money, prosecuted persons, etc.) to get an estimation of the latent variable. However – as the authors explicitly stressed – one big difficulty is that one gets only a relative estimated value of the size and development of ML and one has to use other estimations of absolute values in order to transform/calibrate the relative values from the DYMIMIC estimation into absolute ones.

(E) Finally, a promising line of research is represented by Chong and Lopez-de-Silanes (2006). The authors made a systematic effort to assess ML volume around the world, using six different methodologies to estimate, as a proxy of ML, the main sources of the illegal revenues that have to be laundered. The first three measures they calculated estimate proxies for ML indirectly by measuring the underground economy as the discrepancy between the official (or declared) value of a macro series and its actual (or estimated) value. Furthermore, since these macro estimates of ML have potential measurement problems, the authors complemented these figures with subjective indicators from opinion surveys. Under the three proxies of the underground economy, the dimension of ML ranges from 19 (15)% to 31 (32)% of GDP for the average (median) country.

If the figures for the world ML industry are few and uncertain, the estimates of the economic effects of this crime are even more problematic. Unger and Rawlings (2005) did the first systematic research on the effects of ML. They distinguished the direct effects of crime – losses to the victims and gains to the perpetrator – from the indirect effects – economic (real and financial) indirect effects, social indirect effects – distinguishing also between short-term and long-term effects. They classified twenty-five different effects of money laundering, on business activities, relative prices, consumption, saving, taxes, output, employment, growth, etc. Unfortunately, their classification is just a qualitative one.

Again, an exception is represented by the Chong and Lopez-de-Silanes paper. They estimated the impact of regulation and enforcement on ML. In particular, a two standard deviation increase in the efficiency of the legal system is associated with a decrease of ML that ranges from 10.85% to 14.1%, depending on the definition of ML volume. Also, ML regulation has a statistically significant impact on ML.

2.2 The solution

Masciandaro (1999) proposed a theoretical model of the relationship between illegal market revenues and ML activities, which Unger (forthcoming) recently used to estimate the situation in The Netherlands.

The model determines the economic value of ML, from the point of view of the users, i.e. the criminal organisations. The framework is simple: starting from the initial crime that produces some dirty revenues, the laundering process allows – given some laundering costs – such capitals to be re-invested in the legal and illegal sectors of the economy, minimising the risks of prosecution. The share which is destined for the illegal sector will further produce some other dirty revenues to undergo the laundering process; the money-laundering cycle has therefore taken off and each step – provided that no obstacle hinders the process – contributes to increasing the economic value of effective ML activities.

The lower the cost of the ML services, the higher the economic value of ML and the bigger the amount of re-investment in illegal activities, as well as the need to finance this re-investment with clean liquidity; also increased are the differential of the expected return from illegal activities and the initial amount of the revenues from the illegal economic activity.

Now, in order to provide estimations, let us use a simpler formulation of this model, claiming that it is not necessary to clean the money for re-investment in the illegal sector. The gross value of the money laundering activities (GML), given the initial illegal revenues (IR), can be calculated using the multiplier formula, and it is equal to (provided that $0 < q(1+r) < 1$[1]):

$$GML = \frac{y\,IR}{1-q(1+r)} = \delta\,IR$$

where y is the proportion of illegal revenues that needs to be laundered; c, the costs of laundering; q, the proportion of laundered money reinvested in the illegal economy; r, the average return from illegal activities; δ, the gross multiplier. Furthermore, if c is the cost of laundering (the laundering fee is equal to a share of the laundered money, with $0 < c < 1$), the net value of the money laundering (NML) – i.e. the product of IR and the net multiplier – is equal to:

$$NML = (1-c)GML = \frac{(1-c)y\,IR}{1-q(1+r)} - \beta\,IR$$

Now we build up our estimates on three crucial assumptions. First of all, we assume that: (1) the net value of the ML activity represents *a public bad*. In other words, given the absence of robust empirical analyses on the spill-over effect that, in a given country, goes from criminal money to macroeconomic performance, we adopt a *conservative view*.

Secondly we assume that: (2) other things being equal, the cost of ML depends on the *effectiveness of the anti-money-laundering*

---

[1] Note that this condition is more likely to occur in the legal than in the illegal economy, given that q is always a share, while the expected illegal rate of return is in general higher than the legal one, with basically no 'natural' restriction.

regulation, given that the legal regulations and their enforcement increase the transaction costs. We can conclude that every improvement in the effectiveness of the anti-money-laundering regulation – given its cost — will produce a decrease in the ML multiplier, consequently in the value of the ML activity, and therefore an increase in the overall public benefits.

Finally, following this line of reasoning, let us highlight that: (3) the goal of the regulation has to be to eliminate the multiplier effect – i.e. the optimal value of β is 1 – rather than the ML activity. In fact, if the multiplier is less than one, this means that the ML activity destroys economic value – the NML is lower than the initial illegal revenues – and the likely consequence is a change in the behaviour of the criminal sector – for example, in terms of the proportion of illegal revenues to be laundered, the amount of reinvestment in the illegal economy and its diversification – in order to avoid the value destruction. Therefore we assume the existence of an *illegal no-value-destruction constraint*. In other words, if the volume of the criminal activities is independent from the ML activities – i.e. the initial amount of IR is an exogenous variable – the anti-money-laundering regulation can impact in a stable way only on the value of the multiplier, not on its existence. But how to estimate this model?

Using the very scarce data, let us adopt, as an estimate of the initial illegal revenues to be laundered at the beginning of each year, the 2003 value – i.e. the most recent one available – of revenues from the underground economy. Choosing the overall underground economy can be consistent with the definition of ML activity. As was stressed in section 1, the demand for money laundering is potentially generated by the revenues of any activity characterised by the probability of discovery, and consequently of prosecution. The broadest definition of underground economy includes those economic activities that circumvent government laws and regulations and the income derived from them. Therefore – at least from a theoretical point of view – the revenues of all underground activity might need to be cleaned.

The world value of the underground economy for the year 2003 can be assumed to be equal to US$15.07 trillion, summing up the estimates of both the grey and the *black economy*.[2] However, in order to produce

---

[2] The broadest definition of underground economy considers illegal revenues (the black economy) and the legal revenues unreported to the state in order to avoid

a conservative estimation, let us consider just the criminal (black) economy, which is equal to US$2.1 trillion. Regarding the multiplier effect, let us assume that – given a time horizon of one year (using in all but item 4 the average values of Unger's (forthcoming) hypothetical parameter range):

1) the fixed proportion of illegal revenues that needs to be laundered has a value of 0.75 (in a range between 70% and 80%);
2) the fixed proportion of transaction costs of laundering has a value of 0.25 (in a range between 5% and 50%);
3) the fixed share of reinvestment in illegal activities is equal to 35% (in a range between 20% and 50%);
4) adopting again a conservative viewpoint, the rate of return from illegal activities has a value of 100% (in a range between 50% and 600% – the latter for drugs such as heroin).

Therefore, the average gross multiplier is equal to 2.5, and the gross value of the ML activity is US$7.5 trillion (18% of the 2004 world GDP, which is equal to US$41.43 trillion), while the average net multiplier is equal to 1.8, and the *net value of money laundering is US$ 3.78 trillion* (9% of the 2004 world GDP).

The multiplier formula can show the potential benefits in combating ML for different assumptions regarding the parameters. For example, Figure 3.1 below displays how big the public bad can be if, other things being equal, the rate of return from the illegal activities changes. If the average illegal rate of return increases from 0 to 180%, the multiplier increases from 0.86 to 28 times the initial illegal revenues. In other words, the net value of money laundering can theoretically range, other things being equal, from US$1.8 trillion (4% of the 2004 world GDP) up to US$33.6 trillion (81% of the 2004 world GDP). In reality, the

laws and regulations of different types (the grey – or shadow – economy). Schneider and Windischbauer (2006) reports that the total revenues of organised crime (the black economy) reached the figure of US$2.1 trillion in 2003, while Schneider (2004) calculated estimates of the shadow economy in the main 145 countries: the global average size of the shadow economy (as a percentage of official GDP) for 2002/2003 is 35.2%, equal to US$12.97 trillion. Chong and Lopez-de-Silanes (2006) group the main sources of ML into three categories: criminal activities, underground economy, and tax evasion. However, these three categories can be summarised in our broadest definition of underground economy, given that tax evasion is a crime whose income can increase the probability of detection and prosecution.

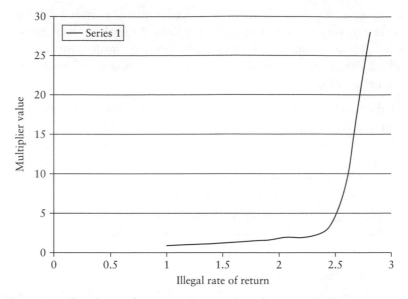

Figure 3.1. Illegal rate of return and money-laundering multiplier

rate of return from all crime except the heroin trade is likely to be much lower than 300%, so, on average, estimates closer to the lower limit are likely to be more realistic.

At the same time, we can show the impact of effective anti-money-laundering regulation on the black money markets activity, through the effect on the laundering costs. Figure 3.2 illustrates how big the public bad is if, other things remaining equal, the cost of ML changes. If the average cost of laundering increases from 10% to 60% of the laundered amount – due to an increase of regulatory effectiveness – the multiplier falls from 2.25 times the initial criminal revenues to 1. Note that, in our simulation, the effect of the increase in the legal system's efficiency – a decrease of money laundering that ranges from 10.85% to 14.1% – simulated by Chong and Lopez-de-Silanes can be obtained with an increase in the cost of money laundering equal to 2.5%.

Now we have all the information to calculate the benefits of the proposed solution. If the goal of the anti-money-laundering-regulation is to eliminate the multiplier effect, i.e. to reduce the multiplier value from 1.8 to 1, the cost of money laundering has to be increased from 25% to 60% of the laundered money. The corresponding benefits are equal to *US$1.68 trillion* (3% of the 2004 world GDP).

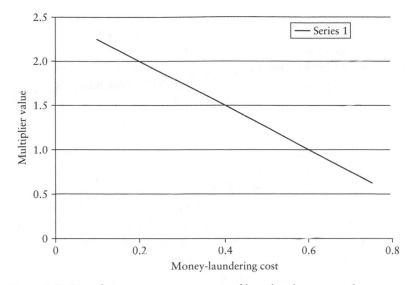

Figure 3.2. Laundering cost as percentage of laundered money and money-laundering multiplier

Table 3.1. *Expected benefits: the present discount value (PDV) of the socially optimal money-laundering cost*

Discount rate	3.00% (low)	6.00% (high)
Lags in years		
No lag	US$1.68 trillion	US$1.68 trillion
1 year	US$1.63 trillion	US$1.58 trillion
2 years	US$1.58 trillion	US$1.50 trillion
3 years	US$1.54 trillion	US$1.41 trillion

To the best of our knowledge, no studies exist on the time taken for a change in the cost of money laundering. Therefore in Table 3.1 we mimic the delayed effect of more expensive ML operations, calculating the Present Discount Value (PDV) of the socially optimal level of money-laundering cost (i.e. 60% of the laundered money). We consider the potential benefit at different points in time, using – as do all the Copenhagen Consensus 2008 Problem Papers – 'low' (3%) and 'high' (6%) discount rates. Regarding the time lags, note that we cannot use the time periods that Copenhagen Consensus 2008 usually suggests be considered (10, 40, 60, 100 years) given that these horizons are too long with respect to the dynamic of the financial markets, and therefore the crucial 'other-things-being-equal' hypothesis is really unrealistic. Furthermore, given that the primary effects of the solution are not embedded in persons – other than the relatively short time lags – we do not need to calculate any survival probability for individuals (in DALYs).

Now, how to calculate the expected costs of the solution to the ML phenomenon? Consistent with the modern theory of financial regulation[3] – i.e. the Coase principle – the case for (or against) money-laundering regulation would be made on the basis of an overall costs and benefits analysis. Unfortunately there are two main problems, given that no estimates exist: (a) of the relationship between ML costs and the effectiveness of anti-money-laundering regulation; (b) on the compliance costs of the anti-money-laundering regulations.[4]

On the relationship between ML costs and the effectiveness of anti-money-laundering regulation, we have already postulated a causal link: more effective regulation produces increasing costs for the criminal organisation. In other words, given the results obtained by Chong and Lopez-de-Silanes (2006), we propose a positive response to the question of whether regulation matters in fighting the black finance phenomena. I must stress that this assumption is still controversial, given, for example, the traditional theory of regulation – Coase (1960) and Stigler (1964) – which claims that the regulatory effort can be either irrelevant or counterproductive.

Regarding the compliance costs of anti-money-laundering regulation for the legal sector, Masciandaro (1998) proposed a model which shows that anti-money-laundering regulation can negatively impact the efficiency of the banking and financial system, taking into account the potential costs that affect the financial service industry and its clients; the relationship was tested in the field on the situation in Italy (Filotto and Masciandaro 2001). Therefore, we have to accept that the effectiveness of money-laundering regulation is not a free lunch: a trade-off exists between the effectiveness of regulation and the efficiency of the financial system. At the same time, this approach is again

---

[3] For a review essay, see Zingales (2004).
[4] Yeandle *et al.* (2005) proposed tentative average estimations of anti-money-laundering costs for five countries only: USA (£1.2 billion), UK (£0.253 billion), Germany (£0.150 billion), France (£0.085 billion) and Italy (£0.70 billion).

Table 3.2. *Expected costs: the PDV of anti-money-laundering regulation*

Discount rate	3.00% (low)	6.00% (high)
Lags in years		
No lag	US$0.53 trillion	US$0.53 trillion
1 year	US$0.51 trillion	US$0.50 trillion
2 years	US$0.50 trillion	US$0.47 trillion
3 years	US$0.48 trillion	US$0.44 trillion

a cautious one, given that it does not take into account the fact that designing and implementing a regulation incurs costs for the government too.

Therefore our overall position on the economic features of anti-money-laundering regulation is: regulation matters, but it is expensive. However, given the absence of any estimation of the trade-off between public effectiveness and private efficiency, we can propose just an upper limit – or an extreme benchmark, if that sounds more appropriate – for the compliance costs of anti-money-laundering regulation: the total amount of world banking profits. The intuition is simple: the total costs of implementing the public financial solution to money laundering cannot be greater than total private financial profits, in order to avoid destruction of economic value. We impose the existence of a *legal no-value-destruction constraint*.

Now, given that in 2004 the total amount of world banking profits was equal to *US$0.53 trillion*, in Table 3.2 we can simulate the different effects of more effective anti-money-laundering regulation, from the point of view of the private sector. We calculate the PDV of the maximum cost of the optimal level of anti–money-laundering regulation.

The calculation of the benefit/cost (B/C) ratio is equal to 3.16.

Let us summarise the main findings: in order to eliminate just the world multiplier effect of ML activity (benefit: US$1.68 trillion, i.e. 3% of the 2004 world GDP) – not the money-laundering activity itself – it is necessary to produce an increase in laundering costs equal to US$0.875 trillion. If we assume that the optimal increase in laundering costs can be caused by effective anti-money-laundering regulation, and the optimal compliance costs of regulation cannot be greater than US$0.53 trillion (the bank profits amount, equal to 45% of the banking operational costs in the same year), the net benefits will be 3.16 times the net costs. This methodology is conservative from at least three different points of view: (a) we do not calculate the macroeconomic spillover effects of ML; (b) we consider only the revenues to be laundered which are generated by the criminal sector, instead of considering the overall underground economy; (c) the applied rate of return from criminal activities is 100%, given a range between 50% and 600%.

3. Conclusions and caveats

In the previous section I proposed an economic analysis of the benefits and costs of a worldwide fight against ML, using a consistent model, and formulating prudent estimations. The identified solution is a more effective global anti-money-laundering regulation. But the discussion would be partial and incomplete without considering the political economic perspective on designing an optimal regulation. In other words, we can evaluate not only the overall economic feasibility, but also the political feasibility, both at national and international levels. In this respect, it can again be useful to treat regulation against money laundering as a product, with a demand and a supply schedule.

Let us assume that the policymaker in a given country has not yet decided the direction it will impose on its financial regulation against black money. The policymaker may thus decide to implement regulations that create serious obstacles to black money, or it may decide – at the other extreme – to make the opposite choice, devising lax regulation.

As we have already noted, black money generates costs as well as benefits. The key point is that the distribution of costs and benefits hits different constituencies at different points in time. We can identify at least four different macro categories of actors potentially interested in regulation: (a) the policymakers; (b) criminal organisations, deriving utility from the possibility of black money; (c) those who bear the costs of black money; (d) the financial community and, in general, the citizens who receive benefits from the inflow of foreign black and grey capital.

Starting with this last category, (d), it seems difficult to predict which side the financial community will take. In general, we tend to think that the utility function of financial intermediaries does not appear to be affected by whether profits stem from legal or illegal financial activities (*pecunia non olet* – '*money does not smell*'). We think that they simply maximise the expected revenues.

It is useful to start the analysis by examining the case of lax intermediaries, through whose transactions third parties may attempt ML manoeuvres. Money-laundering techniques can leave traces and constitute anomalies in banking and financial accounts, and the authorities find it efficient to ask the banks to collaborate in producing these. The more effective the collaboration is, the lower the ML risk will be, while for crooked intermediaries the central theme is *deterrence*. The effectiveness of regulation thus depends on the ability to influence the interest alignment. The possibility that regulation generates counterproductive effects dependent on the degree to which it is accepted by the regulated intermediaries is a general phenomenon, given the existence at least of the *compliance costs*.

The interests of (b) and (c) are obviously incompatible, as the gains of the former depend on the losses of the latter; (a) appears to be caught in the middle, having to decide which demand schedule to follow. As long as the costs and benefits of a decision fall within the boundaries of the policymaker's area of influence, we expect to have an efficient decision. Policymakers in countries where crime is pervasive will tend to bear at least some of the costs associated with a decision to favour black money.

Countries where organised crime is pervasive might appear to play a minor role in the offer of black or grey financial services at the international level, because they are sensitive to crime-related national costs. This might be so because the widespread presence of organised crime or terrorism in the country increases, for the lawmaker, the cost of regulations that favour black money.

The public will bear the costs of the decision and will hold the policymaker responsible. Entering the international market for black money services has a greater potential for countries that are immune from criminal activities. Such countries will almost be able to externalise the costs associated with the increase of predicate offences. As a result of this process, some countries which do not bear the costs associated with black money become predisposed to adopting lax regulations.

In the light of these considerations, is it possible to suggest final common guidelines for the design of international rules for the financial war on illegal activities, organised crime and terrorism? The possible indications, useful on both the microeconomic and macroeconomic levels, revolve around two fundamental words: information and incentives.

First it is evident that the more widespread information asymmetries, to the detriment of various categories of authorities in the financial industry are, the more developed and effective ML will be. A necessary, but not sufficient, condition for designing effective rules and enforcement at both the national and international levels is the generation and collection of relevant information.

But the production and collection of relevant information can never reach satisfactory levels unless we recognise the need to provide proper incentives for the various players involved, starting with the individual intermediaries and operators, passing through the authorities and arriving at the countries, be they onshore or offshore. Combating ML must be beneficial at all the various levels that are potentially involved in the rather complex operation of laundering dirty money. Designing incentive-compatible regulations – at both national and international levels – is the challenge for the future in increasing the economic and political feasibility of the proposed solution.

References

Argentieri, A., Bagella, M. and Busato F., (2006), Money Laundering in a Two Sector Cash-In-Advance Model, mimeo, August.

Boorman, J. and Ingves, S. (2001), *Financial System Abuse, Financial Crime and Money Laundering*. IMF Background Paper, Washington D.C.: International Monetary Fund.

Chong, A. and Lopez-de-Silanes, F. (2006), Money Laundering and its Regulation, unpublished Working Paper, no. 590, Research Dept, Inter-American Development Bank, Washington D.C..

Coase, R. (1960), The Nature of the Firm, *Economica*, 6, 386.

Errico, L. and Musalem, A. (1999), *Offshore Banking: An Analysis of Micro- and Macro-Prudential Issues*. Working Paper of the International Monetary Fund, no. 5, Washington D.C., IMF.

Filotto, U. and Masciandaro D. (2001), Money Laundering Regulation and Bank Compliance Costs. Economics and Italian Experience, *Journal of Money Laundering Control*, 2, 133.

Financial Action Task Force (1990), *The Forty Recommendations*, Paris: OECD.

    (2000), *Review of Non-Co-operative Countries or Territories: Increasing the Worldwide Effectiveness of Anti-Money Laundering Measures*, Paris: OECD.

Hampton, M .P. and Christensen, J. (2002), Offshore Pariahs? Small Island Economies, Tax Havens, and the Re-configuration of Global Finance, *World Development*, 30, (9), 1657.

Levi, M. (2002), Money Laundering and Its Regulation, *Annals of the American Academy of Political and Social Science*, 582, July.

Masciandaro, D. (1998), Money Laundering Regulation: the Microeconomics, *Journal of Money Laundering Control*, 2, 49.

(1999), Money Laundering: the Economics of Regulation, *European Journal of Law and Economics*, 3, 245.

(ed.) (2004), *Global Financial Crime. Terrorism, Money Laundering and Offshore Centres*, Aldershot:Ashgate.

(2005), False and Reluctant Friends? National Money Laundering Regulation, International Compliance and Non-Cooperative Countries, *European Journal of Law and Economics*, 20, 17.

(2006), *Offshore Financial Centres and International Soft Laws: Explaining the Regulation Gap*. Asset Management Forum Working Paper, no. 3, Milan: Bocconi University.

Masciandaro, D., Takats, E. and Unger, B. (forthcoming), *Black Finance. The Economics of Money Laundering*, Cheltenham: Edward Elgar.

Quirk, P. J. (1996). *Macroeconomic Implications of Money Laundering*, Washington: IMF.

(1997). *Money Laundering: Muddying the Macroeconomy*, Washington: IMF.

Schneider, F. and Windischbauer, U. (2006), Money Laundering: Some Preliminary Empirical Findings, mimeo, August.

Stigler, G. (1964), Public Regulation of the Securities Markets, *Journal of Business*, 37, 117.

Takats, E. (2005), A Theory of 'Crying Wolf': The Economics of Money Laundering Enforcement, Princeton University, mimeo.

Tanzi, V. (2000), Money Laundering and the International Financial System, in *Policies, Institutions and the Dark Side of Economics*, Cheltenham: Edward Elgar, 186.

Truman, E. M. and Reuter, P. (2004), *Chasing Dirty Money: Progress on Anti-Money Laundering*, Washington D.C.: Institute for International Economics.

Unger, B. (forthcoming), International Economics, in D. Masciandaro, E. Takats and B. Unger, *Black Finance. The Economics of Money Laundering*, Cheltenham: Edward Elgar.

Unger, B. and Rawlings, G. (2005), The Amount and the Effects of Money Laundering, mimeo.

(2006) *Competing for Criminal Money*. Working Paper of the Tjaling Koopmans Institute, Utrecht School of Economics, July.

Walker, J. (1999), How Big is the Global Money-Laundering? *Journal of Money Laundering Control*, 3, 1.

Yeandle, M., Mainelli, M., Berendt, A. and Healy, B. (2005), *Anti-Money Laundering Requirements: Costs, Benefits and Perceptions*, City Research Series, no. 6, London: Corporation of London.

Zingales, L. (2004), *The Costs and Benefits of Financial Market Regulation*. ECGI Working Paper Series in Law, no. 21, April, Brussels: European Governance Institute.

4 | Subsidies and Trade Barriers

KYM ANDERSON*

Despite the net economic and social benefits of reducing most government subsidies and opening economies to trade, almost every national government intervenes in markets for goods and services in ways that distort international commerce. Those interventions have been reduced considerably over the past two decades, but many remain. Distortionary policies harm most the economies imposing them, but the worst of them (in agriculture and clothing) are particularly harmful to the world's poorest people. This paper focuses on how costly those anti-poor policies are and examines possible strategies to reduce remaining distortions, including via the Doha Development Agenda of the World Trade Organization (WTO) and sub-global preferential reforms such as the Free Trade Area of the Americas (FTAA) initiative.

Arguments for removing trade barriers

The standard comparative static analysis of national gains from international trade emphasises the economic benefits from production specialization and exchange so as to exploit comparative advantage in situations where a nation's costs of production and/or preferences differ from those in the rest of the world. Domestic industries become more productive as those with a comparative advantage expand by drawing resources from those previously protected or subsidized industries that grow slower or contract following reform. The static gains from trade tend to be greater as a share of national output the smaller the economy, particularly where economies of scale in production have not been fully

* This draws on my earlier 2004 Copenhagen Consensus paper which appears as Chapter 10 in *Global Crises, Global Solutions*, edited by B. Lomborg, Cambridge University Press, 2004. Helpful computational assistance for Table 4.2 from Ernesto Valenzuela is gratefully acknowledged. The views expressed are my own and not necessarily those of the World Bank.

exploited and where consumers (including firms importing intermediate inputs) value variety so that intra- as well as inter-industry trade can flourish.

To the standard comparative static analysis needs to be added links between trade and economic growth. Channels through which openness to trade can affect an economy's growth rate include the scale of the market when knowledge is embodied in the products traded, the degree of redundant knowledge creation that is avoided through openness, and the effect of knowledge spillovers. Economies that commit to less market intervention tend to attract more investment funds too, and greater competition spurs innovation (Aghion and Griffith 2005), leading to higher *rates* of capital accumulation and productivity growth (Lumenga-Neso, Olarreaga, and Schiff 2005). Wacziarg and Welch (2003) show that countries that have liberalized their trade (raising their trade-to-GDP ratio by 5+ percentage points) have enjoyed 1.5 percentage points higher GDP growth compared with their pre-reform rate.

Opportunities for reducing subsidies and trade barriers

Among the more feasible opportunities available today for encouraging trade negotiations to stimulate significant market opening, the most obvious is a non-preferential legally binding partial trade liberalization following the WTO's current round of multilateral trade negotiations, the Doha Development Agenda (DDA).

A second type of trade-negotiating opportunity involving a subset of the world's economies is a reciprocal preferential agreement. Efforts are also being made to negotiate a Free Trade Area of the Americas (FTAA), which potentially would bring together all the economies of North, Central, and South America. This is by far the largest and most ambitious preferential agreement currently in prospect: it dwarfs the bilateral FTA negotiations the United States and the European Union (EU) are each having with a range of other countries. It is examined both without and with the prospect of an EU–Mercosur FTA.

There is also the opportunity for high-income countries to offer least-developed countries duty-free access to their markets, but this opportunity involves only a very small volume of global trade, so estimates of its benefits are not included.

Economic benefits from reducing subsidies and trade barriers

Empirical comparative static studies of the economic welfare gains from multilateral trade liberalization typically generate positive gains for the world and for most participating countries. When economies of scale and monopolistic competition (IRS/MC) are assumed instead of constant returns to scale and perfect competition (CRS/PC), and when trade in not just goods but also services is liberalized, the estimates of potential gains can be increased severalfold. Economists have also begun to examine the effects of lowering barriers to temporary labor movements across borders.

Table 4.1 reports estimates of the economic benefits associated with removing all trade barriers and agricultural subsidies. The AMV study (Anderson, Martin, and van der Mensbrugghe 2006) provides the simplest scenario: global liberalization of just merchandise trade using the latest version of the World Bank's Linkage model, assuming constant returns to scale and perfect competition in all product and factor markets. The GTAP Version 6 database, which provides trade and protection data for 2001, is used in that study to generate a new baseline first for 2005 (allowing for recent policy changes including the completion of implementation of the Uruguay Round, the EU expansion to twenty-five members, and the accession of new members such as China and Taiwan to the WTO), and to project the world economy forward a decade assuming no further trade policy reforms. This baseline for 2015 is then compared with how it would look after full adjustment following the removal of all countries' trade barriers and agricultural subsidies. The economic welfare gain is estimated to be US$287 billion per year in 2001 dollars as of 2015 (and hence slightly more each year thereafter as the global economy expands). Of that, $86 billion per year is estimated to accrue to developing countries. These are the lowest of the estimates summarized in Table 4.1.

The BKS study (Brown, Kiyota, and Stern 2005) uses the GTAP Version 4 database projected to 2005, but they embed it in the authors' static Michigan Model of World Production and Trade (www.ssp. umich.edu/rsie/model) to produce the highest of the surveyed estimates of global welfare gains from complete removal of trade barriers and agricultural subsidies: $2417 billion per year. This much larger estimate is the result of several features of this study: not having China and Taiwan's implementation of their WTO accession commitments in the

Table 4.1. *Comparative static estimates of economic welfare gains from full global liberalization of goods and services trade*

Study	Market assumptions[a]	Sectors liberalized	Baseline year (of EV welfare measure)	Welfare gain, non-OECD (US$ billions)	Welfare gain, global (US$ billions)	Year of currency (US dollars)
AMV (2006)	CRS/PC	Goods only	2015	142	287	2001
BKS (2005)	IRS/MC	Goods, services and FDI	1997	na	2417	1997
HRT (2002)	CRS/PC	Goods only	1995	100	456	1995
WBGEP (2003)	CRS/PC plus productivity boost	Goods only	2015	539	832	1997
WBGEP (2006)	CRS/PC	Labor migration	2025	623[b]	674	2001

[a] Constant returns to scale/perfect competition and increasing returns to scale/monopolistic competition/firm-level differentiated products.

[b] Includes $481 billion to new migrants who move to OECD countries and raise the labor force in the OECD by 3 percent.

Sources: Anderson, Martin, and van der Mensbrugghe (2006); Brown, Kiyota, and Stern (2005); Francois, van Meijl and van Tongeren (2005); and World Bank (2003, 2006).

baseline; the inclusion of increasing returns to scale and monopolistic competition (IRS/MC) for non-agricultural sectors and therefore product heterogeneity at the level of the firm rather than the national industry; liberalization of services in addition to goods trade (with IRS/MC assumed for the huge services sector); and the inclusion in services liberalization of the opening to foreign direct investment. The last of these boosts substantially the gains from services liberalization, which account for nearly two-thirds of this study's estimated total gains.

All other estimates of the gains from complete trade liberalization are between these two extremes. The HRT (Harrison, Rutherford, and Tarr 2002) study uses much larger trade elasticities than other models and so gets a considerable gain even using a 1995 base. WBGEP (World Bank 2003) uses the World Bank's Linkage model to 2015. It assumes liberalization boosts factor productivity in each industry according to the extent of growth in the share of production exported by the industry. The case presented suggests the gains would be $832 billion per year. That model is also used by the World Bank in its study of the potential gains from international migration, drawing on a new bilateral migration and remittances database (WBGEP – see World Bank 2006). Even assuming that the flow of migrants from developing to OECD countries amounts to just a 3 percent boost in the latter's labor force, it estimates the global gains would amount to $674 billion per year, most of which would be enjoyed by current citizens of developing countries (including those who migrate).

Implications for the Doha Round

Anderson, Martin, and van der Mensbrugghe (2006) examine the options that have been canvassed in the Doha Round and show that welfare gains from goods trade liberalization could range from a minimalist reform (in which no more is achieved other than the phase-out of export subsidies and the reduction in agricultural tariff and domestic support binding overhang) to $96 billion per year by 2015 (0.2 percent of GDP) if agricultural tariffs are cut by an average of about one-third and non-agricultural tariffs by one-half, or even to $120 billion if developing countries fully engaged rather than cutting by only two-thirds as much as OECD countries. Since this is only for goods, this value of 0.2 percent globally (0.3 percent for developing countries) represents a conservative or lower-bound estimate of possible comparative static gains from the DDA. As for an upper bound on comparative static gains, the results in Table 4.1 suggest it could be many times greater, depending on the extent to which investment is also liberalized and on the strength of influence of imperfect competition and economies of scale. We chose an upper bound of five times the lower bound, or 1.0 percent of GDP globally (1.4 percent for developing countries). We also assume that those gains will accrue fully after an eight-year phase-in period from 2008, prior to which the gains will begin in 2008 at one-eighth the full amount as of 2015 and rise by a further one-eighth each year until 2015.

There are dynamic gains from trade to consider in addition to those comparative static ones. The experiences of successful reformers such as Korea, China, India, and Chile suggest trade opening immediately boosts GDP growth rates by several percentage points. A conservative estimate might be that reform boosts GDP growth rates – projected to 2015 by the World Bank (2006) to be 2.7 percent for developed countries and 4.6 percent for developing countries – by one-sixth for developed countries and one-third for developing countries, that is, to 3.1 and 6.1 percent, respectively and hence from 3.2 to 3.8 percent globally.

Comparison with just removing intra-American trade barriers

The negotiations to create a Free Trade Area of the Americas (FTAA) – the largest such FTA negotiations currently under way – have run into political problems so it is not clear if/when they might conclude. It is nonetheless worth considering that opportunity so as to point out that the potential global gains from such an FTA are only a small fraction of those obtainable from multilateral negotiation. Two studies that examine both multilateral reform and the FTAA are the BKS study and one by Harrison, Rutherford, Tarr, and Gurgel (HRTG, 2004). The BKS study estimates the gains from the FTAA to be just one twenty-fifth that from a full multilateral trade liberalization, and for the HRTG study the difference is even greater (although its gains are somewhat higher when its estimated benefits from adding an EU–Mercosur FTA are included on top of the FTAA). Hence even if several such large FTAs were to be agreed, their potential contribution to world welfare would remain only a fraction of what is potentially achievable via multilateral negotiations. Furthermore, these FTA studies take no account of the dampening effect of the rules of origin that almost invariably constrain the extent to which firms can take advantage of any FTA's removal of bilateral tariffs.

Economic costs of trade reform

The above benefits from reform are not costless. Expenditure on negotiating, and on supporting policy think tanks and the like to develop and disseminate a convincing case for reform, would be needed. But more significant in many people's eyes are the private costs of adjustment for firms and workers, as reform forces some industries to downsize or close to allow others to expand (Matusz and Tarr 2000; François 2003). Those costs are ignored in the CGE (computable general equilibrium) models discussed above, where the aggregate level of employment is held constant. There are also social costs to consider. They include social safety-net provisions in so far as such schemes are developed/drawn on by losers from reform (e.g., unemployment payments plus training grants to build up new skills so displaced workers can earn the same wage as before).

Those one-off costs, which need to be weighed against the non-stop flow of economic benefits from reform, tend to be smaller, the longer the phase-in period or smaller the tariff or subsidy cut per year (Furusawa and Lai 1999). The adjustment required also tends to be small when compared with the changes due to exchange rate fluctuations, technological improvements, preference shifts, and other economic shocks and structural developments associated with normal economic growth (Anderson et al. 1997). In recent debates about trade and labor, analysts have not found a significant link between import expansion and increased unemployment. One example is a study of the four largest EU economies' imports from East Asia (Bentivogli and Pagano 1999). Another is a study of the UK footwear industry which found liberalizing that market would incur unemployment costs only in the first year, because of the high job turnover in that industry, and they were less than 1.5 percent of the estimated benefits from cutting that protection (Winters and Takacs 1991). For developing countries also the evidence seems to suggest low costs of adjustment, not least because trade reform typically causes a growth spurt (Krueger 1983). In a study of thirteen liberalization efforts for nine developing countries, Michaely, Papageorgiou, and Choksi (1991) found only one example where employment was not higher within a year.

So as not to exaggerate the net gains from trade reform, it is assumed here that there would be an adjustment period of eight years following the beginning of liberalization in 2008, and that in each of those years the adjustment costs would be 15 percent of the annual comparative static benefits as of 2015 (and zero thereafter) in the high case, and 5 percent in the low case when much less adjustment would be needed. That amounts to $71 billion per year during 2008 to 2015 globally, of which $24 billion is expended in developing countries, when expressed in 2005 US dollars by using the projection to 2015 of global GDP provided by the World Bank (2006).

Benefit/cost calculus

With these numbers fed into a spreadsheet, the range of net present value benefits and costs, using both 3 and 6 percent as the discount rate, are summarized in Table 4.2. The "low gains" case refers to gains of just 0.2 percent of GDP while the "high gains" case refers to gains

Table 4.2. *Summary of net present value (in 2005 dollars) of benefits and costs to 2100, and benefit/cost ratios, for liberalizing subsidies and trade barriers globally under the WTO's Doha Development Agenda*

(US$ billion)

(a) Costs and benefits (NPV 2005)

	3% discount rate				6% discount rate			
	Low gains		High gains		Low gains		High gains	
	Benefit	Cost	Benefit	Cost	Benefit	Cost	Benefit	Cost
World	27867	150	115320	442	9011	134	38338	396

(b) Benefit/cost ratios

	3% discount rate		6% discount rate	
	Low	High	Low	High
World	186	261	67	97

Source: Author's calculations based on assumptions in text.

five times that lower benefit. In all cases the benefits are estimated to the year 2100. In present value terms the net benefit of the DDA ranges from $9,000 billion to $38,000 billion at the higher discount rate and about three times that at the lower discount rate. The costs range from $130 billion to $440 billion, but they are mostly private rather than government costs and are dwarfed by the benefits. The benefit/cost ratios are between 67 and 97 in the higher discount rate case and between 180 and 260 in the lower discount rate case. This is clearly a very high payoff activity, if only the political will to bring about a successful conclusion to the DDA can be found.

References

Aghion, P. and R. Griffith (2005), *Competition and Growth: Reconciling Theory and Evidence*, Cambridge, MA: MIT Press.

Anderson, K., B. Dimaranan, T. Hertel, and W. Martin (1997), "Economic Growth and Policy Reforms in the APEC Region: Trade and Welfare Implications by 2005," *Asia-Pacific Economic Review* 3(1): 1–18, April.

Anderson, K., W. Martin, and D. van der Mensbrugghe (2006), "Market and Welfare Implications of the Doha Reform Scenarios," in *Agricultural Trade Reform and the Doha Development Agenda*, edited by K. Anderson and W. Martin, London: Palgrave Macmillan (co-published with the World Bank).

Bentivogli, C. and P. Pagano (1999), "Trade, Job Destruction and Job Creation in European Manufacturing," *Open Economies Review* 10: 156–84.

Brown, D. K., K. Kiyota, and R. M. Stern (2005), "Computational Analysis of the Free Trade Area of the Americas (FTAA)," *North American Journal of Economics and Finance* 16: 153–85.

François, J. F. (2003), "Assessing the Impact of Trade Policy on Labour Markets and Production," pp. 61–88 in *Methodological Tools for SIA*, CEPII Working Paper No. 2003-19, Paris: CEPII.

François, J. F., H. van Meijl, and F. van Tongeren (2005), "Trade Liberalization in the Doha Round," *Economic Policy* 20: 349–91.

Furusawa, T. and E. L. C. Lai (1999), "Adjustment Costs and Gradual Trade Liberalization," *Journal of International Economics* 49: 333–61.

Harrison, G. W., T. F. Rutherford, and D. G. Tarr (2002), "Trade Policy Options for Chile: The Importance of Market Access," *World Bank Economic Review* 16(1): 49–79.

Harrison, G. W., T. F. Rutherford, D. G. Tarr, and A. Gurgel (2004), "Trade Policy and Poverty Reduction in Brazil," *World Bank Economic Review* 18(3): 289–317.

Krueger, A. O. (1983), *Trade and Employment in Developing Countries*, Volume III: *Synthesis and Conclusions*, Chicago: University of Chicago Press for NBER.

Lumenga-Neso, O., M. Olarreaga, and M. Schiff (2005), "On 'Indirect' Trade-Related R&D Spillovers," *European Economic Review* 49(7): 1785–98, October.

Matusz, S. and D. Tarr (2000), "Adjusting to Trade Policy Reform," in *Economic Policy Reform: The Second Stage*, edited by A. O. Krueger, Chicago: University of Chicago Press.

Michaely, M., D. Papageorgiou, and A. Choksi (eds.) (1991), *Liberalizing Foreign Trade, 7: Lessons of Experience in the Developing World*, Cambridge, MA and Oxford: Basil Blackwell.

Wacziarg, R. and K. H. Welch (2003), "Trade Liberalization and Growth: New Evidence," NBER Working Paper 10152, Cambridge, MA, December.

Winters, L. A. and W. E. Takacs (1991), "Labour Adjustment Costs and British Footwear Protection," *Oxford Economic Papers* 43: 479–501.

World Bank (2003), *Global Economic Prospects 2004: Realizing the Development Promise of the Doha Agenda*, Washington, DC: World Bank.

World Bank (2006), *Global Economic Prospects 2006: Economic Implications of Remittances and Migration*, Washington, DC: World Bank.

PART II

Environment

5 | *Air Pollution*

GUY HUTTON

The problem

Air pollution in its broadest sense refers to suspended particulate matter (dust, fumes, mist, and smoke), gaseous pollutants and odours [1]. A large proportion of air pollution worldwide is due to human activity, from combustion of fuels for transportation, energy generation, energy-intensive industrial operations, resource extraction and processing industries, and domestic cooking and heating, among others. Air pollution has many impacts, most importantly affecting human and animal health, buildings and materials, crops, and visibility.

In addressing the multiple burdens of air pollution, its related causes, and the solutions, a broad distinction is necessary between indoor and outdoor air pollution:

• Human-induced *indoor air pollution* is caused by the household use of biomass for cooking and heating, usually involving open fires or traditional stoves in conditions of low combustion efficiency and poor ventilation. Indoor air pollution also originates from other "modern" indoor air pollutants associated with industrialization, with a variety of suspected health effects such as sick-building syndrome. However, from a global burden of disease point of view, these modern indoor air pollutants are relatively minor; hence this study focuses on air pollution from solid fuel use. Owing to the close proximity and low or zero cost of biomass in most rural areas, indoor air pollution is more of an issue in rural than in urban areas, although in many urban areas coal and charcoal are common household energy sources. Indoor air pollution from solid fuel use is particularly hazardous given that pollution concentrations exceed World Health Organization (WHO) guidelines by a factor of more than 100. The "rule of 1000" states that a pollutant released indoors is 1,000 times more likely to reach people's lungs than a pollutant

released outdoors. Indoor air pollution is also related to environmental tobacco smoke ("passive smoking") and exposure to chemicals and gases in indoor workplaces.

• Human-induced *outdoor air pollution* occurs mainly in or around
cities and in industrial areas, and is caused by the combustion of
petroleum products or coal by motor vehicles, industry, and power
generation. Outdoor air pollution is fundamentally a problem of
advancing economic development but also implies a corresponding
underdevelopment in terms of affording technological solutions that
reduce pollution, subsidizing more energy-efficient public transport
schemes, and enforcing regulations governing energy use.

Rates of exposure to these two types of air pollution therefore vary
greatly between rural and urban areas, and between developing regions,
given variations in vehicles ownership and use, extent and location of
industrial areas and power generation facilities, fuel availability, purchasing power, climate and topology, among others. Indoor sources
also contribute to outdoor air pollution, particularly in developing
countries; vice versa outdoor air pollution in industrialized countries
may contribute to pollution exposure in the indoor environment [1].

In the year 2003, at least 3 billion people were estimated to depend
on solid fuels, including biomass and coal, to meet their basic energy
needs: cooking, boiling water, and heating [2]. In rural areas, use of
improved domestic fuels varies from under 15 percent in sub-Saharan
Africa and Southeast Asia, to 33 percent in the Western Pacific developing region, and closer to 50 percent in Eastern Mediterranean and
Latin American countries. The main types of unimproved fuels used in
rural areas are firewood, dung, and other agricultural residues, followed by charcoal and coal/lignite [3]. The global number of annual
deaths due to solid fuel use within the home is estimated at more than
1.5 million, the majority of which are from acute lower respiratory
infection in children under five, and chronic obstructive pulmonary
disease in adults over thirty years of age. The total disease burden,
including morbidity, is estimated at 38.5 million Disability-Adjusted
Life-Years (DALYs) [4]. Indoor air pollution from solid fuel use is generalized throughout the developing world. However, the actual health
impact will depend on many factors, including whether fuel is burned
in indoor areas, cooking practices and proximity to stove, type and efficiency of stoves, and the presence of routes for smoke evacuation or

dissemination (depending on household features such as room size and height, chimney).

According to the World Health Organization, PM_{10} concentrations in urban outdoor air from industries and vehicles may trigger some 800,000 premature deaths a year with 65 percent occurring in the developing countries of Asia [5]. Outdoor air pollution is estimated to contribute as much as 0.6 to 1.4 percent of the burden of disease in developing regions [6]. This excludes pollution from lead in water, air, and soil, which may contribute a further 0.9 percent. It also excludes air pollution caused by forest fires (e.g. Indonesia in 1997), and serious accidents causing release of organic chemical substances (such as Bhopal, India, in 1984) or radioactive pollution (such as Chernobyl in 1986).

The solution

Indoor air pollution. There exists a range of solutions to reduce exposure to indoor air pollution, which includes reducing the source of pollution and altering the living environment and user behavior. Source reduction covers improved cooking devices (with or without flue attached), cleaner burning fuel, and reduced need for fire. Alterations to the living environment include improved ventilation and improved kitchen design and stove placement. Altered user behavior includes fuel drying, stove and chimney maintenance, use of pot lids to conserve heat, and keeping children away from the smoke [7]. While there are many options available for reducing exposure to indoor air pollution, there is limited evidence on their effectiveness in real-life conditions for modeling the cost–benefit of these options. Hence a global cost-effectiveness analysis (CEA) conducted by the WHO modeled only switching to modern fuels and using improved biomass stoves, separately as well as in combination [8]. A more recent global cost–benefit analysis, conducted in collaboration with the WHO, chose a similar set of interventions, but also included biofuel (ethanol) as an option as well as a pro-poor option [9]. The results of three interventions from this latter study are presented in this paper:[1]

---

[1] In addition to these scenarios, the following were presented in the global cost–benefit analysis: 50% of individuals to LPG pro-poor; 50% of individuals to biofuels pro-poor (ethanol); 100% of individuals to LPG; 100% of individuals to biofuels (ethanol); and 100% of individuals to improved stove.

1. Switching 50 percent of the population using solid fuels to liquefied petroleum gas (LPG)
2. Switching 50 percent of the population using solid fuels to ethanol
3. For 50 percent of those using a traditional stove for cooking with solid fuels, switch to a cleaner burning and more efficient improved stove

Outdoor air pollution. According to Kjellstrom et al., reducing air pollution exposure is largely a technical issue, and includes removing pollution at its source and filtering pollution away from the source [1]. These technical solutions are implemented in policy environments which may either make it illegal to use fuels which contain specific polluting substances (e.g. bans on leaded gasoline), or increase the costs of using polluting fuels (polluter pays principle). Governments may also make available information on and encourage best practices with regard to the use of technologies that reduce emissions of polluting substances. However, applying these policies is often more an economic than a technical issue. In the case of air pollution caused by vehicles, the solution may be in the form of a catalytic converter to use lead-free gasoline (at the same time reducing PM_{10}, CO, NO_x, and hydrocarbon emissions), reduced sulfur-content diesel fuel, more fuel-efficient vehicles, or more expensive use of roads (road tax, congestion tax, or fuel tax). Power plants and industrial plants that burn fossil fuels can reduce emissions through filtering and scrubbing methods, changing fuel sources to natural gas, or building high chimneys to dilute pollutants and reduce pollution concentration locally [1]. However, high chimneys may simply relocate the problem rather than solve it.

The choice of solutions, or interventions, to be presented in this present paper is, however, highly dependent on what studies have been previously conducted. As documented below, the literature reveals a considerable diversity of studies – national and city-level studies, comprehensive outdoor air pollution control versus single regulatory measures, single versus multiple pollutant interventions, and industry-wide versus single industry measures. Hence, the interventions that are presented here are many and diverse.

Cost–benefit analysis

Indoor air pollution. Given the availability of a global study which models the costs, economic benefits, and benefit–cost ratio of a selection of interventions to reduce exposure to indoor air pollution, this present paper draws heavily on this study [9]. Except for a global cost-effectiveness analysis, which evaluated the cost per DALY averted for the same set of interventions [8], it is the only global economic evaluation study in the field of indoor air pollution. In this study, the benefit–cost ratio is calculated as the annual average economic benefits of the intervention divided by the annual average economic gross costs of the intervention. Intervention costs include stove purchase cost spread over an assumed length of life, programme costs, and recurrent fuel costs based on expected consumption levels. Health impacts include pneumonia among children, and chronic obstructive pulmonary disease and lung cancer among adults. Economic benefits include reduced health expenditure related to less illness, the value of assumed productivity gains due to less illness and death, time savings due to less time spent on fuel collection and cooking, cost savings as a result of switching away from traditional fuels or using less fuel due to efficiency gains, and environmental impacts at the local and global level. Local environmental effects are assessed as fewer trees cut down, while global environmental effects considered are lower CO_2 and CH_4 emissions, valued using current market values of emission reductions on the European carbon market. The base year used in the study was 2005, and the first year of intervention is the year 2006, giving an intervention period of ten years until the end of the year 2015. As the global benefit–cost study did not calculate DALYs, the annual DALY gain from these interventions is extracted from the previous CEA [8].

A summary of the costs, health benefits, economic benefits and resulting benefit–cost ratios are presented in Table 5.1, for eleven WHO developing country subregions and all developing country subregions combined. The global cost of reducing by half those without modern cooking fuels by switching to LPG is US$23.6 billion annually, while averting 10 billion DALYs per year and saving US$10.4 billion fuel costs from traditional fuels no longer purchased. The contributors to overall economic benefits at global level are the following: time savings (48.6%), health-related productivity (44.5%), environmental benefits (6.7%), and health care savings (0.2%). The benefit–cost ratio ranges from 3.0 (BCR1) to 4.3 (BCR3) to 4.7 (BCR2). When biofuel (ethanol) is used instead of LPG, the cost leaps to US$53 billion annually, due to the higher purchase cost and lower burning efficiency assumptions. Hence the BCR drops to around 2.0 (BCR2 and BCR3) and as low as 1.3 (BCR1).

Table 5.1. *Results of global cost–benefit analysis: costs, benefits and benefit–cost ratio, for eleven developing world subregions*

Interventions and variables	Africa		The Americas		E Mediterranean		Europe		SE Asia		W Pacific	Developing World
	AFR-D	AFR-E	AMR-B	AMR-D	EMR-B	EMR-D	EUR-B	EUR-C	SEAR-B	SEAR-D	WPR-B	World
Total population in 2015 (million)	487	481	531	93	184	189	238	223	473	1,689	1,488	6,076
1. Reduce by half those without modern cooking fuel by switching to LPG (all US$ values annually in *millions*)												
1.1 Costs (US$)	1,838	2,033	2,058	465	771	1,225	611	399	1,964	5,928	6,271	23,563
1.2 DALYs averted ('000 DALY)	310	564	61	60	1	255	52	n/a	184	2,186	6,284	9,957
1.3 Fuel cost savings	905	1,388	444	270	7	502	324	363	518	1,323	4,398	10,441
1.4 Health cost savings (US$)	21	29	5	4	1	22	1	0	8	49	35	174
1.5 Productivity (morbidity) (US$)	172	146	67	21	11	49	14	1	103	238	638	1,459
1.6 VOSL (mortality) (US$)	1,437	1,361	620	61	15	326	108	96	274	1,451	32,980	38,729
1.7 Time savings (US$)	3,028	4,986	5,464	506	3,354	1,467	1,192	734	3,399	5,305	14,542	43,977
1.8 Environmental benefit	955	1,352	429	69	31	229	130	80	556	1,008	1,229	6,066
1.9 BCR1 (DALY at US$1,000)	2.8	4.1	3.1	2.0	4.4	2.0	2.8	n/a	2.4	1.7	4.2	3.0

1.10 BCR2 (DALY at US$5,000)	3.5	5.2	3.2	2.5	4.4	2.9	3.1	n/a	2.8	3.1	8.2	4.7
1.11 BCR3 (Productivity & VOSL)	3.5	4.6	3.4	2.0	4.4	2.1	2.9	3.2	2.5	1.6	8.6	4.3
2. Reduce by half those without modern cooking fuel by switching to biofuel (ethanol) (all US$ values annually in *millions*)												
2.1 Costs (US$)	4,019	4,461	4,972	1,125	1,795	2,479	1,427	924	4,130	14,257	13,546	53,136
2.2 DALYs averted ('000 DALY)	310	564	61	60	1	255	52	n/a	184	2,186	6,284	9,957
2.3 Fuel cost savings	905	1,388	444	270	7	502	324	363	518	1,323	4,398	10,441
2.4 Health cost savings (US$)	21	29	5	4	1	22	1	0	8	49	35	174
2.5 Productivity (morbidity) (US$)	172	146	67	21	11	49	14	1	103	238	638	1,459
2.6 VOSL (mortality) (US$)	1,437	1,361	620	61	15	326	108	96	274	1,451	32,980	38,729
2.7 Time savings (US$)	3,028	4,986	5,464	506	3,354	1,467	1,192	734	3,399	5,305	14,542	43,977
2.8 Environmental benefit	924	1,318	388	60	15	209	117	72	524	881	1,103	5,612
2.9 BCR1 (DALY at US$1,000)	1.3	1.9	1.3	0.8	1.9	1.0	1.2	n/a	1.1	0.7	1.9	1.3
2.10 BCR2 (DALY at US$5,000)	1.6	2.4	1.3	1.0	1.9	1.4	1.3	n/a	1.3	1.3	3.8	2.1
2.11 BCR3 (Productivity & VOSL)	1.6	2.1	1.4	0.8	1.9	1.0	1.2	1.4	1.2	0.6	4.0	1.9

Table 5.1. *(cont.)*

Interventions and variables	Africa		The Americas		E Mediterran		Europe		SE Asia		W Pacific	Developing World
	AFR-D	AFR-E	AMR-B	AMR-D	EMR-B	EMR-D	EUR-B	EUR-C	SEAR-B	SEAR-D	WPR-B	
3. Reduce by half those without improved stove (all US$ values annually in *millions*)												
3.1 Costs (US$)	168	210	415	46	103	156	42	22	122	487	546	2,319
3.2 DALYs averted ('000 DALY)	201	395	n/a	30	n/a	133	n/a	n/a	113	1516	132	2,520
3.3 Fuel cost savings	1,367	2,724	4,245	1,305	35	2,232	1,915	814	1,613	5,312	15,124	36,687
3.4 Health cost savings (US$)	3	4	1	1	0	3	0	0	2	9	9	32
3.5 Productivity (morbidity) (US$)	60	51	24	7	4	17	5	0	36	83	223	511
3.6 VOSL (mortality) (US$)	503	476	217	21	5	114	38	34	96	508	11,543	13,555
3.7 Time savings (US$)	3,072	5,314	16,707	1,211	7,862	2,963	2,443	912	4,280	8,717	34,620	88,100
3.8 Environmental benefit	344	482	169	29	19	89	51	32	208	413	489	2,324
3.9 BCR1 (DALY at US$1,000)	29.7	42.5	n/a	56.0	n/a	34.7	n/a	n/a	51.0	32.8	92.3	55.9
3.10 BCR2 (DALY at US$5,000)	34.5	50.0	n/a	58.6	n/a	38.2	n/a	n/a	54.7	45.2	93.2	60.3
3.11 BCR3 (Productivity & VOSL)	31.8	43.1	51.5	56.0	76.9	34.7	106.0	81.5	51.1	30.9	113.6	60.9

BCR: benefit–cost ratio; VOSL: value of a saved life; DALY: disability-adjusted life-year

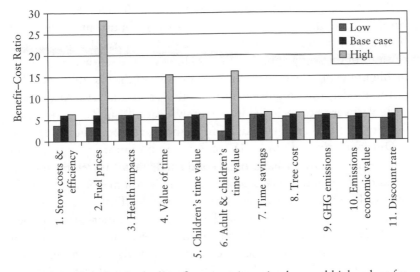

Figure 5.1. Variation in the benefit–cost ratios using low and high values for scenario I (LPG) in AFR-D

The global cost of reducing by half those without improved stoves is US$2.3 billion annually. The fuel cost savings due to greater fuel efficiency is considerably greater, at US$36.7 billion annually. Hence the fuel savings alone justify the intervention. Additionally, time savings of US$88.1 billion annually and mortality savings of US$13.6 annually give the intervention a very high benefit–cost ratio of at least 55. The contributors to overall economic benefits at global level are the following: time savings (84.3%) and health-related productivity (13.5%) represent the major economic benefits, followed by environmental benefits (2.2%), and health care savings (<0.1%). There is considerable variation between WHO subregions and scenarios.

Sensitivity analysis was performed to evaluate the impact of changes in assumptions on results and conclusions. Eleven different sensitivity analyses were run based on changing one or two input values for key variables. As shown in Figure 5.1, these analyses revealed a high level of sensitivity in the benefit–cost ratios in subregion AFR-D.[2] However,

[2] The benefit–cost ratio for the results in Figure 5.1 is calculated with fuel cost savings subtracted from interventions costs in the denominator; in Table 5.1, fuel cost savings are added to economic benefits in the numerator. However, Figure 5.1 is illustrative of the confidence around the base case results.

within the range of optimistic and pessimistic alternatives tested, the base case results turn out to be relatively robust in terms of a benefit–cost ratio that remains above 2.0. Therefore, the overall conclusions of the study appear realistic. However, the sensitivity analyses highlight the high level of uncertainty in some of the variables included in the model, thus requiring further study and analysis. Also, some variables were not included in the analysis at all, such as greenhouse gases other than carbon dioxide and methane, and other health effects.

Outdoor air pollution. Despite its importance, very few full cost–benefit analyses have been conducted on measures to address outdoor air pollution. Most studies are single country or single city in nature. Hence no global estimates are possible. Table 5.2 presents a selection of seven cost–benefit studies [10–16] and others are described briefly below. While no global study exists, these studies cover several major industrialized countries or economic areas (USA, Europe, Japan, Canada, UK) or heavily polluted cities located in developing countries (Mexico City, Jakarta, Shanghai). These setting-specific studies are highly indicative of the costs and benefits that are likely in other – similar – settings. Differences that may reduce transferability of results include different economic levels (e.g. for the valuation of health benefits, using a proxy measure such as national income per capita) and different pollution levels. In most studies, economic gains measured are limited to reductions in premature deaths, lower health care costs and workdays gained due to less morbidity. In only few studies were other economic benefits included, such as avoided damage to agriculture and ecosystems, or avoided damage to infrastructure and public buildings from corrosive pollutants. The benefit–cost ratios are highly variable, depending on contextual factors as well as the assumptions used in the analysis. Most studies present a wide range on benefit–cost ratio, and in some cases costs exceed the benefits. However, benefit–cost ratios are commonly above 3.0, thus giving a return of 3 currency units per currency unit spent. Studies that calculate net present value show a net positive return on investment; however, only one study presents expected annual rate of return.

Other cost–benefit studies of outdoor air pollution control not reported in Table 5.2 include:

- Aunan et al. estimate the costs and health and environmental benefits from air pollution reductions in Hungary [17]. Benefit–cost

Table 5.2. *Results of cost–benefit studies of policies and measures to control outdoor air pollution*

Study	US Federal Regulations [10]	United States EPA Clean Air Act [11]	European Commission [12]	UK Air Quality Strategy review [13]	China natural gas project [14]	Shanghai emissions control [15]	Japan SO_2 emissions control [16]
Location	US-wide	US-wide	Europe-wide	UK-wide	China (2 cities)	Shanghai	Japan-wide
Policies evaluated	National emissions standards for hazardous air pollutants	Clean Air Act (i) attain national ambient AQS; (ii) mobile source provisions; (iii) hazardous air pollutants; (iv) acid rain; (v) operating permits	Reductions in emissions to meet air quality targets for CO/Benzene, heavy metals, ozone, hydrocarbons	17 different policy measures to achieve AQS objectives (reported here: meeting European standards, low and high intensity)	Beijing (B) and Chongqing (C) natural gas projects (substituting natural gas for coal)	Emissions control (C1) power and (C2) industrial sectors	SO_2 emissions control in 3 policy epochs 1968–73 (stage 1); 1974–83 (stage 2); and 1984–93 (stage 3)
Period evaluated	1994–2004	1990–2010	NA	Until 2020	20 years	2010–2020	1968–1993
Cost data	2001; US$	1990; US$	Various years; Euro	2005; £	1998; RMB	1998; US$	1993; Yen
Discount rate	7%	5%	2%–6%	HM Treasury rate 12%	5%	2.5% Capital

Table 5.2. *(cont.)*

Study	US Federal Regulations [10]	United States EPA Clean Air Act [11]	European Commission [12]	UK Air Quality Strategy review [13]	China natural gas project [14]	Shanghai Emission Control [15]	Japan SO$_2$ emissions control [16]
Costs included	Compliance & monitoring	R&D, capital, operations and maintenance	NA	Capital and recurrent	Equipment and fuel minus costs saved of old fuel source	Regulations, facility closure, equipment	investment, fuel conversion and running
Cost results	US$15,171 mn –US$16,765 mn annually	US$19,000 mn p.a. in 2000, rising to US$27,000 mn in 2010	Euro 7 billion	Low: £374 mn p.a. High: £866 mn p.a.	Capital investment B: 3,509 mn RBM C: 703 mn RMB	C1: US$395 mn C2: US$94 mn p.a.	1. 5,576 bn Yen 2. 15,991 bn Yen 3. 9,354 bn Yen
Benefits included	Health benefits	Health, ecological (crop damage from acid deposition), and visibility benefits	Less premature deaths & morbidity, hospital admissions; labour productivity	Health effects (1%, 3%, and 6% hazard rates reported; optimistic 6% reported here)	Health impact	Mortality, morbidity and loss of workdays	Medical expenses, labor losses avoided, adjusted by WTP factor

Benefit results	US$41,292 mn – US$217,721 mn annually	US$71,000 mn p.a. in 2000 US$110,000 mn p.a. in 2010	Euro 42 billion	L: £566 mn–£1410 mn p.a. at 6% hazard H: £812–£2021 mn p.a. 6% hazard	B: 2,150 mn RMB annually C: 4,930 mn RMB annually	C1: US$417 mn p.a. (US$ 190–1,162) C2: US$266 mn p.a. (US$ 121–714)	1. 30,058 bn Yen 2. 18,818 bn Yen 3. 3,854 bn Yen
Benefit–cost ratio	2.72–13.0	3.8	6.0	L: 1.5–3.8 H: 0.9–2.3	NA	C1: 1.1 (0.5–2.9) C2: 2.8 (1.3–7.6)	1. 5.39 2. 1.18 3. 0.41
Net Present Value	NA	US$52,000 mn p.a. rising to US$83,000 mn p.a. in 2010	Various	L: £190 mn to £1039 mn H: £63 mn–£1165 mn	B: 6,876 mn RMB C: 18,650 mn RMB	C1: US$22 mn C2: US$172 mn p.a.	NA
IRR	NA	NA	NA	NA	B: 29.4%; C: 74.7%	NA	NA

NA – not available; mn – million; bn – billion; p.a. – per annum; IRR – internal rate of return ratios are presented in terms of the investments different sectors have to make for a given health benefit, ranging from a benefit–cost ratio of around 3.0 (agriculture), 5.0 (industry), 6.0 (transportation; energy), 16.0 (households), and 17.0 (services).

- Netalieva, Wesseler, and Heijman estimate the costs and health benefits of emissions reductions in the oil extraction industry in Kazakhstan [18]. By installing the equipment required, it is estimated that US$2.61 million social health care costs can be avoided annually, comparing with abatement costs of US$0.46 million annually, thus giving a benefit–cost ratio of 5.7.
- Voorhees et al. model the reductions in nitric oxide and NO_2 emissions in Tokyo from 1974 to 1993, and estimate a benefit–cost ratio of 6.0 [19].
- Blackman et al. report that the benefits considerably outweigh the costs of control strategies to reduce PM_{10} emissions from traditional brick kilns in Mexico [20].
- Pandey and Nathwani estimate the benefits of a pollution control program in Canada of US$7.5 billion per year outweigh the costs by three times [21].

In addition to the cost–benefit studies presented above, other studies have examined air pollution-related cost-of-illness and damage costs, and, in some studies, the predicted benefits of successfully implementing certain measures to reduce air pollution [22–30].

Implications and outlook

For a significant proportion of the world's population, air pollution is a daily fact of life, whether it is in the home, in the workplace, or in the urban environment. One of the major tangible effects of air pollution is sickness and premature mortality, which according to global estimates accounts for 2.5 million deaths per year and countless more million episodes of illness. These health effects have important implications for national economic indicators. Poor quality air also has other quality of life as well as economic consequences. This review and summary presentation of the economic costs and benefits of air pollution control options has shown that it is highly cost-beneficial to spend society's resources on air pollution control programs, both in the indoor and outdoor environments.

In interpreting the results of this review, it is important to keep in mind the multiple uncertainties by which cost–benefit analysis is plagued in the field of indoor and outdoor air pollution. First, measuring the impact of air pollution on health is very complex since there are many different pollutants and their effects on health are difficult to discern. Hence, controlled trials in the medical scientific sense are very few in the area of air pollution. Time-series studies are also difficult to interpret, due to seasonal and year-to-year variations in exposure, especially for outdoor air pollution. Second, there exists significant uncertainty in the economic valuation techniques used in these studies, such as the value of life. Different methods and values used between different studies makes it difficult to compare the results of studies reported in the literature.

While the control strategies for indoor and outdoor air quality improvement are largely unrelated, they do have similar basic approaches: (1) fuel switching, (2) emission control, and (3) fuel use efficiency. Each of these options offers different opportunities and drawbacks. General constraints to the implementation of air pollution control measures cover lack of political motivation or competing political priorities, lack of economic (purchasing) power, lack of regulatory frameworks or regulation monitoring, and lack of access of the potential user to the necessary resources or technologies. Hence, government and private sector activities should focus on addressing these barriers, according to their importance in each air pollution context.

References

1. Kjellstrom, T., Lodh, M., McMichael, T., Ranmuthugala, G., Shrestha, R., and Kingsland, S. (2006). Air and water pollution: burden and strategies for control, in *Disease Control Priorities in Developing Countries*, Jamison, D., Breman, J., Measham, A., Alleyne, G., Claeson, M., Evans, D., Jha, P., Mills, A., and Musgrove, P., Editors, New York: Oxford University Press.
2. World Health Organization (2006). *Fuel for Life: Household Energy and Health*. Geneva: World Health Organization.
3. Rehfuess, E., Mehta, S., and Prüss-Üstün, A. (2006). Assessing household solid fuel use – multiple implications for the millennium development goals *Environmental Health Perspectives* 114(3): 373–8.
4. Smith, K., Mehta, S., and Feuz, M. (2004). Indoor smoke from household solid fuels, in *Comparative Quantification of Health Risks: Global and Regional Burden of Disease due to Selected Major Risk Factors*,

vol. II of 3 vols. Ezzati, M., Rodgers, A., Lopez, A., and Murray, C., Editors, Geneva: World Health Organization.

5. United Nations Environment Programme (2006). *Global Environment Outlook Year Book 2006: An Overview of Our Changing Environment*. Nairobi: United Nations Environment Programme.

6. World Health Organization (2002). *World Health Report 2002*. Geneva: World Health Organization.

7. Bruce, N., Rehfuess, E., Mehta, S., Hutton, G., and Smith, K. (2005). Indoor Air Pollution, in *Disease Control Priorities in Developing Countries*, Jamison, D., Breman, J., Measham, A., Alleyne, G., Claeson, M., Evans, D., Jha, P., Mills, A., and Musgrove, P., Editors, New York: Oxford University Press.

8. Mehta, S. and Shahpar, C. (2004). The health benefits of interventions to reduce indoor air pollution from solid fuel use: a cost-effectiveness analysis *Energy for Sustainable Development* 8(3): 53–9.

9. Hutton, G., Rehfuess, E., Tediosi, F., and Weiss, S. (2006). *Global Cost–Benefit Analysis of Household Energy and Health Interventions*. Geneva: Department for the Protection of the Human Environment, World Health Organization.

10. US Office of Budget and Management (2005). *Validating Regulatory Analysis: 2005 Report to Congress on the Costs and Benefits of Federal Regulations and Unfunded Mandates on State, Local and Tribal Entities*. Washington, DC: Office of Budget and Management, December 2005. Available: www.whitehouse.gov/omb/inforeg/2005_cb/final_2005_cb_report.pdf.

11. US Environmental Protection Agency (1999). *The Benefits and Costs of the Clean Air Act: 1990 to 2010*. Environmental Protection Agency, November 1999. Available: www.epa.gov/oar/sect812.

12. Pye, S. and Watkiss, P. (2005). Clean Air for Europe (CAFE) Programme cost–benefit analysis. Baseline analysis 2000 to 2020 Study conducted by AEA Technology Environment for the European Commission, DG Environment.

13. UK Department for Environment, Food and Rural Affairs (2006). Economic analysis to inform the air quality strategy review consultation: third report of the Interdepartmental Group on Costs and Benefits Department for Environment, Food and Rural Affairs, London, April 2006.

14. Mao. X., Guo, X., Chang, Y., and Peng, Y. (2005). Improving air quality in large cities by substituting natural gas for coal in China: changing idea and incentive policy implications *Energy Policy* 33: 307–18.

15. Li, J., Guttikunda, S., Carmichael, G., Streets, D., Chang, Y-S, and Fung, V. (2004). Quantifying the human health benefits of curbing air

pollution in Shanghai *Journal of Environmental Management* 70: 49–62.

16. Kochi, I., Matsuoka, S., Memon, M. A., and Shirakawa,. H (2001). Cost–benefit analysis of the sulfur dioxide emissions control policy in Japan *Environmental Economics and Policy Studies* 4: 219–33.

17. Aunan, K., Patzay, G., Asbjorn Aaheim, H., and Martin, Seip H. (1998). Health and environmental benefits from air pollution reductions in Hungary. *Science of the Total Environment* 212: 245–68.

18. Netalieva, I., Wesseler, J., and Heijman, W. (2005). Health costs caused by oil extraction emissions and the benefits from abatement: the case of Kazakhstan *Energy Policy* 33: 1169–77.

19. Voorhees, A., Araki, S., Sakai, R., and Sato, H. (2000). An ex post cost–benefit analysis of the nitrogen dioxide air pollution program in Tokyo *Journal of the Air and Waste Management Association* 50: 391–410.

20. Blackman, A., Newbold, S., Shih, J., and Cook, J. (2000). The benefits and costs of informal sector pollution control: Mexican brick kilns Discussion Paper 00–46, Resources for the Future, Washington, DC.

21. Pandey, M. and Nathwani, J. (2003). Canada wide standard for particulate matter and ozone: cost–benefit analysis using a life quality index *Risk Analysis* 23(1): 55–67.

22. Pearce, D. (1996). Economic valuation and health damage from air pollution in the developing world *Energy Policy* 24(7): 627–30.

23. Mexico Air Quality Management Team (2002). Improving air quality in Metropolitan Mexico City: an economic valuation Policy Research Working Paper 2785. World Bank, Washington, DC, February 2002.

24. Pearce, D. and Crowards, T. (1995). Assessing the health costs of particulate air pollution in the UK. CSERGE Working Paper GEC 95–27, Centre for Social and Economic Research on the Global Environment, University of East Anglia.

25. Maddison, D. (1998). Valuing changes in life expectancy in England and Wales caused by ambient concentrations of particulate matter. CSERGE Working Paper GEC 98–06, Centre for Social and Economic Research on the Global Environment, University of East Anglia.

26. Dubourg, W. (1995). A note on estimating the mortality costs of lead emissions in England and Wales *Resources Policy* 21(2): 107–12.

27. UK Department of Health (1999). *Economic Appraisal of the Health Effects of Air Pollution*. Department of Health. Norwich, UK: Stationery Office.

28. Seethaler, R. (1999). Health costs due to road traffic-related air pollution: an impact assessment project of Austria, France and Switzerland.

Synthesis report, prepared for the WHO Ministerial Conference on Environment and Health, London, June 1999.

29. Ostro, B. (1983). The effects of air pollution on work loss and morbidity *Journal of Environmental Economics and Management* 10: 371–82.

30. Lvovsky, K., Hughes, G., Maddison, D., Ostro, B., and Pearce, D. (2000). *Environmental Costs of Fossil Fuels: A Rapid Assessment Method with Application to Six Cities*. Pollution Management Series, Paper No. 78. World Bank, Washington, DC.

6 | *Climate Change*

GARY YOHE

Scoping the problem

The Intergovernmental Panel on Climate Change (IPCC, 2001) offered perhaps the most efficient presentation of the climate change problem with its "burning ember" diagram; it is replicated here as Figure 6.1.

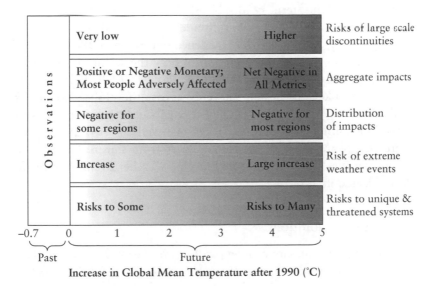

Increase in Global Mean Temperature after 1990 (°C)

Figure 6.1. Sources of concern and shaded indications of vulnerability

Source: Figure 19-8-1 in IPCC (2001). Relative levels of vulnerability along five "Lines of Evidence" or "Sources of Concerned" and their sensitivity to increases in global mean temperature were assessed based on the literature available through the middle of 2000. Low vulnerability was indicated by a white or very pale yellow coloration, here indicated by light grey. High vulnerability was highlighted by red coloration, here indicated by very dark grey; and intermediate vulnerabilities by various shades of yellow and orange.

The diagram identifies five "Lines of Evidence" with color-coded indicators of economic, social, and natural vulnerabilities. Two are essentially economic indicators of aggregate impacts at the global and regional levels. They are dominated by estimates of the economic damage of climate impacts in market-based sectors such as real estate, agricultural, and energy, and they increase with the global mean temperature. They include, to some degree, evaluations of how various nations and even communities within nations might adapt to climate-related stress driven by higher temperatures as well as the cost of undertaking those adaptations.

In its recently released Fourth Assessment Report (IPCC, 2007), the IPCC concluded that new knowledge supports moving the thresholds of color change indicating increasing risk in the embers to the left – toward lower temperature ranges. It follows that potentially significant impacts are looming in the nearer term. Table 6.1 replicates table 6.1 in Stern, *et al.* (2006). Based on background work reported in Warren, *et al.* (2006), it adds texture and content to the moving embers, and it provides evidence that the new IPCC conclusion is an appropriate interpretation of how the science is evolving. Notice, in particular, how Table 6.1 shows clearly that climate impacts are likely to be felt unevenly across the globe. Notice, as well, that the remaining rows in Figure 6.1 focus attention on ecosystems (and other non-market risks), as well as two potentially more significant areas of concern: "Risks from Future Large-Scale Discontinuities" and "Risks from Extreme Weather Events"; both are also reflected in Table 6.1.

Scoping some solutions

Even though the climate problem will not be "solved," it is, though, possible to describe responses that could at least partially ameliorate additional damages. Estimates of economic cost are, of course, key components of such descriptions. While economists disagree on what the future might hold, they agree that "the social cost of carbon" is a useful measure with which to summarize both the size of the problem and efficient responses to the associated risks – i.e., the damage caused over time by releasing an additional tonne of carbon in the atmosphere discounted back to the year of its emission. The social cost of carbon therefore represents the "marginal cost" of emissions. Alternatively, it

Table 6.1. *Highlights of possible climate effects*

A summary of the recent science on climate impacts calibrated by increases in global mean temperature for major sectors of interest.

Temp rise (°C)	Water	Food	Health	Land	Environment	Abrupt and Large-Scale Impacts
1°C	Small glaciers in the Andes disappear completely, threatening water supplies for 50 million people	Modest increases in cereal yields in temperate regions	At least 300,000 people each year die from climate-related diseases (predominantly diarrhoea, malaria, and malnutrition) Reduction in winter mortality in higher latitudes (Northern Europe, USA)	Permafrost thawing damages buildings and roads in parts of Canada and Russia	At least 10% of land species facing extinction (according to one estimate) 80% bleaching of coral reefs, including Great Barrier Reef	Atlantic Thermohaline Circulation starts to weaken
2°C	Potentially 20–30% decrease in water availability in some vulnerable regions, e.g.	Sharp declines in crop yield in tropical regions (5–10% in Africa)	40–60 million more people exposed to malaria in Africa	Up to 10 million more people affected by coastal flooding each year	15–40% of species facing extinction (according to one estimate) High risk of extinction of	Potential for Greenland Ice Sheet to begin melting irreversibly, accelerating sea

Table 6.1. (*cont.*)

Temp rise (°C)	Water	Food	Health	Land	Environment	Abrupt and Large-Scale Impacts
	Southern Africa and Mediterranean				Arctic species, including polar bear and caribou	level rise and committing world to an eventual 7 m sea level rise
3°C	In Southern Europe, serious droughts occur once every 10 years 1–4 billion more people suffer water shortages, while 1–5 billion gain water, which may increase flood risk	150–550 additional millions at risk of hunger (if carbon fertilisation weak) Agricultural yields in higher latitudes likely to peak	1–3 million more people die from malnutrition (if carbon fertilisation weak)	1–170 million more people affected by coastal flooding each year	20–50% of species facing extinction (according to one estimate), including 25–60% mammals, 30–40% birds and 15–70% butterflies in South Africa Onset of Amazon forest collapse (some models only)	Rising risk of abrupt changes to atmospheric circulations, e.g. the monsoon Rising risk of collapse of West Antarctic Ice Sheet Rising risk of collapse of Atlantic Thermohaline Circulation
4°C	Potentially 30–50% decrease in	Agricultural yields decline by 15–	Up to 80 million more people	7–300 million more people affected by	Loss of around half Arctic tundra	

	water availability in Southern Africa and Mediterranean	35% in Africa, and entire regions out of production (e.g. parts of Australia)	exposed to malaria in Africa	coastal flooding each year	Around half of all the world's nature reserves cannot fulfill objectives
5°C	Possible disappearance of large glaciers in Himalayas, affecting one-quarter of China's population and hundreds of millions in India	Continued increase in ocean acidity seriously disrupting marine ecosystems and possibly fish stocks		Sea level rise threatens small islands, low-living coastal areas (Florida) and major world cities such as New York, London, and Tokyo	
More than 5°C	The latest science suggests that the Earth's average temperature will rise by even more than 5 or 6°C if emissions continue to grow and positive feedbacks amplify the warming effect of greenhouse gases (e.g. release of carbon dioxide from soils or methane from permafrost). This level of global temperature rise would be equivalent to the amount of warming that occurred between the last ice age and today – and is likely to lead to major disruption and large-scale movement of population. Such "socially contingent" effects could be catastrophic, but are currently very hard to capture with current models as temperatures would be so far outside human experience.				

Source: Stern et al. (2006), ch. 3.

represents the "marginal benefit" of unit of carbon emissions reduction, and it can serve as an estimate of the appropriate carbon tax.

More than 100 estimates of the social cost of carbon currently available in the published literature were surveyed by Tol (2005). The median estimate is $13 per tonne of carbon. The mean is $43 per tonne, and the upper end of the range lies above $350 per tonne of carbon. How should all of this disagreement be interpreted? Richard Tol, the economist who prepared the survey, read the range to mean that roughly $50 per tonne should be interpreted as representative of the highest reasonable "best" estimate of the social cost of carbon. Thomas Downing (2005), a geographer from the Stockholm Environment Institute, looked through the lens of his enormous experience in developing countries where changes in climate produce enormous displacement and other transitional effects that cannot be quantified in terms of currency. He read the data to mean that $50 per tonne should be interpreted as representative of the lowest reasonable estimate of the true social cost of carbon.

But why is the range so large? Which of the "Lines of Evidence" do the estimates include, and which do they miss? What combinations of underlying factors produce low or high estimates of social cost? Answers to these questions can be enormously revealing. The choice of discount rate and the incorporation of equity weights are extremely important, and both lie within the purview of decision-makers. High (low) discount rates sustain low (high) estimates because future damages become insignificant (are exaggerated). Meanwhile, strong (weak) equity weighting across the globe support high (low) estimates because poor developing countries are most vulnerable.

It turns out, however, that several scientific parameters over which decision-makers have no discretion are even more important in explaining the variability in the estimates. Climate sensitivity (the increase in global mean temperature that would result from a doubling of greenhouse gas concentrations from pre-industrial levels) is the largest source of variation; see Hope (2006). Valuation of non-market impacts ranks second. In fact, it is possible to derive high estimates for the social cost of carbon even if you assume low discount rates and almost no equity weighting. All that is required is the assumption that the climate sensitivity lies at the high range of the latest range of estimates. Andronova and Schlesinger (2001) find that the historical record could easily be explained with climate sensitivities as high as

9°C (even though the TAR reported an upper bound of 5.5°C); both admit that a sensitivity below 1.5°C is impossible. Moreover, none of the estimates included in the survey include *any* internally consistent reflection of economic costs of "Risks from Extreme Climate Events" or "Risks from Future Large-Scale Discontinuities."

To understand the significance of these omissions, consider the possibility that the Atlantic Thermohaline Circulation might weaken significantly or even suddenly collapse. The climate research community has not yet prepared comprehensive portraits of the implications of such a collapse, but there is consensus in the view that impacts would be abrupt (occurring within a decade or two) and felt across the globe (i.e., not just in Europe). It is, as well, widely held that finding out what would happen is not really an experiment that should be conducted on our only planet (since the collapse would likely be irreversible). Schlesinger, *et al.* (2006) put the chance of collapse at 50% if the global mean temperature were to climb by another 2°C beyond 1990 levels. Put another way, Yohe, *et al.* (2006c) show a 45% chance of collapse by 2105 along a "middle of the road" emissions scenario across the full range of climate sensitivities. Imposing a *global policy* targeted at a $50 per tonne social cost of carbon would reduce that likelihood to 30% if it were initiated immediately; but only to 40% if the policy intervention were delayed by 30 years.

To be clear, adding on a static $50 per tonne carbon tax (adding something like $5 to the price of a barrel of oil) would not do the trick over the long term. Watkiss (2005) has shown that the social cost of carbon, and thus the appropriate tax, should increase in real terms by 2% or 3% per year – approximately the endogenously determined real rate of interest. This is the critical component of the policy; that is, *it is the persistent and predictable ratcheting-up of the effective price of carbon* that would give the policy traction at all.

Evaluating solutions – imposing a $50 per tonne carbon tax (or its equivalent)

What else can be said about a $50 per tonne tax on carbon? Since it lies close to the mean of the published estimates in Tol's survey, it is certain that its estimated benefits would exceed its estimated costs for some combinations of discount rate, equity weighting, and scientific variables. Low discounting, high equity weighting, and high climate

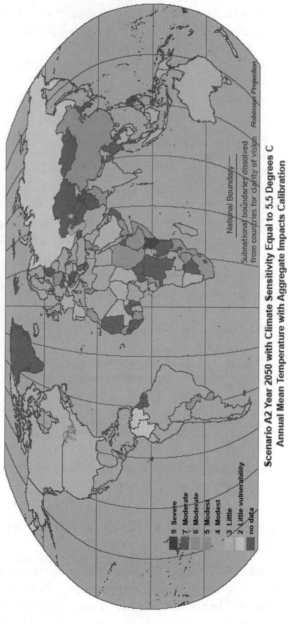

Global Distribution of Vulnerability to Climate Change
Combined National Indices of Exposure and Sensitivity

9 Severe
7 Moderate
6 Moderate
5 Modest
4 Modest
3 Little
2 Little vulnerability
no data

National Boundary
Subnational boundaries dissolved
from countries for clarity of vision

Robinson Projection

Scenario A2 Year 2050 with Climate Sensitivity Equal to 5.5 Degrees C
Annual Mean Temperature with Aggregate Impacts Calibration

http://ciesin.columbia.edu/data/climate/

©2006 Wesleyan University and Columbia University

Figure 6.2. Geographical distribution of vulnerability in 2050 with a climate sensitivity of 5.5°C.

Source: Yohe, et al. (2006a) and (2006b).

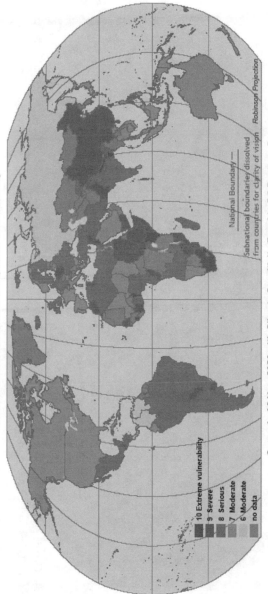

Global Distribution of Vulnerability to Climate Change
Combined National Indices of Exposure and Sensitivity

10 Extreme vulnerability
9 Severe
8 Serious
7 Moderate
6 Moderate
no data

Scenario A2 Year 2050 with Climate Sensitivity Equal to 5.5 Degrees C
Annual Mean Temperature with Extreme Events Calibration

National Boundary
Subnational boundaries dissolved
from countries for clarity of vision   Robinson Projection

http://ciesin.columbia.edu/data/climate/   ©2006 Wesleyan University and Columbia University

Figure 6.3. Geographical distribution of vulnerability in 2050 with a climate sensitivity of 5.5°C.

Source: Yohe, et al. (2006a) and (2006b).

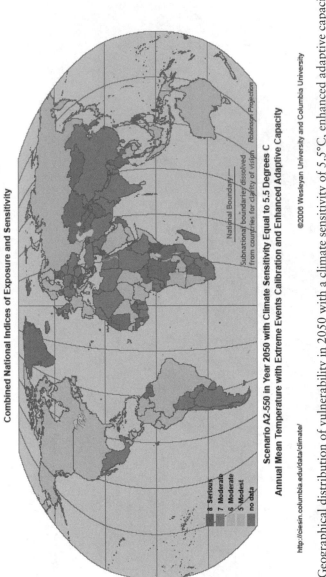

Figure 6.4. Geographical distribution of vulnerability in 2050 with a climate sensitivity of 5.5°C, enhanced adaptive capacity alone and combined with concentrations of greenhouse gases limited to 550 ppm in carbon dioxide equivalents

Source: Yohe, et al. (2006a) and (2006b).

sensitivities would do the trick. Of course, costs would dominate benefits for other combinations characterized by more aggressive discounting, less concern about equity, and low climate sensitivities.

Given the wide range of impacts that are not included in the calculations of benefits, however, a strong case can be made that we simply do not know enough to be at all confident in comparisons based on incomplete statistics; see Yohe (2004) and Tol (2003). For present purposes, these shortcomings mean that any evaluation of the benefits of a $50 per tonne tax will simply miss many of the most important benefits simply because they have not been quantified in terms of currency.

Table 6.2 tries to offer some insight into the scope of these omitted benefits for five different cases after it records gross and net (available partial estimates of the economic value of damages avoided deducted from gross costs) in Columns (1) and (2). Column (3) reports net costs as a fraction of discounted GDP through 2105, and it also indicates abatement costs for the first 10 years (when avoided damages are likely to be minimal) as a percentage of then current GDP. Evidence-constrained benefit–cost ratios are reported in Column (4). All of these estimates are derived from the baseline emissions scenario generated by the DICE integrated assessment model and described by Nordhaus and Boyer (2000).

Insights into omitted benefits are recorded in Columns (5) through (7). They are derived from Arnell, *et al.* (2002) for alternative evaluative metrics that track three measures of risk of climate change: millions at risk of hunger, millions at risk of water scarcity, and millions at risk of coastal flooding. Their work has shown that limiting the increase of global mean temperature to 1.2°C (above the average of the last third of the twentieth century) rather than allowing an unregulated 2.9°C warming through 2080 would remove 43 million, 2,070 million, and 74 million people from those risks, respectively, if the climate sensitivity were something like 3°C. Columns (5) through (7), in fact, report the per capita expense of achieving these reductions.

Case 1, described in the first row of Table 6.2, considers implementing the $50 per tonne tax in 2006 and reports the various evaluative metrics under the assumption that the climate sensitivity is, in fact, 3°C. The high (low) discount case sets the pure rate of time preference at 3% (0%) so that the Ramsey discount rate falls over time from near 5% (2%) to something closer to 4% (1%) by 2105. Notice that the per-capita costs of reduced risk of hunger, water scarcity, and coastal

Table 6.2. *Comparative statistics for five alternative cases*
Calculations indicating costs and benefits for alternative policy approaches designed to reduce greenhouse gas emissions over the near term into the more distant future.

	(1)[a] Cost present value through 2105	(2)[b] Net cost present value through 2100	(3)[c] Net cost %GDP through 2100 (first 10 yrs)	(4)[d] Lower bound for the B/C ratio	(5)[e] Risk of hunger (in 2080)	(6)[f] Risk of water scarcity (in 2080)	(7)[g] Risk of coastal flooding (in 2080)
(1) Case 1 (3°)							
$50/tonne							
Begin in 2006							
High discount[h]	$12.73	$0.46	0.04%	>> 0.96	$17,692	$222	$6,216
Low discount[i]	$110.81	$0.76	0.02% (0.22%)	>> 0.99	$29,231	$367	$10,270
(2) Case 2 (1.5°)							
$5/tonne							
Begin in 2006							
High discount[h]	$0.22	$0.44	0.04%	>> 2.00	$24,444	$379	$27,500
Low discount[i]	$2.22	$0.20	0.00% (0.00%)	>> 0.99	$1,111	$17	$1,250

(3) Case 3 (5.5°)							
$75/tonne							
Begin in 2006							
High discount[h]	$19.23	$0.74	0.06%	>> 0.96	$15,417	$266	$9,737
Low discount[i]	$141.52	$1.07	0.03%	>> 0.99	$22,292	$385	$14,079
			(0.47%)				
(4) Case 4 (3°)							
$100/tonne							
Begin in 2016							
High discount[h]	$16.14	$0.59	0.05%	>> 0.96	$22,692	$285	$7,973
Low discount[i]	$129.43	$0.95	0.02%	>> 0.99	$36,538	$459	$12,838
			(0.58%)				
(5) Case 5 (1.5°)							
$8/tonne							
Begin in 2016							
High discount[h]	$0.73	$0.44	0.04%	>> 1.91	$24,444	$204	$27,500
Low discount[i]	$2.33	$0.02	0.00%	>> 0.99	$1,111	$9	$1,250
			(0.00%)				

Notes:

[a] Derived from DICE (Nordhaus and Boyer, 2000) in trillions of dollars (1995$).

Table 6.2 (cont.)

b Net costs derived from DICE (Nordhaus and Boyer, 2000); includes estimates of climate damages avoided with little recognition of damage associated with climate-related extreme events and valuation of unique systems. Abrupt climate change is included in terms of an estimate of the willingness to pay to avoid such events.

c Net costs as a percentage of discounted GDP through 2105; in parenthesis, abatement costs during the first ten years of implementation (i.e., through 2016 for cases 1, 2 and 3 but from 2016 until 2026 for cases 4 and 5).

d Benefits computed by comparing columns (1) and (2); the ratio uses column (1) as a denominator. Since so many benefits of climate change have not yet been quantified (and may never really be quantified), these ratios represent lower bounds of the appropriate ratios since the numerator could be much larger.

e Derived from Arnell, *et al.* (2002) estimates of number of people removed from risk. Options 1 and 4 reduce exposure from 69 million to 43 million in 2080; Options 2 and 5, from 61 million to 42 million; and Option 3, from 91 to 43 million.

f Derived from Arnell, *et al.* (2002) estimates of number of people removed from risk. Options 1 and 4 reduce exposure from 2.83 billion to 760 million in 2080; Options 2 and 5, from 1.92 billion to 760 million; and Option 3, from 3.44 billion to 760 million.

g Derived from Arnell, *et al.* (2002) estimates of number of people removed from risk. Options 1 and 4 reduce exposure from 79 million to 5 million in 2080; Options 2 and 5, from 21 million to 5 million; and Option 3, from 81 to 5 million.

h High discounting set the pure rate of time preference for Ramsey discounting equal to 3%; with DICE employing a logarithmic utility function, this amounts to real discount rates between something close to 5% and, later in the century, 4%.

i Low discounting set the pure rate of time preference for Ramsey discounting equal to 0%; with DICE employing a logarithmic utility function, this amounts to real discount rates between something close to 2% and, later in the century, 1%.

flooding are all less than $30,000 in discounted terms – a level that compares favorably to estimates of $300,000 to $104 million per life saved from existing Occupational, Safety and Health Administration (OSHA), National Highway Traffic Safety Administration (NHTSA), and the Environmental Protection Agency (EPA) regulations on everything from passive restraints in automobiles to asbestos exposure; see Viscusi (1996).

Since so much has been made of uncertainty in our estimates of climate sensitivity, Cases (2) and (3) of Table 6.2 record the results of repeating the exercise for 1.5°C and 5.5°C, respectively. In both cases, the initial tax is adjusted to achieve 1.2°C temperature increase benchmark in 2080 so that the Arnell, *et al.* (2002) estimates of risk reduction can be employed; estimates for the unregulated baselines were adjusted, as well, from their work. Notice that the initial tax and all aggregate cost metrics are higher for the higher sensitivity and lower for the lower sensitivity. The costs of reduced risk are lower for the lower climate sensitivity, but they are also lower for the higher sensitivity; this is because high climate sensitivities exaggerate the risk associated with the unregulated benchmark scenario so that the benefit is enlarged.

And what if implementation of the policy were delayed by 10 years? Cases (4) and (5) indicate that costs would be uniformly higher (by as much as 50%) for climate sensitivities equal to 3°C and 1.5°C. For a sensitivity of 5°C, however, the news is even worse; the 10-year delay in implementation means that the 1.2 degree warming benchmark in 2080 becomes unachievable with *any economically palatable climate policy.*

Results

Table 6.2 presents some of the economic consequences of imposing a tax on the carbon content of fossil fuel. The specific policy offered in Case 1 would charge $50 per tonne beginning in 2006 and allow this charge to increase at the rate of interest through 2105. Alternatives were offered, but they were contingent on climate sensitivity and the date of implementation. All would effectively limit the increase in temperature through 2080 to 1.2°C; the version described in Case 1 for a climate sensitivity of 3°C would restrict atmospheric concentrations of greenhouse gases to 550 ppm in carbon dioxide equivalents.

In addition to economically quantified benefits that never fell below 90% of abatement cost for any case examined, implementing any of the alternatives would produce a 33% reduction in the likelihood of a collapse of the Atlantic thermohaline circulation. Reductions in risk to hunger, water scarcity, and coastal flooding in 2080 never rose above $30,000 per person.

These benefits must, of course, be viewed in the context of opportunity cost – investments in progress toward the other challenges identified by the Copenhagen Consensus. How, in particular, would climate policy participate as part of a portfolio of initiatives designed to effectively spend $75 billion on global welfare? Yohe, et al. (2006a and 2006b) have shown that the benefits of climate policy are seen most strikingly in countries where the other challenges are largest – the developing countries of Africa, southern Asia, and South America. There is synergy across approaches to these challenges that should be exploited. Moreover, many of the goals embodied in the other challenges are, in fact, underlying determinants of adaptive and mitigative capacities; see Yohe and Tol (2002) and Yohe (2001), for example. Progress in overcoming these challenges will make climate policy more effective.

Should climate policy be part of the Copenhagen Consensus portfolio of responses? Declining the opportunity to respond to the climate change challenge would make achieving other goals more difficult; accepting the challenge as described here would offer the chance of exploiting significant synergies. At what cost? Since the carbon tax policy could be self-sufficient (e.g., by allocating some tax revenue to administering, negotiating and monitoring or by imposing a very modest Tobin tax on carbon permit transactions under a cap and trade system) the question is how much to deduct from the Copenhagen Consensus bottom line. The economic costs reported in Column (1) are *not* the appropriate charges. These are economic costs, but they are not administrative costs. To compute the latter, suppose that donations to the $100 billion budget were to decline in proportion to abatement cost expressed in terms of a percentage of discounted global GDP. These are the values reported in Column (3) of Table 6.2, and none of those values exceeds 1% even for a climate sensitivity of 5.5°C. Taking the range seriously, the $50 per tonne carbon tax proposal advanced here would cost the Copenhagen Consensus bottom line no more than $1 billion regardless of the discount rate applied. In short, devoting no more than 1% of the Consensus budget would help assure that the other $99 billion does not "swim upstream" against climate damages. Seems like too good a deal to refuse.

Caveats, context and design

It is important, in thinking about how to respond to the risks posed by climate change, to recognize that setting near-term policy can be an exercise in determining the appropriate short-term incentives for carbon-saving investments and energy conservation rather than an exercise in "solving" the climate problem once and for all. The options described above are all extended 100 years into the future, and their specifications depend, to some degree, on the discount rate (a parameter over which decision-makers have some authority). They also depend, to a large degree, on climate sensitivity. This is one of many parameters over which only Mother Nature has purview, and she has not been particularly forthcoming about what value is most appropriate. Given that she is likely to remain "tight-lipped" about climate sensitivity and other climate system details for a long time, it is perhaps desirable to step out from under the burden of trying to address the unmanageable long-term problem. Perhaps, instead, we should agree to confront the more tractable near-term question of what to do over the next few decades while still preserving our ability to make progress toward an ultimate response to climate risk.

A good answer to the "What to do now?" question is simple to describe. Design something that will (1) discourage long-term investments in energy, transportation, and construction that would lock in high carbon intensities for decades to come, and (2) encourage development of alternative energy sources, carbon sequestration technologies and efficiency, while (3) not causing enormous economic harm (and thereby impeding our ability to make progress in overcoming the other challenges discussed in the Copenhagen Consensus project). Done correctly, such an approach holds the promise of reducing the expected discounted cost of meeting whatever climate policy goal turns out to be appropriate, and so it holds the promise of complementing investments designed to confront those challenges.

As an example of how these short-term objectives might be achieved, one might consider what it would take to make it economically attractive to run existing natural gas-fired electric generators more intensively and coal-fired generators correspondingly less intensively. Why? Because gas-fired generators emit only about half as much carbon per unit of electricity. Natural gas is considerably more expensive than coal, however, so it would take a substantial carbon price to inspire such a change – about $100 per tonne of carbon given current fuel price expectations. This, of course, is larger than the $50 proposal discussed above.

On the other hand, consider pending investments to add new generating capacity across the United States (and the entire world, for that matter) over the next few decades. Much of this capacity is currently planned as conventional coal-fired technology. What would it take, in terms of carbon price, to make it economic to install new gas-fired capacity instead? On current gas price expectations, a carbon price of about $20 per tonne would be sufficient to make new gas-fired generators as economical as new coal-fired plants based on the present value of fixed and variable costs and limited uncertainty. Several confounding economic factors (such as greater price volatility) add uncertainty, though, so it may be necessary to set an initial carbon price somewhere above $20 per tonne to achieve the desired economic equivalence (but something lower than $50 per tonne would suffice). Lower costs involved in building a new gas plant can compensate for a large difference in fuel cost.

To make the full step to near zero carbon technologies (e.g., carbon capture and sequestration) would require a somewhat higher price – also estimated at around $100 per tonne of carbon by several sources and included in Pacala and Socolow (2004) as one possible "wedge" of emissions reduction. Meanwhile, a $100 per tonne of carbon tax has been identified as the level for which current sequestration technologies might become economically efficient in many places. McCarl and Sands (2007) estimate that annual terrestrial offsets could total between 1 billion tonnes of carbon dioxide between 2010 and 2035 if a $100 per tonne value were assigned to carbon. Some of the detail behind estimates of this sort has been offered by Antle, *et al.* (2007). They show carbon sequestration supply curves for conservation tillage in the agricultural heartland of the United States beginning at carbon dioxide prices that range between $20 and $40 per tonne and reach capacity thresholds between $100 and $200 per tonne.

Bringing these technologies up to scale would take more than a decade, of course, and large investment would be based on the same type of present value calculation outlined above. It is here where the

Hotelling rule helps. Since power generators and sequestration projects last 30 to 40 years or more, increasing the carbon price at the rate of interest can make CCS technologies attractive in the present value calculation even if it does not reach the economic "tipping point" for some time. The $50 per tonne charge in 2007 proposed above would, for example, reach $100 just around 2021 (at a 5% interest rate), and that should be sufficient to affect even the retrofitting switch in most places and inspire appropriate development of enhanced sequestration techniques.

A carbon tax would not, of course, provide any incentive to sequester carbon by itself; doing that would require a targeted use of some of the tax revenue. Yohe (1989) describes how some of the revenue might be used to "buy back" carbon that was removed from the end of the effluent stream at a price that equals the tax applied at the beginning. Doing so would mean that the marginal cost of bringing in the last tonne would equal the marginal cost of taking it out – an efficiency criterion that "closes the loop."

And what about policy design? Cap and trade systems have become the stock in trade of many who try to advocate climate policy, but this preference may be based on little more than an allergic reaction to the use of the word "tax." Since concentrations depend on cumulative emissions over long periods of time, there is no Weitzman (1974) reason to favor a policy that would fix annual emissions. Yohe (1992) noted, more specifically, that fixing total emissions of any pollutant only makes sense if period-to-period variability around a targeted mean (that would improve economic efficiency) would unnecessarily increase expected social costs; and he argued that this is clearly not the case for carbon emissions. In addition, Newell, *et al.* (2005), among others, have expressed concerns that the prices which clear cap and trade permit markets can be volatile. Volatility has certainly been the hallmark of the sulfur permit markets in the United States and the nascent carbon markets of the European Union. Pizer (2002) responded to the threat of incapacitating volatility by proposing "safety valve" limits on the price of permits. Others have argued that volatility can be diminished by appropriate banking provisions. The fundamental problem with either solution is that appropriate climate policy requires a clear signal that carbon will always be more expensive next year than it is today. Even a modest amount of volatility can obscure that signal.

On other hand, a tax, increasing at the rate of interest à la Hotelling, would produce a persistent and predictable increase in the cost of using carbon that would inspire cost-reducing innovation and fuel switching in the transportation, building, and energy supply sectors of our economy. If carbon were taxed at the point it entered an economy (a couple of thousand sources in the United States, for example, as opposed to millions of end-users), then it would be dispersed appropriately throughout the economy with relative prices of thousands of goods changing in proportion to the underlying carbon intensities. Moreover, it would generate revenue. A $60 per tonne of carbon dioxide tax would, for example, generate something like $90 billion in tax revenue in the United States in 2007 if it were paid on every tonne of carbon embodied in every unit of fossil fuel consumed. This is revenue that could be used to offset the regressive nature of the carbon tax itself, by underwriting tax credits for citizens with taxable incomes below a specified level. The substitution effect would still apply, of course, so carbon conservation could be expected even from the beneficiaries of the credits. Tax revenue could also be used to reduce other distortional taxes. It could even be used to fund research into alternative energy sources.

References

Andronova, N. G. and M. E. Schlesinger (2001), "Objective Estimates of the Probability Density Function for Climate Sensitivity," *Journal of Geophysical Research* 106 (D19): 22605.

Antle, J. M., S. M. Capalbo, K. Paustian and M. K. Ali (2007), "Estimating the Economic Potential for Agricultural Soil Carbon Sequestration in the Central United States using an Aggregate Econometric-Process Simulation Model," *Climatic Change* 80: 145–171.

Arnell, N., M. Cannell, M. Hulme, R. Kovats, J. Mitchell, R. Nicholls, M. Parry, M. Livermore, and A. White (2002), "The Consequences of CO_2 Stabilization for the Impacts of Climate Change," *Climatic Change* 53: 413–446.

Downing, T. (2005), "Social Cost of Carbon: A Closer Look at Uncertainty, Final Report," Stockholm Environment Institute for the United Kingdom Department for Environment, Food, and Rural Affairs.

Hope, C. (2006), "The Marginal Impact of CO_2 from PAGE2002: An Integrated Assessment Model Incorporating the IPCC's Five Reasons for Concern," *Integrated Assessment* 6: 1–16.

Intergovernmental Panel on Climate Change (IPCC) (2001), *Climate Change 2001: Impacts, Adaptation and Vulnerability,* Cambridge University Press, Cambridge.

Intergovernmental Panel on Climate Change (IPCC) (2007), *Climate Change 2007: Impacts, Adaptation and Vulnerability,* Cambridge University Press, Cambridge.

McCarl, B. A. and R. D. Sands (2007), "Competitiveness of Terrestrial Greenhouse Gas Offsets: Are they a Bridge to the Future?," *Climatic Change* 80: 109–126.

Newell, R., W. Pizer, and J. Zhang (2005), "Managing Permit Markets to Stabilize Prices," *Environmental and Resource Economics* 31: 133–157.

Nordhaus, W. and J. Boyer (2000), *Warming the World – Economic Models of Global Warming,* MIT Press, Cambridge, MA, 232 pp.

Pacala, S. and R. Socolow (2004), "Stabilization Wedges: Solving the Climate Problem for the Next 50 Years with Current Technologies," *Science* 305: 968–972.

Pizer, W. (2002), "Combining Price and Quantity Controls to Mitigate Global Climate Change," *Journal of Public Economics* 85: 409–434.

Schlesinger, M. E., J. Yin, G. W. Yohe, N. G. Andronova, S. Malyshev, and B. Li (2006), "Assessing the Risk of a Collapse of the Atlantic Thermohaline Circulation," in *Avoiding Dangerous Climate Change,* Cambridge University Press, Cambridge, ch. 5.

Stern, N., S. Peters, V. Bakhshi, A. Bowen, C. Cameron, S. Catovsky, D. Crane, S. Cruickshank, S. Dietz, N. Edmonson, S.-L. Garbett, L. Hamid, G. Hoffman, D. Ingram, B. Jones, N. Patmore, H. Radcliffe, R. Sathiyarajah, M. Stock, C. Taylor, T. Vernon, H. Wanjie, and D. Zenghelis (2006), *Stern Review: The Economics of Climate Change,* Cambridge University Press, Cambridge.

Tol, R. S. J. (2003), "Is the Uncertainty about Climate Change too Large for Expected Cost-Benefit Analysis?," *Climatic Change* 56: 265–289.

Tol, R. S. J. (2005), "The Marginal Damage Costs of Carbon Dioxide Emissions: An Assessment of the Uncertainties," *Energy Policy* 33: 2064–2074.

Viscusi, K. (1996), "Economic Foundation of the Current Regulatory Reform Efforts," *Journal of Economic Perspectives* 10: 38–52.

Warren, R., N. Arnell, R. Nicholls, P. Levy, and J. Price (2006), "Understanding the Regional Impacts of Climate Change," Tyndall Centre for Climate Change Research, Working Paper 90 (www.hm-treasury.gov.uk/independent_reviews).

Watkiss, P. (2005), "The Social Costs of Carbon (SCC) Review – Methodological Approaches for Using SCC Estimates in Policy

Assessment, Final Report," for the United Kingdom Department for Environment, Food, and Rural Affairs.

Weitzman, M. (1974), "Prices versus Quantities," *Review of Economic Studies* 41: 50–65.

Yohe, G. (1989), "More on the Properties of a Tax Cum Subsidy Pollution Control Strategy," *Economic Letters* 31: 193–198.

Yohe, G. (1992), "Carbon Emissions Taxes: Their Comparative Advantage under Uncertainty," *Annual Review of Energy* 17: 301–326.

Yohe, G., E. Malone, A. Brenkert, M. Schlesinger, H. Meij, X. Xing, and D. Lee (2006a), "A Synthetic Assessment of the Global Distribution of Vulnerability to Climate Change from an IPCC Perspective that Reflects Exposure and Adaptive Capacity," Center for International Earth Science Information Network, Palisades, NY. Available at (http://ciesin.columbia.edu/data/climate)

Yohe, G., E. Malone, A. Brenkert, M. Schlesinger, H. Meij, and X. Xing, (2006b), "Global Distributions of Vulnerability to Climate Change," *Integrated Assessment Journal* 20: 1–10.

Yohe, G. W., M. E. Schlesinger and N. G. Andronova (2006c), "Reducing the Risk of a Collapse of the Atlantic Thermohaline Circulation," *Integrated Assessment Journal* 20: 1–17.

Yohe, G. W. and R. S. J. Tol (2002), "Indicators for Social and Economic Coping Capacity – Moving toward a Working Definition of Adaptive Capacity," *Global Environmental Change* 12: 25–40.

Yohe, G. W. (2001), "Mitigative Capacity – The Mirror Image of Adaptive Capacity on the Emissions Side," *Climatic Change* 49: 247–262.

Yohe, G. W. (2004), "Some Thoughts on Perspective," *Global Environmental Change* 14: 283–286.

Yohe, G. W., N. G. Andronova, and M. E. Schlesinger (2004), "To Hedge or Not against an Uncertain Climate Future," *Science* 306: 416–417.

7 | Deforestation

HENK FOLMER AND G. CORNELIS
VAN KOOTEN*

Deforestation occurs as a result of fire, disease, wind and other natural means, or as a consequence of human activities related to the harvest of timber for commercial purposes and/or clearing of land for agriculture. Global patterns of deforestation are indicated in Table 7.1. Between 2000 and 2005, the majority of countries in the Caribbean, Europe, North America, Oceania, and Western and Central Asia had no significant changes in forested area, while in Africa nearly all countries lost forestland to agriculture (Kauppi et al. 2006). The countries with the greatest losses in forest averaged a net loss of 8.2 million ha per year, with Brazil (3.1 mil ha yr^{-1}) and Indonesia (1.9 mil ha yr^{-1}) leading the way. The ten countries with the greatest net gains in forest area averaged gains of 5.1 million ha yr^{-1}, with China accounting for the most (4.1 mil ha yr^{-1}). As Table 7.1 shows, forests in temperate and boreal areas have actually expanded. Thus, we conclude that deforestation is mainly a problem of tropical deforestation, but that rates of deforestation appear to be falling.

Tropical deforestation

The UN's Food and Agricultural Organisation (FAO) defines tropical forest ecosystems as having a minimum of 10% crown canopy of trees and/or bamboo; they are generally associated with wild flora, fauna and natural soil conditions and not subject to agricultural practices. Tropical forests cover a large portion of the globe's land surface between 23° north and south of the Equator, and range from open savannahs where precipitation is limited, to dense tropical rainforests. Tropical deforestation is defined to occur when canopy cover

* Van Kooten would like to thank Canada's Sustainable Forest Management Network for research support.

Table 7.1. *Forest area and rates of deforestation, 1981–2005*

| Region/country | Forest cover 2000 (10^6 ha) | Average annual change in forest cover | | | | | | | |
| | | 1981–90 | | 1990–95 | | 1990–2000 | | 2000–2005[a] | |
		Area (10^3 ha)	Rate (%)	Area (10^3 ha)	Rate (%)	Area (10^3 ha)	Rate (%)	Area (10^3 ha)	Rate (%)
Africa	*649.9*	*–4,100*	*–0.7*	*–3,748*	*–0.7*	*–5,264*	*–0.7*	*–2,898*	*–0.4*
Tropical	634.2	n.a.	–0.7	–3,695	–0.7	–5,295	–0.8	–2,299	–0.4
Nontropical	15.7	n.a.	–0.8	–53	–0.3	31	0.2	–120	–0.8
Asia	*524.1*	*n.a.*	*n.a.*	*–3,328*	*–0.7*	*–651*	*–0.1*	*n.a.*	*n.a.*
Tropical	288.6	–3,791	–1.2	–3,055	–1.1	–2,427	–0.8	–1,599	–0.6
– South Asia	76.7	–551	–0.8	–141	–0.2	–98	–0.1	+41	0.1
– SE Asia	211.9	–3,240	–1.4	–2,914	–1.3	–2,329	–1.0	–1,640	–0.8
Europe	*998.1*	*n.a.*	*n.a.*	*+389*	*+0.3*	*+424*	*+0.3*	*+661*	*+0.1*
Northern	70.3	n.a.	n.a.	+8	+0.0	+40	+0.1	+95	+0.1
Western	32.6	n.a.	n.a.	+358	+0.6	+311	+0.5	+51	+0.1
Eastern	848.8	n.a.	n.a.	+23	+0.1	+73	+0.2	–28	≈0
Former USSR	*901.4*	*n.a.*	*n.a.*	*+557*	*+0.1*	*+739*	*+0.1*	*–3,704*	*–0.4*
Canada	*244.6*	*n.a.*	*n.a.*	*+175*	*+0.1*	*0*	*0.0*	*+2,621*	*+1.1*
USA	*226.0*	*n.a.*	*n.a.*	*+589*	*+0.3*	*+388*	*+0.2*	*+3,084*	*+1.3*
Central Am. & Mexico	*73.0*	*–1,112*	*–1.5*	*–959*	*–1.2*	*–971*	*–1.2*	*+546*	*+0.7*

Caribbean	5.7	−122	−0.3	−78	−1.7	+13	+0.2	+11	+0.2
South America	885.6	n.a.	n.a.	−4,774	−0.5	−3,711	−0.4	−4,513	−0.5
Tropical	834.1	−6,173	−0.7	−4,655	−0.6	−3,456	−0.4	−4,251	−0.5
Brazil	543.9	−3,671	−0.6	−2,554	−0.5	−2,309	−0.4	−3,103	−0.6
Temperate	51.5	n.a.	n.a.	−119	−0.3	−255	−0.5	n.a.	n.a.
Oceania	197.6	n.a.	n.a.	−91	−0.1	−365	−0.2	+346	+0.2
Tropical	35.1	−113	−0.3	−151	−0.4	−122	−0.3	n.a.	n.a.
Temperate	162.5	n.a.	n.a.	+60	+0.1	−243	−0.1	n.a.	n.a.
Global total[b]	**3,869.5**	n.a.	n.a.	**−11,269**	**−0.3**	**−9,397**	**−0.2**	**−7,317**	**−0.2**

Notes:

n.a. implies not available or not applicable.

[a] Preliminary and based on authors' calculations

[b] Totals may not tally due to rounding

Source: FAO (1993, 1997, 2001, 2006); www.mongabay.com/forest_types_tab.e.htm

is reduced to less than 10%. This implies that significant forest degradation can take place without being considered as deforestation. Nonetheless, the FAO definition is generally used because of its consistency and reliability.

In 1995, tropical forests were estimated to cover about 1,733.9 million ha, or about 13.4 percent of the globe's land area excluding Antarctica and Greenland. This was down from an estimated 1,756.3 million ha in 1990 and 1,910.4 million ha in 1981. During the 1990s, some 5.8 million ha of humid tropical forest were lost each year (or 0.5%), although re-growth reduced this by 1 million ha (Mayaux *et al.* 2005). However, rates of deforestation have varied substantially throughout the tropics (see Table 7.1). Perhaps surprisingly, the tropical rainforest, which is the forest type of most concern to the international community, experiences relatively slower rates of deforestation than other tropical forests (FAO 1993). Indeed, the highest rates of deforestation in tropical regions appear to occur in (moist or dry) upland forests.

Even at the current rate of tropical deforestation, the world's tropical forests would continue to exist through the entire twenty-first century and well into the twenty-second century. Of course, the current rate of tropical deforestation will almost surely change over time. Moreover, deforestation is generally a reversible process, but appears irreversible because of the long time required to restore forests to their original state. In many respects, tropical deforestation today is not dramatically different from temperate deforestation that occurred centuries earlier. In the past, expanding populations led to greater use of wood for fuel and construction and an expansion of agricultural land, resulting in large-scale deforestation in many regions of Europe and North America.

Economic benefits of tropical forests

Forests provide many values to humans. We distinguish between production functions (production of timber and non-timber forest products), regulatory functions (e.g., carbon sink, watershed protection) and wildlife habitat/biodiversity functions, where the latter include non-use values associated with preservation. Preservation values are associated with the knowledge that tropical forests exist now (existence value) and in the future (option and bequest value).

Production functions of tropical forests

Tropical stands contain some 200 m³ to 400 m³ of timber per ha (Pearce and Warford 1993, p. 130), but much of this consists of non-commercial species, so clear felling does not usually occur. Nonetheless, if 30 to 40 percent of the harvest is usable and for stumpage values of US$30 m⁻³, clear felling yields a rent (or social surplus) of $1,800–$4,800 per ha, not including returns from subsequent land uses. Subsequent use of the land in forestry yields a positive but small return (less than US$1 ha⁻¹ yr⁻¹ for artificially regenerated stands), while managed plantations frequently yield negative returns and proceed only with government subsidies (Sedjo 1992).

Estimates of the value of sustainable selective logging per ha vary considerably, with differences due to (among other things) discount rates, stumpage prices, management costs, site conditions and productivity (see e.g., Vincent 1990; Pearce and Warford 1993). Vincent (1990) provides estimates of present value ranging from +US$850 down to −$130 per ha, with the outcome of the most realistic scenario in the vicinity of $250 ha⁻¹.

Small-scale gathering of non-timber forest products (NTFPs) is competitive with commercial logging only in some regions. The values provided by rattan, oils, fruits, nuts and bush meat can be large on occasion (Peters *et al.* 1989) and, in some cases, large numbers of forest dwellers depend critically on them for survival. However, one cannot simply extrapolate these high figures to large stretches of tropical forests due to downward sloping demand, uncertainty concerning sustainable supply, and increasing costs of production and transportation.

Although tropical rainforests are generally not very attractive to tourists because of the humid climate and their limited scenic value (compared to say, East African game parks), recreation and tourism have the potential to become sources of foreign exchange. However, the role of eco-tourism in the promotion of forest conservation will likely remain small, and per ha values fall, as more regions are available for tropical forest recreation.

Regulatory functions of tropical forests

Regulatory services consist of watershed protection, waste assimilation, soil conservation, carbon storage, and the like. Since these services do not have prices, non-market valuation methods (see e.g, Van Kooten and Folmer, 2004) are needed to gain insight into their values. Postel and Heisse (1988) estimate that deforestation in Costa Rica resulted in revenue losses of $133–$274 million from sedimentation behind one dam, while Ruitenbeek (1989) computes the fishery and agricultural benefits of forest conservation in one region of Costa Rica to amount to some $3/ha/yr. Ruitenbeek (1989) estimates the present value of the watershed function to be US$23 ha^{-1} of forest protected in Costa Rica.

It is important to recognize that it is not deforestation *per se* that leads to the loss of regulatory functions, but rather the nature of the succeeding land use. Agricultural practices that leave soils exposed during the wet season create erosion problems and nutrient losses, but land uses that provide crop cover all year long (e.g., pasture, coffee plantations) experience rates of erosion not much worse than forestland.

Release of CO_2 is an important cost of deforestation, with estimates of the potential damage from tropical deforestation ranging from $25 to $175 ha^{-1} yr^{-1} (IPCC 1996). But without knowledge of the shadow price of CO_2 in the atmosphere, it is impossible to determine unambiguously this component of the costs of tropical deforestation. Therefore, we employ several estimates of CO_2 prices in the cost–benefit analysis below.

Habitat, biodiversity and non-use values

Tropical deforestation is considered a major contributing factor to loss of species, with claims of annual loss ranging from 14,000 to 40,000 species to as many as 16 million (Hughes *et al.* 1997). Even under the most optimistic assumptions, the present value of marginal species is small, less than $10,000. As the number of extant species increases, the value of marginal species falls – from almost $3,000 when there are 250,000 species, to a negligible amount when there are more than 1 million (Simpson *et al.* 1996). If the value of marginal species is small, then, by extension, so is the value of a marginal hectare. While the economic value of species in biodiversity prospecting may be modest at the margin, ecosystem stability may nonetheless be positively linked to diversity; but ecosystem stability and services from ecosystems may not depend on the uniqueness of the species mix.

Non-use values related to biodiversity (species) are likely more important than use values. Based on data from contingent valuation

Table 7.2. *Summary of the economic values of tropical forests (US$ ha⁻¹ yr⁻¹)*

Item	Marginal[a]	Average[c]
Commercial logging		
Clear felling	72–192	not calculated
Natural forest management	≈ 1	315 (all raw materials)
Agriculture[b]	120–140	not calculated
Sustainable land use		
Selective logging	10–145	not calculated
Nontimber forest products	≈ 10	32
Tourism	≈ 1	112 (all outdoor recreation, incl. tourism)
Preservation		
Watershed protection[b]	≈ 2	8
Prevention of soil loss	≈ 3	245
Flood prevention	≈ 1	6
Other	not calculated	1,024
Global climate change	2–140	223
Biodiversity prospecting	1–2	41
Non-use value	1–4	2

Notes:
[a] Unless otherwise indicated, these data are based on discussion in the text. Values are annualized using a 4% discount rate.
[b] *Source:* van Soest (1998, p.25).
[c] *Source:* Costanza *et al.* (1997). Not all categories correspond to those in the marginal column.

studies cited by Pearce and Warford (1993, pp. 131–32), we estimate that the annual existence value for the total tropical forest is approximately $3 per ha, and no more than $6 per ha for the tropical rainforest. As we show below, whatever value is chosen, it is likely small compared to commercial values. Further, since non-use values decline as the forest stock increases, the marginal preservation value is probably much lower than indicated here.

A summary of the marginal values of tropical forests is provided in Table 7.2. For comparison, estimates of the average economic values of tropical forests, as calculated by Costanza *et al.* (1997), are also provided. While it is true that tropical forests provide a wide range of ecosystem services and other non-timber amenities, their marginal values are small compared to commercial values of the forest. Nonetheless, as more of the tropical forest is converted to other land uses, it is likely that the costs of further conversion (the value of foregone ecosystem and other non-timber amenities) will increase as well.

Causes of tropical deforestation

The causes of tropical deforestation are complex and not well understood. Identification of causes is influenced by poor-quality data, the approach employed (normative, positive, statistical, structural, etc.), the level of analysis (local, country-level or cross-country comparisons), different definitions of terms such as "deforestation" and "shifting cultivation", and failure to distinguish between types of logged areas. Moreover, explanations of tropical deforestation are situation dependent. Because of these differences, there is often no consensus about the actual causes of deforestation. Nonetheless, we investigate some of the main factors that have been raised.

Commercial logging

A common but simplistic view, now largely rejected by most analysts, is that tropical deforestation is due to commercial logging (Kaimowitz and Angelsen 2001). Commercial logging in the tropics rarely results in significant direct land conversion. Unlike logging in the temperate forest, in the tropics it almost never involves clear felling; – because of the high diversity of tree species, only a relatively small number of all trees in a tropical forest are commercially suitable (Panayotou and Sungsuwan 1994). It should be observed that selective logging is generally conducive to forest regeneration and regret. The most damaging aspect of the harvesting process may be the construction of roads (Panayotou and Ashton 1992). Estimates of the direct contribution of commercial logging to deforestation are therefore modest, typically varying from 2 to 10 percent (Amelung and Diehl 1992). However, logging often facilitates conversion of forestland to agriculture. Illegal logging is also important and is estimated to deprive governments of some $15 billion annually in royalties, and depress timber prices by some 7–16 percent (*The Economist* 2006).

Conversion to agriculture

Deforestation is primarily caused by a desire to convert forests to agriculture, which is particularly true in Africa and Latin America but less so in Asia. A fundamental distinction needs to be made between "shifting cultivators" and "forest pioneers", with numerous possibilities between these extremes (Sunderlin and Resosudarmo 1997). Shifting cultivators clear the forest, cultivate the land for a short period and then leave it fallow for sufficient time to enable the land to revert back to natural forest. Traditional shifting cultivation can be sustainable, with products consisting of low-yield crops and a wide range of timber and non-timber products. Forest pioneers, on the other hand, clear the forest with the intention of establishing permanent or semi-permanent agricultural production. Forests are converted to both permanent and shifting agriculture as a result of factors, such as high agricultural prices, conversion subsidies, access roads, population pressure, and lack of tenure security, but the significance of the various factors varies.

Income and deforestation

The relation between income and deforestation is complex and ambiguous, having direct and indirect effects (Palo 1994). The environmental Kuznets curve (EKC) hypothesis views deforestation initially as an engine for economic growth when income is low, but, as income rises, deforestation falls (and afforestation may occur) as people demand more of the amenities associated with natural forests in addition to wood products. Moreover, higher education levels (and potentially less corruption in resource management) are associated with increases in per capita income, improved land tenure arrangements, fewer individuals engaged in primary production (agriculture and forestry) as a proportion of the population, and general improvements in the economy as a result of technical changes (e.g., Cropper and Griffiths 1994; Naidoo 2004). But empirical evidence for an EKC for tropical deforestation is mixed, partly due to the way empirical models are specified, partly because deforestation is defined differently across studies, and because mainly poor tropical countries are investigated. For studies where an inverted-U relation is found, turning points vary from annual incomes of US$500 to $3,500 to $5,000 (Meyer, van Kooten and Wang 2003; Scrieciu 2006).

Population and deforestation

The effect of population growth and population density on rates of deforestation is not well understood, mainly because of two opposing views. Those subscribing to the neo-Malthusian view generally find evidence of a positive relation between population and deforestation (Scrieciu 2006; Saxena *et al.* 1997). Studies of population change that take a more optimistic view find that increased population density leads to less erosion and more forests (Tiffen and Mortimore 1994), and that wood scarcity leads to increased tree planting (Hyde and Seve 1991). Many studies find neither population density nor growth to have any effect on deforestation (Cropper and Griffiths 1994). The overall picture remains unclear, primarily because the direction of causality has not been identified (Sunderlin and Resosudarmo 1997; Brown and Pearce 1994), although Scrieciu (2006) finds population pressure to be the driver of agricultural expansion, which he equates (probably erroneously) to deforestation. Nonetheless, a cursory examination of Ethiopia, which has a high and growing population, indicates that population must play a role – its rate of deforestation is some 37 percent with fuelwood needs, not agricultural expansion, as the primary cause.

Ultimate causes

Policy failure is usually a more important driver of tropical deforestation than market failure. Panayotou (1993) and Mendelsohn (1994), among others, demonstrate that government policies, whether deliberate or inadvertent, can result in deforestation at the cost of reducing society's welfare. Major forms of policy failure include (Sunderlin and Resosudarmo 1997; Repetto 1997): (1) direct subsidies to cut down forests; (2) indirect subsidies to forest companies through forest concessions that fail to capture all of the available rents and encourage excessive harvesting and wasteful rent seeking; (3) creation and protection of an inefficient ("log wasting") domestic forest industry; (4) direct subsidies to cattle ranchers to generate foreign exchange; (5) generous investment tax credits; (6) exemption of agricultural income from taxation; (7) subsidized credit for agriculture; (8) rules on public land allocation that favour large land holders or require 'development' of land to demonstrate ownership; (9) development of public infrastructure (e.g., access roads); and (10) overpopulation and migration policies (sometimes rooted in ethnic politics).

Reasons why governments may choose to promote deforestation include:

- Governments overstate the value of forests for timber and under-state the value of non-timber products, and their regulatory and habitat functions.
- The value of forest soils for agriculture is often overstated, with soils quickly depleted by cropping.
- Forest regions sometimes serve as an outlet for crowded popula-tions, with peasants encouraged to move into forested regions rather than the cities, thereby avoiding social unrest (Reed 1992).
- Investment in the forestry sector may be promoted to secure doubt-ful employment and other benefits (Osgood 1994).
- The value of minor forest products is systematically ignored because the majority of economic benefits accrue to powerless social groups (de Beer and McDermott 1989).
- Forests are not considered essential for economic development and may even be viewed as an asset to be liquidated in order to diversify the economy. Sometimes resource prices are kept artificially low to encourage industrial and agricultural activity, and economic growth.

For a democratic market economy to function properly, or for market-oriented economic policies to have effect, at least two criteria beyond well-functioning markets and well-defined property rights are required (Fukuyama 2002). First, a country must have institutions within which policy change can occur. Second, public economic policies can only be carried out by the state. However, the state must be able to enforce the rule of law, be competent and sufficiently transparent in formulating policy, and with enough legitimacy to be able to make painful deci-sions. Good governments protect property rights and individual free-doms, impose optimal regulations on businesses, provide an adequate (efficient) level of public goods (e.g., infrastructure, schools, health care, police protection, a court system), and are run by bureaucrats who are generally competent and not corrupt (La Porta *et al.* 1999; De Soto 2000). Unfortunately, in developing countries regulatory agencies often prevent market entry, courts resolve disputes arbitrarily and sometimes dishonestly, and politicians use government property to benefit their supporters rather than the population at large (Shleifer and Vishny 1998, p. 8). Consequently, illegal logging is often rampant in developing countries.

Is tropical deforestation excessive?

As a result of market and government failures, it is often assumed that current rates of deforestation must be excessive (Barbier and Burgess 1997). But conservation of tropical forests involves considerable opportunity costs – the foregone benefits from log sales and subsequent returns to agriculture. What then is the optimal stock of tropical forest that a country (global community) should protect? In one of only a few studies, Ehui and Hertel (1989) compute an optimal tropical forest stock for Côte d'Ivoire, which had the highest rate of deforestation of any nation during the 1980s, but also achieved the fastest agricultural growth in sub-Saharan Africa. They found that the optimal forest stock ranged from 5.4 million hectares (for a discount rate of 3%) to 1.9 million hectares (discount rate of 11%). Their estimates of the optimal forest stock exceeded the actual 1990 forest stock of approximately 3.2 million ha for discount rates below 8 percent. Clearly, the optimal stock of forests in Côte d'Ivoire and elsewhere depends on the discount rate, with further deforestation optimal when discount rates exceed about 10 percent (if one leaves some room for uncertainty). Whether this is the case more generally is an open question, but one should note that extant real rates of discount exceed 20 percent in most developing countries.

Ehui and Hertel conclude that they underestimate the true optimal forest stock because positive externalities like preservation and ecosystem benefits are ignored, as are non-timber forest products, possibilities for eco-tourism and existence values. One suspects that their inclusion would lead to higher optimal forest stocks, but, as we saw above, these values are generally quite small at the margin. Empirical support for this conclusion is provided for Costa Rica by Bulte et al. (2002).

Our own cost–benefit analysis reported in Tables 7.3 and 7.4 yields an ambiguous conclusion. Using the most recent information on global forest resources (FAO 2006), we calculated the annual benefits and costs of logging activities and fuel wood acquisition activities for the period 2000–2005. Benefits are given by the value of harvested logs plus the net discounted value of the deforested areas in agriculture, while costs are measured by the discounted loss of non-market amenities (including ecosystem services) and shadow damage caused by emissions of CO_2

from land use change. (Note that we assume that net revenues from logging are consumed, rather than invested in productive activities.) The results indicate that the worldwide net benefits of logging activities might have amounted to some $22.1 billion per year (optimistic scenario). In that case, global society is actually better off when countries deforest forestlands at the margin. If damages from release of CO_2 and losses of other ecosystem services are sufficiently high (pessimistic scenario), deforestation is an inefficient activity, with the potential to damage global welfare by as much as $126.4 billion. Similar results hold for regions.

There are three important qualifiers. First, it is assumed that deforestation releases all of the CO_2 stored in harvested timber. However, some of the carbon might remain sequestered in products. Further, the subsequent land use (e.g., coffee plantation, high-yielding forest plantation, agroforestry) might result in the sequestration of carbon to offset that released by deforestation. Second, the cost–benefit analysis presented in Tables 7.3 and 7.4 relates to the period 2000–2005 for forest covers (as presented in the two last columns of Table 7.1). For further deforestation, the costs are likely to increase and the cost–benefit ratio of logging is going to fall. Third, in making decisions about how much deforestation to permit, developing countries are usually given no, or inadequate, compensation for CO_2 released to the atmosphere by deforestation activities. Hence, release of CO_2 does not enter into their decision calculus.

International forest conservation measures

Roughly speaking, two types of trade measures are possible – those that reduce the level of logging (such as trade bans and import levies) and those that affect the way exploitation takes place (e.g., certification of forest management practices). The effects of trade measures on deforestation are probably modest. Barbier *et al.* (1994, p. 8) argue that the share of trade in total tropical roundwood production is small: only 17 percent of the tropical wood is used for industrial purposes, with most of the remainder consumed as fuelwood. Of the industrial wood, no more than 31 percent is subsequently exported (with an increasing share involved in South-South trade), so exports account for only about 6 percent of total tropical roundwood production. Since commercial logging accounts for only a small proportion of deforestation, it is evident that the direct

Table 7.3. *Cost–benefit analysis of deforestation in developing regions (2000–2005)*

Region	Annual change in forest area 2000–2005a	Estimated carbon removed	Estimated cost of CO2 emissions for offset prices[b]		Net value of logs removed[a]
			$5/tCo2	$30/ tCO2	
	million ha	tC/ha			
Eastern & Southern Africa	−1.702	86	2675.1	16050.6	488.3
Northern Africa	−0.982	36	650.2	3901.3	1461.0
West & Central Africa	−1.356	193	4799.1	28794.3	2644.4
East Asia	3.840	43	−3051.6	−18309.7	0.0
South & Southeast Asia	−2.851	119	6200.9	37205.4	
Western & Central Asia	0.014	56	−14.3	−85.6	0.0
Carribean	0.054	136	−134.9	−809.4	0.0
Central America	−0.285	119	622.0	3732.2	427.6
Ocenia[f]	−0.356	52	336.4	2018.6	1838.8
South America	−4.251	167	13019.0	78113.8	5628.3
WORLD	**−7.875**	**1006.342**	**25101.9**	**150611.5**	**19810.3**

Notes:

[a] *Source:* FAO (2006)

[b] CO_2 offset values obtained from (as viewed 18 October 2006): www.ecobusinesslinks.com/carbon_offset_wind_credits_carbon_reduction.htm Annual value = price ($/tCO$_2$) × carbon released (tC/ha) × area deforested (ha) × conversion of carbon to CO_2 (44 tCO$_2$/12 tC). Negative values indicate possible gain from afforestation.

[c] Annual land value from Table 7.2, discounted at a social rate of 5% to obtain discounted value.

[d] Marginal values range from Table 7.2, discounted at 5% rate. Negative values indicate possible gain to afforestation.

[e] Negative values indicate that deforestation provides negative benefits to society; n.a. = not applicable since afforestation occurs.

[f] Includes New Zealand and Australia, but also many developing countries.

Value of land in agriculture[c]		Estimated value of marginal plus non-timber benefits[d]		Estimated annual net benefits of logging[e]		Benefit–cost ratio of deforestation	
$120/ ha/yr	$140/ ha/yr	$10/ ha/yr	$20/ ha/yr	High	Low	High	Low
US$ millions						ratio	
4084.8	4765.6	340.4	680.8	2238.4	−12158.3	1.74	0.27
2356.8	2749.6	196.4	392.8	3364.0	−476.3	4.97	0.89
3254.4	3796.8	271.2	542.4	1370.9	−23437.9	1.27	0.20
−9216.0	−10752.0	−768.0	−1536.0	n.a.	n.a.	n.a.	n.a.
6842.4	7982.8	570.2	1140.4	8533.6	−24181.5	2.26	0.37
−33.6	−39.2	−2.8	−5.6	n.a.	n.a.	n.a.	n.a.
−129.6	−151.2	−10.8	−21.6	n.a.	n.a.	n.a.	n.a.
684.0	798.0	57.0	114.0	546.6	−2734.6	1.80	0.29
854.4	996.8	71.2	142.4	2428.0	532.2	6.96	1.25
10202.4	11902.8	850.2	1700.4	3661.9	−63983.5	1.26	0.20
18900.0	22050.0	1575.0	3150.0	22143.4	−126439.9	1.57	0.25

effects of trade measures are relatively modest for most countries. Yet trade measures have some impact because they signal concern.

Trade measures aimed at affecting harvesting practices, specifically to promote sustainable harvesting by preferential treatment, may also impact the land allocation decisions of governments. When selective trade measures reduce the profitability of unsustainable forest management practices, conversion of forests to alternative land uses could be accelerated.

Certification of tropical forestry management practices by the Forest Stewardship Council (FSC), an independent, third party, non-governmental certifier, could reduce deforestation. Since illegal logging

Table 7.4 *Sensitivity analysis: Cost–benefit analysis of tropical deforestation*

	Cost–benefit ratio of deforestation[a]			
	Low discount rate (3%)		High discount rate (6%)	
Region	Optimistic	Pessimistic	Optimistic	Pessimistic
E & Southern Africa	2.60	0.42	1.51	0.23
Northern Africa	6.18	1.18	4.61	0.81
West & Central Africa	1.71	0.27	1.16	0.18
S & SE Asia	2.88	0.48	2.09	0.34
Central America	2.45	0.40	1.63	0.26
Oceania	7.69	1.45	6.74	1.19
South America	1.76	0.28	1.13	0.18
World	**2.04**	**0.33**	**1.45**	**0.23**

[a] Optimistic and pessimistic assumptions regarding economic values discussed in text.

is big business and wood products from illegal logs enter legal channels (often with the complicity of corrupt government officials), the only way to prevent it is to ensure that any product sold is certified by a third party. Unfortunately, while the area of timberland certified outside developing countries has grown phenomenally since the FSC was formed in 1994, certification of forests in developing countries lags behind.

The preferred approach for controlling tropical deforestation is to provide direct subsidies that cause forestland owners to take into account the non-use benefits of tropical forests (Barbier and Rauscher 1994). They may also increase with efforts to increase carbon storage in terrestrial carbon sinks. Such transfers should take the form of lump-sum payments to prevent development of a resource, technical assistance and/or loans for environmentally benign projects, or debt relief in return for sustainable resource management.

In theory, a direct international transfer should unambiguously increase the long-run equilibrium forest stock. The reason is that imports must be paid for with foreign exchange, which can be earned by selling tropical timber (among other products). Transfers will ease the stringency of the foreign exchange constraint, which implies that more imports can be purchased. As a result, the marginal value of these imports falls. The marginal value of deforestation should also fall, thus the steady-state forest cover should increase. However, it is an open question to what extent this is the case in the real world.

When transfers are directly coupled to the size of the conserved forest stock (i.e., a greater forest stock implies more funding), the expectation is that funding unambiguously increases the forest stock in developing countries. However, Stahler (1996) has demonstrated that this may not be the case, due to strategic behaviour by governments in developing countries. As marginal external benefits are probably declining in stock size (so that the demand curve for forest conservation is downward sloping), governments of some recipient countries are in a position to increase the compensation per hectare (and thereby their total revenues) by reducing their forest stock. Thus, it is possible that compensating for external benefits will produce the adverse result of smaller stocks and high compensation per hectare. Further, as our calculations in Tables 7.3 and 7.4 demonstrate, failure to transfer funds for not releasing CO_2 from logging activities could lead developing countries to ignore forest protection, although this conclusion is case specific and may not always hold.

Finally, a word of caution is necessary for the debt-relief option. Despite some well-publicized successes in the past, debt relief may not be a very good mechanism for attaining the desired aims of the international community. The reason is that the money markets are trading the debt of developing countries at a discount that takes into account the expected ability to repay. The problem of debt-for-nature swaps is that, while in some cases they protect vulnerable ecosystems, the large nominal reductions in debt barely touch real burdens of these nations, and may even increase expected repayments.

Conclusions

There is no consensus on what causes tropical deforestation, although change in land use is its identifying characteristic. While logging is not the major factor, it is certainly a catalyst as it opens up natural forests to peasants seeking land for growing agricultural crops. Countries with tropical forests might well be reducing their stocks of forests because they are going through development stages similar to those experienced by developed countries. For the period 2000–2005, our crude analysis indicates the cost–benefit ratio of deforestation on a global scale for a high discount rate can be as low as 0.23 (a ratio smaller than 1 means it is better not to deforest the land) if the value of CO_2 offsets is high, marginal non-market plus non-timber values of deforested land are also high, but the value of land converted to agriculture is low. For the case of low CO_2-offset prices, low ecosystem values, high agricultural opportunities and low discount rates, the global cost–benefit ratio exceeds 2.0. Regionally, the cost–benefit ratio varies from a low of 0.18 to a high of 7.69 (there are large payoffs to harvesting trees), suggesting that decisions to continue deforestation are dependent on local conditions. If deforestation continues, however, cost–benefit ratios will inevitably decline, perhaps slowing or halting deforestation in the process. It is important to note that conclusions about the social desirability or feasibility of further deforestation are based to a large extent on the potential contribution that the release of CO_2 makes towards global climate change. But it is clear that, in the absence of massive global transfers to tropical nations to encourage them to preserve forests (e.g., via Kyoto's Clean Development Mechanism), deforestation will likely continue.

We also pointed out that market failure might be less of a factor in deforestation than policy failure. Government policies in many developing countries encourage deforestation for development and revenue purposes, and for political reasons (e.g., as an outlet for expanding populations). Sound economic policy, including much less of the types of intervention by governments that encourage deforestation, may enable humans to protect tropical forest ecosystems and the amenities associated with them. The benefits of this change of policy definitely outweigh its costs. The main problem, however, is to induce countries to adopt such a transition path. International institutions like the World Bank, and the international community in general could play an important role.

References

Amelung, T. and M. Diehl, 1992. *Deforestation of Tropical Rain Forests: Economic Causes and Impact on Development.* Tubingen: J.C.B. Mohr.
Angelsen, A. and D. Kaimowitz, 1999. Rethinking the Causes of Deforestation: Lessons from Economic Models, *World Bank Research Observer* 14(1): 73–98.

Barbier, E. B. and B. Aylward, 1996. Capturing the Pharmaceutical Value of Biodiversity in a Developing Country, *Environmental and Resource Economics* 8: 157–81.

Barbier, E. B. and J. Burgess, 1997. The Economics of Tropical Forest Land Use Options, *Land Economics* 73: 174–95.

Barbier, E. B. and M. Rauscher, 1994. Trade, Tropical Deforestation and Policy Interventions. *Environmental and Resource Economics*, 4: 75–90.

Brown, K. and D. W. Pearce (eds.), 1994. *The Causes of Tropical Deforestation*. London: UCL Press.

Bulte, E. H., D. P. van Soest, G. C. van Kooten and R. Schipper, 2002. Forest Conservation in Costa Rica: Optimal Forest Stocks under Uncertainty and Rising Nonuse Benefits, *American Journal of Agricultural Economics* 84: 150–60.

Costanza, R., R. d'Arge, R. de Groot, S. Farber, M. Grasso, B. Hannon, K. Limburg, S. Naeem, R. V. O'Neill, J. Paruelo, R. G. Raskin, P. Sutton and M. van den Belt, 1997. The Value of the World's Ecosystem Services and Natural Capital, *Nature* 387: 253–61.

Cropper, M. and C. Griffiths, 1994. The Interaction of Population Growth and Environmental Quality, *American Economic Review* 84 (May): 250–54.

De Beer, J. H. and M. J. McDermott, 1989. *The Economic Value of Nontimber Forest Products in Southeast Asia*. Amsterdam: Netherlands Committee for the IUNC.

De Soto, Hernando, 2000. *The Mystery of Capital. Why Capitalism Triumphs in the West and Fails Everywhere Else*. New York, NY: Basic Books.

The Economist, 2006. Down in the woods. *The Economist*, March 25, pp. 73–5.

Ehui, S. K. and T. W. Hertel, 1989. Deforestation and Agricultural Productivity in the Côte d'Ivoire, *American Journal of Agricultural Economics* 70 (August): 703–11.

Ehui, S. K., T. W. Hertel and P. V. Preckel, 1990. Forest Resource Depletion, Soil Dynamics and Agricultural Dynamics in the Tropics, *Journal of Environmental Economics and Management* 18: 136–54.

FAO, 2006. *Global Forest Resources Assessment 2005: Progress Towards Sustainable Forest Management*. FAO Forestry Paper 147. Rome: United Nations' Food and Agricultural Organization. 348pp.

FAO, 2001. State of the World's Forests 2001. Rome: Food and Agriculture Organization.

FAO, 1997. State of the World's Forests 1997. Rome: Food and Agriculture Organization of the United Nations.

FAO, 1993. Forest Resources Assessment 1990. Paper 112. Rome: Food and Agriculture Organization of the United Nations.

Fukuyama, F., 2002. Social Capital and Development: The Coming Agenda, *SAIS Review* 22 (1 Winter–Spring): 23–37.

Hughes, J. B., G. C. Daily and P. R. Ehrlich, 1997. Population Diversity: Its Extent and Extinction, *Science* 278: 689–92.

Hyde, W. F. and J. E. Seve, 1991. 'Malawi: A Rapid Economic Appraisal of Smallholder Response to Severe Deforestation', in R. Haynes, P. Harou and J. Mirowski (eds.), Pre-proceedings of Working Groups S6.03–03 and S6.10–00; Meetings at the 10th World Congress. Paris: International Union of Forest Research Organizations.

IPCC (Intergovernmental Panel on Climate Change), 1996. *Climate Change 1995: Economic and Social Dimensions of Climate Change.* New York: Cambridge University Press.

Kaimowitz, D. and A. Angelsen (eds.), 2001. *Agricultural Technologies and Tropical Deforestation.* Wallingford, UK: CAB International.

Kauppi, P. E., J. H. Ausubel, J. Fan, A. S. Mather, R. A. Sedjo and P. W. Waggoner, 2006. Returning Forests Analyzed with the Forest Identity, *PNAS* 103 (46 14 Nov): 17574–79.

La Porta, R., F. Lopez-de-Silanes, A. Shleifer and R. W. Vishny, 1999. The Quality of the Government, *Journal of Law, Economics & Organization* 15: 222–79.

Mayaux, P., P. Holmgren, F. Achard, H. Eva, H-J. Stibig, and A. Branthomme, 2005. Tropical Forest Cover Change in the 1990s and Options for Future Monitoring, *Philosophical Transactions: Biological Sciences (Royal Society of London)* 360(1454): 373–84.

Mendelsohn, R., 1994. Property Rights and Tropical Deforestation, *Oxford Economic Papers* 46: 750–56.

Meyer, A. L., G. C. van Kooten and S. Wang, 2003. Institutional, Social and Economic Roots of Deforestation: Further Evidence of an Environmental Kuznets Relation? *International Forestry Review* 5(1 March): 29–37.

Naidoo, R., 2004. Economic Growth and Liquidation of Natural Capital: The Case of Forest Clearance, *Land Economics* 80 (May): 194–208.

Osgood, D., 1994. Government Failure and Deforestation in Indonesia. In D. W. Pearce and K. Brown (eds.), *The Causes of Tropical Deforestation.* London: UCL Press.

Panayotou, T., 1993. Empirical Tests and Policy Analysis of Environmental Degradation at Different Stages of Economic Development. Working Paper WP238, Technology and Employment Program. Geneva: International Labor Office.

Panayotou, T. and P. Ashton, 1992. *Not by Timber Alone: Economics and Ecology for Sustaining Tropical Forests.* Washington, DC: Island Press.

Panayotou, T. and S. Sungsuwan, 1994. An Econometric Analysis of the Causes of Tropical Deforestation. In D. W. Pearce and K. Brown (eds.), *The Causes of Tropical Deforestation.* London: UCL Press.

Pearce, D. W. and J. J. Warford, 1993. *World without End*. New York: Oxford University Press.

Peters, C., A. Gentry and R. Mendelsohn, 1989. Valuation of an Amazonian Rainforest, *Nature* 339: 655–56.

Postel, S. and L. Heisse, 1988. Reforesting the Earth. Worldwatch Paper No. 83.

Reed, D., 1992. *Structural Adjustment and the Environment*. London: Earthscan Publications.

Repetto, R., 1997. Macroeconomic Policies and Deforestation. In P.S. Dasgupta and K. G Mäler (eds.), *The Environment and Emerging Development Issues, Vol. 2*. Oxford, UK: Clarendon Press.

Ruitenbeek, H. J., 1989. Social Cost Benefit Analysis of the Korup Project. Report prepared for the Worldwide Fund for Nature and the Republic of Cameroon. London: WWF.

Saxena, A. K., J. C. Nautiyal and D. K. Foote, 1997. Analyzing Deforestation and Exploring Policies for its Amelioration: A Case Study of India, *Journal of Forest Economics* 3(3): 253–89.

Scrieciu, S. S., 2006. Can Economic Causes of Tropical Deforestation be identified at a Global Level? *Ecological Economics* doi:10.1016/j.ecolecon.2006.07.028

Sedjo, R. A., 1992. Can Tropical Forest Management Systems be Economic? In P. N. Nemetz (ed.), *Emerging Issues in Forest Policy*. Vancouver: UBC Press, pp. 505–17.

Shleifer, A. and R. W. Vishny, 1998. *The Grabbing Hand: Government Pathologies and their Cures*. Cambridge, MA: Harvard University Press.

Simpson, R. D., R. A. Sedjo and J. W. Reid, 1996. Valuing Biodiversity for Use in Pharmaceutical Research, *Journal of Political Economy* 104: 163–85.

Stahler, F., 1996. On International Compensation for Environmental Stocks, *Environmental and Resource Economics* 8: 1–13.

Sunderlin, W. D. and I. A. P. Resosudarmo, 1997. Rate and Causes of Deforestation in Indonesia: Towards a Resolution of Ambiguities. Occasional Paper No. 9. Jakarta: CIFOR.

Tiffen, M. and M. Mortimore, 1994. Malthus Converted: The Role of Capital and Technology and Environmental Recovery in Kenya, *World Development* 22: 997–1010.

Van Kooten and H. Folmer, 2004. *Land and Forest Economics*. Cheltenham, UK: Edward Elgar.

van Soest, D, 1998. *Tropical Deforestation: An Economic Perspective*. Groningen, NL: Rijksuniversiteit Groningen, Graduate School of Systems, Organisations and Mangement. 268pp.

Vincent, J. R., 1990. Rent Capture and the Feasibility of Tropical Forest Management, *Land Economics* 66: 212–23.

8 | Land Degradation

IAN COXHEAD AND RAGNAR ØYGARD

1. Definition

"Land degradation" means reduction or loss of the biological or economic productivity and complexity of rainfed cropland, irrigated cropland, or range, pasture, forest and woodlands resulting from land uses
or from a process or combination of processes, including processes
arising from human activities and habitation patterns, such as:

(i) soil erosion caused by wind and/or water;
(ii) deterioration of the physical, chemical and biological or economic properties of soil; and
(iii) long-term loss of natural vegetation. [33]

Disregarding the issue of long-term loss of natural vegetation (which
will be covered in this project under the headings of deforestation and
biodiversity), land degradation primarily relates to a reduction in soil
quality and quantity as an input to the production of agricultural crops.
But there are also off-site effects, such as loss of watershed function.

Soil quality relates to the chemical, physical, and biological properties of the soil, and how these are distributed throughout the soil
profile. Scientists use an array of indicators to describe soil quality:
pH, organic matter content, plant-available nutrients, porosity, grain
size distribution, water permeability and retention capacity, topsoil
depth, presence of chemicals toxic to plants or plant consumers, etc.
These properties vary vertically within the soil profile and horizon-
tally from site to site. They also interact. Therefore, soil quality
cannot easily be described by one variable or an index. Crop yields
alone are not a good proxy as they depend on water, fertilizer, seed
variety, and crop management practices in addition to soil quality.
However, measuring yield *trends* while controlling for other inputs
and management can provide an observable and credible measure of
trends in soil quality.

Agricultural practices fundamentally influence soil characteristics over time. Farmers improve soil nutrient levels by adding manure or fertilizer; reduce acidity by adding lime; and optimize water availability through drainage or irrigation. However, agriculture also entails degradation processes:

- Soil erosion: clearing of natural vegetation, weeds, and previous crop remains for seedbed preparation leaves the soil with sparse plant cover or root mass to protect it from wind and rainwater impact and surface water flows. The result is more loss of topsoil and plant nutrients than would be the case were the land not cleared, or were it under a cropping system with perennial crops or dense plant cover. Intensive grazing may also reduce vegetation and increase erosion.
- Soil compaction and crusting can result from cultivation with heavy machinery and/or depletion of soil organic matter.
- Nutrient depletion or nutrient mining results from removal of plant nutrients with crops removed from fields without replacement through manure or fertilizer. Removing plant residues also reduces soil organic matter content.
- Salinization occurs on irrigated land under arid conditions, when salts are added by irrigation water and not washed away by rainfall.
- Waterlogging may result from irrigation with poor water control.
- Pollution, acidification, alkalization, and waterlogging are often important locally.

Soils vary in their resilience to these forms of degradation depending on characteristics such as slope, soil texture, climate, and cropping pattern. Some aspects of land degradation are less easily reversed than others. Thus, terrain deformation by gully erosion, or total topsoil loss from erosion, or the wiping out of native soil fauna is more irreversible than a negative nutrient balance, or surface sealing and crusting.

Off-site and downstream effects include siltation of dams and waterways, nutrient runoff causing eutrophication, and pesticide runoff. In some locations, wind-blown soils inflict damage on wide areas. Reduction of soil organic matter also releases CO_2 and CH_4 to the atmosphere, contributing to global warming.

2. Extent and trends of land degradation

During the last half-century the global extent of agriculture has increased vastly at the expense of natural forests, rangelands, wetlands, and even desert. Some of the increased land degradation associated with this expansion is compensated **for** by farmers' investment in soils, such as fertilization, terracing, and tree planting. New soil formation also occurs through natural processes, but in general these proceed too slowly to compensate for human-induced degradation.

No developing country has installed a system for monitoring soil quality at a national scale. Existing assessments are based on consultation with experts, extrapolation from case studies, field experiments and other micro studies, or inferences from land use patterns [28]. While little is known about current status, even less is known about trends, and to what extent the degradation processes are human-induced.

The most influential assessment of aggregate land degradation has been the GLASOD study, in which 250 experts contributed assessments of land degradation in their countries since the mid 1940s [25]. The results suggest that about 560 million ha of farmland had been degraded – or 38 percent of the total. Permanent loss of farmland due to human-induced land degradation was estimated to be 5–6 million ha per year, or about 0.3 to 0.5 percent of the world's arable land area. However, since this was based on expert judgment, it may "reflect unsubstantiated biases and assumptions" [28]. Thus, Lindert [24] found clear evidence of overstated soil degradation in GLASOD for China and Indonesia, as well as confusion between soil quality in general and human-induced degradation.

Within specific agro-ecological environments, experimental data from plot and field scale allow soil degradation processes to be observed with greater precision. Long-term data series indicate that intensive farming can cause yield reductions of 50 percent and more in some environments [16]. Even under best varietal selections and management practices, yields have stagnated and even fallen under long-term intensive monoculture for irrigated rice [9] and rainfed corn [23]. The data underlying these results are, however, limited to a few experimental plots, and the basis for extrapolation to farmers' fields is weak.

A review [28] of sixteen studies to assess the global extent, rate, and effects of soil degradation concluded that soil quality on three-quarters of the world's agricultural lands has been fairly stable over the last fifty years, but that on the remaining share land degradation is widespread and has accelerated. Productivity has declined substantially on about 16 percent of agricultural land in developing countries, especially cropland in Africa and Central America, pasture in Africa, and forests in Central America. Land areas of 5 to 8 million hectares have gone out of production each year. These are primarily lands at the margin of cultivation, especially at desert margins and in steeply sloping and high-altitude areas.

Soil nutrient mining is particularly acute in Africa. In 2002/2004 about 85 percent of African farmland had nutrient mining rates at more than 30 kg nutrients (NPK) per hectare per year (ha/yr), and 40 percent had rates greater than 60 kg/ha/yr [22]. Partly as a consequence, sub-Sahara African cereal yields are the lowest in the world, averaging about 1 ton per hectare – about the same as twenty years ago.

Patterns of degradation vary according to agro-ecological conditions, farming systems, levels of intensification, and resource endowments, but these also interact in important ways with social and economic systems. Temperate lands, for example, are generally more resilient to degradation but are also associated with societies that have more resources for investing in maintaining and rehabilitating land quality – and for developing alternative sources of livelihood for their citizens. Thus, the areas for prime concern are the tropical and subtropical marginal lands, which have low physical resilience to land degradation and are also associated with societies in which property rights are weakly defined, information systems are weak, and managerial capacity is low. For poor people, income from land accounts for a larger share of total income, thus making them more vulnerable to degradation. They also have fewer resources for alleviating degradation and are especially susceptible to the credit market failures and land tenure insecurity which can raise time discount rates and reduce planning horizons, leading to faster soil mining.

World agriculture is likely to expand in area to cater for population growth and increased demand for food and industrial crops. The Food and Agricultural Organisation (FAO) [8] estimates that the area for arable agriculture will expand by 8 percent over the next quarter century, with most of the expansion occurring in developing countries, and much of it from the clearing of tropical forests. Continued degradation of existing lands will also raise the land clearing rate. Under current technologies and practices, this will have high local costs but is less likely to lead to large agricultural commodity price increases – or to threaten global food supplies within the next couple of decades [28].

3. What can be achieved and what does it cost?

The main environmental principles for reducing land degradation are to maximize vegetation cover to prevent erosion; replace nutrients removed; prevent accumulation of harmful substances; and put in place structures (terraces, bunds, vegetation strips) to reduce the speed and volumes of water flow over the soil. From this perspective tree crops and perennial crops are preferred, as are intercropping and reduced-tillage systems. High-yielding crops cover the soil better than low-yielding crops [29]. Moreover, obtaining high yields on the best lands reduces the profitability of cultivating marginal lands, leaving more land to be returned to nature (when crop prices decline in response to the increased production).

Most land users exert efforts to maintain future productivity of the land. Our knowledge of what these efforts result in, in terms of degradation and yield losses avoided, is very incomplete. There is limited knowledge of how differences in land use influence land degradation, and of how land degradation in turn influences current and future yield [16]. Our understanding of how changed policies will affect land use decisions by land users is also incomplete. Land management is the result of decisions of millions of small-scale and large-scale land users. It is therefore extremely expensive to attempt to alter land degradation through direct interventions at the farm or community scale, since the interventions must be replicated many times over to effect large aggregate changes. However, farmers' decisions are shaped by economic incentives, and thus to the extent that markets are pervasive, the decisions of many land users can simultaneously be influenced by policies that alter prices.

In the following, we rank interventions broadly according to increasing cost of wide-scale implementation.

3.1 Price and trade policy reforms

Many countries explicitly or implicitly subsidize practices that increase land degradation, or tax activities that tend to reduce degradation. Examples are subsidies on cultivation of upland crops that drive expansion into the marginal lands; subsidies on water and energy in irrigation schemes; tariff protection for land-degrading crops; and export taxes on more environmentally benign crops. Reversal of these policies will have very high benefit–cost ratio, since their net cost is low, zero, or even negative. Numerous studies of tariff reduction demonstrate that the short-run costs of policy implementation, adjustment in factor markets, and revenue losses to governments are minuscule in relation to the long-run benefit streams they generate, and that even these frictional costs are zero or negative in a large number of cases (Anderson [4] provides an excellent survey of this literature). Examples of cases in which abandoning or "tarifficating" import bans or reducing existing levels of protection generate unambiguous social gains include US sugar import quotas, which promote farmland expansion in areas like the Florida Everglades, and developing-country corn import barriers, which have contributed to land expansion and increased intensity of cultivation in ecologically fragile upper-watershed areas of countries like India and the Philippines. Developing countries in particular have undertaken extensive reform of trade policies in manufacturing sectors, driven both by unilateral goals and by the need to conform to international obligations as signatories to regional and multilateral trade agreements. Agricultural trade reform has lagged behind this process, with the result that average agricultural tariffs are now equal to or greater than those on non-agricultural goods in developing countries [3, Table 8.1].

In general equilibrium simulation experiments, implementation of a mid-1990s package of trade liberalization measures in the Philippines, including a modest reduction in cereals prices, are found to exert a substantial effect on land use. The price of corn, the major annual crop grown in uplands, falls in these experiments by about 0.55 percent; this fall, along with rises in wages and some input prices, causes a contraction of about 0.5 percent in demand for upland land for seasonal crops. If corn land is primarily responsible for erosion from upland fields [11] and the base annual soil loss from upland farms is 74–81 million t./yr [19], then the trade reforms could save about 407,000–445,000 t/yr once permanent ground cover is reestablished – assuming that this is what happens after corn production ceases. Earlier Philippine studies valued the nutrients lost in soil erosion at US\$0.60/ton; adopting that as a very conservative indicator of the total value of soil lost, the experiment yields a direct, on-site gain of roughly US\$250,000 – in addition to the other benefits that trade liberalization brings to the economy.

The effects of global trade reform are potentially far higher than can be achieved by this modest trade reform. The Philippines is the world's eleventh-ranked country by corn area, with 1.55 percent of the total harvested area [18]; its average agricultural tariff was 47 percent in 2001 [5]. The scope for trade policy liberalization is large. India is another relevant case; it has nearly 5 percent of the world's corn area (7.8 m. ha), and an average tariff on cereals of 21.5 percent in 2005 [27]. If we assume an elasticity of area planted with respect to price of 1.0, eliminating the tariff will reduce area planted by about 15.6 million hectares. Supposing that the average erosion from corn land is 75 t/ha/yr valued at US$1/ton in nutrient losses alone, and that this falls to 25 t/ha/yr under an alternative land use, the policy change would generate immediate savings of US$7.8m plus the value of any off-site savings, and about US$100m in direct savings over a thirty-year period, using a discount rate of 6 percent.

In these and similar tropical economies, substantive trade liberalization will result in major land use changes. Relaxing protectionist policies on crops that contribute to land degradation in the tropics will shift their production to countries and environments where they can be grown at lower environmental cost [12]. In the case of subsidies, their relaxation creates fiscal savings that provide an opportunity to compensate upland farmers, who are often extremely poor. For environmental taxes, e.g. on activities that lead to downstream siltation, the challenge is to monitor and assess such widely dispersed activities.

Addressing policy-induced distortions that operate through markets to promote land-degrading activities is the most efficient single means to address land degradation in large areas of the developing world. The success of policy reforms, however, relies on the pervasiveness of markets and the feasibility of market-based instruments. Nor are trade policy reforms on their own a panacea for environmental damage; in countries with comparative advantage in land-degrading crops, greater trade openness without complementary environmental protection policies may lead to rapid worsening of land degradation.

3.2 Capital market failures

Liquidity constraints under imperfect credit markets prevent landowners from undertaking otherwise profitable conservation investments.

For poor rural households, financial market failures are pervasive. They face severe liquidity constraints and have very high discount rates. Most estimates of the discount rates of rural poor in developing countries indicate that these rates are far higher than 6 percent. We can therefore surely say that the "business as usual trend" scenario implies land degradation rates that are higher than would be optimal from a social point of view (as reflected in discount rates of 3 percent or 6 percent).

A rough estimate of the marginal rate of return on conservation activities might be obtained by assuming that land users carry out those projects where the expected rate of return is higher than their reservation rate of return, i.e. their discount rate. Assuming that rural households order their investment projects according to expected private returns, and also that households do undertake some land conservation or investment activities, this implies that the marginal land conservation or improvement investment has a return roughly equal to their discount rate. Typical estimates of rates of return for poor rural households in developing countries are surprisingly high: 60 percent in rural Ghana [32], for example, while a recent survey of empirical studies from South Asia and Africa finds rates varying over a range of 22 percent to 100 percent [6]. The primary explanation for these high rates of return is "financial market imperfections that hinder flows of capital into the informal sector" [32].

Analyzing the consequences of an economy-wide easing of capital constraints for the rural poor certainly requires general equilibrium models. Production costs would decline, leading to expanded output, which would likely lead to lower prices and a dampening effect on supply response. The net effect on land use is ambiguous.

Improving the functioning of financial markets will facilitate land-conserving investments but may also increase total agricultural investment, leading to an expansion of cultivated area. The net effect of capital market development on land degradation is therefore ambiguous.

3.3 Property rights, land tenure, market failures, and externalities

If security of land tenure is weak or absent, land is treated as an open-access resource. It is then difficult to reclaim or to bequeath the value of soil improvements or conservation measures, so land users lack incentives to invest in maintaining long-term soil productivity [7]. In areas of low population density, land is abandoned when it has been degraded, and farmers move on to clear new land, leaving the degraded land as a negative externality.

Some current research indicates that secure rights do indeed induce higher investment and productivity in developing countries [13–15, 30]. One source suggests that more secure land rights in Ethiopia might induce investments (e.g. in terracing) that increase the value of the land by 5 percent [15], while land-titling in Ethiopia has been conducted at a cost of only about US$3.50 per household. In some cases of communal or open-access land tenure, however, there may be strong incentives for investing in the land, since such investments can be a means of obtaining permanent private use rights [31], meaning that investment in tree planting or terracing might actually be higher under less secure tenure. Clearly, the effects on land investment from securing and formalizing land tenure are highly dependent on other aspects of institutions. A recent illustration of this point, and of the costs of associated loss of land quality, comes from villages in Ghana [20]. On croplands owned by kinship groups and allocated among members according to the principle that everyone in the group who needs land should have access to it, the duration of fallowing by women, who seldom hold office within the kinship group, was found to be much lower than that by men. Since fallowing is an effective means to restore and maintain soil fertility, the welfare costs of women's uncertainty over returns to fallowing, based on the concern that fallowed land is more susceptible to resumption and reallocation than land that is actively cropped, were estimated at 1.4 percent to 2.1 percent of Ghanaian GDP.

Land use rights need not be assigned to individuals in order to capture the benefits of secure tenure. In drylands, reducing grazing intensity can be necessary to halt land degradation. This has in some cases been achieved through empowering local communities to manage rangelands as commons, in others through assigning individual land use rights. Impediments to developing and enforcing tenure regimes that give incentives for sustainable land management are primarily political, but poor capacity in public administration frequently contributes.

Assigning property rights can increase investment in land [15] but is not a sufficient condition for sustainable land use. Soil quality is hard to observe and may therefore be poorly captured in land transactions, reducing the return to such investments relative to more easily observable investments. There are also limits to what property rights can do to prevent land degradation as long as soil generation processes work slowly and land users have a positive time preference for consumption [21]. Finally, the success or otherwise of any efforts to confer more secure property rights in land are entirely dependent on the robustness of national legal systems, without which a certificate of land title has no practical meaning.

3.4 Technology development and productivity growth

The costs of conservation agriculture and nutrient replacement practices may be reduced, and adoption increased by developing new technologies that raise returns to nutrient inputs, or reduce the costs of conservation practices. There is a particularly important role for international and national agricultural research to develop farming systems that conserve or improve soil quality, while being attractive to farmers. Past agricultural research has yielded very high returns [17]. While fixed costs of research can be high, results are often widely applied at very low marginal cost. A meta-analysis of 289 studies of rates of return [1] reported mean rates of return of 47 percent for agricultural research and extension combined. However, the authors express skepticism to the validity of these estimates, worrying that they are overestimated [2]. To be on the safe side, we will therefore assume that mean returns are only half of what was found in these studies. Of course, most of these returns have been related to the value of increased productivity and the concomitant reduced price of food. But pervasive yield increases imply that the current global crop can be grown on a smaller land area than would have been needed to grow the same amount of produce with lower average yields. In this sense, increases in yields have also contributed to sparing land for nature [34] – preserving the land from the degrading effects of agriculture.

Nor is this phenomenon limited to agricultural productivity increases. Thailand's transition from agrarian to industrialized economic structure due to a boom in domestic and foreign investment directed at labor-intensive manufacturing sectors was associated, over the decade 1985–95, with a 17 percent reduction in the size of the agricultural labor force. This enormous migration, a response to higher labor productivity and thus wages in the manufacturing sectors, resulted in the retirement of large areas of marginal agricultural land previously used for subsistence cultivation [10].

3.5 Direct land use interventions

Many countries have tried measures such as set-aside programs, land use zoning and establishment of conservation areas, bans on "degrading activities," and public reforestation projects. China's Sloping Land Conversion Program, which with a target area of almost 15 million hectares and a budget of US$40 billion is the world's largest and most ambitious land conservation program. Its 2010 target is an increase in China's forested area by 10–20 percent and an 11 percent decrease in cultivated area. The current program, however, lacks "voluntarism" in participation and therefore suffers from low cost-effectiveness and high cost of performance monitoring and evaluation [36]. In general, it is very difficult and costly to police and enforce bans against common and widely dispersed practices when these practices are profitable to land users – or perhaps even necessary for survival. Still, in some cases they may be the only practical approach [35].

Project-based payment for environmental services (PES) schemes provide a means to influence land use by paying compensation (i.e. bribes) to farmers for desisting from environmentally undesirable activities [26]. But since there is no internal mechanism for decreasing-cost replication of PES measures, in benefit–cost terms these are expensive interventions if they are to be widely applied – even before counting the costs of contract enforcement and monitoring.

Preventing or reversing waterlogging and salinization on irrigated areas requires improved water management and, in some cases, installation of drainage systems. Correcting design and engineering mistakes, and ending water and energy subsidies that encourage waste of water are good first steps. The costs of drainage systems are, however, very high.

4. Summing up benefits and costs

To attempt a benefit–cost analysis of the above remediation measures is strictly futile due to the heterogeneity of the projects according to place, time, nature, and extent of implementation. There are no "typical" numbers. Option 3.1, removing subsidies that promote land degradation, could have B/C ratios that are infinite, as already argued – if the political costs are disregarded. Option 3.2, assigning and extending private land rights, involves administrative costs, but the benefits are highly uncertain.

Table 8.1. *Rates of return on approaches[a] to reducing land degradation*

Opportunity or solution	Rate of return
Price and trade policy reforms reducing subsidies on land-degrading crops	Infinite (only benefits, no cost[b])
Correcting credit market failures	> 20%
Property rights formalization in land tenure and turning open-access pastures into commons	Wide range
Technology development and dissemination	> 20%
Direct land use interventions	Wide range

[a] Activities additional to business-as-usual trends.
[b] When disregarding political costs. Example: Corn trade liberalization in India, 15.6m ha land reverts to less erosive use.

In the discussion above we have presented rates of return rather than B/C ratios for actions to reduce land degradation. Measures to counteract land degradation do not lend themselves to be organized as projects, where total project costs and benefits can be assessed. However, rates of return can be recalculated as B/C ratios. E.g. a rate of return of 20 percent is equivalent to a B/C ratio of 3.32, if we assume equal annual returns, a discount rate of 6 percent, and a time horizon of 100 years.

Rough estimates of rates of return are given in Table 8.1. These are recalculated as B/C ratios in Table 8.2.

5. Conclusion and broader discussion

Problems of valuation, and even of assigning causality, make it impossible to compute accurate benefit–cost ratios for reducing land degradation. This does not, however, mean that nothing should be done. A precautionary approach, taking account of the relative magnitude of the problem, the relative importance of land degradation to the poor, and the relative weakness of existing institutional and market-based mechanisms to deal with on-site degradation and externalities, indicates that efforts to reduce land degradation should focus on sloping lands and forest/desert margin areas in developing countries, and

Table 8.2. *Benefit–cost* ratios of approaches[a] to reducing land degradation*

Opportunity or solution	Discount rate LOW	Discount rate HIGH
Price and trade policy reforms	Infinite (only benefits, no cost[b])	Infinite (only benefits, no cost[b])
Correcting credit market failures	>6.3	>3.3
Property rights formalization in land tenure, turning open-access pastures into commons	Wide range	Wide range
Technology development and dissemination	>6.3	>3.3
Direct land use interventions	Wide range	Wide range

* Based on a 100-year time horizon, "Low rate" is 3 percent, "High rate" is 6 percent
[a] Activities additional to business-as-usual trends
[b] When disregarding political costs. Example: Corn trade liberalization in India, 15.6m ha land reverts to less erosive use.

should depend mainly (though not exclusively) on market-based instruments, accompanied by efforts to ease capital constraints, to assign and protect property rights in land, and to increase investment in the development of technologies for sustainable agriculture.

We conclude with two points that link land degradation to broader issues. First, as noted above, land degradation is proportionally and absolutely most severe in the tropics, where it represents a loss of long-run earning power for farmers and negative externalities for larger rural populations. Monetary values aside, therefore, the problem of land degradation becomes more acute when the welfare of the poor is given higher priority.

Second, it is important to note that the same policy instruments (economic policy reforms, strengthening property rights) that we have advanced as the best means to alleviate land degradation are also components of reform packages with much broader economic development aims. In this sense our land degradation proposals are "bundled with" measures that deliver gains that extend well beyond the environment. Recent policy initiatives in China, where in early 2007 the national legislative body began considering proposals for a broad strengthening of property rights in land, give hope for a closer match between the pace of economic growth and that of institutional reform in fast-growing developing countries. Such institutional strengthening is essential if exploitation of new market opportunities by the poor, whose rate of time discount is high, is not to worsen existing rates of land degradation.

References

1. Alston, J. M., M. C. Marra, P. G. Pardey, and T. J. Wyatt, 2000, Research returns redux: a meta-analysis of the returns to agricultural R&D. *Australian Journal of Agricultural and Resource Economics* 44 (2): 185–215.
2. Alston, J. M. and P. G. Pardey, 2001, Attribution and other problems in assessing returns to agricultural R&D. *Agricultural Economics* 25 (2–3): 141–152.
3. Anderson, K., 2006, Reducing distortions to agricultural incentives: progress, pitfalls and prospects. *American Journal of Agricultural Economics* 88 (5): 1135–1146.
4. Anderson, K., 2007, Reducing Subsidies and Trade Barriers, this volume.
5. Anderson, K. and W. Martin, 2005, Scenarios for global trade reform, in T. W. Hertel and L. A. Winters, Eds. *Poverty and the WTO: Impacts of the Doha Development Agenda*. Hamphsire, UK: Palgrave MacMillan; Washington, DC: World Bank.
6. Banerjee, A. V. and E. Duflo, 2005, Growth Theory through the Lens of Development Economics, in P. Aghion and S. N. Durlauf, eds., *Handbook of Economic Growth*. Amsterdam: Elsevier.
7. Barbier, E. B., 2005, *Natural Resources and Economic Development*. Cambridge, UK: Cambridge University Press.
8. Bruinsma, J., ed. 2003, *World Agriculture: Towards 2015/2030: An FAO Perspective*. Rome: FAO; London: Earthscan.
9. Cassman, K. G. and P. L. Pingali, 1995, Intensification of irrigated rice systems: learning from the past to meet future challenges. *Geo-Journal* 35: 299–305.
10. Coxhead, I. and J. Plangpraphan, 1998, *Thailand's Economic Boom and Agricultural Bust*. Madison, WI: University of Wisconsin-Madison.
11. Coxhead, I. and G. S. Shively, 2006, Economic incentives and agricultural outcomes in upland settings, in I. Coxhead and G. S. Shively, eds. *Land Use Change in Tropical Watersheds: Evidence, Causes and Consequences*. Wallingford, UK: CABI Publishing.

12. Coxhead, I. A. and S. Jayasuria, 2003, *The Open Economy and the Environment: Development, Trade and Resources in Asia.* Cheltenham, UK: Edward Elgar.

13. Deininger, K. and J. S. Chamorro, 2004, Investment and equity effects of land regularisation: the case of Nicaragua. *Agricultural Economics* 30 (2): 101–116.

14. Deininger, K. and S. Jin, 2005, The potential of land rental markets in the process of economic development: evidence from China. *Journal of Development Economics* 78 (1): 241.

15. Deininger, K. and S. Jin, 2006, Tenure security and land-related investment: evidence from Ethiopia. *European Economic Review* 50 (5): 1245–1277.

16. Eswaran, H., R. Lal, and P. F. Reich, 2001, Land degradation: an overview, in *Responses to Land Degradation: 2nd International Conference on Land Degradation and Desertification.* New Delhi: Oxford University Press.

17. Evenson, R. E. and D. Gollin, 2003, Assessing the impact of the Green Revolution, 1960 to 2000. *Science* 300 (5620): 758–762.

18. FAO. *FAOSTAT – Agriculture.* 2007 [cited 13 March 2007]; available from: http://faostat.fao.org.

19. Forest Management Bureau, 1998, *The Philippines Strategy for Improved Watershed Resources Management.* Manila: Philippines Department of Environmental and Natural Resources.

20. Goldstein, M. and C. Udry, 2005, *The Profits of Power: Land Rights and Agricultural Investment in Ghana.* Economic Growth Center Working Papers 929. New Haven: Yale University.

21. Good, D. H. and R. Reuveny, 2006, The fate of Easter Island: the limits of resource management institutions. *Ecological Economics* 58 (3): 473.

22. Henao, J. and C. Baanante, 2006, *Agricultural Production and Soil Nutrient Mining in Africa: Implications for Resource Conservation and Policy Development.* Muscle Shoals, AL: International Fertilizer Development Center.

23. Kim, K., B. L. Barham, and I. Coxhead, 2000, Recovering soil productivity attributes from experimental data: a statistical method and an application to soil productivity dynamics. *Geoderma* 96: 239–259.

24. Lindert, P. H., 2000, *Shifting Ground: The Changing Agricultural Soils of China and Indonesia.* Cambridge, MA: MIT Press.

25. Oldeman, L. R., R. T. A. Hakkeling, and W. G. Sombroek, 1991, *World Map of the Status of Human-Induced Soil Degradation: An Explanatory Note.* Wageningen: International Soil Reference and Information Centre; Nairobi: United Nations Environment Programme.

26. Pagiola, S., J. Bishop, and N. Landell-Mills, eds. 2002, *Selling Forest Environmental Services: Market-Based Mechanisms for Conservation and Development.* London: Earthscan.

27. Sandri, D., E. Valenzuela, and K. Anderson, 2006, *Compendium of Economic and Trade Indicators by Region, 1960 to 2004.* Washington, DC: Development Research Group, World Bank.

28. Scherr, S. J., 1999, *Soil Degradation: A Threat to Developing-Country Food Security by 2020?* Washington, DC: International Food Policy Research Institute.

29. Shaxson, F., M. Tiffen, A. Wood, and C. Turton, 1997, *Better Land Husbandry: Re-thinking Approaches to Land Improvement and the Conservation of Water and Soil.* London: Overseas Development Institute.

30. Shively, G. E., 2001, Poverty, consumption risk, and soil conservation. *Journal of Development Economics* **65** (2): 267–290.

31. Sjaastad, E. and D. Bromley, 1997, Indigenous land rights in sub-Saharan Africa: appropriation, security and investment demand. *World Development* **25** (4): 549–562.

32. Udry, C. and S. Anagol, 2006, The return to capital in Ghana. *American Economic Review* **96** (2): 388–393.

33. United Nations Convention to Combat Desertification, 1996.

34. Waggoner, P. E., 1996, How much land can ten billion people spare for nature? *Dædalus* **125** (3): 73–93.

35. Wunder, S., D. T. Bui, and E. Ibarra, 2005, *Payment is Good, Control is Better: Why Payments for Forest Environmental Services in Vietnam Have So Far Remained Incipient.* Bogor, Indonesia: Center for International Forestry Research.

36. Xu, J., M. T. Bennett, R. Tao, and Z. Xu, 2006, China's Sloping Land Conversion Program: does expansion equal success? Paper presented at 3rd World Congress of Environmental and Resource Economists, Kyoto, Japan, July 3–7.

9 | The Economics of Biodiversity Loss

DAN BILLER

The problem: the extent of biodiversity loss

What is biodiversity?

Biological diversity, or biodiversity, is defined by the Convention on Biological Diversity (CBD)[1] as: "the variability among living organisms from all sources including, inter alia, terrestrial, marine and other aquatic ecosystems and the ecological complexes of which they are part; this includes diversity within species, between species and of ecosystems." Biological resources, which have often been commercialized, are defined as: "genetic resources, organisms or parts thereof, populations, or any other biotic component of ecosystems with actual or potential use or value for humanity" (UNCBD 2000). In this paper, the use of scientific terms broadly follows the CBD definitions unless otherwise indicated; yet, for ease of reference, the term "biodiversity" encompasses biological resources, ecosystems, and habitats.

In economic terms, biodiversity can be metaphorically viewed as "Earth's infrastructure"; therefore, broad policy guidance can be designed in a similar fashion as for man-made infrastructure in public economics. This entails mapping the different economic characteristics that define private and public goods and services against recognized biodiversity products and services[2] (Heal 2000; OECD 2003).

---

[1] One hundred and ninety countries are parties to the CBD, making it one of the most subscribed conventions in the world.

[2] A private good or service is both rival in consumption, that is one person's consumption depletes the good's availability to others, and excludable, that is it is feasible to exclude people (e.g. by charging a price) from consuming the good. A club good or service is excludable but non-rival, and an open access good or service is rival but non-excludable. A public good or service is neither rival nor excludable.

What is being lost?

As implicit in the breadth of its definition, measuring biodiversity is complex and there is a lack of widely accepted and adequate biodiversity indicators. This knowledge gap generates a wide range of estimates of what and how much is being lost. The available proxy indicators seem to indicate that the extinction of species is increasing and the rate of extinction is between 100 and 10,000 times more than their would-be natural rate (IUCN website). Natural habitats are also severely degraded: between 1980 and 2000, about 25 percent of the mangrove area worldwide was lost; 20 percent of the world's coral reefs have been destroyed, 24 percent are under imminent risk of collapse, and 26 percent are under a longer-term threat of collapse (Wilkinson 2004); the worldwide loss of tropical rainforest, home to biodiversity of large significance, caused by human intervention is around 15 million hectares per year, and if recent rates of tropical forest loss continue for the next twenty-five years, it is estimated that the number of species in forests would be reduced by 4 to 8 percent (Waller-Hunter and Biller 2001). Several fisheries are under severe threat of collapse due to over-fishing and environmental degradation, and threats related to climate change and invasive species (mostly introduced by humans) significantly compound the odds against biodiversity. Only a few ecosystems around the world have not suffered from human intervention, but the full consequences of this intervention are minimally understood. Overall, it appears that biodiversity is already under severe distress or may be in the foreseeable future.

Whether in a developed or developing country, societies rely directly or indirectly on biodiversity, but its value is predominantly implicit rather than explicit. The absence of an economic, or rather, an easily monetized value combined with absent or poorly defined, enforced, and traded property rights provide the conditions for overexploitation and unregulated use. In addition, increasing development pressures have led to the problem exemplified above of an unprecedented rate of biodiversity loss directly or indirectly caused by humans. Many of the biodiversity-rich areas are located in economically poor countries. Since biodiversity has strong public good characteristics, is difficult to measure and value, and defies simple description, quantification, and monitoring, its conservation and sustainable use are often disregarded when conflicting priorities in the selection of development paths are being faced. Alternatively, it is difficult to conceive a world without biodiversity that can sustain human life.

Why place economic values on biodiversity?

Placing a value on any public good or service is complex. This complexity is expanded for biodiversity due to the difficulties in measuring it and its components. For example, does diversity per se have value or would one focus on the individual components of biodiversity?[3]

This lack of clarity, among other factors, may suggest that biodiversity conservation policies are of low priority simply because biodiversity defies easy description and quantification. The absence of quantification and the difficulty in monitoring and evaluating biodiversity policies thus provide justification to regard the loss of biodiversity as a necessary outcome of development, creating an extra requirement to substantiate designing and implementing policies that address biodiversity conservation or sustainable use.

Similar to other goods and services that face market failures,[4] especially those related to environmental externalities,[5] placing economic values on biodiversity is nonetheless important since it (OECD 2001; Nunes, van den Bergh, and Nijkamp 2003):

a. Supports cost–benefit analysis (CBA) of investment projects and policies, which properly incorporates environmental costs and benefits, and this is essential to enable policymakers to choose the investment or policy option that maximizes total net benefits to society.

b. Assists on environmental accounting at the national level (green national accounts), local level (community green accounts), and firm level (environmental reporting), which adjusts the gross domestic

---

[3] For a theoretical analysis of diversity, see Weitzman (1992). OECD (2002) also provides a discussion of less theoretical focus.

[4] Failure of market forces to allocate the socially optimal level of biodiversity conservation or sustainable use. The four main sources of market failures are: (1) public good/public bad, (2) externality, (3) imperfect information, and (4) monopoly (OECD 2003).

[5] Externalities can be defined as costs or benefits that result from an activity, but accrue to other than those undertaking the activity in the first place without any mechanism to impute these costs or benefits to the original causers (OECD 2003).

product (GDP) and other standard ways of measuring final outputs to take into account any depreciation in the environmental base of the economy and hence improve planning.

c. Enables proper valuation of the benefits (costs) provided by biodiversity and other environmental public goods (bads) in the absence of markets, which is useful in the design of policy instruments to address market failures and essential in order to level the playing field between conservation and economic development.

d. Facilitates Natural Resource Damage Assessment (NRDA) where relevant due to laws resulting in compensation payments for natural resource damage from man-made accidents such as pollution spills, among others.

How to place economic values on biodiversity?

The value of biodiversity is measured through the concept of Total Economic Value (TEV), which is the sum of its use and non-use values. Use values encompass the value of direct use (extractive – e.g. timber and non-extractive – e.g. bird-watching); the value of indirect use (e.g. environmental services such as flood protection); and the option value of personally enjoying direct and/or indirect use in the future. Non-use values encompass the notions of altruism, bequest, and existence; that is, others including future generations enjoying biodiversity and the fact that the existence of biodiversity has a value even when people do not derive or intend to derive direct or indirect uses of it (e.g. knowing that the Siberian Tiger roams the wild while realizing that one will never see one or use Siberian Tiger products). Since estimating the world's biodiversity TEV is very difficult, uncertain, and controversial,[6] research usually focuses on estimating the benefits of conserving or using biodiversity in a sustainable way in a particular ecosystem or through specific species. In addition, a large share of biodiversity's TEV comes from non-use values. These can be global in nature and are closely linked to biodiversity's public good attributes, making the valuation exercise especially challenging. On the other hand, since the

---

[6] Costanza et al. (1997) estimate the minimum biosphere's economic value to be US$33 trillion per year compared to the total GDP worldwide at the same time of US$18 trillion per year. The study was criticized on various grounds but mostly for using marginal values to estimate the value of the Earth's total stock of biological resources.

costs of biodiversity conservation and sustainable use of its components are primarily locally borne, cost estimations have been largely absent from the literature.

While the term biodiversity is broadly encompassing, as indicated in OECD (2001 and 2002), finding out the precise object to be valued is a key challenge in valuation exercises in general and when specifically valuing biodiversity or a part of it. As discussed, there is a clear distinction between biological resources and biological diversity, but many valuation studies do not make this distinction. They tend to value biological resources rather than biological diversity, which could lead to suboptimal programs to support biodiversity. Projects targeting single species, such as the spotted owl or the tiger, may in biological diversity terms be suboptimal, if these species have a close genetic relative that is not endangered. Moreover, to be relevant for policy-making, economic valuation of biodiversity should measure marginal or discrete local changes in the availability of biodiversity. For example, land use changes, increased tourism, and increased pollution affect the future flow of services from an ecosystem. It is important to value the impact on this flow when deciding whether to engage in a specific development policy or not.

Examples of economic valuation of biodiversity and its components

Regardless of the shortcomings described above, there is a vast literature on the economic valuation of some benefits linked to biodiversity. Table 9.1 provides some valuation examples divided in major clusters that capture most valuation studies. On the use value side, they include the benefits of conservation and sustainable use and the costs of degrading biodiversity (forgone benefits of conservation – another way of calculating the benefits of conservation). On the non-use value side, examples of valuing the existence of species are provided. The methods and units used,[7] especially for use values, greatly vary. For non-use values of single and multiple species, the stated preference approach is

---

[7] Economic valuation methods of environmental issues can be generally divided into cost–benefit approach, revealed preference approach, and stated preference approach. Detailed analysis of each approach is beyond the scope of this paper, but there are several papers and handbooks that address this (see OECD 2006 and Alberini and Kahn 2006 for the most recent).

Table 9.1. *Examples of economic valuation of biodiversity*

Area studied and source	Benefits included	Cost included	Estimates	Timeframe discount rate
Protected Areas in Madagascar Carret and Loyer (2003)	Biodiversity, tourism, water supply	Management, opportunity	B= US$88.3/ha C= US$72.6/ha	15 years 10%
Portland Blight Protected Area in Jamaica Cesar (2000)	Fisheries, forestry, tourism, carbon fixation, coastal protection, biodiversity	Management (no opportunity cost)	C= US$19m B= US$41m or 53m depending on the tourism scenario	25 years 10%
Leuser National Park, Indonesia Van Beukering et al. (2003)	Water supply, fisheries, flood and drought prevention, agriculture, hydro-electricity, tourism, biodiversity, carbon sequestration, NTFP and timber	No cost included formerly but they compare the benefits for three scenarios: deforestation (D), conservation (C) and selective use (SU).	NPV(C)=US$9.5bn NPV(D)=US$7bn NPV(SU)=US$9.1bn	30 years 4%
Mangrove conservation, Thailand Sathirathai (1998)	Direct-use values by local communities and indirect-use values for offshore fisheries and coastline protection	Assess benefits from conversion to shrimp farming (i.e. opportunity cost)	NPV(Conservation) >NPV(Conversion to shrimp farming)	20 years 6–10%

Table 9.1. (*cont.*)

Area studied and source	Benefits included	Cost included	Estimates	Timeframe discount rate
Coral reefs in Indonesia – the case of blast fishing Cesar (2000)	Tourism, coastal protection, net-benefit non-destructive fishing	Net private benefits of blast fishing	Net loss to society from blast fishing =US$33.9m–306.8m per km^2 of coral reef Economic loss to society=4*net private benefits to blast fishers	20 years 10%
Coral mining in Indonesia Cesar (2000)	Sales of lime, side-payments	Coastal erosion, increase wood prices, forgone tourism, net fishery loss	B= US$355,000 C= US$389,000– 1.1m depending on the tourism scenario	30 years 9%
Giant panda in China (Wolong Reserve) Kontoleon et al. (2002)	Potential for increase in eco-tourism by estimating the demand high-quality eco-tourism		B= US$145–210/ha per year. Lower bound estimate assumes only 30 tourists per day for 6 months/year	
Black rhinoceros in Namibia. Swanson et al. (2002) Gray whale. Loomis and Larson (1994)	Non-use values of UK residents		WTP= 5 pounds per household per year. WTP=US$16–18 per household per year	

Source: author

commonly used and values are expressed in monetary currency/per household/year or per person/year.[8] As it is apparent from the list and references, only a few studies provide cost figures and hence the opportunity for calculating B/C ratios.

The solution: a generalized guide for policies to curtail biodiversity loss

Biodiversity is under threat due to pressures caused outside the sphere of influence of biodiversity policies but often linked to human activity. These include: destruction and degradation of natural habitat (through land use changes, urban expansion, deforestation, changes of use in the coastal zone, overuse of marine and riverine ecosystems), the introduction of non-indigenous species, overhunting and overfishing, pollution (e.g. industrial, human, and animal waste discharges), and climate change.

Figure 9.1 provides a schematic representation of different biodiversity goods and services according to their different economic attributes. This assists in building the different policy options to mitigate suboptimal biodiversity loss, starting with the option that has the largest net benefit. All options would benefit from the establishment of a core set of biodiversity indicators to facilitate monitoring and evaluation of biodiversity policies, and diminish uncertainty related to erroneous policies such as the case of most introductions of non-indigenous species, which could actually work if better information were available.[9] Yet, it should be noted that improving the scientific information set of the policymaker alone is not sufficient to mitigate biodiversity loss and hence is not discussed here as an option in itself.

---

[8] See Pearce, Pearce, and Palmer 2002 and Nunes, van den Bergh, and Nijkamp 2003 for additional examples.

[9] As mentioned in Hill and Greathead (2000), the introduction of non-indigenous species (known as classical biological control – CBC) to combat pests and weeds is normally perceived by policymakers as a public good policy. Yet, given the substantial failure rate of CBCs, overall the intervention could be considered a failure. Nonetheless, twenty-seven published ex-post analyses of CBCs yielded significant benefit–cost ratios (B/C ratios ranged from 1 to over 1,000), some of which were significantly higher than comparable programs and even public goods investment projects.

Option 1: *Eliminate perverse incentives*

Rationale: Perverse incentives are the source of many environmental problems. They encourage environmental damage and biodiversity loss but have little economic basis. They often take the form of different subsidies that encourage environmentally harmful activities, increasing public bads such as pollution (e.g. hydrocarbon-based energy subsidies). Yet, they may also include direct payments from government budgets, tax exemptions or reductions, or the subsidized provision of private and public services (e.g. urban sprawl, road infrastructure). Regarding biodiversity, perverse incentives can be especially harmful by generating rents through the consumption of natural resource-intensive goods or supporting detrimental activities in important biodiversity economic sectors. For example, direct subsidies to agriculture in OECD countries were estimated to be as much as US$361 billion in 1999, while government support for marine capture fisheries amounted to US$6.3 billion, and for coal production it was US$6.2 billion. While some of these funds were used to reduce pressures on biodiversity and the environment, most contribute to destroying further the natural resource base, degradation of the coastal zone, and pollution generation. Some of this support is crucial to explain the collapse of different fisheries. Even climate change, which may have very detrimental impacts on biodiversity by severely altering ecosystems, is at least in part related to perverse incentives. Perverse incentives deplete scarce government budgets, can be regressive in income, affecting the poor more than the rich, and discourage efficient markets by promoting rent-seeking behavior[10] (OECD 2003).

Benefits: Major benefits include diminishing rent seeking behavior, decreasing incentives that generate public bads like pollution and biodiversity loss, increasing economic efficiency, among others.

Costs: These are the opportunity costs of negotiating outcomes such as potential temporary agreements towards sunset clauses related to the disappearance of the perverse incentives/subsidies.

---

[10] Rent-seeking behavior can be defined as "expenditure of resources to bring about an uncompensated transfer of goods or services from another person or persons to one's self as the result of a 'favorable' decision on some public policy" (OECD 2003).

Note: If perverse incentives are clearly identified, the net benefit of this option is likely to be very large as the impacts of their elimination will benefit several sectors of the economy. Freeing scarce public resources to be devoted to the provision of public goods is likely to improve the productivity of public spending. Yet, as government attempts indicate, powerful vested interests may be difficult to change.

Option 2: Privatize the biodiversity that is feasible and involve local communities

Rationale: Biodiversity as a whole is often treated as a public good when in fact there are benefits that can be privately captured and/or provided. When the different attributes of biodiversity are not recognized, there is scope for under-provision and degradation. Potential providers of ecosystem services have little incentive to provide them. Potential guardians of biological resources become poachers and destroyers of habitats. By taking advantage of the excludability of some biodiversity goods and services, clearly establishing enforceable property rights over them and allowing for trade, policymakers can potentially transform destroyers into conservationists.

Benefits: Major benefits include decreasing incentives that generate public bads like pollution and biodiversity loss, increasing economic efficiency, improving monitoring and enforcement by local communities, improving technical skills of individuals within communities, harnessing international and national private financing by facilitating sustainable use, among others.

Costs: These are mainly those related to technical assistance and information provision to increase the likelihood that private biodiversity provision is sustainable.

Note: There are several examples in developing and developed countries with variable degrees of success signaling high net benefit. These include private parks in South Africa, local communities in Africa facilitating viewing safaris and controlled trophy hunting, indigenous communities being paid for the provision of ecosystem services such as conservation of watersheds in Mexico. Once again, this option frees scarce public resources to be devoted to the provision of public goods.

Option 3: Bundle non-excludable attributes of biodiversity with its private goods and club goods and design economic instruments that take advantage of markets to deliver these attributes

Rationale: In policies targeting man-made infrastructure, a common goal is to unbundle service provision. This promotes competition and may drive technological change. Yet, in the case of biodiversity, certain goods and services are not easily divisible from others and carry significant public good attributes. Enjoying marketable services together with positive externalities or additional public good aspects may justify some kind of government support or regulation rather than a direct attempt to unbundle biodiversity goods and services (OECD 2003).

Benefits: Major benefits include securing the optimal provision of public goods related to biodiversity, while taking advantage of market forces. Depending on the chosen instrument, this may even generate public funds.

Costs: Depending on the instrument choice (e.g. subsidies), there is potential for rent seeking. Yet, this could be mitigated by sunset clauses, periodic revisions, and provision of funds against the delivery of public goods measured by clearly defined indicators.

Note: There are a number of examples that have successfully used markets to enforce regulations (e.g. tradable fishing quotas, tradable hunting quotas, etc.). Even public payments if well designed can successfully diminish threats to biodiversity, while diminishing the potential for rent seeking.

Option 4: Ensure the provision of biodiversity-related public goods

Rationale: As discussed above, the benefits of biodiversity conservation are still not well understood. This uncertainty is in part responsible for inaction – if one cannot measure it properly, how can it be prioritized adequately? Yet, extinction is in principle irreversible, and policymakers may wish to secure a certain minimum level of biodiversity to avoid it. This suggests that a certain degree of precaution is advisable even if standard tools of economic analysis such as CBA may be biased against it.

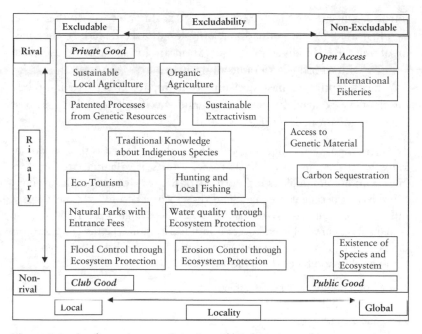

Figure 9.1. A schematic representation of biodiversity and its economic attributes

Source: OECD 2003.

Benefits: Major benefits include securing the minimum provision of public goods related to biodiversity. As information is attained, closer to optimal provision is possible.

Costs: Other policy interventions are sacrificed.

Note: If the outcome is irreversible, it may be justifiable to apply the precautionary principle. This is particularly relevant when securing the existence of species and ecosystems, where non-use values are likely to play a major role.

Conclusions and caveats

Demonstrating the value of biodiversity is a fundamental step in its conservation and sustainable use, because it allows biodiversity to participate on the same basis with other competing calls on public funding. In addition, the threats to biodiversity are significant, and engaging in valuation of biodiversity increases the chances that policymakers will introduce incentives for conservation and sustainable use. In this sense, as illustrated by the valuation examples above, including the ones involving CBA, biodiversity conservation and/or sustainable use often comply with rigorous economic analysis.

Yet, attempting to base decisions that impact directly or indirectly biodiversity exclusively on valuation and specifically on CBA is at best dicey. As mentioned in OECD (2006):

The central problem is one of uncertainty – the basic fact is that we do not know what these losses are likely to be. Efforts at valuation are therefore important but are unlikely to inform us of the scale of "tolerable" change. Moreover, if decisions are made and they turn out to be extremely costly, little can be done to reverse them. Finally, if ecologists are right and the systems have thresholds and other non-linearities, maybe the consequences of losing even modest ecosystem areas could be large. Ecosystem [biodiversity] loss thus combines several features:

- A potential large "scale" effect;
- Irreversibility;
- Uncertainty.

Economists have long known that this combination dictates a "precautionary" approach (e.g. Dasgupta 1982). To these features we need to add another:

- Few ecosystems undisturbed by human activity exist.

The relevance of this last point is that the world no longer has a "reserve" of ecosystems [biodiversity] subject only to natural variation and to which it could turn for genetic and other information. In effect, the information stored over millions of years of evolution is at risk.

Nonetheless, OECD (2006) also explains how CBA could be made compatible with the precautionary principle in the context of decision making:

- It would operate within the constraints of strong sustainability.[11]
- As a safe minimum standard; i.e. the B/C ratio for deciding on the loss of biodiversity is much greater than one.

---

[11] "Strong sustainability starts from the assertion that certain natural assets are so important or critical (for future, and perhaps current, generations) so as to warrant protection at current or above some other target level. If individual preferences cannot be counted on to fully reflect this importance, there is a paternal role for decision-makers in providing this protection" (OECD 2006).

- As an option value, i.e. the forgone costs of not waiting for additional information on the benefits of biodiversity conservation.

Since the importance of biodiversity is self-evident, it is also unclear why, when comparing with alternative policies in other areas, the "burden of proof" is often placed on biodiversity policies. Biodiversity conservation and sustainable use should neither be penalized due to the lack of information associated with it nor punished because it is a new concern among development issues. As discussed, policymakers should be cognizant that the potential for a large-scale effect, the irreversibility and uncertainty related to biodiversity, may require a precautionary approach rather than dismissal for absence of information or novelty.

Finally, it should be remembered that options that secure the greatest biodiversity gains are likely to coincide with those that also increase economic efficiency. The most important option, likely to generate the largest net benefit, does not exclusively target biodiversity loss. Yet, by eliminating perverse incentives, policymakers have a unique opportunity to prevent biodiversity loss while improving economic gains. This is likely to do society a lot of good.

References

Alberini, A. and J. R. Kahn (2006), *Handbook On Contingent Valuation*, Cheltenham, Edward Elgar Publishing.

Carret, J. C. and D. Loyer (2003), "Comment financer durablement les aires protégées a Madagascar? Apport de l'analyse économique," Agence Française de Développement.

Cesar, H. (2000), Collected Essays on the Economics of Coral Reefs. CORDIO, Kalmar University, Sweden.

Costanza, R., R. D'Arge, R. De Groot, S. Farber, M. Grasso, B. Hannon, K. Limburg, S. Naeem, R. O'Neill, J. Paruelo, R. Raskin, P. Sutton and M Van den Belt (1997), "The value of the world's ecosystem services and natural capital," *Nature*, 387, May 15, 253–260.

Dasgupta, P. (1982), *The Control of Resources*, Oxford, Blackwell.

Heal, G. (2000), *Nature and the Marketplace*, 1st edition, Washington DC, Island Press.

Hill, G. and D. Greathead (2000), "Economic evaluation in classical biological control," in C. Perrings, M. Williamson, and S. Dalmazzone, *The Economics of Biological Invasions*, Cheltenham, Edward Elgar Publishing.

Kontoleon, A. et al. (2002), "Optimal ecotourism: the economic value of the giant panda in China," in Pearce, Pearce and Palmer (eds.), *Valuing the Environment in Developing Countries: Case Studies*, Cheltenham, Edward Elgar Publishing.

Loomis, J. B. and D. M. Larson (1994), "Total economic value of increasing Gray Whale populations: results from a contingent valuation survey of visitors and households," *Marine Resource Economics*, 9, 275–286.

Nunes, P., J. van den Bergh, and P. Nijkamp (2003), *The Ecological Economics of Biodiversity: Methods and Policy Applications*, Cheltenham, Edward Elgar Publishing.

OECD (2001), *Valuation of Biodiversity Benefits: Selected Studies*, Paris, OECD.

OECD (2002), *Handbook of Biodiversity Valuation: A Guide for Policy Makers*, Paris, OECD.

OECD (2003), *Harnessing Markets for Biodiversity: Towards Conservation and Sustainable Use*, Paris, OECD.

OECD (2006), *Cost–Benefit Analysis and the Environment: Recent Developments*, Paris, OECD.

Pearce, D., C. Pearce, and C. Palmer, eds. (2002), *Valuing the Environment in Developing Countries: Case Studies*, Cheltenham, Edward Elgar Publishing.

Sathirathai, S. (1998), *Economic Valuation of Mangroves and the Roles of Local Communities in the Conservation of Natural Resources: Case Study of Surat Thani, South of Thailand*, EEPSEA Research Report Series, Economy and Environment Program for Southeast Asia, Singapore.

Swanson, T. et al. (2002), "Conflicts in conservation: the many values of the black rhinoceros" in Pearce, Pearce, and Palmer (eds.), *Valuing the Environment in Developing Countries: Case Studies*, Cheltenham, Edward Elgar Publishing.

UNCBD (2000). The Convention on Biological Diversity, Text and Annexes. Montreal, Quebec.

Van Beukering et al. (2003), "Economic valuation of the Leuser National Park on Sumatra, Indonesia," *Ecological Economics*, 44, 43–62.

WRI, UNEP, UNDP and the World Bank (2000), World Resources 2000–2001 – People and Ecosystems: The Fraying Web of Life, Washington, DC.

Waller-Hunter, J. and D. Biller (2001), "Valuing ecosystems: a key prerequisite for the sustainable management of natural resources," Fifth International Conference on the Environmental Management of Enclosed Coastal Seas, EMECS Proceedings, November 19–23, Kobe, Japan.

Weitzman, M. (1992), "On diversity," *Quarterly Journal of Economics*, 57, 363–405.

Wilkinson, C. (2004), "Status of coral reefs of the world 2004," Global Coral Reef Monitoring Network.

10 | *Vulnerability to Natural Disasters*

ROGER A. PIELKE, JR.

The challenge: global disaster losses are increasing

A wide range of datasets from around the world paint a consistent picture: disaster losses have been increasing rapidly in recent decades. Figure 10.1, produced by Munich Re, is illustrative of the more general conclusions.[1] It is important to recognize that disaster losses do not increase in every region at a constant rate. Some regions may see decreasing trends. Disaster losses typically come in discrete, large values and the trend record is driven by the increase in the costs of the largest disasters, such as hurricanes in the United States.

The economic costs of disasters have largely been driven by events in developed countries, due to their greater wealth. However, disasters in developing countries with smaller loss totals can have much larger effects as they may represent a much larger portion of a country's overall economic activity. Loss of life with respect to disasters has decreased significantly over the past century (Figure 10.2).[2] Much of the human toll of natural disasters occurs in developing countries. For example, the December 2005 Indian Ocean Tsunami killed more than 275,000 people across the region, while Hurricane Katrina, the deadliest natural disaster in the United States in many decades, killed fewer than 1,500 people.

The trend of increasing disaster losses has been driven largely by damage associated with earthquakes, floods, and storms.[3] Figure 10.3

---

[1] P. Höppe and R. A. Pielke, Jr. (eds.), 2006. Workshop on Climate Change and Disaster Losses: Understanding and Attributing Trends and Projections, Final Workshop Report. Hohenkammer, Germany, 25–26 May. http://sciencepolicy. colorado.edu/sparc/research/projects/extreme_events/munich_workshop/work-shop_report.html

[2] www.em-dat.net/documents/figures/global_trends/nb_kill_global.jpg

[3] Red Cross World Disasters Report, 2000–2005. www.ifrc.org/publicat/catalog/ autogen/4517.asp. The same is the case with respect to insured damages, see Association of British Insurers, 2005. www.abi.org.uk/Display/File/Child/552/ Financial_Risks_of_Climate_Change.pdf

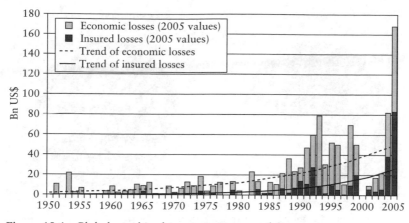

Figure 10.1. Global trend in the economic costs of disasters

©2006 Nat CatSERVICE, Geo Risk Research, Munich Re

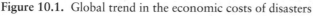

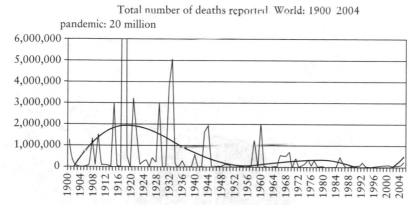

Figure 10.2. Global trend in loss of life disasters. *Source:* www.cred.be.

Equation for time-trend line: y=0,0002×6−0,0666×5+5,6467×4−
94,031×3−8332,1×2+301972×−732338, R2=0,0824

Source: EM-DAT. The OFDA/CRED International Disaster Database, www.em-
dat.net-Université Catholique de Louvain-Brussels-Belgium

indicates that the vast majority of weather-related losses (both insured
and total) between 1970 and 2004 are the result of floods and storms.[4]

[4] Association of British Insurers, 2005. www.abi.org.uk/Display/File/Child/552/
Financial_Risks_of_Climate_Change.pdf

i. Distribution of total losses
1970–2004

ii. Distribution of insured losses
1970–2004

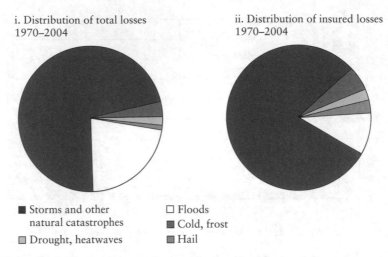

■ Storms and other   □ Floods
   natural catastrophes   ■ Cold, frost
□ Drought, heatwaves   ■ Hail

Figure 10.3 Total and insured costs of atmospheric-related disasters
worldwide 1970–1994. *Source:* ABI, 2005.

Note: Since 1970 weather-related catastrophes resulted in about $345 bn in total
damage, of which $300 bn was insured.

Source: Sigma Date. Swiss Re.

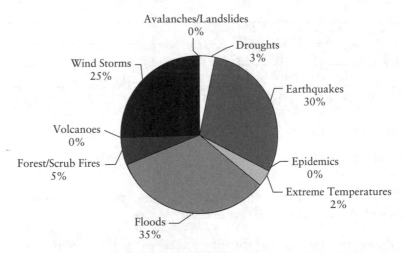

Figure 10.4a Total disaster losses in the 1990s by cause (IFRC, 2000)

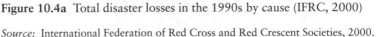

Source: International Federation of Red Cross and Red Crescent Societies, 2000.

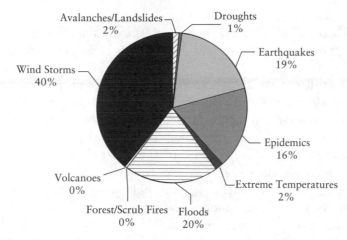

Figures 10.4b Total deaths in the 1990s by cause (IFRC, 2000)

Source: International Federation of Red Cross and Red Crescent Societies, 2000.

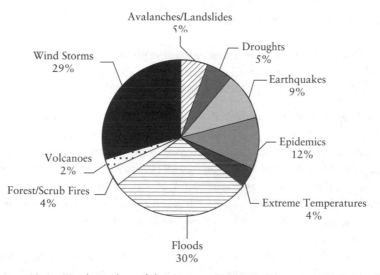

Figures 10.4c Total number of disasters in the 1990s by cause (IFRC, 2000)

Source: International Federation of Red Cross and Red Crescent Societies, 2000.

Figures 10.4a–c show the distribution of disasters by phenomena in terms of the total damage, loss of life, and number of disasters for the decade of the 1990s.[5] A consistent picture emerges from this

[5] Data from the Red Cross World Disasters Report, 2000. www.ifrc.org/publicat/catalog/autogen/4517.asp

data – earthquakes, floods, and windstorms are the primary phenomena responsible for disasters around the world according to each of
these metrics.

The challenge facing policymakers in the face of increasing costs
of natural disasters and a significant human toll is that many cost-
effective solutions are understood and in-hand but remain unimple-
mented in developed and developing countries alike. A significant part
of the challenge is to frame the natural disaster challenge properly as
one of reducing vulnerability in exposed locations, rather than ineffective efforts to modulate events themselves. This challenge appears
to have been well understood in the context of earthquakes, but less
so with respect to atmospheric hazards. The challenge of reducing vulnerability is difficult, in part, because of the lack of understanding of
the benefits and costs of improving resilience to extreme events.

Solutions, costs, and benefits

1. Properly frame the disaster challenge as one of reducing vulnerability, and not modulating extreme events via energy policies

The impacts of climate on society result from the interaction of a
climate event and societal vulnerability to experiencing impacts. To
understand this interaction requires a comprehensive perspective on
the drivers of disaster losses. Such a perspective can be achieved via a
sensitivity analysis of the integrated effects of drivers on loss totals
(Pielke, in press). The goal of such a sensitivity analysis methodology
is to examine various combinations of climate change and societal conditions (and the relationship of the two) to assess future economic
impacts. Here we use the global economic impacts of tropical cyclones
to illustrate the relative potential for different approaches to their mitigation. The goal of such a sensitivity analysis is not to perform a
cost–benefit analysis of policy options. Nor is the goal to predict future
impacts or to select arbitrarily among different scientific understand-
ings. Rather the goal is to explore the potential effectiveness of alternative approaches to addressing future tropical cyclone losses in the
context of a wide range of assumptions about the future.

In order to assess possible future damage due to tropical cyclones relative to today requires a number of assumptions. Pielke (in press) uses

Table 10.1. *Assumptions of the sensitivity analysis in Pielke (in press) to 2050*

Societal change
Annual combined increase in wealth and population (based on expert projections):
    2.5% and 4.7%
Climate change
Total increase in tropical cyclone intensity
    18% (based on an expert elicitation): and 36% (twice highest value)
Relationship of climate change to damage
Damage varies as (based on a literature review):
    3rd, 6th, 9th power of the storm intensity

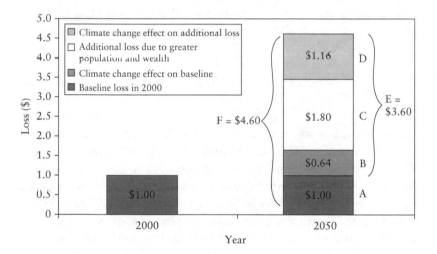

Figure 10.5. Display of values presented in Table 10.1

assumptions about societal change, climate change, and the relationship of climate change to damage. Table 10.1 summarizes these assumptions, which are documented in detail in Pielke (in press).[6] The various assumptions result in a two by two by three table of results,

---

[6] Note that the assumptions in Nordhaus (2006), cited by Stern, are within the bounds of the assumptions used by Pielke (in press).

which are intended to encompass the range of present expectations for the future.

The analysis begins with $1.00 in damages today and asks how that will increase by 2050. Table 10.1 and Figure 10.5 illustrate the analysis step by step by assuming that all tropical cyclones increase in intensity by 18 percent by 2050, population/wealth increases by 180 percent above today's levels, and damage is proportional to the cube of the intensity. From Table 10.1, of total costs of tropical cyclone damage in 2050, the fraction that can be addressed, in principle, if the intensity of tropical cyclones is intentionally modulated by stabilizing the climate such that intensities remain at their current levels is $1.80 (B + D), and the part that can be addressed, in principle, by reducing vulnerability is $4.60 (F). Assuming (unrealistically) (a) an instantaneous reduction of greenhouse gases to 2006 levels, and (b) no commitment to climate change due to past emissions, then at the theoretical limit, climate stabilization policies could reduce the increase in future damages from $3.60 to $1.80, that is, a 50 percent reduction.

A more realistic exercise would focus on the potential effectiveness of more realistic policy proposals. Here we illustrate the potential effectiveness of efforts to reduce greenhouse gas emissions with a hypothetical emissions reduction policy that leads to a 10 percent reduction in the projected increase in atmospheric greenhouse gas concentrations in 2050. Carbon dioxide concentrations are about 380 parts per million (ppm) in 2006, and assuming that carbon dioxide concentrations will be 500 ppm in 2050 under business as usual, a 10 percent reduction equates to a 12 ppm decrease (i.e., 10 percent $= 12/[500 - 380]$).[7] Assuming that greenhouse gas reductions have an instantaneous (i.e., contemporaneous with the reductions) and proportional (i.e., a 50 percent decrease in emissions decreases the projected increase in tropical cyclone intensity by 50 percent) effect on tropical cyclone intensity,[8] then policies that lead to a 10 percent decrease in atmospheric carbon dioxide concentrations in 2050 would (under the assumptions here)

---

[7] By contrast under the Kyoto Protocol if fully and successfully implemented by 2012 (including participation of the United States and Australia), the corresponding carbon dioxide reduction would be 2 ppm by 2012 and, absent other policies, about 2.5 ppm by 2050.

[8] Of course, the real climate system does not work in this way, and the effects of mitigation on hurricane behavior remains poorly understood, but it is certainly less direct than the oversimplification offered here.

Table 10.2. *An overview of the approach in Pielke (in press)*

Assumptions for 2050:
1. Change in tropical cyclone intensity = 18%
2. Change in population and wealth above present baseline = 180%
3. Damage function = cubic

A = tropical cyclone damages today = $1.00
B = increase in tropical cyclone damages in 2050 = 64%, i.e., damage
    increase = (($1.00 * 0.18))^3-$1.00 = $0.64
C = increase in tropical cyclone damage in 2050 = Today's damage + 180%
    increase = $1.00 * 1.80 = $1.80
D = combined effect of B and C = $1.80 * 0.64 = $1.16
E = Total increase in costs = B + C + D = $0.64 + $1.80 + $1.16 = $3.60
F = Total tropical cyclone economic damage in 2050 = A + E = $4.60

---

decrease the projected increase in hurricane intensities by 10 percent in 2050. The corresponding reduction in projected damages as described in Table 10.2 would be therefore about $0.21 (i.e., the increase in intensity would be reduced from 18 to 16.2 percent, see Table 10.3 details) reducing losses in 2050 from $4.60 to $4.39, a reduction of about 4.5 percent. Under these assumptions 100 percent success in implementation of a policy about five times more ambitious than Kyoto is the equivalent in its effect of about a 4.5 percent success rate in addressing ever-increasing vulnerability through efforts to build societal resilience.

Greenhouse gas mitigation may certainly be justified for other reasons, such as its cost-effectiveness, but if the case of tropical cyclones is representative of other disaster-related phenomena, then even if greenhouse gas mitigation polices were cost-free, vulnerability reduction would still have far greater potential to address the mounting toll of disaster losses because emissions reduction policies can address only a subset of the multiple causes of increasing losses. It should be underscored that this exercise was conducted using conservative projected societal changes (i.e., wealth, population) as well as unrealistic assumptions about climate behavior. Using larger societal changes and more realistic assumptions about climate science would result in a larger potential effectiveness ratio in favor of vulnerability reduction. Thus, the effectiveness of mitigation is certainly overstated in this analysis. These results are robust even under the full range of assumptions about changes in tropical cyclone intensities.

Table 10.3. *Various scenarios for future economic losses from tropical cyclones in 2050, as a function of climate change, societal change, and windspeed-loss damage function*

10.3a. 18% increase in intensity by 2050

Societal change	180%	180%	180%	600%	600%	600%
Damage function	Cubic	6th power	9th power	Cubic	6th power	9th power
Climate	0.64	1.70	3.44	0.64	1.70	3.44
Society	1.80	1.80	1.80	6.00	6.00	6.00
Climate/Society	1.16	3.06	6.18	3.86	10.20	20.61
Total damage	4.60	7.56	12.42	11.50	18.90	31.05
Maximum effect of 10% reduction in 2050 CO_2 concentrations	0.21	0.67	1.60	0.52	1.66	4.01
Maximum mitigation	1.80	4.76	9.62	4.50	11.90	24.05
Maximum vulnerability reduction	4.60	7.56	12.42	11.50	18.90	31.05

10.3b. 36% increase in intensity by 2050

Societal change	180%	180%	180%	600%	600%	600%
Damage function	Cubic	6th power	9th power	Cubic	6th power	9th power
Climate	1.52	5.33	14.92	1.52	5.33	14.92
Society	1.80	1.80	1.80	6.00	6.00	6.00
Climate/Society	2.73	9.59	26.85	9.09	31.97	89.50
Total damage	7.04	17.72	44.57	17.61	44.29	111.42
Maximum effect of 10% reduction in 2050 CO_2 concentrations	0.54	2.63	9.56	1.36	6.59	23.90
Maximum mitigation	4.24	14.92	41.77	10.61	37.29	104.42
Maximum vulnerability reduction	7.04	17.72	44.57	17.61	44.29	111.42

For a range of assumptions about intensity change and changes in population/ wealth, the growth of $1.00 in global tropical cyclone damage today into damage in 2050 using damage functions that assume damage as being proportional to the 3rd, 6th, and 9th powers of windspeed. The first column of Table 10.3a shows the values from Table 10.2. Values expressed in constant 2007 dollars.

Table 10.3 illustrates the results under a range of different assumptions. The column headings refer to the assumptions used in the calculations about increase in tropical cyclone intensity and growth in combined population and wealth. The first column of Table 10.3a provides the values presented in Table 10.2 and Figure 10.1. Within the table the values presented reflect three different damage functions.

Under these various assumptions, the largest *maximum potential effectiveness* of a 10 percent reduction in the projected increase in greenhouse gas concentrations by 2050 for reducing future global tropical cyclone damage is far less than the maximum potential effectiveness of adaptation (i.e., reducing the vulnerability of people and property) by a ratio of about 8 to 1 under the maximum change in intensity resulting from the expert elicitation and about 5 to 1 when arbitrarily doubling the maximum change in intensity. Alternatively, under the assumptions most favorable to vulnerability reduction, the ratios are 22 to 1 and 13 to 1.

Table 10.3 also shows the potential effectiveness of instantaneous climate stabilization at 2006 values. Under no scenario does this form of mitigation result in a greater potential effectiveness than vulnerability reduction. It is therefore appropriate to conclude that vulnerability reduction is potentially more effective under any theoretically possible mitigation scenario. Under any plausible mitigation scenario, vulnerability reduction vastly exceeds mitigation in terms of its potential effectiveness. These conclusions are qualitatively insensitive to the magnitude of the projected increase in tropical cyclone intensity or population scenarios. The longer the timescale, the greater the role of the societal factors, assuming continued growth in wealth and/or population.

To emphasize, the analysis presented here should not be interpreted as an argument against mitigation of greenhouse gases. And there is no suggestion here that human-caused climate change is not real or should not be of concern. Instead, this simple analysis under the most favorable assumptions for mitigation indicates that in the coming decades any realistically achievable mitigation policies can have at best only a very small and perhaps imperceptible effect on global tropical cyclone damage, whatever the costs of those policies might happen to be. This reality explains why adaptation necessarily must be at the center of climate policy discussions and must be viewed as a complement to mitigation policies, rather than simply as the costs of failed mitigation, as suggested, for example, by the Stern Review on the Economics of

Climate Change. It also helps to explain why mitigation policies in the short term necessarily must be focused on their non-climate benefits.

Most importantly these results show how misleading it is to use tropical cyclone damage as a reason for greenhouse gas mitigation when other actions have far more potential effectiveness. The images of storm-spawned death and destruction are no doubt compelling, but it is misleading or disingenuous to suggest that energy policies can have an appreciable effect on future damages. The only way to arrive at tropical cyclone damages that exceed the societal factors is to hold societal change constant and focus only on the climate component, which is in fact what some studies have done in the past. Climate change is real and policy action on mitigation makes sense, but when compared with available alternatives for addressing the escalating costs of tropical cyclones. Those interested in honest advocacy and effective policy should keep these issues separate.

2. There is a pressing need for improved information on the costs and benefits of vulnerability reduction policies and practices, the impacts of natural disasters, as well as the relative vulnerability of different countries and communities, in order to prioritize disaster mitigation projects and programs more effectively

If reducing vulnerability is preferred to efforts to modulate extreme events through energy policies, then what are specific examples of beneficial vulnerability reduction policies?

Formal evaluation of specific options for reducing disaster vulnerability remains difficult because "natural hazards and related vulnerability are rarely considered in the design and appraisal of development projects. Similarly, monitoring and evaluation are still relatively neglected in disaster reduction, especially where impact evaluation is concerned."[9] There are a number of benefit–cost estimates that circulate in the disaster community that suggest that "disaster mitigation pays," typically by a ratio of 3 to 1 or higher. Of such estimates Benson and Twigg (2004, pp. 13–14)[10] write:

---

[9] C. Benson and J. Twigg, 2004. 'Measuring Mitigation': Methodologies for assessing natural hazard risks and the net benefits of mitigation – A scoping study, ProVention Consortium. www.proventionconsortium.org/themes/default/pdfs/MM_scoping_study.pdf.   [10] Ibid.

However, there is surprisingly little evidence in support of many broad-brush statements. Detailed underlying calculations are not available, suggesting that they may, in fact, be no more than "back-of the-envelope" – if informed – estimates. Even if they are based on more extensive calculations, the fact that the workings underlying them are not readily available can cast doubts on their legitimacy, particularly if figures involve some valuation of non-tangibles. Of course, financial analysis of loss and the cost of investments needed to avoid loss may not be sufficient to ensure greater attention to natural hazard risk, as demonstrated from experience elsewhere (for instance, in relation to disease, water pollution and illiteracy). But proof of net financial benefits is almost undoubtedly a first, very necessary step in making a case for the importance of analysing hazard-related risks.

The lack of a well-developed body of cost–benefit analyses of the value of disaster mitigation sets the stage for a chicken-and-egg problem. Because such studies do not exist, it can be difficult to compare projects or policies focused on disaster mitigation with other sorts of development policies; hence disaster mitigation policies are at risk of being overlooked in any systematic comparison of costs and benefits across different policy alternatives. But if such projects are overlooked, then there is less incentive to call for and support rigorous cost–benefit studies. One consequence of this dynamic is that funds for disaster relief in the aftermath of a horrific disaster are, in many cases, easier to secure than funds for long-term reduction of vulnerability to disasters, which may have supported efforts that would have reduced the need for post-disaster relief. This vicious cycle is well appreciated by observers of disaster policy but remains entrenched.[11]

Thus, one recommendation is for increasing attention to the need for rigorous cost–benefit analyses of disaster mitigation policy alternatives and practices. To put this another way, irrespective of how such studies turn out (in terms of relative costs and benefits), there is a substantial benefit to decision making related to disasters to be gained from a more rigorous understanding of the value of disaster mitigation. More fundamentally, there is also a pressing need for more rigorous information on the impacts of disasters,[12] as well as indicators of relative

[11] B. Wisner, P. Blaikie, T. Cannon, and I. Davis, 2004, *At Risk: Natural Hazards, People's Vulnerability and Disasters*. Wiltshire: Routledge.

[12] For example, C. Benson and E. Clay, 2004, *Understanding the Economic and Financial Impacts of Natural Disasters*. Disaster Risk Management Series No.4.

vulnerability[13] in order to help prioritize disaster mitigation investments. Even in the United States and Europe, where response to disasters is generally quite successful as measured by lives lost and
community recovery from disasters, there is exceedingly little information available on the costs and benefits of disaster mitigation, as
well as the role of government investments in disasters on outcomes.[14]

3. Even in the absence of well-developed studies of the costs and benefits of disaster mitigation, there are many proven and promising options for cost-effective disaster mitigation

Actions to reduce the impacts of natural disasters are many and varied
around the world. Some of these actions are developed in the longer term,
such as building codes, evacuation plans, and emergency response plans.
Some of these longer-term plans require additional action in the short
term in the face of an impending threat, such as an order of evacuation.

In some instances not only has a cost–benefit analysis not been
attempted, but neither has a more general risk assessment. Hurricane
evacuation in the United States is an example of such a situation.
Hurricane forecasts of storm tracks have improved steadily over the past
three decades or so, yet at the same time the area of coastline warned per
storm has increased over the same time period. This suggests that decision makers (including forecasters and emergency managers) have possibly become more risk-averse over time and have used advances in the
science of forecasting to reduce the chances of leaving part of the population unwarned. Of course, such strategies have costs, in the form of a
greater number of people warned unnecessarily. But to date there has
been little demand for the quantification of the costs, benefits, and risks
associated with different approaches to the challenge of hurricane evacuation in the face of uncertainty.[15] Arguably, the case of hurricane

Footnote 12 (cont.)
  Washington DC: World Bank. www-wds.worldbank.org/servlet/WDS_IBank_
  Servlet?pcont=details&eid=000012009_20040420135752
[13] UNDRO, 1990, *Preliminary Study on the Identification of Disaster-Prone
  Countries Based on Economic Impact.* New York/Geneva: United Nations
  Disaster Relief Organization.
[14] C. Meade and M. Abbott, 2003, *Assessing Federal Research and Development
  for Hazard Loss Reduction*, RAND, Santa Monica, CA.
[15] R. A. Pielke, Jr., 1999, Hurricane Forecasting. *Science*, 284, 1123.

evacuation is representative of the broader challenges of evaluating existing disaster mitigation policies in terms of their costs, benefits, and risks.

There are new and innovative policy options that have been proposed for disaster mitigation that will likely stimulate demand for greater attention to costs and benefits. Among these are the securitization of risk through financial products such as catastrophe bonds and derivatives[16] and the provision of micro-finance[17] in developing countries as a tool of disaster recovery in ways that reduce long-term vulnerabilities. One example is a reinsurance contract developed by Axa Re to underwrite the possibility of drought in Ethiopia for the World Food Programme.[18] The way that the program works is that Axa Re and the World Food Programme agree upon a specific climate metric that can be objectively measured, such as seasonal rainfall total in a particular region. Such measures should ideally be closely correlated with the impact of concern, in this case famine. The World Food Programme pays a premium calculated on the expected probability of the anomalous rainfall. If the rainfall exceeds the threshold, then Axa Re keeps the premium, and if it falls below the threshold, Axa Re pays out on the contract, freeing up resources for famine relief. In this manner risks can be shared and the World Food Programme can free resources for other activities knowing that it has hedged its risks. This program serves as a model that might be applied in other areas, tapping the risk sharing and liquidity of financial markets to hedge against the uncertainty of negative outcomes. Such policies are not widespread, however, and they have not been subject to rigorous evaluation of costs and benefits. Nonetheless, they have strong support among many disaster experts.

4. There are large ancillary benefits associated with more general progress with respect to human development and poverty reduction associated with vulnerability reduction related to natural disasters

Simply because the financial costs of natural disasters are increasing does not necessarily reflect an underlying policy problem, or if a

---

[16] www.axa.com/lib/axa/uploads/cpsocietes/2006/United_nations_PR_20060306.pdf

[17] www.proventionconsortium.org/themes/default/pdfs/microfin_guidebook.pdf

[18] www.wfp.org/english/?ModuleID=137&Key=2030

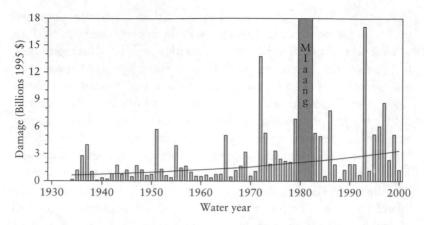

Figure 10.6a. Trends in US flood damage, 1934–2000, adjusted for inflation.

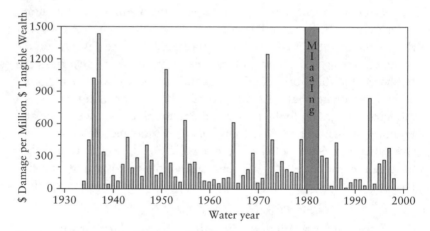

Figure 10.6b. Trends in US flood damage per unit of wealth, 1934–1998.

problem does exist, the magnitude of the challenge. The case of flood damage in the United States provides some insights to this perhaps counterintuitive situation. Figures 10.6a and 10.6b show two different perspectives on flood damage in the United States from 1934 to 2000. In Figure 10.6a the data is simply adjusted for inflation, showing a clear upward trend in damage. However, Figure 10.6b shows the same data expressed in terms of per-unit-national-wealth, and shows no trend.

This figure provides some evidence that overall growth in national wealth is an important factor in how we think about the impacts of natural disasters. Although damage may be rising, this is due to the fact that there is more to be damaged, and floods may in some cases have a decreasing effect on the economy even as losses increase. Of course, disaster mitigation policies likely have played some role in shaping trends in various metrics of damage.

Such an analysis is significant in particular for thinking about the impacts of disasters on developing countries, where disasters may be smaller in absolute terms than in developed countries, but far greater as a fraction of national economic activity. This suggests that there are considerable ancillary benefits to development and economic growth, particularly if done in a manner cognizant with disaster risks. Hazards scholar Dennis Mileti has frequently called for disaster mitigation to occupy a more central role in all of development planning, rather than as a separate category of policy activity.[19]

Conclusions

Once we understand that the chief reason for increasing disaster losses is the role of demographics in making a country vulnerable to disaster, we can better focus responses on managing vulnerability. But the narrow focus of the climate debate to date on emissions reductions has worked against a clear focus on vulnerability. The UN Framework Convention, for example, has refused to fund disaster preparedness efforts unless states could demonstrate exactly how the disasters they feared were linked to climate change. Consider, too, the amount spent on scientific research. According to a recent RAND study, US funding for disaster loss-reduction research in 2003 amounted to about $127 million – only 7 percent of the amount invested in climate-change research for that year.

This is not to say that many thousands of people and hundreds of organizations worldwide are not productively confronting disaster vulnerability, but their efforts do not begin to address the magnitude of the problem. Thousands of participants from most of the world's nations, along with scientists and political advocates, have come together every year since 1995 to work toward concerted international

[19] D. Mileti, 1999, *Disasters by Design*. Washington, DC: Joseph Henry Press.

action on climate change. But, when the UN World Conference on Disaster Reduction met in January 2005, it was the first such meeting in more than a decade.

Yet we know that effective action is possible to reduce disaster losses even in the face of poverty and dense population. During the 2004 hurricane season, Haiti and the Dominican Republic, both on the island of Hispaniola, provided a powerful lesson in this regard. As Julia Taft of the UN Development Program explained: "In the Dominican Republic, which has invested in hurricane shelters and emergency evacuation networks, the death toll was fewer than ten, as compared to an estimated two thousand in Haiti . . . Haitians were a hundred times more likely to die in an equivalent storm than Dominicans." Most tools needed to reduce disaster vulnerability already exist, such as risk assessment techniques, better building codes and code enforcement, land-use standards, and emergency-preparedness plans. The question is: Why is disaster vulnerability so low on the list of global development priorities? Says Brian Tucker, president of GeoHazards International: "The most serious flaw in our current efforts is the lack of a globally accepted standard of acceptable disaster vulnerability, and an action plan to put every country on course to achieve this standard. Then we would have a means to measure progress and to make it clear which countries are doing well and which are not. We need a natural disaster equivalent to the Kyoto Protocol."[20]

In principle, fruitful action on both climate change and disasters should proceed simultaneously. In practice, this will not happen until the issues of climate change and disaster vulnerability are clearly separated in the eyes of the media, the public, environmental activists, scientists, and policymakers. The accompanying text box presents twenty consensus recommendations at a workshop organized by Munich Re in spring 2006 on disasters and climate change. There are good reasons for more substantial action on energy policies, particularly in the United States; and there are good reasons for concern about the growing toll of disaster losses around the world. But suggestions that the escalating disaster losses should motivate action on energy policy simply cannot lead to an effective approach to disaster management.

[20] D. Sarewitz, and R. A. Pielke, Jr., 2005, Rising Tide, *The New Republic*, January 6.

Text Box: Consensus (unanimous) statements of the
Hohenkammer workshop (Höppe and Pielke 2006):[21]

1. Climate change is real, and has a significant human component related to greenhouse gases.
2. Direct economic losses of global disasters have increased in recent decades with particularly large increases since the 1980s.
3. The increases in disaster losses primarily result from weather-related events, in particular storms and floods.
4. Climate change and variability are factors which influence trends in disasters.
5. Although there are peer-reviewed papers indicating trends in storms and floods there is still scientific debate over the attribution to anthropogenic climate change or natural climate variability. There is also concern over geophysical data quality.
6. IPCC (2001) did not achieve detection and attribution of trends in extreme events at the global level.
7. High-quality long-term disaster loss records exist, some of which are suitable for research purposes, such as to identify the effects of climate and/or climate change on the loss records.
8. Analyses of long-term records of disaster losses indicate that societal change and economic development are the principal factors responsible for the documented increasing losses to date.
9. The vulnerability of communities to natural disasters is determined by their economic development and other social characteristics.
10. There is evidence that changing patterns of extreme events are drivers for recent increases in global losses.
11. Because of issues related to data quality, the stochastic nature of extreme event impacts, length of time series, and various societal factors present in the disaster loss record, it is still not possible to determine the portion of the increase in damages that might be attributed to climate change due to GHG emissions
12. For future decades the IPCC (2001) expects increases in the occurrence and/or intensity of some extreme events as a result

of anthropogenic climate change. Such increases will further increase losses in the absence of disaster reduction measures.

13. In the near future the quantitative link (attribution) of trends in storm and flood losses to climate changes related to GHG emissions is unlikely to be answered unequivocally.

Policy implications identified by the workshop participants

14. Adaptation to extreme weather events should play a central role in reducing societal vulnerabilities to climate and climate change.

15. Mitigation of GHG emissions should also play a central role in response to anthropogenic climate change, though it does not have an effect for several decades on the hazard risk.

16. We recommend further research on different combinations of adaptation and mitigation policies.

17. We recommend the creation of an open-source disaster database according to agreed-upon standards.

18. In addition to fundamental research on climate, research priorities should consider needs of decision makers in areas related to both adaptation and mitigation.

19. For improved understanding of loss trends, there is a need to continue to collect and improve long-term and homogenous datasets related to both climate parameters and disaster losses.

20. The community needs to agree upon peer-reviewed procedures for normalizing economic loss data.

[21] P. Höppe and R. Pielke, Jr., 2006, *Workshop on Climate Change and Disaster Losses*.

PART III

Governance

11 | *Arms Proliferation*

J. PAUL DUNNE*

The problem

To proliferate normally means to increase rapidly in number or quantity, or to grow or reproduce by rapid production of new parts (biological). When used in the case of arms, proliferation has tended to relate to nuclear weapons, where it means the spread of production technology to nations that do not already have it. More recently concerns have been raised about the spread of other dangerous technologies (chemical and biological) and of weapons themselves. For large weapons systems it can be the spread of production technology, but increasingly it is simply the spread of weapons per se. In this case we can distinguish qualitative and quantitative proliferation, the former being the increase in the number of agents that have more advanced weaponry (or technology) than is generally available through receiving it from another country, for example missiles or missile technologies, the latter being the increase in the numbers of weapons available, such as the increase in the number of small arms being supplied to countries (often cascading to groups other than the military). This means that proliferation is not simply the supply of arms per se. If we start from a particular status quo (balance) it would mean an increase in the spread of more advanced arms or arms technology across countries, or a marked growth in the quantity of arms available.

Arms proliferation is an issue of real concern for the world as it can increase the potential lethality of any conflict and could increase the probability of conflict. It can also increase the economic burden on countries, particularly developing ones. Conversely, reducing arms proliferation holds the promise of increasing security, reducing conflict, and improving economic performance and moving people out of poverty.

* I am grateful to Sam Perlo-Freeman, Elisabeth Skons and Ron Smith for comments, but the usual disclaimer applies.

There are problems in measuring proliferation, as there are not even reliable measures of arms.[1] In fact, in looking at proliferation it is the transfer of arms that is most important, but there are problems with this data.[2] It will tend to underestimate proliferation as it will not pickup illicit arms and small arms and it might perhaps be more important to look at the size and technological nature of deals than trends in import values.[3] Despite the fact that arms expenditures may seem to have fallen, the nature of the weapons has changed and one can expect more 'bangs per buck', so the lethality may even have gone up beyond that reflected in the SIPRI data. Another concern is the role of stocks of armaments and the importance of upgrades, which may constitute proliferation, but are not as obvious or transparent as a new system.[4] Complete weapons systems, final weapons systems, or platforms are usually the main focus of analysis of arms proliferation, but increasingly it is trade in components, services and technology that is important. Indeed, it is mainly the proliferation of technologies that is of concern rather than the actual weapons.

Controlling arms proliferation is gradually becoming more difficult with the internationalisation of the industry, giving a range of countries access to at least parts of the technologies involved in advanced systems and reducing transparency. In addition, there is also an increasing range of services that were once provided by the military being outsourced. Mercenaries have always been important, but not the type of companies that provide security services in conflict zones these days (Dunne and Surry, 2006). More recently the problems of arms proliferation have changed as suicide bombers have turned civil products into instruments of death and destruction using improvised explosive devices. This

---

[1] Military spending, an input measure is, often used as an indicator of output. It actually reflects the potential increase in arms. Total military spending trends showed a marked decline after the Cold War, up to the late 1990s, but since then have been rising. This does of course hide considerable regional variation.

[2] SIPRI provide arms transfer data based on volume measures of major weapons deliveries, which picks up trends, but omits a range of weapons. BVC provides some value of arms imports and exports, but the latest data is now over five years old and the quality of some of the data, based on CIA estimates, can be questioned.

[3] Arms exports and import trends are difficult to search for, as they can be very lumpy with one large deal such as the UK Al Yamamah making for a lumpy series over time and also hide changes in composition.

[4] For example adding smart systems on to dumb bombs.

is an extreme example of asymmetric conflict where the dominance of one adversary can force the other to change their approach to conflict – proliferation may not increase security.[5] Similarly, it is important to bear in mind proliferation to non state actors such as rebel groups, terrorists, major criminals and small criminals as increasing their firepower can have important and sometimes devastating effects on countries. It is often not clear where one draws the line.

Three categories of weapons can be identified which show rather different characteristics: non-conventional weapons, major conventional weapons and small arms.

Non-conventional weapons proliferation

Much of the discussion about proliferation concerns nuclear weapons. The end of the cold war saw some nations such as South Africa go non-nuclear, but others have still striven for nuclear weapons capability.[6] The possibility exists of states and non-state actors getting hold of weapons grade plutonium that could be made to produce weapons and ballistic missile technologies that could be used to deliver them.[7] The costs of attaining nuclear weapons status are high, partly because of existing international agreements and restrictions, but also because of the high fixed costs involved. Once these are paid, if they are treated as sunk costs the cost of nuclear weapons defence can become cheap by comparison to conventional ones. However, it is not only nuclear weapons that have the potential for mass destruction. Biological and chemical weapons also have the potential to be equally devastating to life. There is international concern that these technologies might fall into the 'wrong hands', which has led to a number of supplier group control regimes being set up, for example MTCR and Wassenaar.[8]

Non-conventional weapons of mass destruction are little used in reality and are generally not traded. This means that preventing

---

[5] See Dunne et al. (2006)
[6] The response of the US to Iran's nuclear programme, to Iraq's attempts and to developments in North Korea, makes it evident that there is an intense international concern that nuclear weapons technology should not proliferate.
[7] Though it is possible to make 'dirty' bombs.
[8] See Smith and Udis (2003) and various SIPRI Yearbooks. Technological advances have in fact blurred the distinction between smaller nuclear devices and larger non-nuclear ones, such as airburst weapons.

proliferation has only minor economic costs to the economies that hold the technologies in the form of lost trade. But there are real costs in providing treaties, policing and incentives to maintain agreements.[9] If controls on proliferation fail then there are the very real costs of counter-proliferation measures – which could entail military action and, if the offending states have already perfected the weapons, could itself lead to catastrophe.[10] While alternatives to military action are available, such as economic and other sanctions, they may be unsuccessful.

Major conventional weapons systems

When concerns are raised about conventional arms proliferation, it is normally the major weapons systems that are involved – tanks, planes, warships, submarines (platforms that can support any number of weapons). These can provide necessary defensive capabilities in the face of aggression and provide support for allies, but they can also start and escalate conflicts by giving one side a clear advantage. They can also lead to regional arms races and wasteful expenditure. Most of the concern here is the arms trade and production and the proliferation of advanced technologies which, as mentioned, can create imbalances and a higher level of lethality. No countries are completely self-sufficient in arms production, so trade is necessary, even if it is only at the level of

[9] "The Missile Technology Control Regime is an informal and voluntary association of countries which share the goals of non-proliferation of unmanned delivery systems capable of delivering weapons of mass destruction, and which seek to coordinate national export licensing efforts aimed at preventing their proliferation. The MTCR was originally established in 1987 by Canada, France, Germany, Italy, Japan, the United Kingdom and the United States. Since that time, the number of MTCR partners has increased to a total of thirty-four countries, all of which have equal standing within the Regime". http://www.mtcr. info/english/index.html "The Wassenaar Arrangement has been established in order to contribute to regional and international security and stability, by promoting transparency and greater responsibility in transfers of conventional arms and dual-use goods and technologies, thus preventing destabilising accumulations. Participating States seek, through their national policies, to ensure that transfers of these items do not contribute to the development or enhancement of military capabilities which undermine these goals, and are not diverted to support such capabilities." http://www.wassenaar.org/introduction/index.html

[10] Even with controls and treaties there is always the issue that current nuclear states will still have the knowledge of how to produce nuclear weapons. Though if they were to restart production it would be obvious to the international community.

components. Increasingly it is the growth of components, technology and people that are important sources of proliferation.

The SIPRI trend measure of the volume of major weapons transfers showed an increase in 2003, but the five-year moving average shows a trend decline after a slight upward trend in the 1990s (SIPRI Yearbook 2005). The main suppliers are Russia and the USA, with their transfers both twice that of the next three, France, Germany and the UK combined. Losing the trade in arms would impact upon Russia and Ukraine rather more than the US and European countries for whom the share of exports is small (e.g., less than 1% of exports in the UK). The list of recipients is somewhat different, but the fact that there are not many low-income countries should not blind us to the fact that many such countries spend significant fractions of their foreign exchange on weapons.

Small arms and light weapons

Recently, considerable research has been generated on issues around small arms, as it came to be recognised that they are the main security concern in the developing world. It is small arms that kill most people. While larger weapons can be important for power projection, small arms create the most social disintegration and casualties. They are used frequently by both state and non-state actors and the Graduate Institute of International Studies (SAS 2001, p. 1) estimates that 500,000 people are killed each year by small arms and light weapons. This is equivalent to a number of major wars being fought each year.

Small arms are relatively easy to manufacture and difficult to control. Even with proliferation controls of the legal trade there will be an illicit trade[11] and even with control of new weapons there is a massive and well organised second-hand market. There has also been a fragmentation of market through the collapse of various states, especially ex-Soviet Union countries. It is also important to recognise that weapons need not be technologically advanced to be lethal.[12]

---

[11] Most recently there is evidence that Austrian pistols exported for the Iraqi army have ended up in Turkey and in the hands of insurgents.

[12] The import of large numbers of Chinese manufactured machetes to Rwanda preceded the massacres in which they were the major tool of slaughter. Of course guns played important role for organisers. In some cases guns are mainly for show as the cost and scarcity of ammunition is such that they are not loaded. It is of course easier for local industry to produce ammunition than weapons.

Costs

In attempting to measure the direct costs of proliferation, the first stop must be military spending, which, while a measure of input rather than output, is used as a measure of military effort in the absence of output measures. Proliferation could be considered as increasing the military spending of the countries involved, to import weapons, import technology, or develop their own. The fraction of military spending that is spent on arms and the development of arms–procurement varies from country to country, with poorer countries tending to spend more on wages and personnel. World military spending in 2004 was estimated by SIPRI to be $975 billion at 2003 constant prices and exchange rates and $1003 billion at current prices. This was 6% lower than at the peak of the Cold War in 1987–8 and corresponds to $162 per capita as a global average or 2.6% of world GDP (Yearbook, 2005, p. 307). The main change has been in the US, which has 47% of the world total. The estimated value of the arms trade, which will include the large weapon systems and small arms, is estimated by SIPRI at $38–43 billion or only 0.5–0.6% of world trade. Clearly it is not significant. So any reduction in arms proliferation is unlikely to have any significant effects on the international economy through reduced trade.

Of course the big problem of using these measures is that the secrecy surrounding military spending means we do not know how reliable or comparable the figures are, particularly when we try to distinguish different weapons programmes and types of weapons.[13] In addition, military spending per se is not the cost of proliferation, which is likely to be only a fraction of total military spending and of the total arms trade, but to distinguish the expenditure that is related to proliferation is rather difficult. We could argue that any military spending above say, 1.5% of world GDP reflects a response to proliferation. This would give direct cost of proliferation for 2003 of around $412bn in 2003 constant prices,[14] though as many countries spend less than 1.5%, 500bn might seem a reasonable estimate.[15]

---

[13] Not only might allocations be misleading, but there may also be off budget inputs to the development of weapons systems, or monies used going through non defence categories.

[14] Based on a $975bn constant 2003 figure for world milex, which is 2.6% of world GDP, decreased to 1.5% of GDP.

[15] Of this, $321bn is the USA.

In addition to the direct cost in terms of military spending on proliferation, there are also the indirect economic effects on the economy. There are clear opportunity costs for countries that produce arms, in that the resources could be used to more effect in the civil sector, while there are more important costs for countries, especially developing countries, that import all of their arms. It is also possible that the success of proliferation reductions is an increase in domestic expenditure by countries attempting to develop their own technologies and weapons. In this case there could even be an increase in military spending, making the opportunity cost higher.

If reductions in arms proliferation are combined with disarmament treaties and international agreements then it is likely that defence spending will decline and will also mean that defence exports will decline. The fact that this will mainly affect the richer countries and the magnitudes involved is not suggestive of a large economic impact on the arms producers. The reduction in military spending since the end of the Cold War has not led to particular economic problems and while there may be problems of adjustment within countries because of local dependence, research suggests these will not be problematic. Indeed, if the spending is reallocated to other forms of government spending is likely to be beneficial producing a 'peace dividend' (Gleditsch et al., 1996).

In principle, reducing or preventing arms proliferation could result in a reduction of security for individual countries, but there is little direct evidence that this is likely to be the case and no real way of measuring the effect.[16] If proliferation was stopped for one adversary and not another it could lead to conflict, at a cost to the international community. If it simply sparks an arms race, no country actually benefits and all will lose in terms of the opportunity cost of their military spending.[17] There is also the issue of whether military security actually works, especially in the developing world.[18]

---

[16] An arms embargo in Bosnia meant the Serbs had weapons but the Muslims did not (until Arab states smuggled weapons to them) which resulted in a slaughter of the latter.

[17] This does, however, suggest that mutual reductions in arms could lead to increase in security.

[18] Security sector reform is important in developing countries, allowing arms transfers only to where there is competent and accountable military and enforcement agencies. While this is control of arms trade rather than proliferation, it would be expected that competence and accountability would lead to building up necessary defensive force rather than being part of proliferation.

Arms proliferation can upset strategic balances and lead to an increased probability of conflict and, with the increased lethality of weapons, a more devastating conflict.[19] Conflict will have internal costs to the economy as well as spill-over effects on neighbours and the international community. The end of the Cold War saw a reduction in superpower involvement in conflicts, a marked reduction in their explicit role in arms proliferation, and so reduced the intensity of conflict, though they continue to dominate the arms trade. There are, however, still considerable numbers of conflicts taking place and there is still considerable loss of life and destruction, particularly in the form of internal conflict.

If proliferation leads to arms races, in the sense that one country responds to another country increasing their stock of arms, then the impact and costs of proliferation can be considerably higher and the probability of conflict increased. An arms race between two countries can also lead to higher arms spending in neighbouring countries.

It is important to distinguish the costs of reducing arms proliferation from the legacy cost of arms. For example, if a treaty leads to reduction in warheads, which results in clean-up costs, these are not the costs of conversion, but the costs of the arms – they would have been paid later anyway.[20]

Benefits

All of the above can be considered the costs of proliferation, but there can also be benefits. These are, potentially, the provision of security, either through providing a level playing field or assisting in the maintenance of hegemonic power (e.g., the US being the technological leader with everyone else dependent on its technology). It is also prestigious – having nuclear weapons allows countries to be on the Security Council. This means that the UK and France can punch above their weight.[21] There is no clear way to value any of these benefits in monetary terms and it is not clear that these benefits could not be achieved without proliferation.

---

[19] While there is no evidence of a link between proliferation and conflict, one is suspected and there are cases that suggest one. What is undeniable is that proliferation can increase the intensity and possible duration of conflict.

[20] In fact these can be identified in the Russian budget.

[21] Although India and Pakistan have still not made it to the Security Council.

In some countries there are expectations that arms imports will provide support for local industry, investment and technology transfer through offset agreements. But there is no evidence that countries really do gain net benefits from these deals (see Brauer and Dunne, 2004). There are also questions as to what are legitimate security needs and how security can legitimately be achieved through proliferation, what spill over and linkage effects there are, and if countries are just trying to gain influence with the exporters, or whether it is just about making money for elites (corruption).

The solutions

In considering the solutions, there will be costs of the reduction process, management, policing and surveillance and the costs to some countries of not having the weapons. In principle, the cost of reducing/ preventing arms proliferation could be the reduction of security for individual countries, but there is little direct evidence that this is likely to be the case and no real way of measuring the effect. During the Cold War the doctrine of mutual assured destruction resulted in strategic stability (in the advanced economies), but the potential costs were unfathomable.

Solution 1: WMD non-proliferation programmes and nuclear disarmament

The costs are those of nuclear disarmament treaties and decommissioning. Experience from the START I and INF treaties indicates that nuclear disarmament costs can be high, although this depends a lot on the degree of verification required. Projected US costs for dismantlement and verification under these two treaties was approximately $31 billion. However this does not include clean-up costs that could reach more than $365 billion.[22] More recent figures presented below show the total cost in FY 2004 to be around $2bn, though an important component of this is Russian expenditure, which should decline.

---

[22] The full cost for the dismantling and destroying nuclear weapons, disposing of fissile material and cleaning up nuclear sites is impossible to determine with any accuracy. It depends on a number of policy decisions including the speed of the process, the types and complexity of verification systems and the methods for dealing with the fissile material.

Major non-proliferation programmes FY 2004 appropriation

US Department of Defense Cooperative threat reduction programme:	$450.8 m
US Department of Energy non-proliferation programs	$1,330.5 m
US State Department non-proliferation programs	$187.4 m
Total	$1,968.7 m

Source: www.armscontrolcenter.org/archives/000676.php

It is also important to recognise that these are not costs of disarmament, but legacy costs of the systems that were not factored in at the outset. Anyway, regardless of the cost, a disarmament programme would be cheaper than maintenance and modernisation, which merely both delay these costs and potentially add extra ones. The US continues to spend around $35 billion annually on nuclear weapons programs.

Costs of international bodies also need to be added to this, though this may involve some double counting, such as:

UNMOVIC[23]	£ 80 m
IAEA[24]	£303 m
UNSCOM[25]	£ 50 m

[23] "The United Nations Monitoring, Verification and Inspection Commission (UNMOVIC) was created through the adoption of Security Council resolution 1284 of 17 December 1999. UNMOVIC was to replace the former UN Special Commission (UNSCOM) and continue with the latter's mandate to disarm Iraq of its weapons of mass destruction (chemical, biological weapons and missiles with a range of more than 150 km), and to operate a system of ongoing monitoring and verification to check Iraq's compliance with its obligations not to reacquire the same weapons prohibited to it by the Security Council. The Secretary-General of the United Nations appointed Dr. Hans Blix of Sweden to be the Commission's Executive Chairman." (http://www.unmovic.org/) *Source*: http://www.public.iastate.edu/~hoyj/WMD.html

[24] International Atomic Energy Agency. "The IAEA is the world's center of cooperation in the nuclear field. It was set up as the world's 'Atoms for Peace' organization in 1957 within the United Nations family. The Agency works with its Member States and multiple partners worldwide to promote safe, secure and peaceful nuclear technologies." (http://www.iaea.org/). *Source*: http://www.public.iastate.edu/~hoyj/WMD.html

[25] United Nations Special Commission. By its resolution 687 of 3 April 1991, the United Nations Security Council established the terms and conditions for the formal cease-fire between Iraq and the coalition of Member States co-operating with Kuwait. Section C of this resolution called for the elimination, under international supervision, of Iraq's weapons of mass destruction and ballistic missiles with a range greater than 150 kilometres (km), together with related items and

UNMOVIC is the UN Monitoring, Verification, and Inspection Commission, IAEA, the International Atomic Energy Authority, and UNSCOM, the UN Special Commission that was to be replaced by UNMOVIC. Allowing for costs incurred by countries other than the US, a rough estimate of $3bn a year would seem reasonable and an estimate of $6bn generous. The benefits of such a policy are very difficult to evaluate as weapons of mass destruction (WMD) are just that and their impact could be astronomical if their use is not limited. If we assume proliferation increases the probability of their use, we could consider an estimate of 5% of world GDP per annum and 30% for a less controlled conflict. This may seem something of an underestimate, but it serves as a starting point.

Benefits and cost per year (US $ bn)

	Benefits	Costs
Low	1,525	6
High	10,250	3

Solution 2: Conflict prevention measures

Another solution to the effects of proliferation is to reduce the probability of it leading to conflict by using conflict prevention policy initiatives as discussed by Cranna (1994). These would establish clear principles for international action and respond to sparks of conflict – hopefully picked up by early warning systems. Economic sanctions could then be applied and UN troops deployed in preventive roles, as peacekeepers, to undertake humanitarian actions, to shift the military balance, to provide safe havens and to possibly create UN Trust territories. To undertake such roles properly would require a larger and better-resourced UN force than exists at present, as the ineffectiveness of the UN troops in Lebanon illustrated.

Klein (2006) discusses the cost of setting up a UN rapid reaction force and the benefits of it, which in Klein and Marwah (1996) was

production facilities. It also called for measures to ensure that the acquisition and production of prohibited items were not resumed. The United Nations Special Commission (UNSCOM) was set up to implement the non-nuclear provisions of the resolution and to assist the International Atomic Energy Agency (IAEA) in the nuclear areas. *Source*: http://www.un.org/Depts/unscom/General/basicfacts.html

costed at \$50bn for 1 million persons. A more modest rapid reaction force would be say 45,000 with back up and would cost \$30bn (50,000 per person per year). Chalmers (2004) looks at a number of conflict prevention packages for a number of conflicts in an attempt to evaluate the cost effectiveness of conflict prevention.[26] He estimates NPV costs at 2004 prices of between \$0.2bn and \$139.4bn, the latter being for Afghanistan. Based on this we use a range for the costs of peacekeeping of between \$2bn and \$50bn.

Appendix 1 presents a valuation for the cost of conflict using figures for civil wars by Collier and Hoeffler which suggests that the NPV costs of conflict is around 250% of initial GDP. In a review of the cost of conflict, Skons (2006) suggests external costs of \$4.5–54bn. We assume that proliferation's contribution to the costs is its impact on the probability, intensity and duration of conflict, plus the opportunity cost for importers, and take low and high estimates of 5% and 20% respectively. Taking the figure of \$37,500bn constant 2003 figure for world GDP gives figures of \$375bn and \$1875bn for the benefits of control of proliferation.

Benefits and cost per year (US \$ bn)

	Benefits	Costs
Low	375	2
High	1,875	50

Solution 3: Counter arms proliferation measures

The issues here are similar to those above, but instead of attempting to prevent proliferation taking place, attempts are made to counter its impact. This can take the form of diplomacy, sanctions, threats and military action, or a mixture of the four. The experience of the US in dealing with Libya, Iran, and North Korea provides good examples of the first three, while Iraq gives a good example of the last.

---

[26] He estimates the likely probability that particular conflict prevention policies, military and non-military actions, would have stopped the conflict. He then considers the actual cost of the conflict to the international community and works out the breakeven probability. It turns out to be very low. The study estimates that £1 on conflict prevention generates savings of £4.1 to the international community, with range £1.2–7.1 based on the case studies.

The costs of the first three are marginal, but the initial costs to the advanced economies of the supposed countering of proliferation in Iraq was estimated to be more than £80bn and a total cost to the US estimated as $268 billion by February 2005 (Skons, 2006).[27] So an estimate of attempts to counter proliferation through military means and impose disarmament is likely to be around the initial costs of the Iraq war, so say £80bn pa +.[28] The benefits will be lower than the previous solution because such a policy will impact directly on the country being dealt with and if there is a war there will be damage, so we reduce the benefits by the amount of the costs as a gross approximation.

It is possible that this policy could act as a deterrent and so the chance of having to undertake counter proliferation actions could become less, so the solution would cost less over time. Also to estimate the benefits, each individual invasion is implicitly assumed to reduce the probability and consequences of conflict to the same degree as the US/Russian arsenals and whatever else was considered in the WMD anti-proliferation scenario. This is rather generous and should probably be reduced. For the moment we ignore both of these, suggesting the costs and benefits below.

Benefits and cost per year (US $ bn)

	Benefits	Costs
Low	365	10
High	1,795	80

Solution 4: Controlling the trade in conventional arms: arms trade treaty

Proliferation can be dealt with as part of the policies that have been proposed to control the arms trade per se. At one level these are the maintenance of already existing frameworks and regulations, such as the UN arms trade register, with some individual countries maintaining there

---

[27] Bilmes and Stiglitz attempted to measure the full cost and come up with a much greater figure, $1–2 trillion.

[28] We are just trying to capture the annual cost of continuous incursions with aims to reduce proliferation with no other motive. There are still concerns as to how successful this can be in reducing proliferation below what it would have been and in forces being able to exit countries once the primary aim has been achieved. We are also not considering other possible costs of the aftermath of conflict, such as reconstruction.

own registers.[29] At another level are the attempts to make the system more rigorous and developing an 'arms trade treaty' to determine the nature and degree of the arms trade and to assist in policing arms export control policies. The arms trade treaty proposals aim to curtail the arms trade, get all countries to adopt a code of conduct, introduce greater transparency, reduce the use of landmines and include a commitment to uphold human rights.[30]

The costs of this solution are the additional costs of strengthening the agreements in existence, surveillance and policing and any costs of sanctions required against countries that break the treaty. There will also be some costs to arms producing countries of the reduced arms exports, but these will not be significant.

The benefits will be the economic benefits of reduced arms imports, reduced probability and lethality of conflict, and reduced escalation through arms races. Using the benefit figures from the previous solution and recognising that the costs for activities such as policing, surveillance and developing necessary organisations are likely to be considerably higher than for WDM, suggests costs in the in the region of $15–50bn.

Benefits and cost per year (US $ bn)

	Benefits	Costs
Low	375	15
High	1,875	50

Solution 5: Taxing arms transfers

This is a proposal that has been around for a while, but was recently suggested to the G8 summit by the Brazilian president, only to be ignored. The basic line is that arms exports should be taxed and the

---

[29] "On 6 December 1991, the General Assembly adopted resolution 46/36 L entitled 'Transparency in armaments', which requested the Secretary-General to establish and maintain at United Nations Headquarters in New York a universal and non-discriminatory Register of Conventional Arms, to include data on international arms transfers as well as information provided by Member States on military holdings, procurement through national production and relevant policies." *Source*: http://disarmament.un.org/cab/ register.html

[30] See the control arms campaign http://www.controlarms.org/ and http://www. armstradetreaty.com/

money raised used for a development fund, which will assist developing countries to improve their economic performance and reduce poverty and inequality. The increase in the price of arms should reduce proliferation as well as benefiting developing countries, but if it does so, it will reduce tax revenues.[31]

Burrows estimated in 2000 that an arms trade tax of 1% would provide revenue of $326m and one of 10%, around $3bn.[32] The ILO suggested that a 10% tax would raise $2bn and a 25% tax $5bn for 1994.[33] There would then be multiplier effects of say double the size if the money was allocated to development (likely to be very much an underestimate, but there is clearly a risk in how well the money is used). The costs of running such a programme would be relatively cheap, say around 0.5bn or less.

Benefits and cost per year (US $ bn)

	Benefits	Costs
Low	6	0.2
High	66	0.5

Conclusions

This chapter has considered the challenge of reducing arms proliferation and found this to be a much more complex subject of inquiry than is at first apparent. It is clearly difficult to define arms proliferation and many of the issues involved differ across different types of weapons. It is also extremely difficult to estimate the costs and benefits of counter-proliferation policies. The solutions considered were the following:

- Non-proliferation programmes and nuclear disarmament
- Conflict prevention measures
- Counter arms proliferation measures
- Arms trade treaty
- Taxing arms transfers.

[31] See Brzoska (2004).
[32] Burrows, G: *Arms and the Taxman* http://www.globalpolicy.org/socecon/glotax/general/0701arms.htm. Also see Corporate Watch *The Summit: the G8 and the arms trade* http://www.corporatewatch.org/?lid=1293
[33] ILO: *Arms Trade Taxes* http://www.ilo.org/dyn/idea/ideasheet.display?p_idea_id=63

Subject to numerous provisos the benefits and costs of these solutions on a per annum basis were:

Benefits and cost per year (US $ bn)

| | | Per annum | |
		Benefits	Costs
Solution 1	Low	1,525	6
	High	10,250	3
Solution 2	Low	375	2
	High	1,875	50
Solution 3	Low	365	10
	High	1,795	80
Solution 4	Low	375	15
	High	1,875	50
Solution 5	Low	6	0.2
	High	66	0.5

Discounting these over any period of time is fraught with difficulties, as the time paths cannot be estimated and guesses might suggest spurious accuracy. Rather it is better to simply assume they are constant values over a period of time and work out the NPV based on that. This gives the results below:

NPV of benefits and costs over 20 years (US $ bn)

| | | Low discount rate (3%) | | High discount rate (6%) | |
		Benefits	Costs	Benefits	Costs
Solution 1	Low	22,688	89	17,492	69
	High	152,494	45	117,567	34
Solution 2	Low	5,579	30	4,301	23
	High	27,895	744	21,506	573
Solution 3	Low	5,430	149	4,187	115
	High	26,705	1190	20,589	918

NPV of benefits and costs over 20 years (cont.)

		Low discount rate (3%)		High discount rate (6%)	
		Benefits	Costs	Benefits	Costs
Solution 4	Low	5,579	223	4,301	172
	High	27,895	744	21,506	573
Solution 5	Low	89	3	69	2
	High	982	7	757	6

One of the solutions, counter-proliferation policy is clearly the most expensive and probably the most risky. It could lead to much greater costs and much lower benefits than suggested in the table.

The sensible solution seems to combine the others, which have different foci. Solution 1 is particularly aimed at nuclear proliferation and should be seen as important in its own right. Solution 4, the arms trade treaty, could be combined with Solution 2, which would deal with the failures of proliferation controls and would be relevant for both large conventional weapons systems and small arms. The tax on the arms trade is a nice idea, but does have limitations and would need to be an adjunct to the other two.

What is clear is that the potential costs of arms proliferation are extremely high and that with sensible policies to control it, the world could be a safer and more prosperous place at little cost to the arms supplying nations.

Appendix 1: Costs of conflict

A major benefit of reduced arms proliferation, particularly of conventional arms is the reduction of the probability of conflict, the intensity of conflict and probably the duration of conflict. Collier and Hoeffler (2002) estimate the costs of civil war. This gives a useful benchmark for the costs of conventional arms proliferation, as it is more likely to affect civil wars and relatively low income country wars than major wars, although the Gulf Wars did see the allies being confronted by weapons that they had provided (during the proliferation around the Iran–Iraq war). Their figures suggest:

Economic growth NPV costs:	105% initial GDP
Increase milex during and after conflicts NPV:	18% initial GDP
Deterioration in health (0.5 DALYs pa @ $1th)	£5m
Spillover effects on neighbours	115% initial GDP
Increase milex neighbours	12% initial GDP
Total:	**250% initial GDP**
Benefit of averting war to a low income country	= £54bn
Conflict trap cost	= £10.2bn
Total	**= £64.2bn**

These are lower bound and only deal with civil wars, so as a starting point we can use them as an estimate of a cost of arms proliferation worldwide.

In another study, Hess (2003) estimates a lower bound of the cost of war at an average cost of $72 per person. This gives a total world cost of conflict in 1985 US$ and 1985 population of $399.12 bn, a permanent payment growing with population.[34] To get figures for 1985–2006, one can increase this amount by the growth in world population of around 2% pa (the 2000 figure).

One cannot really add in the costs of war on terror to the costs of proliferation as it was not clearly an effect of arms proliferation.

The measures here are estimates of the total cost of conflict, but there is no evidence that arms proliferation causes conflict. It is reasonable to assume that it intensifies conflict through increasing lethality and possible duration of conflict and possibly increases the probability (Brzoska and Pearson, 1994). For this reason we only use a fraction of the costs of conflict in the analysis.

References

D. Scott Bennett and Allan C. Stam (2004) *The Behavioural Origins of War*, University of Michigan Press.

---

[34] This is based on estimating the amount of consumption individuals would lose through conflict and hence would be willing to pay to prevent conflict. A Lucas-type new classical model was used.

Bennis, Phyllis, and the IPS Iraq Task Force (2004) 'Paying the Price: The Mounting Costs of the Iraq War', Washington DC: The Institute for Policy Studies and Foreign Policy in Focus.

Bennis, Phyllis, and the IPS Iraq Task Force (2005) 'The Iraq Quagmire: The Mounting Costs of War and the Case for Bringing Home the Troops', Washington DC: The Institute for Policy Studies and Foreign Policy in Focus, 31 August.

Bilmes and Stiglitz (2006) 'Economic Costs of the Iraq War'. Paper presented to the Allied Social Sciences Society Conference, Chicago, January. http://www2.gsb.columbia.edu/faculty/jstiglitz/cost_of_war_in_iraq.pdf

Brauer, Jurgen (2007, forthcoming) 'Arms industries, arms trade and developing countries.' In Hartley, K and T Sandler (eds.) *Handbook of defense economics, Vol 2*. North Holland: Elsevier.

Brauer, Jurgen and J. P. Dunne (2004) *Arms trade and economic development: Theory, policy, and cases in arms trade offsets*. London: Routledge.

Brauer, Jurgen and J. P. Dunne (2002) *Arming the South: The economics of military expenditures, arms production and trade in developing countries*. London: Palgrave Macmillan.

Brito, D. L. and M. D. Intriligator (1995) 'Arms races and proliferation.' In K. Hartley and T. Sandler (eds.) *Handbook of defense economics*. North Holland: Elsevier.

Brown, Michael E., and Richard N. Rosecrance (eds.) (1999) *The costs of conflict: Prevention and cure in the global arena*. Lanham, MD: Rowman and Littlefield.

Brzoska, Michael (2004) 'Taxation of the Global Arms Trade? An Overview of the Issues', *Kyklos*, 57(2) 149–72.

Brzoska, Michael, Pearson, Frederic S. (1994) *Arms and warfare: Escalation, de-escalation and negotiation*. University of South Carolina Press.

Chalmers (2004) 'Spending to Save? An Analysis of the Cost Effectiveness of Conflict Prevention'. Report for DFID.

Collier, Paul (1999) 'On the Economic Consequences of Civil War', *Oxford Economic Papers* 51: 168–83.

Collier, Paul and Anke Hoeffler, (2004a) 'Greed and Grievance in Civil War', *Oxford Economic Papers* 56: 563–95.

Collier, Paul, and Anke Hoeffler (2004b) 'The Challenge of Reducing the Global Incidence of Civil War.' Challenge Paper. Copenhagen Consensus, Copenhagen. http://www.copenhagenconsensus.com/Files/Filer/CC/Papers/Conflicts_230404.pdf.

Collier, Paul, V. L. Elliot, Håvard Hegre, Anke Hoeffler, Marta Reynal-Querol and Nicholas Sambanis (2005) 'Breaking the Conflict Trap: Civil War and Development Policy'. Washington DC: World Bank. [This report is also published by Oxford University Press.]

Cranna M. (1994) *The true cost of conflict*. London: Earthscan.

Dunne, John P. and Sam Perlo Freeman (2006) 'The opportunity cost of the Trident replacement'. Mimeo.

Dunne, John P. and Eamon Surry (2006) 'Arms Production.' In *SIPRI Yearbook, 2006: Armaments, disarmaments and international security*. Stockholm International Peace Research Institute. http://www.sipri.org/contents/milap/milex/publications/recent_publications.html

Dunne, J. Paul, Maria Garcia-Alonso, Paul Levine and Ron Smith (2006) 'Managing Asymmetric Conflict.' *Oxford Economic Papers* 58: 183–208.

Dwan, Renata (2004.) 'Major armed conflicts.' In *SIPRI Yearbook 2004: Armaments, disarmament and international security*. Stockholm International Peace Research Institute. Oxford: Oxford University Press.

Eriksson, Mikael, and Wallensteen, Peter (2004a) 'Armed Conflict, 1989–2000.' *Journal of Peace Research* 41(5) 625–36.

Eriksson, Mikael, and Wallensteen, Peter (2004b) 'Patterns of major armed conflicts, 1990–2003.' In *SIPRI Yearbook 2004: Armaments, disarmament and international security*. Stockholm International Peace Research Institute. Oxford: Oxford University Press.

Ghobhara, H.A., P. Huth, and B. Russett, (2003) 'Civil Wars Kill and Maim People – Long after the Shooting Stops', *American Political Science Review* 97 (2).

Gleditsch, Nils Petter, Adne Cappelen, Olav Bjerkholt, Ron Smith and Paul Dunne (eds.) (1996) *The peace dividend*. Amsterdam: North Holland.

Greenpeace (2006) 'Counting the costs: Military counter proliferation versus non proliferation.' Greenpeace Briefing.

Hess, Gregory D. (2003) 'The Economic Welfare Cost of Conflict: An Empirical Assessment.' *Claremont College Working Papers in Economics*.

Hess, P. (1989) 'The Military Burden, Economic Growth and the Human Suffering Index', *Cambridge Journal of Economics* 13(4), 497–515.

Klein, L. R. (2006) 'Peacekeeping operations: from the birth of the United Nations onward', *Economics of Peace and Security Journal* 1/2.

Klein, L. R. and Marwah, K. (1996) 'Capital Inflow and Economic Growth', *Carleton Economic Papers*, 96–04.

Knight, M., N. Loayza, and D. Villanueva. (1996) 'The Peace Dividend: Military Spending Cuts and Economic Growth', *IMF Staff Papers* 43 (1): 1–37.

Lal, Deepak (1995) 'Arms and the Man: The Costs and Benefits of Defense Expenditure', UCLA Department of Economics, Working Paper No. 747.

Leach, Graeme (2003) 'War and the World Economy', IoD economic paper. London: Institute of Directors.

Murdoch, J. C. and T. Sandler (2002) 'Economic Growth, Civil Wars, and Spatial Spillovers.' *Journal of Conflict Resolution* 46: 91–110.

Nordhaus, William D. (2002) 'The economic consequences of a war with Iraq.' In Carl Kaysen, Steven Miller, Martin Malin, William Nordhaus and John Steinbruner (eds.), *War with Iraq: Costs, consequences and alternatives*. Cambridge, Mass.: American Academy of Arts and Sciences. www.amacad.org/ publications/occasional.htm.

SIPRI (various years) *SIPRI Yearbook: Armaments, disarmament and international security*. Oxford: Oxford University Press.

Skons, Elisabeth (2006) 'The Costs of Armed Conflict.' Paper prepared for the International Task Force on Global Public Goods. Mimeo. Sweden: Stockholm.

Small Arms Survey (2001) *Small Arms Survey: Profiling the Problem.*

Smith, Ron and Bernard Udis (2003) 'New challenges to export control: Wither Wassenar?' In Ron Smith and Paul Levine (eds.) (2003) *Arms trade, security and conflict*. London: Routledge.

Soares, R. R. (2003) *The welfare cost of violence*. University of Maryland. Mimeo.

Stewart, Frances (1993) 'War and Underdevelopment: Can Economic Analysis Help Reduce the Costs?' Oxford: International Development Centre.

Stewart, Frances, and Valpy FitzGerald (2001) 'The costs of war in poor countries: Conclusions and policy recommendations.' In Frances Stewart and Valpy FitzGerald (eds.) *War and underdevelopment, Vol. 1: The economic and social consequences of conflict*. Oxford: Oxford University Press.

12 | Conflicts

PAUL COLLIER

Introduction

The high profile of the security challenges facing rich countries has tended to crowd out the rather different security challenges facing poor countries. A discourse on international security that does not address these challenges is one-sided and less likely to gain acceptance.

The key security challenges facing poor countries are civil wars and coups. Currently, governments respond to these risks by military spending. Both the risks and the response are highly costly. If there were cost-effective international interventions that would substantially reduce the risks of wars and coups and reduce military spending, the payoff to poor countries would be enormous. Yet even among the international interventions designed to help such countries, security has received less policy attention than 'photogenic' topics like health and education. International security interventions, though numerous and expensive, have not been guided by cost–benefit analysis. With the establishment of a permanent UN Peacebuilding Commission in September 2005, there is a real opportunity for more informed and coherent international action. There is the potential to build on recent advances in the quantitative study of security issues in poor countries as exemplified by the contributions to the new *Handbook of Defense Economics* (Hartley and Sandler, 2007).

This chapter will first estimate the costs of these phenomena in poor countries and then investigate four possible ways of ameliorating them: increasing aid; making aid conditional upon limits to military spending; expanding peacekeeping forces and guaranteeing security using 'over-the-horizon' measures. Given the constraints of space the chapter merely sketches the results derived from recent research.

Other than the costs of civil war, the results presented here are new rather than a repetition of our previous work for the *Copenhagen*

Consensus (Collier and Hoeffler, 2004). Since that was written we have completed five new studies that are used as building blocks. Using the most recent data, we have quantified how military spending, aid, coups, the risk of war and peacekeeping forces are interlinked. From these new studies we are able to estimate the costs and benefits of the four proposed interventions. Since these are the first such estimates, not only will they directly inform policy, but they will also open up a new area for future research which, over time, will reveal a credible range of answers.

The three scourges: civil wars, coups, and military spending

Civil war

Civil war is far more likely to break out in poor countries, and once started, they tend to last longer and are more likely to recur. International wars, although capturing the headlines, are rarely long and drawn-out, whereas civil conflicts may persist for many years or even decades. During this time, in addition to the direct cost in deaths and injuries, a country's economy can be devastated and large sections of the population displaced. The costs of civil conflict are enormous, both to the country itself and to its neighbours. In our previous study for the *Copenhagen Consensus* we estimated the cost of a typical civil war in a poor country at around $64bn (Collier and Hoeffler, 2004). The risks of civil war have now been estimated quantitatively by scholars and the results published in reputable, peer-reviewed journals (Fearon and Laitin, 2003; Miguel *et al.*, 2004; Collier and Hoeffler, 2004a).

These studies largely agree. From them we can infer that three recent international developments have raised the risk of new outbreaks: the discovery of oil in fragile states (such as Chad), the current high international prices for primary commodities, and the recent fragile settlements that have brought a number of civil wars to an end (such as Sudan). The reasoning behind this is simple. Mineral resources are generally found only in particular regions of a country, but the local population is often not a primary beneficiary. It may suffer the disadvantages and disruption of mining or oil drilling, but will experience little direct benefit. In situations where ethnic differences are involved, militias and guerrilla groups can be formed which aim to secede from, or take over, the state. The mineral resources provide a means of funding the troops, and this is made easier at a time of rising commodity prices. A typical case in point is that of 'blood diamonds' in Sierra Leone. The apparent endings of civil wars can also be less than durable unless there are real incentives for the combatants to maintain the peace and credible and effective sanctions are available to use against those who may break agreements. A country that has suffered a civil war remains at a significantly higher risk of further violence for years to come. To some extent, this may be due to the continued presence of poor and brutalized sectors of the population for whom fighting has become a way of life. And the tensions and strains which initially led to the conflict are rarely more than suppressed by the victory of one side. In these circumstances, building a prosperous and stable state may take many years.

The immediate costs of civil wars are of course borne by the country itself. Not only is there a direct cost to the economy, which persists for some years, but government expenditure also becomes skewed towards military spending (see below). This, of course, is in addition to the human cost in terms of loss of life, increased disease and forced migration. Such population movements are one aspect of the regional impact of civil wars. More generally, there can be a destabilising effect on neighbouring countries, a small but widespread negative impact on economic growth in the region and an escalation of military expenditure. Individual civil wars can also have a global impact. Scourges such as the trade in hard drugs, the AIDS epidemic and international terrorism have certainly been made worse by particular civil conflicts. Both terrorism and drugs production thrive on territory that is outside the control of a recognized government. Thus, Afghanistan harboured Al Qaida, and Colombia became a key producer of hard drugs. There is credible though not decisive evidence that the AIDS pandemic originated in an African civil war due to the dangerous conjunction of mass rape and mass migration.

Coups

In Africa alone, there have been over 200 coup attempts in the past thirty years. Coups continue to plague the region: for example, recent successful coups have occurred in Mauritania (2005), the Central African Republic (2003), and a failed coup led to the present civil war in Cote d'Ivoire. This phenomenon can now be researched using quantitative techniques thanks to a comprehensive dataset compiled by McGowan (2003). Coups are costly: they sharply reduce growth, by around 3% of GDP during the year of the coup, and this loss is long lasting (Collier, Goderis and Hoeffler, 2006). Further, even when a coup does not transpire, the very threat of one inflicts costs. In low-income countries governments respond to the threat of a coup by pre-emptively increasing military spending (Collier and Hoeffler, 2006b). These costs are concentrated in low-income countries: coups, like civil war, are far more likely at low levels of income. Unfortunately, the risk of a coup is significantly and substantially increased by aid, a factor that evidently complicates policy interventions.

The distinction between coups and civil wars is often blurred. Unsuccessful coups may result in continued fighting rather than complete defeat for the insurgents. Equally, successful coups may create continued military opposition from supporters of the previous government. And the root causes are generally similar: instability, poverty and the disaffection of a section of the community with the means to arm itself. In the case of coups, these may be initiated by factions within the army, and have little effective armed opposition, which is why they do not necessarily lead to civil war. Successful coups can also lead to relatively stable, if despotic, government. It is still worthwhile to make the distinction from civil wars, because coups – whether successful or not – have a different degree of impact than the massive effects of a drawn-out civil conflict.

Military spending

Military spending in low-income countries has recently been the subject of some substantial published quantitative studies (Dunne and Freeman, 2003; Collier and Hoeffler, 2006a, 2006b). They find that military spending does not in general reduce the risk of civil war: on the contrary, in post-conflict conditions it sharply increases the risk. Increased spending by one country produces a response from its neighbours and this ricochets around the region. Around 11% of aid inadvertently leaks into military budgets, so that in low-income Africa around 40% of military budgets are aid-financed – this makes aid interventions problematic. Hence, there is a grim interconnection between aid, coups, military spending, and civil war.

Military spending in countries where civil war has broken out is typically increased by 1.8% of GDP. At the end of the war, expenditure drops in general by only around 0.5%. At a time when a country needs all possible resources to rebuild itself, an increased proportion of the national income is spent in ways that do nothing to raise the welfare level of the population. Since poor countries are far more prone to civil conflict than rich ones, anything that depresses development and income becomes a risk factor for further violence. Little wonder, then, that in post-conflict nations, there is a much greater risk of a new war breaking out.

Possible international interventions

In an ideal world we should, of course, strive to prevent the outbreak of war in the first case. However, short of stimulating economic growth and good governance, there is little that can be done to reduce the overall risks. Since countries that are experiencing civil wars remain destabilised and at increased risk of further conflict, we suggest opportunities to encourage the development of stability and prosperity and hence lessen the chance of a recurrence of violence.

Increasing aid

As will be apparent, increasing aid is a double-edged sword. In post-conflict situations it is very effective in helping to rebuild the economy (Collier and Hoeffler, 2004b). Economic recovery is the surest way of reducing the risks of further conflict. However, aid also increases the threat of a coup, and inadvertently finances additional military spending, both of which reduce peace prospects. The ideal is therefore either to redesign aid in post-conflict situations (the next proposal), or to combine aid with other interventions (the remaining two proposals).

International finance for rebuilding is necessary and can be effective, but it must be controlled to ensure that it does not have perverse effects. In the early post-conflict years, institutions are normally so weak that aid cannot be spent particularly effectively, and it is at this stage where particular attention must be paid to the potential channelling of the money into military and other unintended purposes. Beyond this, as institutions strengthen, post-conflict aid is normally unusually productive.

Introducing new conditions for aid

Potentially, in post-conflict situations, aid could be made conditional on the government not exceeding a particular level of military spending. Guidelines on government military spending in post-conflict conditions could be set by the new UN Peacebuilding Commission and would enable a coordinated donor response. Eliminating the adverse effect of aid through increased military spending, leaves a large positive effect of aid on security. We estimate the cost–benefit ratio at better than 1:2.

A government in control of a country at the end of a civil war will inevitably be very aware of future security needs and will wish to consolidate its own grip on power. In these situations, particularly when governance is weak, there will be a natural tendency to maintain a high level of military expenditure. Typically, this still accounts for an extra 1.2% of GDP than before the war. To force this down, not only should aid be made conditional, but practical intervention may also be needed to maintain stability.

Expanding the role of peacekeeping forces

The most useful replacement of increased military spending by a post-war government is an international peacekeeping force. By bringing in well-equipped, disciplined, professional soldiers from countries with no allegiance to any warring factor, the benefits of a strong military presence can be gained, without the destabilising downside.

We are the first researchers to have received comprehensive data on peacekeeping expenditure from the UN. From this we have been able to estimate the efficacy of peacekeeping. Despite some failures, the more that is spent on peacekeeping forces in post-conflict situations, the lower the risk of further conflict (Collier, Hoeffler and Soderbom, 2007). On average, doubling expenditure on international peacekeepers from $5 to $10 per inhabitant per year over a decade reduces the risk of renewed conflict by around 15 percentage points. We estimate that given the cost of a typical civil war in a post-conflict country this reduction is worth around $8bn. Its cost is around $1.1bn, yielding a cost–benefit ratio of around 1:7.

This is hard evidence that investment in effective peacekeeping is easy to justify in economic terms. The problem is that we tend to hear more about failures than success in this area: new wars are news;

the absence of war is not. The message is that peacekeeping forces must be of sufficient size and capability to do the job they are mandated to do.

Guaranteeing security from 'over the horizon'

The supply of effective peacekeeping troops is limited. A simple way of economizing is to have the troops based in their home countries, but to provide 'over the horizon' guarantees of rapid intervention should this be necessary. As peace has taken hold in Sierra Leone, following several years during which peacekeeping forces were needed on the ground, the peacekeepers are being withdrawn. However, the UK has provided an 'over the horizon' guarantee for the next ten years. This reinvents and refines a much older strategy of the French government, which until the late-1990s provided a less explicit security safeguard for the whole of Francophone Africa. Because this French policy was in place over a large area for a long period it is possible to evaluate its effect quantitatively. Using the new models of conflict risk we have quantified the efficacy of the French guarantee. We find that it was highly significant and effective in reducing the risk of civil war in Francophone Africa. Over the entire period of 1965–2005, the risk facing these countries was only one quarter of what it would have been otherwise (Collier, Hoeffler and Roemer, 2007). There are thirteen Franc Zone countries, so this reduction in risk across so many countries is worth a substantial amount – in the order of $5bn. One estimate of the costs, which is probably on the high side, puts them at around $1bn., so that the cost–benefit ratio would have been around 1:5. It provides a reasonable guide to the payoff from introducing a more general and international security guarantee.

In practical terms, such an approach can be both effective and politically feasible. With military expenditure predicated partly on a defined back-up role to maintain security in specific countries or regions, countries such as the UK and France can justifiably retain a flexible and effective military capability without having to commit troops to immediate and costly foreign interventions. Unfortunately, it is not always possible to put such a system in place to prevent civil war in the first place, but it is certainly an effective second stage following initial intervention, as is the case in Sierra Leone.

Packaging interventions

As will be apparent, these interventions are far more cost-effective as packages. There are numerous complementarities. Peacekeeping and post-conflict aid reinforce each other. Ceilings on military spending and aid reinforce each other. Security guarantees and aid reinforce each other. Security guarantees eventually become cheaper substitutes for peacekeeping. Both peacekeeping forces and security guarantees complement the imposition of ceilings on military spending by the governments of low-income countries.

The key factor is to be able to address the needs of a country torn by civil war, which are primarily for stability and reconstruction. Rebuilding the economy needs external resources if it is to be accomplished reasonably quickly, but these resources can only be used effectively if security is guaranteed. The population needs peace and stability to give it an opportunity to rebuild lives and the economy. These two factors are inextricably linked.

This chapter can only point to these complementarities. However, in a more complete discussion we would be able to quantify them and apply the techniques of cost–benefit analysis. We would be able to show that these packages are highly attractive opportunities for enhancing the security of the poorest countries. We believe there is a strong economic case for such effective interventions.

References

Collier, P. and A. Hoeffler, 2004, Conflicts. In B. Lomborg (ed.), *Global Crises: Global Solutions*, Cambridge: Cambridge University Press.

2004a, Greed and Grievance in Civil War, *Oxford Economic Papers*, 56: 663–95.

2004b, Aid, Policy and Growth in Post-Conflict Societies, *European Economic Review*, 48: 1125–45.

2006a, Military Spending In Post-Conflict Societies, *Economics of Governance*, 7: 89–107.

2006b, Grand Extortion: Coup Risk and Military Spending, Mimeo, Department of Economics, Oxford University.

2007, Unintended Consequences: Does Aid Promote Arms Races? *Oxford Bulletin of Economics and Statistics*, 69: 1–27.

Collier, P., B. Goderis and A. Hoeffler, 2006, Shocks and Growth in Low-Income Countries, Mimeo, Department of Economics, Oxford University.

Collier, P., A. Hoeffler and D. Roemer, 2007, Beyond Greed and Grievance: Feasibility and Civil War, Mimeo, Department of Economics, Oxford University.

Collier, P., A. Hoeffler and M. Soderbom, 2007, Post Conflict Risks, *Journal of Peace Research* (forthcoming).

Dunne, P. and S. P. Freeman, 2003, The Demand for Military Spending in Developing Countries: A Dynamic Panel Analysis. *Defence and Peace Economics*, Vol. 14, No. 6, 461–74.

Fearon, J. and D. Laitin, 2003, Ethnicity, Insurgency, and Civil War, *American Journal of Political Science*, **97**: 75–90.

Hartley, K. and T. Sandler, (eds.) 2007, *Handbook of Defense Economics*, Amsterdam: North Holland.

McGowan, P. J. 2003, African Military Coups d'Etats, *Journal of Modern African Studies*, **31**: 339–70.

Miguel, E., S. Satyanath, and E. Sergenti, 2004, Economic Shocks and Civil Conflict: an Instrumental Variables Approach, *Journal of Political Economy*, **112**: 725–53.

13 | *Corruption*

SUSAN ROSE-ACKERMAN[1]

Effective solutions to pressing global problems depend upon both good policies and effective institutions. No policy can succeed if a country's public and private institutions are corrupt and dysfunctional. True, some countries are able to function in spite of pervasive corruption, but corruption and poverty go together, and even viable corrupt countries would do much better with more effective institutions.

Varieties of corruption

Corruption occurs where private wealth and public power overlap. I differentiate between low-level opportunistic payoffs and systemic corruption, which implicates an entire bureaucratic hierarchy, electoral system, or governmental structure from top to bottom.

Low-level corruption occurs within a framework where basic laws and regulations are in place, and officials and private individuals seize upon opportunities to benefit personally. There are several generic situations.

First, a benefit may be scarce, and officials may have discretion to assign it to applicants. This would seem the least problematic case. The obvious policy response is to sell the benefit legally. However, even that may not work. Officials may pocket the proceeds or steal the goods outright. In Uganda, a study found that 68–77 percent of user charges paid for pharmaceuticals were pocketed by clinic workers, and 40 –94 percent of drugs simply disappeared (McPake et al. 1999, 855–56). In Brazil, federal police authorities estimate that embezzlement in the pharmaceutical sector totals $637 million per year (Colitt 2004).

Second, low-level officials may be required to select only qualified applicants. The officials' discretion frequently permits them to collect bribes from both the qualified and the unqualified. Services that are

---

[1] This chapter draws on Rose-Ackerman (1978, 1999, 2004, 2006), sources that include comprehensive references to the literature in the field.

supposed to be provided free to the needy are rationed by the ability to pay, for example, in the case of publicly provided health care (McPake et al. 1999, 855). Alternatively, government workers may simply steal the benefit. For example, at least 18 percent of the rice disappeared in an Indonesian program designed to provide food aid to the poor; in one-third of the villages, 43 percent disappeared (Olken 2003).

Third, a benefit, such as pharmaceuticals, may be hard for benefi- ciaries to evaluate. Those in charge of distribution may provide sub- standard goods and keep the high quality drugs for private resale. According to one estimate, 25 percent of drugs consumed in poor countries are counterfeit or substandard.[2]

Fourth, bureaucratic processes may be a source of delay creating corrupt incentives. Officials may create more delay as a means of extracting more bribes. According to survey evidence, businesses gen- erally spend more, not less, time dealing with officials when corruption is common (Fries, Lysneko, and Polanec 2003).

Fifth, some government programs impose costs – for example, tax and customs collection or the possibility of arrest by the police. Officials can then extract payoffs in return for tolerating illegal activities. Odd- Helge Fjeldstad (2005) reports that at least half of tax collections are lost to corruption in some countries. A study in Bolivia estimates that 42 percent of VAT was lost in 2001 – this fell to 29 percent in 2004 after reforms (Zuleta, Leyton and Ivanovic 2007, 351). In 2004, Russia reported losing $4.5 billion in duties on goods imported from Europe.[3] In 2000, Bangladesh lost duties equal to 5 percent of GDP, and that figure omits the discouragement of potential investors caused by the corrupt regime (OECD 2003, 9). Reforms can have dramatic results. When Peru reformed customs collection, tariff revenues went from 23 percent of revenues in 1990 to 35 percent in 1996 and increased four- fold in dollar terms, despite reductions in duties (OECD 2003, 9). Additional benefits include streamlined customs procedures that save importers and exporters valuable time. In Peru average clearance times fell from two days to two hours, and in Costa Rica, times fell from six days to 12 minutes (OECD 2003, 22). Costs per dollar collected are

---

[2] WHO Counterfeit and Substandard Medicines. /www.who.int/mediacentre/ factsheets/fs275/en/ (accessed September 12, 2006).

[3] RIA Novosti Moscow, December 8, 2005, at http://en.rian.ru/business (accessed September 13, 2006).

quite low. In Mozambique, for example, they ranged from 1.86 percent to 3.42 percent of revenues in 1997–2000. In Angola, reform cost $84 million over two years, and revenues increased from $230 million to $345 million (OECD 2003, 22).

"Grand" corruption shares some features with low-level payoffs, but it can be more deeply destructive of state functioning – bringing the state to the edge of outright failure and undermining the economy. I have distinguished three varieties.

First, a branch of the public sector may be organized as a bribe generating machine. For example, top police officials may organize corrupt systems in collaboration with organized crime groups. Government positions can be sold to applicants, and some who obtain jobs never show up for work and may simply collect paychecks. This problem is particularly harmful in education where teacher absenteeism rates are very high in some countries. One study of seven countries calculated the annual direct costs to be $2.5 billion annually, an estimate that excludes the longer term costs of poorly educated citizens (Patrinos and Kagia 2007, 70).

Second, a nominal democracy may have a corrupt electoral system. Corruption can undermine limits on spending, get around limits on the types of spending permitted, and subvert controls on the sources of funds.

Third, corruption can influence the award of contracts for construction projects, the allocation of natural resource concessions, and the privatization of state-owned firms. The costs of corruption and illegal activity can be large. For example, in the forestry sector alone the World Bank estimates that illegal logging costs at least $10 billion a year – much of this is facilitated by corruption (World Bank 2004, 1, 31, A-23–A-28). Similarly, corruption in the construction of water and sanitary projects inflated the value of winning bids by at least 15 percent in South Asia; factoring in the use of substandard materials, the cost inflation rises to almost 20 percent (Davis 2003, 57–9). Some procurement reforms have been very beneficial. Such reforms saved South Korea over $2.5 billion in recent years at a budgetary cost of $26 million.[4] In Mexico, the government estimated that every dollar

---

[4] "Korea's move to e-procurement," PREMnotes, No 90, July 2004, World Bank, http://siteresources.worldbank.org/INTPEAM/Resources/premnote90.pdf (accessed September 13, 2006).

invested in an internet procurement system earned a social return of 4 dollars.[5] However, a technological fix is unlikely to be sufficient. For example, a study of water and sanitation projects showed that successful reforms combined monitoring with heightened staff motivation and grassroots oversight (Davis 2003, 61–5).

Consequences and causes of corruption

Researchers at the World Bank Institute estimate that worldwide bribery totals at least $1 trillion per year or just over 3 percent of world income in 2002.[6] This is an estimate of the volume of bribes, not the impact of corruption. The economic costs are the distortions induced by these payoffs. Those costs may be many orders of magnitude higher than the volume of bribes themselves.

Richer countries and those with high growth rates generally have less reported corruption and better functioning governments (Kaufmann 2003). However, it is unclear whether low levels of income and growth are a consequence or a cause of corruption. Most likely, the causal arrow runs both ways, creating vicious or virtuous spirals.

High levels of corruption are associated with lower levels of investment and growth, and corruption discourages both capital inflows and direct foreign investment. According to Wei (2000), an increase in the corruption level from relatively clean Singapore to relatively corrupt Mexico is the equivalent of an increase in the tax rate of over twenty percentage points. Corruption lowers productivity, reduces the effectiveness of industrial policies, and encourages business to operate in the unofficial sector. Highly corrupt countries tend to spend less on education, to over-invest in public infrastructure, and to have lower environmental quality levels.

High levels of corruption produce a more unequal distribution of income and can undermine programs designed to help the poor.

---

[5] Robert Kossick, "Best Practice Profile: CompraNet," May 10, 2004 (accessed September 13, 2006). www.undp.org/surf-panama/egov/docs/programme_ activities/bpractices/e-procurement_in_mexico-compranet.pdf (accessed September 13, 2006).

[6] World Bank, "The costs of corruption," Press Release, available at: http://web.worldbank.org/WBSITE/EXTERNAL/NEWS/0,,contentMDK:2019 0187~menuPK:34457~pagePK:34370~piPK:34424~theSitePK:4607,00.html (accessed September 13, 2006).

Inequality has a negative effect on growth that may be the result of its impact on corruption. An unequal system may be maintained by corrupt links between wealthy elites and the state.

Corrupt governments also lack political legitimacy. As a result, high levels of perceived corruption are associated with tax evasion. As a consequence, corrupt governments tend to be smaller than more honest governments. Trade openness and other measures of competitiveness appear to reduce corruption, and weak law and order and insecure property rights encourage corruption, which in turn discourages foreign capital inflows. Conversely, corrupt opportunities could produce a political coalition in favor of limited competitive pressures and weak institutions.[7]

One way to get at the costs of corruption is to look at the other Copenhagen Consensus papers where benefits and costs have been calculated under the assumption that corruption will not mar the implementation of programs. Suppose that corruption adds 10, 20 or 30 percent to the cost of programs. How many would still be worthwhile?

As an example, one study estimates that, if funds were allocated to fulfill the Millennium Development Goals in water and sanitation in Sub-Saharan Africa in the next decade and if 30 percent were lost to corruption, the excess costs would total $20 billion over the next decade (Plummer and Cross 2007, 222). In considering hunger and malnutrition, suppose that the costs will be 20 percent above estimates because of corruption – close to the loss Olken (2006) found in an Indonesian rice program. If such leakage occurs, which interventions would still be worthwhile? Options with high net benefits, such as vitamin supplements, would still survive, but interventions with lower benefit/cost ratios and more complex implementation problems, such as reducing low birth-weight babies, would only be worthwhile if corruption can be controlled.

Reform proposals

Corruption is a symptom of dysfunctional state–society relations. Thus, most reforms must be accomplished inside particular countries, each with its own economic, political, and social realities. However, in addition to a basic concern with the way corruption can undermine other challenges, one must also focus on global solutions.

[7] Sources for the claims in the text are available in Rose-Ackerman (1999, 2004).

My analysis suggests four policies: (1) an international effort to help countries streamline government operations, including procurement, regulation and taxation; (2) efforts to encourage the ratification and enforcement of international treaties; (3) agreements between investors and poor, resource-rich countries designed to circumvent corrupt pressures; and (4) stronger controls on money laundering. None of these proposals would involve large outlays, and all promise large benefits if they succeed. Lacking definitive measures of costs and benefits, the best response, if one had $75 billion to spend, would be to allocate, say, $5 billion to put these initiatives in place in a way that includes a budget for ex post evaluation. Given the estimated $1 trillion lost to bribes each year and the impact of these payments on growth, investment and poverty, this seems a reasonable gamble. If the $5 billion reduced bribes by just 10 percent, that would be a fall of $100 billion. Factoring in the gains in real economic variables, the benefits could be substantial.

Procurement, regulation, and revenue collection

Entrepreneurship is discouraged by excess regulation, and those who persevere are pushed into corrupt and off-the-books operations by the tediousness and expense of complying with the law. One study of the business environment in Asia, for example, estimated that if Calcutta had the investment climate of Shanghai, the share of firms exporting would nearly double from 24 percent to 47 percent and the share of foreign-invested firms would increase from 2.5 percent to 3.9 percent (Dollar, Hallward-Driemeier and Mengiste 2003, 7). Wasteful and corrupt procurement and revenue collection impose huge costs. Millions of dollars in revenue are lost, and government overpays for goods and services. Furthermore, corruption can lead to distorted choices of substandard or inappropriate products and poorly targeted and enforced regulatory policies.

Successful reform models exist. Reductions in red tape can save businesses time and money, and internet-based procurement and customs reform systems have worked well in many cases. For the government, benefit/cost ratios range between 3 to 1 and 100 to 1 for some experiments in procurement and revenue reform. Those calculations beg the question of the appropriate size of the government budget, but however that issue is decided, corrupt procurement and revenue collection is inefficient. The same holds true for corruptly administered business regulations. However, simply redesigning programs or introducing computer software will seldom be sufficient. Policies must also seek to retrain, motivate, and monitor officials.

International treaties

Several international treaties seek to control corruption – most notably at the Organization for Economic Cooperation and Development (OECD) and the United Nations.[8] These documents reflect the salience of the issue, but their impact depends upon their ability to change the discourse of international business in ways that also changes behavior. They will have an effect only when combined with strong domestic efforts in both home and host countries.

More resources should be spent on monitoring country compliance with these treaties. Transparency International is engaged in this effort, but more could be done. No one should expect that these treaties will solve the problem of global corruption, but an effort to publicize them and to push countries and firms to comply could bring benefits with little expenditure.

Multinational investments and the control of corruption

According to *The Economist*, "a handful of states are expected to receive $200 billion in the next decade" from oil and gas exploration.[9] Many of these are poor and have weak or venal government that may divert the benefits into rent-seeking instead of productive activity. Suppose that an investment of $1.25 billion would mean that just 10 percent of this total, or $20 billion, would flow towards the poor citizens of these countries. This would be obviously beneficial and is likely to be an underestimate of the benefits, especially if combined with procurement, regulation, and revenue collection.

One proposal, called the Extractive Industries Transparency Initiative (EITI), seeks to have both firms and countries make public reports of payments. The EITI, now endorsed by over twenty developing countries and number of multinational firms and trade associations,

[8] OECD Convention on Combating Bribery of Foreign Public Officials in International Business Transactions, December 11, 1997; United Nations Convention against Corruption, December 9, 2003.
[9] "Can Oil Ever Help the Poor?" *Economist*, December 4, 2003.

is establishing voluntary pilot programs in a number of resource-dependent countries. Such programs can accomplish their goals only if most multinational and domestic contractors in an industry agree on the procedure. Thus even a "voluntary" procedure needs to have mandatory aspects. Funds could be productively spent developing the proposal, publicizing the idea to the general public, pushing firms to accept its requirements, and managing pilot projects.

Second, efforts are underway to monitor and constrain host-country use of the funds from oil and mineral extraction. The World Bank, which helped finance the Chad–Cameroon pipeline, negotiated a complex system of this kind. The agreement fell apart in late 2005, but was renegotiated in June 2006 in a compromise that requires 70 percent of revenues to go to poverty reduction, but permits other funds to be used for security and administration. This experience is worth studying to learn some lessons – both positive and negative.

Finally, in May 2006 ,OECD members agreed to limit the award of export credits.[10] Members will impose greater due diligence on an exporter that is on the debarment list of a multilateral financial institution, under charge in a national court, or convicted for violation of laws against bribery of foreign public officials within the last five years. This appears to be a promising step that should be monitored and evaluated by anti-corruption watchdogs.

Controlling money laundering

International efforts to control the flow of corrupt receipts into the international financial system should be strengthened. The main international body working on money laundering is the Financial Action Task Force (FATF) set up in 1989. It has a list of forty-nine recommendations that have been adopted by over 100 countries. In addition, in 2000, twelve private global bankers developed the Wolfsberg Principles. These try to balance legitimate demands for privacy against the banks' wish to avoid laundering funds from illicit sources.[11]

Unfortunately, there is little solid information on the impact of anti-money laundering systems on the amount of funds laundered or on the link between money laundering and the level of predicate offenses,

---

[10] http://webdomino1.oecd.org/olis/2006doc.nsf/Linkto/td-ecg(2006)11.
[11] www.wolfsberg-principles.com.

such as corruption. More needs to be done to encourage cross-border cooperation and to protect those who report and investigate corruption and money laundering. Both the formal law and its enforcement need to be strengthened. Here research is needed to test the efficacy of alternative methods to prevent the flow of illicit funds and to enforce legal sanctions against money laundering (Levi, Dakolias, and Greenberg 2007; Reuter and Truman 2004).

Text Box: Options to limit corruption (allocate $5 billion of funds from international sources to these options). If each option received $1.25 billion, a strong beginning could be made to develop new programs and monitor and critique existing efforts. Each program would include funds for evaluation of its impact to develop benchmarks.

Option 1
Cross-country efforts to limit corruption in regulation and in procurement and revenue collection. Special emphasis on automated, computer-based systems for procurement and revenue collection. Examination of regulatory climate for business to eliminate or streamline the rules.

Benefits:
Encourage formation of new businesses and increase economic value of existing businesses. Improve the operation of government. End result is more robust and productive economic growth. For government, better service delivery to those at all income levels.

Costs:
Out-of-pocket costs for technical consultancies and program evaluation. Other costs are close to zero for pure "red tape," but one needs to include benefits forgone from programs with social value. Costs of monitoring and reforming bureaucracies may include improvements in salaries and working conditions for oversight officials.

Benefit/Cost ratios:
Of course, not all programs are successful, but existing cases have B/C ratios as high as 100 to 1 with others in the 3 to 1 or 10 to 1 range.

These ratios ignore the opportunity costs of funds formerly not collected in taxes or going into the pockets of government contractors and officials. It counts as a benefit the reduction in illicit transfers.

Option 2
Urge ratification of international anti-corruption treaties, publicize treaty provisions, and engage in monitoring for compliance.

Benefits:
Less corruption in international business and more inter-state cooperation with corresponding increases in efficiency of production.

Costs:
Out-of-pocket costs for advocacy and publicity. Major costs borne by those formerly engaged in corrupt deals.

Option 3
Develop and monitor initiatives to increase the transparency of and limit corruption in investments in developing countries.

Benefits:
If the threat of disclosure of payments affects behavior, then most of the benefits would flow to developing countries.

Costs:
Administrative costs of setting up such systems that should be only a few percentage points of the value of any project. Substantial costs borne by former beneficiaries of corrupt deals.

Option 4
Increased efforts to control money laundering

Benefits:
Reduced corruption because of higher costs of converting funds to usable forms. Recovery of proceeds from corruption.

Costs:
Expense of an international negotiation to agree on standards. Costs of subsequent monitoring and enforcement.

References

Campos, J. E., and S. Pradhan (eds.) 2007 *The Many Faces of Corruption: Tracking Vulnerabilities at the Sector Level*, Washington DC: The World Bank.

Colitt. R. 2004 Brazil probe reveals decade of corruption in health contracts, *Financial Times*, June 2, 2004.

Davis, J. 2003 Corruption in public service delivery: experience from South Asia's water and sanitation sector, *World Development* 32, 53–71.

Dollar, D., M. Hallward-Driemeier and T. Mengiste 2004 Investment Climate and International Integration, Policy Research Working Paper 3323, Washington DC: World Bank.

Fjeldstad, O-H. 2005 *Revenue Administration and Corruption*. U4 Issue 2, 2005, Bergen, Norway: Chr. Michelson Institute.

Fries, S., T. Lysenko, and S. Polanec 2003 The 2002 Business Environment and Enterprise Performance Survey: Results from a Survey of 6,100 Firms, Working Paper No. 84, London: European Bank for Reconstructions and Development.

Kaufmann, D. 2003 Rethinking governance: Empirical lessons challenge orthodoxy, Discussion draft, World Bank, Washington DC, www.worldbank.org/wbi/governance/pdf/ rethink_gov_standford.pdf

Levi, M., M. Dakolias, and T. S. Greenberg 2007 Money laundering, the highway of grand corruption, in Campos and Pradhan (eds.) *The Many Faces of Corruption: Tracking Vulnerabilities at the Sector Level*. Washington DC: World Bank.

McPake, B., D. Asiimwe, F. Mwesigye, M. Ofumbi, L. Ortenblad, P. Streefland, and A. Turinde 1999 Informal economic activities of public health workers in Uganda· Implications for quality and accessibility of care, *Social Science and Medicine* 49, 849–65.

Olken, B. A. 2003 Corruption and the costs of redistribution: micro evidence from Indonesia, *Journal of Public Economics*, 90, 853–70.

Organization for Economic Cooperation and Development (OECD) 2003 *Trade Facilitation Reforms in the Service of Development*, Trade Committee Working Paper TD/TC/WP(2003)11/FINAL, Paris: OECD.

Patrinos, H. A., and R. Kagia 2007 Maximizing the performance of education systems: the case of teacher absenteeism. In Campos and Pradhan (eds.) *The Many Faces of Corruption: Tracking Vulnerabilities at the Sector Level*. Washington DC: World Bank.

Plummer, J., and P. Cross 2007 Tackling corruption in the water and sanitation sector in Africa: Starting the dialogue. In Campos and Pradhan (eds.) *The Many Faces of Corruption: Tracking Vulnerabilities at the Sector Level*. Washington DC: World Bank.

Pogarska, O., and E. L. Segura 2005 *Ukraine–Macroeconomic Situation, July 2005*, SigmaBleyzer, at http://www.sigmableyzer.com (accessed September 13, 2006).

Reuter, P., and E. M. Truman 2004 *Chasing Dirty Money: The Fight against Money Laundering*, Washington DC: Institute for International Economics.

Rose-Ackerman, S. 1978 *Corruption: A Study in Political Economy*, New York: Academic Press.

Rose-Ackerman, S. 1999 *Corruption and Government: Causes, Consequences and Reform*, Cambridge: Cambridge University Press.

Rose-Ackerman, S. 2004 Governance and corruption. In B. Lomborg (ed.), *Global Crises, Global Solutions*. Cambridge: Cambridge University Press.

Rose-Ackerman, S. (ed.) 2006 *International Handbook on the Economics of Corruption*. Cheltenham UK: Edward Elgar.

Wei, S.-J. 2000 How taxing is corruption on international investors? *Review of Economics and Statistics*, 82: 1–11.

World Bank 2004 *Sustaining Forests: A Development Strategy*, Washington DC: The World Bank.

Zuleta, J. C., A. Leyton and E. F. Ivanovic 2007 Combating corruption in revenue administration: The case of VAT refunds in Bolivia. In Campos and Pradhan (eds.) *The Many Faces of Corruption: Tracking Vulnerabilities at the Sector Level*. Washington DC: World Bank.

14 | Lack of Education

PETER F. ORAZEM*

This chapter reviews the stylized facts regarding the distribution of human capital investments and the returns to those investments in developing countries. It then examines recent evidence regarding which policies can induce increased human capital investments in the most efficient manner, using estimated benefits and costs as a guide. Supply-side strategies such as increasing school access or improving school quality are more costly, have less certain benefits, and have a weak record of success. Demand-side interventions such as school sited health programs, vouchers, and conditional transfers have a greater likelihood of improving literacy in the most cost-effective manner.

1. Benefits

Few empirical relationships have been more frequently investigated than that between years of schooling and earnings. Literally hundreds of studies using alternative data sets from developing and developed countries, spanning many decades, and employing alternative specifications to correct for various potential sources of bias, have derived amazingly consistent estimated private returns per year of schooling.[1] Average returns are almost universally positive and at or above market returns on other investments. Using harmonized household data sets from 48

* Department of Economics, Iowa State University, Ames, IA 50011–1070, pfo@iastate.edu

I thank Amy Damon, Jean Fares, Deon Filmer, Paul Glewwe, Sarojini Hirshberg, Manny Jimenez, Elizabeth King, Claudio Montenegro, Harry Patrinos, Annette Richter, and T. Paul Schultz for their advice on topics, content and relevant literature as I prepared background materials for this paper. Shiva Sikdar provided able research assistance. Opinions expressed are my own and not necessarily those of my colleagues or of the World Bank.

[1] Psacharopoulos and Patrinos (2004) present the most recent review of findings from developing countries. Card (1999) contains an excellent review of the various estimation methods and biases associated with analysis of the returns to schooling.

developing countries, Fares, Montenegro and Orazem (2007) found that returns for women average 9.6% compared to 7.1% for men, and 8.1% for urban residents compared to 7.5% for rural residents. There may be external benefits from schooling beyond those that go to the individual. These social benefits include improved governance due to an educated electorate, improved climate for growth due to agglomerations of skilled individuals, reduced fertility behavior, and improved household health.[2]

The finding of positive returns on schooling across a wide array of countries at all stages of development suggest that education offers consistent returns in almost all economic settings. Nevertheless, a year of schooling will be even more productive in some environments than others. As argued by Schultz (1975), human capital is most valuable in markets experiencing technological, production or price shocks that require adaptation, whether by moving to industries or areas with the strongest labor demand, adopting or developing new technologies, or switching occupations to fulfill market needs.[3] Good adaptive decisions require a reward, and so human capital will be most valuable when social or governmental institutions place few restrictions on mobility or trade, when wages and prices are flexible, and when property rights are enforced.[4] An example of the role of freer markets in enhancing human capital productivity is the rapid increase in returns to schooling observed in virtually all formerly planned economies as they transitioned toward market systems (Fleisher *et al.*, 2005).

[2] Pritchett (2004) questioned the importance of these externalities because of the unstable relationship between growth in measures of aggregate human capital and aggregate output, but there is strong microeconomic evidence that human capital improves household health, lowers fertility, lowers the crime rate, and improves labor mobility, all of which have external as well as individual benefits (Schultz, 2002). Angrist *et al.* (2002) and Schultz (2004) both found that increased schooling from randomly assigned vouchers and conditional cash transfers led to reduced fertility behavior, although the evidence was somewhat weaker in the latter case.

[3] Consistent with that presumption, Fafchamps and Quisumbing (1999) and Godoy, Karlan, Rabindran, and Huanca (2005) find that returns on schooling are apparent in off-farm work but not on traditional farms. On the other hand, in agricultural environments with technological change it is the most educated that adapt first (Huffman and Orazem, 2007) and in India, returns on schooling were highest in areas where Green Revolution technologies were most complementary to local agriculture (Foster and Rosenzweig, 1996).

[4] Acemoglu, Robinson, and Johnson (2001) and Acemoglu, Johnson, and Robinson (2002) have examined the role of institutions that constrain or enhance mobility in retarding or fostering economic growth.

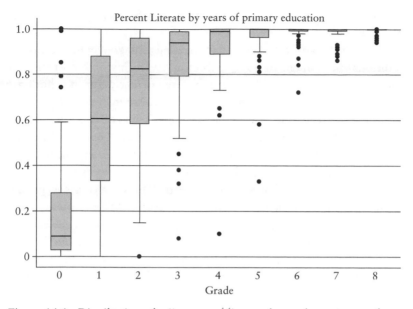

Figure 14.1. Distribution of self-reported literacy by grade attainment for youth aged 15–24, various countries

Source: Author's compilation of summary data from 73 household surveys spanning 57 developing countries provided by Claudio Montenegro of the World Bank.

While years of schooling are consistently associated with higher earnings, time in school is only productive if it enhances cognitive skills. Investments of time and money in a child's schooling that fail to produce basic cognitive skills such as literacy are almost surely wasted.

Studies that include both years of schooling and measures of cognitive skills find that it is the latter and not the former that drive earnings (Glewwe, 2002). Hanushek and Kimko (2000) found that it is average cognitive attainment and not average years of schooling that drives economic growth.

Nevertheless, as shown in Figure 14.1, the probability of attaining self-reported literacy rises with years of schooling, although there is considerable variation in the pattern across countries. Children who complete the primary cycle, about six years of schooling, are almost certain to attain literacy in most countries. While one could argue that these children could have attained literacy without schooling, the figure shows that relatively few literate individuals never attended school. This presumption that schooling is needed for literacy underlies the

Millennium Development Goal of attaining universal primary education (UPE) by 2015.

The World Bank estimates that meeting this goal will require an additional investment of $11–28 billion. Even this high cost may be understated because the children who are currently not in school are disproportionately located in areas that are expensive to reach with schooling services or in households that are less keen to send children to school. Making efficient progress toward the goal requires identifying which illiterate populations can be served most economically.

Many countries have placed an emphasis on raising enrollment rates for girls, and these efforts have succeeded in shrinking the gender enrollment gap over the past twenty years. Across 69 developing countries, the enrollment gap between boys and girls under age 12 exceeds 10 percentage points in only 3 countries. Larger gaps are observed at the secondary schooling level. In contrast, the enrollment gap between urban and rural children under age 12 exceeds 10 percentage points in over half the countries. Filmer and Pritchett (1999) develop estimates of child grade attainment by household wealth status. In almost all countries, the gaps occur even at grade 1, and in all countries, the gaps are larger at higher-grade levels. Therefore, the most underserved populations are the poor and children residing in rural areas.

As shown in Table 14.1, some of the illiteracy problem is due to children who never attend school and the rest from children who drop out before completing the primary cycle. It is the latter group that would be the most cost-effective population to target first in moving toward

Table 14.1. *Reasons for not attaining universal primary education*

Region	Percent never enrolled	Percent not completing Grade 4
West, Central Africa	35.6	37.5
East, South Africa	21.1	34.0
South Asia	23.3	24.7
MENA	15.5	23.5
South America	4.8	17.0

Source: Author's population-weighted averages of data from 49 country household surveys compiled in Lloyd (2005), Appendix Tables 3–5, 3–6, and A.1; pp. 160–163, 658–661. All surveys were conducted in the late 1990s or early 2000s.

UPE and universal literacy. In Southern and Eastern Africa, the Middle East, and Latin America, much of the failure of children to complete even four years of schooling is due to children who drop out after starting school. Getting children who have never attended school, as seems to be a disproportionate share of the illiteracy problems in South Asia and Central and Western Africa, to complete the primary cycle would be much more expensive.

2. Supply-side interventions

Supply-side policies aim to improve the quantity or quality of schooling offered. These policies include direct provision of newly constructed schools or of school supplies by the central government, improving the quality of existing schools, or improving the management of existing schools, but they can also involve the decentralization of school control to local authorities who are believed to be able to allocate resources more efficiently to meet school needs.[5]

While high-quality, well-managed schools would enhance schooling outcomes, there are several reasons why investments in additional schools or improved school materials may fail the cost-effectiveness criteria.

(1) If you build it, they may not come

Building and staffing more schools requires that most expenses are incurred before we find out if parents will send their children to the school. In addition, some of the enrollment at the new schools will be from children already in school who switch to the new school.[6] Duflo's (2001) analysis of Indonesia's massive public works project that doubled the number of primary schools in a six-year period suggests that halving the average distance to school raised years of schooling by about 1.5%.[7]

---

[5] Glewwe and Kremer (2006) and Orazem and King (2007) provide much more detailed discussion of these and other interventions and related evaluation issues.

[6] See Jimenez and Sawada (2001).

[7] Because average distance was cut in half, Duflo's estimates suggest a 3% increase in years of schooling from the doubling of schools. Pitt *et al.* (1993) estimate that the program raised enrollments by 2.5%, very similar to Duflo's estimates of the impact on years of schooling.

Filmer's (2004) analysis of the relationship between distance and enrollments across 21 developing countries generally found very small marginal effects of lowering distance. This does not imply that school provision is unimportant – only that the existing supply is already located in the most dense child populations. New schools will be disproportionately located in relatively remote places where there are relatively few children and relatively high costs.

(2) Quality matters, but we don't know how to foster quality

It is undoubtedly true that higher quality schools enhance human capital production and raise school demand. However, research has failed to identify how to foster improved quality. For example, Rivkin, Hanushek, and Kain (2005) found that good teachers systematically produce better academic outcomes than do bad teachers. Unfortunately, good teachers and bad teachers look very much alike statistically – they have the same education levels, similar demographics, receive the same in-service training and are compensated similarly. In other words, teacher quality matters, but we don't know what matters for teacher quality. As teachers represent 74% of recurring school expenditures in developing countries (Bruns *et al.*, 2003), it would seem that any policy aimed at improving school quality would have to confront teacher quality. The lack of agreement about how to foster teacher quality thwarts any general prescription regarding likely cost-effective avenues for improvement.

(3) Are better managed schools better or are better schools better managed?

The World Bank and other international agencies have made decentralization of school management a central theme of new efforts to improve the efficiency of public service delivery in developing countries (Bardhan, 2005). The clear attraction of the strategy is that it offers the potential of improving school outcomes without spending more on the schools – we simply "spend smarter and not harder," to modify the common aphorism. The available evidence, even that often used by proponents of decentralization, is really too uncertain to engender a high degree of confidence that local management can work in all settings. Studies by Jimenez and Sawada (1999) of the EDUCO[8] schools in El Salvador and by King and Ozler (2001) of the autonomous schools in Nicaragua found that schools that exercised more local autonomy experienced gains in student attendance or test scores compared to other schools. However, participating schools are not randomly drawn – local authorities had to self-select into the programs and would be dropped if they did not fulfill their obligations. It is likely that the schools opting to accept local responsibility differ in ways that could vary school outcomes compared to communities that did not elect to participate in the program. In other words, a finding that autonomous schools outperform schools that do not behave autonomously does not imply that the nonautonomous schools would have better outcomes if they too behaved autonomously.[9]

(4) Returns on increased school supply come at a long lag

Supply-side interventions generally require the allocation of funds up front with the hoped-for child or parental response only becoming apparent later. Once built, there is no economic return to a new school unless children attend, but it may be five years before children attain permanent literacy. It may take some time for parents to react to school quality improvements. Similarly, it may take some time for teachers and students to respond to better local school management. The combination of upfront costs, uncertain response, and delayed benefits place supply-side interventions at a cost–benefit disadvantage compared to the demand-side alternatives we examine next.

---

[8] EDUCO comes from the Spanish acronym "Educacion con Participacion de la Comunidad" or "Community Managed Schools."

[9] Reinikka and Svensson (2004) found that a decentralization program in Uganda dramatically increased the proportion of funds that ended up reaching the schools from 20% in 1995 to 80% in 2001. Pressure to spend more on schools may have been due to publication of the amount of the transfers, making it more difficult to withhold money from the schools, but it may have also come from better central monitoring of the accounts. Whether the resources were then allocated better or whether the schools improved is not clear, but it does suggest that aspects of decentralization can be mandated. Gunnarsson *et al.* (2007) show that most of the variation in the practice of local school autonomy occurs within and not between countries, suggesting that national policies to foster decentralized decisionmaking may be ineffective.

3. Demand-side interventions

Demand-side policies have several distinct advantages over the supply-side efforts to improve literacy. Demand-side stimulus can be targeted to the particular population currently not in school, whereas supply-side interventions will typically result in some redistribution of children already in school to the new schools. Demand-side interventions can also be made contingent on the child being in school, meaning that payment only occurs if the program is working. Finally, demand-side interventions can immediately influence behavior and so they have an advantage relative to the more heavily discounted benefits of supply-side interventions.

There are three types of interventions that I will review: interventions in child health or nutrition that attempt to improve the child's physical or mental ability to learn; efforts to lower the cost of public or private schooling that enhance the household's ability to pay for schooling; and income transfers to the households made conditional on the child's enrollment that enhance the household's ability to afford schooling while lowering the opportunity cost of child time in school. These demand-side strategies work best where there is existing excess capacity of available schools so that more children can be added at low marginal cost.

a: Health and schooling

Numerous mechanisms to influence child health have been introduced through schools including the administration of nutrition supplements, school lunch plans, immunization programs, and health instructions. These programs have been installed from preschool through the schooling cycle, although the most rigorously evaluated have been the ones targeted at younger children.

There is substantial evidence that malnutrition early in life affects both cognitive and physical development that may be only partially reversible by better nutrition later in life. For example, Glewwe, Jacoby, and King (2001) found, in controlling for other household background measures, that children who were malnourished early in life start school later and complete fewer years of schooling. Alderman, Hoddinott, and Kinsey (2003) report similar findings for children who were malnourished because of exposure to civil war and drought in Zimbabwe. Evaluations of efforts to provide nutritional supplements to at-risk preschool children have shown permanent improvements in physical stature and cognitive development, both of which can raise lifetime earnings.

Behrman, Cheng, and Todd (2004) conducted an experimental evaluation of the Proyecto Integral de Desarrollo Infantil (PIDI) program in Bolivia. This program provides support for daycare, nutritional inputs, and preschool activities for low-income children aged 6–72 months. For children exposed to the program for periods exceeding one year, the authors report permanent gains in cognitive development and fine motor skills that they translate to projected lifetime earnings growth with benefit–cost ratios ranging between 1.7 and 3.7. Grantham-McGregor *et al.* (1991) report comparable findings for a similar program aimed at stunted infants in Jamaica, as do Armecin *et al.* (2005) for low-income rural households in the Philippines. Vermeersch and Kremer (2005) found that providing free breakfast to preschoolers raised attendance by 30% in Kenya but did not raise average measured skills. An analysis of a program that combined deworming medication with an iron supplement for preschoolers in India also raised attendance and physical stature.

Nutritional programs can also have benefits at older ages. McGuire (1996) reported that giving iron supplements to secondary children (aged 13–15) in a low-income country can raise cognitive abilities by 5%–25% or the equivalent of 0.05 years of schooling. Knowles and Behrman (2005) estimate that because the cost of the supplement is so small and administration inexpensive, it costs about $11 per added child-year of schooling and even these modest gains in schooling have substantial returns of 32 times the costs.

In a widely publicized study, Miguel and Kremer (2004) examined the impact of a program which administered deworming medicine to schoolchildren in Kenya. The treated children increased their attendance by 0.15 years per pupil, or an implied cost of $3.50 per child-year of schooling.

One reason these health interventions can be viewed as particularly cost-effective in raising schooling investments is that the schooling is a collateral benefit. The main aim for the programs is to improve child health which has a value in itself, raising the benefits side of the equation. On the cost side, expenses are only incurred if the children participate and so there is much less potential for wasted investments than is the case for supply-side interventions.

Can these studies be generalized to other developing country settings? Demographic and Health Survey data suggest that health reasons are less often cited as a reason for children not being in school than are child work inside or outside the home, poverty, or the child's lack of interest in school (Table 14.2). Health is cited more often in Africa and in urban areas of Latin America, but is less often cited elsewhere. Nevertheless, in areas where malnutrition or worm infestations are more common, these interventions offer an inexpensive way to raise attendance, physical and mental capacity, and perhaps length of time in school, all of which would increase the probability that the children attain permanent literacy.

b: Lowering schooling costs

In many countries, parents face significant school costs for their children, ranging from uniforms and school supplies to tuition, fees and after-school tutorials. These expenses can represent a significant share of household income for poor families. Several countries have cut or eliminated the school fees charged by government schools, including Ghana, Kenya, Tanzania, and Uganda. In Tanzania, enrollments rose by 1.2 million children. A program that cut household costs of uniforms and school materials in Kenya increased years of schooling completed by 15% (Kremer, Moulin, and Namunyu, 2003). An evaluation by Deininger (2003) of the Uganda case found that elimination of primary fees lowered average costs by 60% and increased enrollments by 60%, with the largest gains in rural areas. Increased schooling demand led to considerable crowding as school supplies did not keep up. Pupil–teacher ratios rose from 38 to 65.

In many developing countries, students are expected to get tutoring after school with the tutoring often provided by the same teacher they have in class. Poor children cannot afford these services and may fall behind their peers. A program in India hired local women with high school degrees to provide remedial tutoring to grade 3 and 4 children who had fallen behind in school (Banerjee *et al.*, 2003). At a cost of $5 per child, the program raised the likelihood of a child performing at first-grade math level by 11.9 percentage points and at second-grade language levels by 9.9 percentage points. By the end of the two-year program, children were performing on average 0.28 standard deviations higher on the test scores, roughly equivalent to having attained

Table 14.2. *Reasons for not attending school in urban and rural populations, by world region*

	All world regions		Sub-Saharan Africa		North Africa & Middle East		Central Asia & Europe		South & East Asia		Latin America & Caribbean	
	Urban	Rural	Urban	Rural	Urban	Rural	Urban	Rural	Urban	Rural	Urban	Rural
Work outside the home	7.4	4.2	3.3	1.8	0.7	0.7	9.3	7.8	8.7	4.4	18.3	10.0
Housework	7.3	11.5	5.3	7.9	5.6	9.9	6.3	9.3	10.7	19.7	11.7	17.9
Inadequate school supply	1.9	4.9	1.8	3.2	2.0	6.2	1.3	3.0	1.7	2.7	2.6	10.8
Poverty	18.2	18.1	24.1	23.9	4.6	3.4	1.3	0.8	24.2	26.3	11.9	11.3
Lack of interest	47.3	44.0	45.2	42.7	76.6	69.4	65.0	58.2	49.3	41.7	34.0	33.5
Health reasons	6.3	5.0	7.9	7.6	1.2	0.5	0.7	0.4	1.5	0.9	9.4	4.2
Others	11.5	12.3	12.4	12.9	9.3	9.9	16.0	20.5	4.0	4.3	12.1	12.3
Total	100.0	100.0	100.0	100.0	100.0	100.0	100.0	100.0	100.0	100.0	100.0	100.0

Source: Computations provided to the author by Elizabeth King based on data from demographic and health surveys, various years.

one additional year of schooling. The reason the program is so inexpensive is that they hired less-qualified tutors at the market rate rather than mandating teaching certifications and paying the government rate for teachers.

The availability of less-expensive teaching and infrastructure inputs is a major reason to consider private rather than government school options to serve expanding school demand. A program in Balochistan province in Pakistan attempted to spur both school demand for girls and to provide an incentive for private school entry by providing scholarships to girls. Randomly selected neighborhoods were given the option of packaging up to 100 girls' scholarships of 100 rupees per month (equivalent to $3) to try to induce a school operator to open a school in the area. In urban areas, even this modest subsidy was sufficient to get schools to open (Kim, Alderman, and Orazem, 1999) and enrollments for both girls and boys rose relative to enrollments in control neighborhoods. The schools were opened at one quarter of the cost of a public school. A similar program in rural areas enabled schools to open, but the communities were too poor and the number of girls too few to allow the schools to become self-sustaining (Alderman, Kim, and Orazem, 2003). This raises an important lesson for the likely success of private school options to raise enrollments – invariably they will be most successful in areas that would have been able to support private schools in the absence of a subsidy, in other words, places with the greatest elasticity of supply for private schools.

James (1993) reported that private schools are an even more important component of school supply in developing than in developed countries. Often private schools will have excess capacity as measured by the relative numbers of students per teacher in comparison to government schools. If excess private school capacity exists, vouchers are an excellent mechanism by which governments can expand access less expensively than building additional government schools. One example of this strategy was the Colombia PACES program that provided subsidies to municipalities to provide secondary school vouchers to poor children. There was ample evidence that the existing government school supply was insufficient to meet demand, and that private schools could add additional students without requiring additional teachers or classrooms (King, Orazem, and Wohlgemuth, 1999). Angrist *et al.* (2002, 2006) demonstrated that children who were randomly sorted into the program were 10% more likely to complete the eighth grade and also scored 0.2 standard deviations higher on standardized tests, equivalent to adding an additional year of school. For those in doubt about external benefits from education, it is interesting that voucher recipients also were less likely to marry young or cohabit and were less likely to engage in child labor. A follow-up analysis confirmed that educational gains were permanent and not transitory. The voucher costs $228 per recipient including the opportunity cost of the children (Knowles and Behrman, 2005), which is swamped by the lifetime value of the induced additional years of schooling and cognitive attainment.

Programs to reduce the costs of schooling to parents can have dramatic and quick impacts on children's achievement and years of schooling completed. They can take advantage of existing underutilized private school and teaching capacity at a fraction of the cost of building and staffing new schools. Finally, they have the advantage of only using resources if the children use the services.

c: Conditional cash transfers

Latin American countries have moved rapidly to the use of conditional cash transfers to induce parents to send their children to school. These programs transfer income to a household in exchange for the household sending their children to school. Many of these programs include other components, typically adding nutritional supplements and mandating health clinic visits for children and health training for mothers, so the programs are not just aimed at education. Programs have been implemented and evaluated in Argentina, Bangladesh, Brazil, Colombia, Costa Rica, Honduras, Jamaica, Mexico, Nicaragua and Turkey and other programs have been or are being established in Chile, Ecuador, Peru and other countries.

These programs will be most effective in environments in which schooling demand is highly income and child wage elastic and where large numbers of children are not in school. These circumstances naturally fit poor households, neighborhoods and communities and these programs have in fact been aimed at the lowest income strata of society. While they have been tried in urban areas, most notably the *bolsa escola* programs in Brazil, there are significant advantages to using geographic targeting which is easier in less densely populated areas. In urban areas, it can be costly for authorities to try to establish which households qualify on the basis of income and which don't, and such efforts lead to moral hazard problems in which households may take on activities that lower their earned income but increase their chance of getting the government transfer.

Additionally, these programs will be most successful when they are aimed at populations not currently in school. In Brazil, where individual municipalities established their own programs until they were centralized more recently under the federal *bolsa familias*, some programs targeted children who were sufficiently young that the vast majority were already in school. As an example, in Mexico, conditional transfers had almost no impact on primary enrollments because the children were already in school (Schultz, 2004b) while in Nicaragua, enrollment rose by 23 percentage points (Maluccio, 2006). As a rule, the largest effects from conditional transfers have been in rural areas, consistent with the presumption of higher income elasticities and opportunity cost elasticities in rural areas.

IV. Benefit–cost summary

My task in this exercise is to identify the low-lying fruit of educational expansion – what programs will raise returns most per dollar expended. These estimates must be taken with a considerable grain of salt – the returns will depend on the degree of economic freedom and growth in the economy and will depend on whether the program can be successfully targeted to those populations that will respond most elastically to the intervention. As a general rule, these populations will be drawn disproportionately from the poor and rural areas at the primary level. At the secondary level, urban populations may be targeted as well. In designing these programs, efforts to supplement existing supply by working outside the government school system are generally less expensive and subject to fewer regulatory constraints. Such private sector educational programs will be most effective in urban areas where the elasticity of educational supply is greatest. Health programs offer opportunities for collateral educational benefits while improving child welfare. The enrollments of poor and rural children, populations that have higher income and child wage elasticities, will also be particularly sensitive to conditional cash transfers.

My review of returns on literacy and years of schooling demonstrated considerable consistency across countries, gender, and urban and rural markets in the estimated returns on schooling. In the estimates I report, I will assume that the return on schooling is an increase of 8% per year of schooling completed over an estimated average earning for labor in the country. Modest variation in the returns on schooling will not be sufficient to reverse the conclusions regarding whether the interventions are expected to pay for themselves.

I assume a 45-year work career in my estimates. In my projection of lifetime earnings, I am implicitly assuming that the value of time outside the market rises in value at the same rate as the value of time in the labor market. This assumption is particularly suspect in the cases where women are not commonly found in the labor market, as in the Pakistan example. On the other hand, I do not make any adjustments for possible external benefits of women's education which would create a bias in the other direction, and I should further note that the literature has not demonstrated that returns on girls' schooling are substantially lower than are returns on boys' schooling.

I provide summary information on benefit–cost ratios for many of the programs mentioned above. Some of these are compiled personally while others take ratios developed by the authors of those studies. It is important to emphasize that some programs may have very high ratios and yet be only applicable to certain areas and not others. For example, the voucher program that appears to have been successful in urban areas of Colombia could not be implemented in rural areas without preexisting private schools.

Finally, these estimates concentrate on the narrow returns on a year of schooling. This can be misleading in either direction. The reported benefit–cost ratios will be biased downward if increased years of schooling reduced fertility behavior of young women, as was found in Colombia and (less definitively) in Mexico. Incorporating the benefits of delayed fertility increases the benefit–cost ratios substantially, from 3.3 to 25.6 in the case of the Colombia PACES program (Knowles and Behrman, 2005). On the other hand, it is possible that increased time in school will not have the same impact on lifetime earnings if the schools are of atypically poor quality. For example, the results of cognitive tests of the Kenya experiments found that even though students spent more time in school, their performance on cognitive exams did not improve significantly. The increased enrollments in Uganda apparently were only modestly accommodated by increased school materials and so school quality suffered for all children. That raises concerns that these programs did not permanently increase the children's lifetime human capital stock. My view is that the tie between years of schooling and lifetime earnings is sufficiently strong that the benefits will yet become apparent as these children age, even if they do not show immediately. It should be emphasized that in most of the cases summarized in Table 14.3, improved cognitive ability did accompany the increased time in school when both were measured.

Table 14.3. *Overview table of benefit–cost ratios from various efforts to reduce illiteracy*

	Low Discount (3%)			High Discount (5%)		
	Benefit ($)	Cost ($)	BCR	Benefit ($)	Cost ($)	BCR
Health and nutrition programs						
Bolivia PIDI: preschool and nutrition[a]	5,107	1,394	3.66	3,230	301	2.48
Kenya: deworming[b]	2,246!	3.5!	642	1,652!	3.5!	472
Kenya: preschool and nutrition[c]	2,246!	29.13	77	1,652!	28.6!	58
Iron supplements to secondary students[d]	474!	10.49!	45.2	330	10.29!	32.1
Scholarship/voucher programs						
Colombia: PACES secondary school urban voucher[d]	4,287	971	4.41	3,152	953	3.31
Pakistan urban girls' scholarship[e]	3,924!	225!	17.4	2,887!	223!	12.9
Pakistan rural girls' scholarship[e]	3,138!	311!	10.1	2,302!	326!	7.1
India *balsakhis* tutorial program[f]	7,002	9.85!	711	5,152	9.76!	528
Uganda free primary school program[g]	3,675!	140!	26.3	2,703!	140!	19.3

Table 14.3. (*cont.*)

	Low Discount (3%)			High Discount (5%)		
	Benefit ($)	Cost ($)	BCR	Benefit ($)	Cost ($)	BCR
Conditional cash transfers						
Mexico Progresa[h]	17,565!	2,585!	6.8	12,923!	2,535!	5.1
Nicaragua: RED[i]	5,920	1,574!	3.80	4,356	1,574!	2.80

Notes:

[a] Behrman, Cheng and Todd (2004)#
[b] Miguel and Kremer (2004)*
[c] Vermeersch and Kremer (2005)*
[d] Knowles and Behrman (2005)#
[e] Alderman, Kim and Orazem (2003)
[f] Banerjee, Cole, Duflo and Linden (2003)
[g] Deininger (2003)†
[h] Schultz (2004a)
[i] Maluccio (2006)
[#] Benefit–cost ratio computed in the cited paper.
[*] Cost per year of schooling reported in MIT Abdul Latif Jameel Poverty Action Lab. (2005).
[!] Per year of schooling induced.
[†] Assumes that the government expands school space to accommodate additional students at the average cost per primary student.

Estimated benefit–cost ratios for discount rates 3% and 5% are reported in Table 14.3. I use the 5% discount rate because it was the rate most commonly used in the cited literature. I report the estimates of other authors when I assess that they are more carefully done than anything I could do from reading the paper.

It is immediately clear that these benefit–cost ratios are large and some extremely large. The largest returns are from:

(a) very low cost demand-side interventions;
(b) interventions in areas with an atypical need for the intervention such as the schools in Kenya in which 92% of children had worm infestations;

(c) programs with easily identified beneficiaries that would not be able to access the service otherwise, such as the poor children who lacked tutors in India.

The highly selected nature of the sites for the intervention and the children targeted for the programs suggest that these benefit–cost ratios are upper-bound estimates. Were the programs to be expanded, they would be placed in less productive sites and with less needy children. Note that the more broadly distributed interventions such as the conditional cash transfer programs are less selective in terms of the places where the intervention is tried and the uniformity of need among the beneficiaries, and so their benefit–cost ratios are more modest as a result.

The largest benefit–cost ratios are interventions early in the child's life. These interventions are less costly and the opportunity costs of the beneficiaries are very low. In addition, these interventions have the longest potential period of returns. Nevertheless, programs aimed at older children can be successful, such as the Colombia PACES program or the iron supplement aimed at secondary students. Both did not involve building more schools or adding capacity, a key to keeping cost low relative to benefits.

References

Acemoglu, Daron, James A. Robinson and Simon Johnson (2001) "The Colonial Origins of Comparative Development: An Empirical Investigation," *American Economic Review* 91: 1369–401.

Acemoglu, Daron, Simon Johnson and James A. Robinson (2002) "Reversal of Fortune: Geography and Institutions in the Making of the Modern World Income Distribution," *Quarterly Journal of Economics* 117: 1231–94.

Alderman, Harold, John Hoddinott and Bill Kinsey (2003) "Long-Term Consequences of Early Childhood Malnutrition." IFPRI Discussion Paper #168. Washington, DC.

Alderman, H., J. Kim, and P. F. Orazem (2003) "Design, Evaluation, and Sustainability of Private Schools for the Poor: The Pakistan Urban and Rural Fellowship School Experiments," *Economics of Education Review* 22: 265–274.

Angrist, J. D., E. Bettinger, E. Bloom, E. M. King, and M. Kremer (2002) "Vouchers for Private Schooling in Colombia: Evidence from a Randomized Natural Experiment," *American Economic Review* 92 (5, December): 1535–59.

Angrist, Joshua D., Eric Bettinger, and Michael Kremer (2006) "Long-Term Educational Consequences of Secondary School Vouchers: Evidence from Administrative Records in Colombia," *American Economic Review* 96: 847–62.

Armecin, Graeme, Jere R. Behrman, Paulita Duazo, Sharon Ghuman, Socorro Gultiano, Elizabeth M. King, and Nanette Lee (2005) "Early Childhood Development Programs and Children's Development: Evidence from the Philippines." Mimeo, University of Pennsylvania.

Banerjee, Abhijit, Shawn Cole, Esther Duflo and Leigh Linden (2003), "Remedying Education: Evidence from Two Randomized Experiments in India." Mimeo, Massachusetts Institute of Technology.

Bardhan, Pranab (2005) *Scarcity, Conflicts and Coooperation: Essays in the Political and Institutional Economics of Development.* Cambridge, MA: The MIT Press.

Behrman, J. R., Y. Cheng, and P. Todd (2004) "Evaluating Pre-school Programs when Length of Exposure to the Program Varies: A Nonparametric Approach," *Review of Economics and Statistics* 86(1): 108–32.

Bobonis, Gustavo, Edward Miguel and Charu Sharma (2004) "Iron Deficiency Anemia and School Participation," Poverty Action Lab Working Paper No. 7.

Bruns, Barbara, Alain Mingat, and Ramahatra Rakotomalala (2003), "Achieving Universal Primary Education by 2015: A Chance for Every Child." Washington, DC: World Bank.

Card, D. (1999) "The Causal Effect of Education on Earnings," in O. Ashenfelter and D. Card, eds., *Handbook of Labor Economics*, Vol. IIIA. Amsterdam: Elsevier Science BV.

Chaudhury, Nazmul, Jeffrey Hammer, Michael Kremer, Karthik Muralidharan, F. Halsey Rogers (2005) "Missing in Action: Teacher and Health Worker Absence in Developing Countries," *Journal of Economic Perspectives* 19(4, Fall).

Deininger, Klaus (2003) "Does Cost of Schooling Affect Enrollment by the Poor? Universal Primary Education in Uganda," *Economics of Education Review* 22(3): 291–305.

Duflo, E. (2001) "Schooling and Labor Market Consequences of School Construction in Indonesia: Evidence from an Unusual Policy Experiment," *American Economic Review* 91: 795–813.

Fafchamps, Marcel and Agnus Quisumbing (1999) "Human Capital, Productivity, and Labor Allocation in Rural Pakistan," *Journal of Human Resources* 34(2): 369–406.

Fares, Jean, Claudio Montenegro, and Peter Orazem (2007) "Variations in the Returns to Schooling across and within Developing Economies." Mimeo. World Bank.

Filmer, Deon (2004) "If You Build It, Will they Come? School Availability and School Enrollment in 21 Poor Countries," World Bank Policy Research Working Paper 3340, June 2004.

Filmer, Deon, and Lant Pritchett (1999) "The Effect of Household Wealth on Educational Attainment: Evidence from 35 Countries," *Population and Development Review* 25(1).

Fleisher, Belton M., Klara Sabirianova, Xiaojun Wang (2005) "Returns to Skills and the Speed of Reforms: Evidence from Central and Eastern Europe, China and Russia," *Journal of Comparative Economics* 33 (2): 351–70.

Foster, A. D. and M. R. Rosenzweig (1996) "Technical Change and Human-Capital Returns and Investments: Evidence from the Green Revolution." *American Economic Review?*

Glewwe, Paul (2002) "Schools and Skills in Developing Countries: Education Policies and Socioeconomic Outcomes," *Journal of Economic Literature* 40: 436–83.

Glewwe, Paul, Hanan Jacoby and Elizabeth M. King (2001) "Early Childhood Nutrition and Academic Achievement: A Longitudinal Analysis," *Journal of Public Economics* 81: 345–68.

Glewwe, Paul, and Michael Kremer (2006) "Schools, Teachers and Educational Outcomes in Developing Countries,," in E. Hanushek and F. Welch, eds., *Handbook of Economics of Education*. Amsterdam: Elsevier Science BV.

Glewwe, Paul, Michael Kremer and Sylvie Moulin (2003) "Textbooks and Test Scores: Evidence from a Randomized Evaluation in Kenya." Development Research Group, Washington, DC: World Bank.

Godoy, Ricardo, Dean S. Karlan, Shanti Rabindran and Tomás Huanca (2005) "Do Modern Forms of Human Capital Matter in Primitive Economies? Comparative evidence from Bolivia," *Economics of Education Review* 24(1): 45–53.

Grantham-McGregor, S.M., C.A. Powell, S.P. Walker and J.H. Himes (1991) "Nutritional Supplementation, Psychosocial Stimulation, and Mental Development of Stunted Children: The Jamaican Study," *Lancet* 338: 1–5.

Gunnarsson, Victoria, Peter F. Orazem, Mario A. Sánchez, and Aimee Verdisco (2007) "Does School Decentralization Raise Student Outcomes? Theory and Evidence on the Roles of School Autonomy and Community Participation." Iowa State University Working Paper.

Hanushek, Eric A., and Dennis D. Kimko (2000). "Schooling, Labor Force Quality, and the Growth of Nations," *American Economic Review* 90: 1184–208.

Huffman, W. E. and P. F. Orazem (2007) "Agriculture and Human Capital in Economic Growth: Farmers, Schooling and Health," in R. E. Evenson and P. Pingali, eds., *Handbook of Agricultural Economics*, Vol. III. Amsterdam: North Holland.

James, Estelle (1993) "Why Do Different Countries Choose a Different Public-Private Mix of Educational Services?" *Journal of Human Resources* 28(3): 571–92.

Jimenez, Emmanuel and Yasuyuki Sawada (1999) "Do Community-Managed Schools Work? An Evaluation of El Salvador's EDUCO Program." *World Bank Economic Review* 13(3) September).

Jimenez, E. And Y. Sawada (2001) "Public for Private: The Relationship between Public and Private School Enrollment in the Philippines," *Economics of Education Review* 20: 389–99.

Kim, J., H. Alderman and P. F. Orazem (1999) "Can Private School Subsidies Increase Enrollment for the Poor? The Quetta Urban Fellowship Program," *World Bank Economic Review* 13: 443–65.

King, E. M., P. F. Orazem, and D. Wohlgemuth (1999) "Central Mandates and Local Incentives: The Colombia Education Voucher Program," *World Bank Economic Review* 13: 467–91.

King, Elizabeth M. and Berk Ozler (2001) "What's Decentralization Got to Do with Learning? The Case of Nicaragua's School Autonomy Reform," Working Paper Series "Impact Evaluation of Education Reforms," No. 9, Development Research Group, Poverty and Human Resources, Washington, DC: The World Bank.

Knowles, James C. and Jere R. Behrman (2005) "Assessing the Economic Returns to Investing in Youth in Developing Countries," in C. B. Lloyd, J. R. Behrman, N. P. Stromquist and B. Cohen, eds., *The Changing Transitions to Adulthood in Developing Countries: Selected Studies*. Washington, DC: National Academies Press.

Kremer, Michael, Sylvie Moulin and Robert Namunyu (2003) "Decentralization: A Cautionary Tale," Mimeo, Harvard University, April 2003.

Lloyd, Cynthia B., ed. (2005) *Growing up Global: The Changing Transitions to Adulthood in Developing Countries*. Washington, DC: National Academies Press.

Maluccio, John (2006) "Education and Child Labor: Experimental Evidence from a Nicaraguan Conditional Cash Transfer Program," in P. F. Orazem, G. Sedlacek, and P. Z. Tzannatos, eds., *Child Labor and Education in Latin America*. Washington, DC: InterAmerican Development Bank.

McGuire, Judith S. (1996) "The Payoff from Improving Nutrition." Unpublished manuscript. The World Bank.

Miguel, Edward and Michael Kremer (2004) "Worms: Identifying Impacts on Education and Health in the Presence of Treatment Externalities," *Econometrica* 72 (1): 159–217.

MIT Abdul Latif Jameel Poverty Action Lab. (2005) "Fighting Poverty: What Works?" www.povertyactionlab.com/research/Education%20MDGs.pdf

Orazem, Peter F. and Elizabeth M. King (2007) "Schooling in Developing Countries: The Roles of Supply, Demand and Government Policy." Forthcoming in T. P. Schultz and John Strauss, eds., *Handbook of Development Economics, Volume 4*. Amsterdam: North Holland.

Pitt, Mark M., Mark R. Rosenzweig, and Donna Gibbons (1993) "Determinants and Consequences of the Placement of Government Programs in Indonesia," *World Bank Economic Review* 7(3): 319–48.

Pritchett, Lant (2004) "Toward a New Consensus for Addressing the Global Challenge of the Lack of Education," in B. Lomborg, ed., *Global Crises, Global Solutions*. Cambridge: Cambridge University Press.

Psacharopoulos, George and Harry A. Patrinos (2004) "Returns to Investment in Education: A Further Update," *Education Economics* 12: 111–34.

Reinikka, Ritva and Jakob Svensson (2004) "Local Capture: Evidence from a Central Government Transfer Program in Uganda," *Quarterly Journal of Economics* 119(2): 679–705.

Rivkin, Steven G., Eric A. Hanushek, and John F. Kain (2005) "Teachers, Schools, and Academic Achievement," *Econometrica* 73: 417.

Schultz, T. Paul (2002), "Why Governments Should Invest More to Educate Girls," *World Development* 30: 207–25.

Schultz, T. Paul (2004a), "School Subsidies for the Poor: Evaluating the Mexican Progresa Poverty Program," *Journal of Development Economics* 74(1): 199–250.

Schultz, T. Paul. (2004b) "Alternative Perspective on Access to Education," in B. Lomborg, ed., *Global Crises, Global Solutions*. Cambridge: Cambridge University Press.

Schultz, T. W. (1975) "The Value of the Ability to Deal with Disequilibria." *Journal of Economic Literature* 13: 827–46.

Vermeersch, Christel and Michael Kremer (2005) "School Meals, Educational Achievement and School Competition: Evidence from a Randomized Evaluation," Mimeo, Harvard University.

15 | *Terrorism*

DANIEL LINOTTE

Terrorism is one of the main challenges to security and peace. It has become a global problem, and represents a daily menace in many developed and developing countries. Tens of real or hypothetical terror-plot threats and thousands of individuals are under tight surveillance. The human and material costs of terrorism are tremendous. In 2006 alone, there were 6,425 terrorist incidents, with 11,886 fatalities – about 75 percent of them took place in the Middle East/Persian Gulf region.[1] The 1990s saw the emergence of religious factors behind terrorism, and a growing recourse to suicide attacks, which exacerbates tensions between civilizations. In particular, religious terrorism opposes the West to the Muslim world, undermines the integration of foreign communities in immigration countries, and stimulates xenophobia in many places. It may lead to international conflicts, and de facto it delays pacification in specific regions. In the long term, terrorism could reduce the scope for political, social, and economic progress in developing countries, enlarge the North–South divide in terms of wealth and income, and weaken democratic rules and human rights in the richer countries.

This chapter addresses terrorism with a focus on selected economic and policy issues, including a tentative cost–benefit analysis of anti-terrorism based on recent quantitative findings. Considering the vast amount of literature on terrorism published after 9/11, a selection of material had to be made, partly relying on personal preferences. It should be made clear that terrorism is a complex phenomenon that combines many factors such as social conditions, minority and majority status, social stratification and mobility, "territoriality," history, politics, human rights and freedoms, governance and corruption, demographic trends, cultural identity, and modernization.[2]

---

[1] See the Memorial Institute for the Prevention of Terrorism, www.tkb.org

[2] See L. Richardson (ed.), *The Roots of Terrorism*, New York, Routledge, 2006.

Subsequently, for the sake of effectiveness, economic measures that address terrorism must be designed in the context of broad strategies that integrate other and more important dimensions, which goes far beyond the present work.

1. The problem: the costs of terrorism

Definition of terrorism and data collection

There are many definitions of terrorism proposed by the media, experts, academia, research, politicians, governments, and international organizations. Nevertheless, decades ago, experts already predicted that the dispute about a detailed and comprehensive definition of terrorism will not result in consensus.[3] The absence of a universally accepted definition of terrorism matters for policymakers, citizens – particularly in democracies – and the international community, and might have significant economic consequences. For instance, the use of public funds to address so-called terrorism by governments and international organizations has to be justified by those who may advocate costly, risky, and far-reaching responses such as the use of military forces in third countries. Text Box 15.1 presents the US definition of terrorism.

The systematic record of statistical data and other information on what is seen as terrorism is relatively recent; despite shortcomings, documentary bases are used for studying the issue, testing hypotheses, providing explanations, and policy advice. One database is being developed by the so-called ITERATE project in the United States and contains statistics that are used for modeling; another database – interactive – is proposed by the (National) Memorial Institute for the Prevention of Terrorism, MIPT. Both databases are definitely useful and powerful tools. Nevertheless, for some experts, and the former UN Secretary-General, the high figures provided for some countries, Iraq in particular, would be better classified under labels other than terrorism – e.g. civil war.[4]

---

[3] For more details, see Omar Malik, *Enough of the Definition of Terrorism*, Royal Institute of International Affairs, London, 2001.

[4] For Kofi Annan, "the violence in Iraq is (even) worse than civil war," BBC, 4 December 2006.

Text Box 15.1: How do you define terrorism?

The Intelligence Community is guided by the definition of terrorism contained in Title 22 of the US Code, Section 2656f(d):

- The term "terrorism" means premeditated, politically moti-
  vated violence perpetrated against non-combatant targets by
  sub-national groups or clandestine agents, usually intended to
  influence an audience.
- The term "international terrorism" means terrorism involving
  the territory or the citizens of more than one country.
- The term "terrorist group" means any group that practices, or
  has significant subgroups that practice, international terrorism.

Source: CIA website.

History and geography of terrorism

From the 1960s until the late 1980s, the main motives for terrorism
were political. The nature of terrorism changed over time with more
internationalization, the emergence of religious factors in the 1990s,
and the growing recourse to suicide. Figure 15.1, that shows the
number of incidents worldwide over the period 1968–2006, reveals an
exponential trend for recent years, which reflects the Middle East –
especially Iraqi – situation (see table 15.1); the situation in Iraq in terms
of number of incidents, injuries, and deaths, seems to have deteriorated
further in 2007. Nevertheless, as indicated by figure 15.2, all conti-
nents are or have been confronted with the scourges of terrorism,
which has become a global and growing threat.

Research on terrorism

Besides political/ideological statements and common views spread by
the medias, there are research projects. Available studies indicate a
diversity of approaches ranging from simple descriptive works to
sophisticated time series analysis and modeling. From an applied economic perspective, the US experts Enders and Sandler made some of
the most important seminal works on terrorism, which were followed
by other studies with specific geographical coverage and time frames.

Table 15.1. *Basic statistics on terror in 10 countries, 2005*

Country	Incidents	Injuries	Fatalities
Afghanistan	207	328	298
Colombia	101	208	112
India	272	1051	398
Iraq	**2336**	**9399**	**6234**
Nepal	100	104	33
Pakistan	163	398	160
Russia	102	113	51
Thailand	359	984	148
West Bank/Gaza	479	302	74

Source: MIPT – Terrorism Knowledge Base (www.tkb.org)

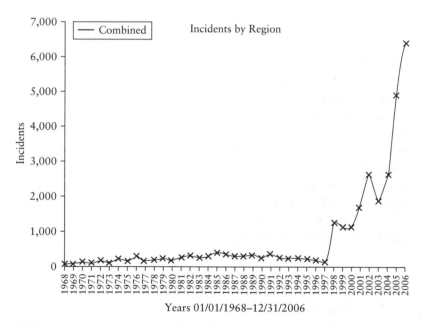

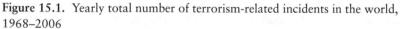

Figure 15.1. Yearly total number of terrorism-related incidents in the world, 1968–2006

Source: MIPT – Terrorism Knowledge Base (www.tkb.org)

The costs of terrorism – the case of 9/11

In addition to the loss of hundreds of lives, permanent disabilities, and suffering, the economic costs of terrorism are manifold and can be tremendous. Considering 9/11, immediate costs corresponded to the destruction of buildings and planes. The destruction of physical assets amounted to about $14 billion for the private sector and $2.2 billion for the public sector. In addition, rescue, cleanup and related costs represented at least $11 billion. The price of most financial assets fell. The insurance business had to disburse up to $58 billion, the largest insurance disbursement in history. In New York, 200,000 jobs were lost or reallocated.[5] Another consequence is the imposition of more controls on the shipping and transportation industry. A third economic outcome of 9/11 is the rise of public expenditures on national security. In addition, the private sector is investing more on security and, as a result, economic growth performance could decrease.[6] The welfare costs in terms of people's utility losses – because, for instance, of higher stress when traveling – should be added.[7] "The costs of misplaced policies, including the use of threat assessments to distort political outcomes" could be considered.[8] The impacts for less-developed economies were and are still far from negligible. Short-term impacts corresponded *inter alia* to wider bonds spreads on financial markets. In the long term, the higher costs of border control will impact on exports; tourism, immigration, and workers' remittances are also affected.[9]

---

[5] For more details, see "Economic Consequences of Terrorism," *OECD Economic Outlook*, No. 71, Chapter 4.

[6] J. Penm, B. Buetre, and Q. T. Tran, "Economic Costs of Terrorism: An Illustration of the Impact of Lower Productivity Growth on World Economic Activity Using GTEM (Global Trade and Environment Model)," Australian Bureau of Agricultural and Resource Economics (ABARE) *e*Report 04.8, Government of Australia, 2004.

[7] B. S. Frey, S. Luechinger, and A. Stutzer, "Calculating Tragedy: Addressing the Costs of Terrorism," University of Zurich, mimeo, July 22, 2004.

[8] This critical view is expressed by D. Gold, "The Costs of Terrorism and the Costs of Countering Terrorism," New School University (New York), International Affairs WP 20050–3, March 2005.

[9] "Economic Consequences of Terrorism," *OECD Economic Outlook*, No. 71, p. 134.

Table 15.2. *GDP gains from less terrorism, 2002*

Country	Reduce incidents per year from:	Gain in GDP million US$
Colombia	13 to 12	87
Egypt	5 to 4	221
France	18 to 17	1,161
India	5 to 4	1,132
Indonesia	2 to 1	1,533
Philippines	9 to 8	122
Spain	1 to 0	92,000
UK	18 to 17	828
US	3 to 2	40,626
World	To zero for 2002	3,600,000

Source: N. Crain and M. Crain, "Terrorized Economies," unpublished manuscript, May 2005

The global cost of terrorism

Nicole and Mark Crain provide a model to estimate the costs of terrorism and the benefits of anti-terrorism, with the use of panel data from the ITERATE project. The model explains real GDP per capita and includes several indicators of terrorism activities, and other "controls" such as the total population in a country, the share of government expenditures in GDP, school enrollment, and the relative importance of trade. They consider 11,723 incidents of terror in 147 countries over the period 1968–2002, with corresponding 37,137 casualties – i.e. the number of individuals killed or injured, with 2002 as the reference year:

The results reveal that the potential gains to a country from reducing terrorism are quite large . . . Most striking is the estimated world cost of terrorism, or the benefit of eliminating all international terrorism. If there were no terrorism incidents in 2002, world GDP would have been *USD3.6 trillion* [emphasis mine] higher than it was that year.[10]

The figure mentioned by Crain and Crain is quite large indeed. It is more than the combined GDP of the United Kingdom and Italy; it

[10] N. Crain and M. Crain, "Terrorized Economies," unpublished manuscript, May 2005, p. 33.

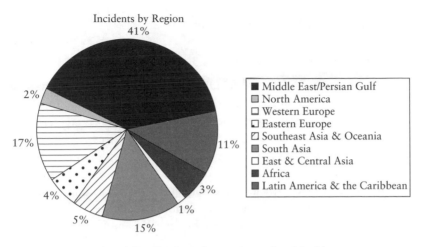

Figure 15.2. Regional distribution of terrorism-related incidents, 1/1/1968–16/01/2007

Source: MIPT – Terrorism Knowledge Base (www.tkb.org)

corresponds to about one-third of US GDP, or 7–9 percent of world GDP. Table 15.2 provides the costs of terrorism for selected rich and less rich countries.

New terror threats

The global costs of terrorism, as provided in the Crains' study, are tremendous. They may rise further with so-called weapons of mass destruction (WMDs), which includes dirty bombs, nuclear, biological, and chemical weapons. Anthrax was already used on a small scale in the United States just after 9/11. A radiological attack is seen as a credible threat and could use materials stored in thousands of facilities located in many countries, rich and poor. Some countries – so-called rogue or failed states – could eventually supply terrorist organizations with WMDs, which would correspond to one of the worst scenarios.[11] Terrorists may also target critical transportation and telecommunication infrastructures, disrupting international trade and the movement of people.

[11] Testimony on Terrorist Nuclear Threat of Dr. Henry Kelly, President, Federation of American Scientists, before the Senate Committee of Foreign Relations, March 6, 2002.

2. Solutions: addressing terrorism

Data analysis and prediction

In a recent work, Enders and Sandler propose a statistical analysis of time series on terrorism. Spectral density functions show that incidents display cyclical patterns with the combination of a primary cycle of 58.18 quarters and a secondary cycle of 23.98 quarters.[12] The detection of cycles could support the making of forecasting models and, as a result, better plan the mobilization of public resources and anti-terrorist forces.[13] Nevertheless, one may question its feasibility because, implicitly, it assumes terrorist groups cannot obtain the relevant information, which is in fact partly available in books and articles.

Suicide terrorism

"Suicide terrorism is the readiness to sacrifice one's life in the process of destroying or attempting to destroy a target to advance a political goal. The aim of the psychologically and physically war-trained terrorist is to die while destroying the enemy target."[14] Confined until recently to a few countries, suicide terrorism is becoming a global and permanent threat, and it represents a category that requires more research for better understanding.[15] Harrison provided an economic explanation to suicide terrorism – "trading life for identity" is what matters.[16] Thus, there would be a rational choice behind suicide terrorism, i.e. a welfare gain by anticipating death, especially when it is going to be covered extensively by medias. As the number of suicide terrorist acts increases, there could be diminishing returns, reducing incentives for suicide. Responses to suicide

---

[12] See W. Enders and T. Sandler, "Is Transnational Terrorism Becoming More Threatening?" *Journal of Conflict Resolution*, Vol. 44, No. 3, June 2000, pp. 307–332.

[13] "Quantitative Analysis Offers Tools to Predict Likely Terrorist Moves," no author, *Wall Street Journal*, Science Section, February 17, 2006, p. B1.

[14] "Suicide Terrorism: A Global Threat," *Jane's Intelligence Review*, October 20, 2000.

[15] See Rohan Gunaratna, "The Employment of Suicide in Terrorism and Guerrilla Warfare," in *"Vers une privatisation des conflits?"* Fondation pour la Recherche Stratégique (Paris), Recherches & Documents, No. 22, April 2001, pp. 43–60.

[16] M. Harrison, "The Eonomics of Martyrdom," Warwick University, research paper, 2003.

terrorism must target sponsors, trainers and their hosting countries, and ideologists who promote hate crimes and mobilize candidates.

Poverty and terrorism

The linkage between terrorism and social conditions is a complex one. Following 9/11, different views were expressed. Those who support an absence of linkage seem to reflect a tradition for which individuals are fully aware of their choices, behave rationally, and should bear the full consequence of their acts.[17] Krueger and Maleckova wrote one of the most representative articles on terrorism in which the impact of economic conditions is minimized.[18] They conclude that econometric models yield little in terms of predictions because non-economic factors such as personal ambitions do also matter to explain terrorism. Abadie reports similar findings.[19] In the case of 9/11, terrorists were far from being poor and were educated; some of them would belong to the middle class.

The above conclusions are challenged by analyses proposed for the Middle East and other regions. For instance, a study proposed by Saleh underlines that beside retaliation and vengeance factors, GDP-related and unemployment variables matter to explain youth violence in the West Bank and Gaza.[20] Considering Chechnya, despite assistance for reconstruction, the region remains characterized by widespread poverty made worse by environmental degradation, and conditions unconducive to business, with high levels of corruption and rampant crime.[21] The world leaders also admit that: "Poverty in all its forms is the greatest single threat to peace, security, democracy, human rights

---

[17] This corresponds to the "Economics of Crime" of Nobel prizewinner G. Becker.

[18] A. Krueger and J. Maleckova, "Education, Poverty and Terrorism: Is there a Causal Connection?" NBER Working Paper No. 9074, July 2002. A version of that paper was also published in the *Journal of Economic Perspectives* in 2003.

[19] A. Abadie, "Poverty, Political Freedom, and the Roots of Terrorism," NBER Working Paper No. 10879, October 2004.

[20] B. A. Saleh, "Economic Conditions as a Determinant of Political Violence in the Palestinian Territories," paper prepared for the Conference "Making Peace Work," organized by the World Institute for Development Economics Research (WIDER), United Nations University, Helsinki, June 4–5, 2004.

[21] D. Linotte and M. Yoshii, "The Reconstruction of Chechnya: A Long-Term and Daunting Task," *Central Asia and the Caucasus, Journal of Social and Political Studies* (Sweden), Vol. 5, No. 23, 2003.

and the environment."[22] Causality can work the other direction too: terrorism negatively impacts on businesses and may cause significant economic decline, as has been the case of the Basque region in Spain. De facto, a case-by-case approach should be the rule when assessing the relationship between social conditions and violence.

Wealth and the sponsoring of terror

Terrorist organizations use money laundering to recycle illicit funds. Money laundering is a complex process by which illicit money is (re-) integrated in the economy to finance legal activities. The al-Qaeda network has used money laundering, relying on the services offered in major financial and offshore centers located in several countries. Some wealthy Islamic donors and charity institutions, where clerics might play key roles, funded al-Qaeda.[23] Moreover, the involvement of Saudi officials, diplomats or their relatives in the funding of 9/11 remains unclear,[24] which indicates that in addition to poverty, and possibly by exploiting unique opportunities created by poverty and distress, oil rents could fund terrorism.[25]

Following 9/11, the international community is better equipped to supervise formal banking operations and detect suspicious transfers. The recommendations of the Financial Action Task Force (FATF) represent a "must" for financial systems, and they are adopted in many countries with IMF support.[26] Nevertheless, more must be done to implement effectively FATF recommendations, especially in developing countries; moreover, terrorist organizations rely on informal banking, and international seed money for terrorism can be complemented and replaced by legal economic activities; in the case of 9/11, the pilot lessons amounted to a few thousands dollars.

---

[22] Statement of M. Moore, head of WTO, at the summit on development held in Monterrey, Mexico. At the same summit, several leaders said that defeating poverty would thwart a major driving force behind international terrorism. See "Poverty Fuelling Terrorism," BBC News, March 22, 2002.

[23] D. Linotte, "Addressing Economic and Financial Aspects of Terrorism," paper prepared for the London International Conference "Stop Money Laundering," February 26–27, 2002.

[24] See "FBI Probes Possible Saudi, 9/11 Money Ties," CNN, November 23, 2002.

[25] The oil and gas rent is also used by Iran to support foreign policy ambitions in the Middle East and finance a controversial nuclear program.

[26] See www.fatf-gafi.org

Trade, terrorism, and security

There are growing concerns about the use of normal trade for carrying arms and weapons of mass destruction to hit targets such as large cities and other populated areas. When the final destination is reached, weapons/bombs can be used or exploded, causing massive damage, killing thousands of people, and disturbing the economy. At the same time, the globalization process requires the adoption of trade facilitation measures and easing the movement of people for business and tourism purposes. In other words, security measures may conflict with the opening of borders and the removal of remaining obstacles to trade, beyond the reduction of import duties within the WTO framework.

The use of modern technologies and the adoption of common security norms and control procedures are required to address risks related to the misuse of trade for terror purposes. That would conciliate the imperative of trade facilitation and the fight against terrorism. Nevertheless, the costs of security measures is large and their imposition could be detrimental to trade and economic growth in the short term. Thus, an OECD study indicates that adopting maritime security measures would cost the shipping industry $1.3 billion, excluding operation, maintenance, and upgrading costs.[27] Developing countries are also lacking resources and expertise to meet security requirements, and assistance will have to be provided by rich countries.

Immigration and terrorism

Immigrants and nationals with foreign roots were involved in 9/11 and the more recent acts of terrorism in Western Europe. These involvements raise concerns about immigration policies and integration in host countries. The fact that some terrorists were born in the West and integrated in their communities with regular jobs, and that some of them had families with children, indicate that full integration is not enough to prevent radicalization and enrollment in complots. Demographic tendencies for Muslim countries and

---

[27] See H. Okayama, "Trade Facilitation and Security," paper presented at the 15th PECC General Meeting, Focus Workshop on Trade, Brunei Darussalam, September 1, 2003.

minority communities in host countries, particularly in Western
Europe, are seen as worrisome by some "native-Europeans," populist
politicians, and journalists – scenarios show Muslims as becoming a
prominent religious group and political force in Europe, which may
impact on anti-terrorism.[28]

Immediate measures could relate to a severing of immigration procedures and border controls and, in countries where they apply, a lowering of quotas to reduce the number of incomers. More controls of
"non-native communities" could also be advocated. However, such
measures may create tensions between domestic and foreign communities in host countries, and could represent a loss of human rights. In
addition, many host/destination countries are characterized by pessimistic demographic tendencies, which implies that immigration is
important for labor supply, and possibly the payment of retirement
benefits. Emigration pressures in home/origin developing countries
should not decrease because of positive demographic trends, political
uncertainties, limited economic prospects, and environmental degradation. In other words, West European countries are confronted with
dilemmas.

Long-term solutions could insist on the assimilation of incomers and
their descents. Thus, a line is often drawn between integration and
assimilation. Broadly speaking, integration refers to the effective inclusion in a society that can be composed of different ethnical, cultural,
and religious segments that may have little in common – they coexist,
most often in peace. Assimilation is more demanding: one cultural
group, very often a minority, is to a large extent absorbed by another
group, the majority one, and adopts new values. Nevertheless, assimilation per se is another sensitive issue in societies that favor tolerance
and mutual respect, as should be the case for Western countries. Social
mobility policies could be enhanced with education programs and more
equal chances for minorities on labor markets – which requires addressing "Islamophobia" in Europe[29] and the United States (see figure 15.3).
Development aid, including support to democratization, human rights,
and the reduction of gender gaps, could also be increased to contain
emigration.

---

[28] Daniel Pipes, "Muslim Europe," *New York Sun*, May 11, 2004.
[29] See "New Report Says Muslims Face Broad Discrimination," Radio Free
Europe/Radio Liberty, December 18, 2006.

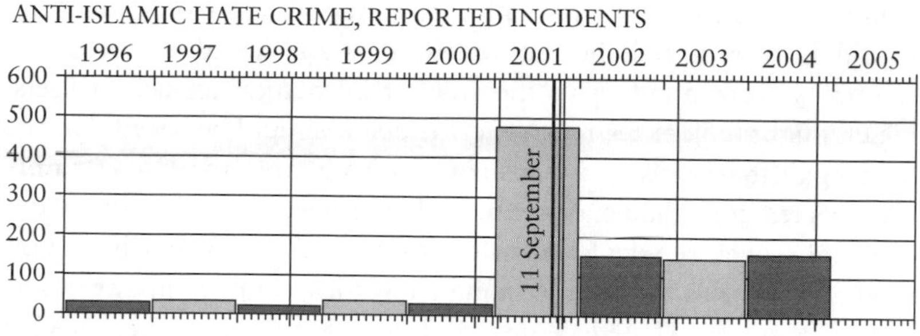

ANTI-ISLAMIC HATE CRIME, REPORTED INCIDENTS

Figure 15.3. The impact of 9/11 on anti-Islamic crimes in the US

Source: FBI.

3. Cost–benefit analysis of anti-terrorism

The calculation of a benefit/cost (B/C) ratio requires the valuation of the gross benefits of anti-terrorism and corresponding costs.

Benefits of no terrorism at all

The Crain and Crain model "provide[s] a foundation to compute the costs of terrorism and the benefits of antiterrorism activities." Thus, estimated equations can be used to estimate the benefits of reducing terrorism from national, regional or global perspectives. As already mentioned, the world GDP would have been $3.6 trillion higher without terrorism at all in the year 2002. The Crains' paper does not provide the cost of eliminating completely terrorism in 2002, the reference year, which would permit the calculation of a B/C ratio. Thus, the proposed figure should be seen as a net benefit. Gross benefits must integrate the total cost of policies and measures that would allow the complete elimination of acts of terror – assuming it can be done!

The costs of anti-terrorism

The actual total cost of all policies and measures that matter in the fight against terror in the world are not known and there seems to be no real attempt to gather adequate information about it. Such information would definitely be useful for governments and international organizations, especially when the rule should be international cooperation and coordination of the fight against terror.

In this paper, I assume that a full elimination of terrorism in 2002 would have required the mobilization of considerable forces and resources corresponding to the sum of all actual defense budgets, which might look excessive. Nevertheless, it should be noted that the fight against terrorism is mobilizing considerable foreign – mainly US – forces in Afghanistan, Iraq, and ex-Soviet Central Asian countries; moreover, the deployment of troops and equipment in distant foreign countries requires complex logistics support in the home country, in the United States and allied countries, i.e. NATO members and some others (such as Austria and Japan); in most countries, several non-military state agencies are also involved in the fight against terrorism, and private companies are investing to increase security levels.

In addition, rich countries are providing aid to many developing countries to help the adoption of new anti-terrorism measures and the acquisition of modern equipment such as patrol boats and computers, and international organizations are involved in the fight against terror. In other words, using the defense budgets as benchmarks does make some sense for a cost–benefit analysis (CBA) of anti-terrorism. In the year 2002, just after the 9/11 events, the total world expenditures on defense amounted to about $0.8 trillion.

Comparing benefits and costs (the B/C ratio)

When adding the "world" defense budget (i.e. $0.8 trillion) to the net benefits of the complete elimination of terrorism in 2002 ($3.6 trillions), the gross benefits value is $4.4 trillions. The corresponding B/C ratio is 5.5 (equal to 4.4/0.8), which could correspond to a low estimate because we believe that the optimal costs of the fight against terrorism could be smaller than actual defense expenditures. Nevertheless, one may also argue that the magnitude of B is somehow too high – in which case, there would be overestimation for the numerator and the denominator.

Limitations of the CBA

Additional data and information about the costs of terrorism and the resources that are needed to fight terrorism are required to provide more precise B/C estimates. Non-economic variables should not be forgotten. Human suffering caused by terrorism is omitted from economic calculations. Military actions in Afghanistan and Iraq are stimulating anti-Western feelings, particularly in the Muslim and developing world. The price of oil has also increased over the last few years, which undermines economic activities in developed and developing countries, and creates more uncertainties about the future of energy security. Moreover, the world is far from homogenous and not all countries are really engaged in the fight against terrorism. In other words, collective preferences differ among countries. When countries are lining up together, there might also be differences in terms of social discount rates and time horizons.

Conclusions and final remarks

As mentioned in the introduction, the roots of terrorism are manifold and do not relate to only economic factors. Nevertheless, economic measures, policies, and strategies can definitely contribute to the fight against terrorism. Table 15.3 underlines that some measures can be quickly (and are de facto already) implemented. Considering the use of CBA to support the decision-making process in the fight against terrorism and our preliminary findings, I believe that corresponding B/C ratios are quite high. Recent calculations in terms of GDP also indicate that huge potential gains can accrue from the reduction of terrorism. Additional research is certainly needed to be more conclusive. Meanwhile, the fight against terrorism should be expected to remain one of the top priorities on the agenda of most governments.

The key issue is *how* best to address and reduce terrorism successfully. Anti-terrorist punitive actions can become counterproductive, especially when they are not restrained and lead to fierce retaliation, which contributes to vicious circles of violence. Whenever possible, military-type operations should be replaced, or at least complemented, by active diplomacy with adequate levels of aid to address the economic, social, and political roots of violence – without compromising with those who advocate intolerance and hate crimes! A long-awaited "Marshall Plan" for the Middle East, that involves all parties, should be seen as a top priority in the fight against terror – which requires the consolidation of the Palestinian Entity, and the recognition of Israel by its neighbors. In the Iraqi case, there seems to be a need to involve Iran and Syria, assuming they are really interested

Table 15.3. *Addressing terrorism – synthesis table*

The issue	Measures/policies	Time frame	Problems and risks
Predicting terrorism with data analysis	Building time series and econometric models	Short term; can be done quickly at low costs	Data are not always available or lack accuracy; terrorists could know publicized forecasts and adjust their plans
Preventing terrorism with poverty reduction	Adoption of poverty alleviation policies and strategies; institutional development; building business-conducive environments	Medium and long term	Lack of resources is an issue and foreign aid does not often fill the gap
Deterring terrorism by fighting dirty money	Adopting measures to better detect and prevent suspicious financial flows and transactions	Short and medium term	Lack of experience and expertise is an issue; external aid required for some countries
Impeding terrorism with trade-related measures	Adopting new control instruments for international commerce in line with trade facilitation measures	Medium term	Low and medium income countries are lacking resources and experience; assistance is required
Diffusing terrorism by better controlling immigration	Enhancing controls on the cross-border movement of people; more assimilation if possible; access to good education and equal chances for all; reducing incentives for emigration	Medium and long term	More hostile attitude against immigrants and minorities in host countries; development aid insufficient

in the building of peace in the region. In many places, significant societal changes and political reforms must contribute to the building of more "open and democratic societies" and, as a result, reduce incentives for terrorism. In that context, the UN should definitely play the leading role to foster multilateralism, universal values, and global governance.

PART IV

Health and Population

16 | *Drugs*

JEFFREY A. MIRON

The challenge of illicit drugs

The challenge of illicit drugs is to balance the negatives of drug use against the negatives of policies that attempt to reduce drug use. Drug use can reduce health and productivity. Drug use can cause traffic and industrial accidents, harm unborn fetuses, and diminish the public purse if drug users make excessive use of government-funded health care. Policies that attempt to reduce drug use, however, have their own costs. These include: black markets, violence, corruption, unwarranted restrictions on use of drugs as medicine, excessive restrictions on civil liberties, aiding terrorism, the increased spread of HIV, enriching criminals, diminished respect for the law, and the direct costs of enforcing these policies. The question is therefore which policy achieves the best balancing of costs and benefits?

The solution

The solution proposed here is to legalize the production, sale, distribution and possession of all illicit drugs. A legalized regime might include a number of auxiliary policies that currently apply to alcohol and tobacco, such as driving-under-the-influence laws, sin taxation, age restrictions, subsidized treatment, advertising restrictions, and the like. The analysis here takes no stand on these auxiliary policies; the conclusions hold under any reasonable set of auxiliary policies so long as these occur in a regime where drugs are legal and not subject to regulation or taxation that drives the market underground.

An analysis of prohibition versus legalization

To assess legalization relative to prohibition I first review prohibition's impacts on drug users, non-users, and society generally. I then consider the implications of these impacts for choosing between prohibition and legalization. I conclude that available evidence makes a compelling case for legalization over prohibition.[1]

Prohibition does not eliminate the market for illicit drugs. Instead, it creates a black market. The key question for analysis of prohibition versus legalization is to what degree the amount of drug consumption in this black market is less than would occur under legalization. To address this issue, I consider the effects of prohibition on the demand for and supply of drugs.

Prohibition affects the demand for drugs in several ways. The mere existence of prohibition might reduce demand if some consumers exhibit respect for the law. The evidence suggests, however, that "respect for the law" exerts only a mild effect, since violation of weakly enforced laws (speeding, tax evasion, blue laws, sodomy laws) is widespread. The penalties for drug purchase or possession might reduce demand by raising the effective price of drug use. Again, however, the evidence does not suggest a major impact given that most such penalties are mild and rarely imposed. And, potentially countering any tendency for prohibition to reduce demand, prohibition might increase demand to the extent it makes drugs a "forbidden fruit."

Prohibition also affects the supply of drugs. Because black market drug suppliers must operate in secret and attempt to avoid detection by law enforcement, they face increased costs of manufacturing, transporting, and distributing drugs. Conditional on operating in secret, however, black market suppliers face low marginal costs of evading tax laws and regulatory policies, and this partially offsets the increased costs of operating in secret. Other differences between a black market and a legal market (e.g., differences in advertising incentives or market power) have ambiguous implications for supply costs under prohibition versus legalization.

The bottom line is that prohibition probably reduces drug consumption, since the direct effects on both supply and demand suggest this outcome. Theory does not dictate that prohibition causes a large reduction in drug use, however. And the evidence suggests prohibition has, at most, a moderate impact on drug consumption. Alcohol

---

[1] The analysis here follows Miron (2004). It is also consistent with the analysis in Becker, Grossman, and Murphy (2004).

Prohibition in the United States, for example, does not appear to have reduced alcohol consumption dramatically. Comparisons of countries with weak versus strongly imposed prohibitions find little evidence of higher drug consumption in the weak enforcement countries. And variations in enforcement of drug prohibition over time in the United States do not appear to have been associated with substantial fluctuations in drug consumption. For example, US enforcement of drug prohibition expanded dramatically between the late 1970s and the present day. Over this time period, drug prices fell substantially, yet consumption was relatively unchanged. Thus the evidence is consistent with the view that drug consumption might increase 25% under legalization, but there is no evidence to suggest it would be increased by orders of magnitude.

In addition to reducing drug consumption, prohibition has numerous other effects. Most of these occur to a substantial degree whether prohibition's impact on drug use is large or small. I describe each of these briefly.

Increased crime

Participants in illegal markets cannot resolve disputes using non-violent mechanisms like courts and lawyers, so they use guns instead; thus prohibition increases violent crime. Violence increased dramatically in the US during Alcohol Prohibition and then decreased just as dramatically upon repeal. The ups and downs of the homicide rate in the US over the past century coincide with the ups and downs in drug prohibition enforcement. Differences in violence across countries correlate well with differences in prohibition enforcement. Also, commodities like prostitution and gambling are associated with violence mainly when they are prohibited.

By raising drug prices, prohibition also encourages income-generating crime such as theft or prostitution, since users need additional income to purchase drugs. And by diverting criminal justice resources to drug prohibition enforcement, prohibition causes reduced deterrence of all kinds of crime. Because participants in a black market must either evade law enforcement authorities or pay them to look the other way, prohibition also encourages corruption.

The conclusion that prohibition causes crime contrasts with the usual claim that drug use causes crime. However, the evidence provides little indication that drug use promotes violence or other criminal behavior. Instead, the evidence makes a compelling case that the causation flows from prohibition to crime and corruption through a variety of mechanisms.

Harm to drugs users

By raising drug prices and creating the threat of arrest and other legal sanctions, prohibition reduces the welfare of those who use drugs. These users also spend more time trying to buy drugs and must deal with criminals in order to do so. These effects may discourage some drug consumption; I discuss below how to account for policy-induced reductions in drug consumption. But the higher prices and legal penalties experienced by those who continue to use drugs are unambiguously costs of prohibition.

Reduced product quality

In a legal market, consumers who purchase faulty goods can punish suppliers by pursuing liability claims, by generating bad publicity, by avoiding repeat purchases, or by complaining to private or government watchdog groups. In a black market, these mechanisms are unavailable or less effective. This means product quality is lower and more uncertain. For example, deaths from adulterated alcohol soared during US Alcohol Prohibition. In current drug markets, variable product quality and purity potentially explain many accidental overdoses and poisonings.

Enriching criminals

In a legal market, the income generated by production and sale of drugs is subject to taxation, and the tax revenues accrue to the government. In a black market, suppliers capture these revenues as profits. Prohibition thus enriches the segment of society most willing to evade the law. The revenue involved is substantial – existing estimates suggest the illicit drug market generates hundreds of billions of dollars in annual income worldwide, so at standard tax rates governments could collect tens of billions of dollars in additional revenue each year by legalizing and taxing currently illegal drugs.

Increased spread of HIV

By increasing drug prices, prohibition increases the incentive to inject drugs since this ingestion method provides a large "bang-for-the-buck." It also encourages restrictions on the sale of syringes. This means an increased incentive to share dirty needles that increases the spread of HIV, hepatitis, and other blood-borne diseases. In recent years a substantial fraction of HIV transmission in developed economies has occurred due to needle sharing.

Restrictions on medicinal uses of drugs

Because of prohibition, marijuana is even more tightly controlled than morphine or cocaine and cannot be used for medical purposes despite abundant evidence that it alleviates nausea, pain, and muscle spasms and symptoms of glaucoma, epilepsy, multiple sclerosis, AIDS, and migraine headaches, among other ailments. Also, because of prohibition, doctors fear legal sanctions for over-prescribing opiates and thus under-treat pain in cancer patients and others with chronic conditions.

Compromised civil liberties

Because drug crimes involve voluntary exchange, enforcement relies on asset seizures, aggressive search tactics, and racial profiling. All these tactics strain accepted notions of civil liberties and generate racial tension.

Aiding terrorism

Prohibition creates a major source of cash income in countries like Colombia and Afghanistan. Terrorist groups that have expertise in "violence" can therefore sell protection services to drug traffickers. Legalization would not by itself eliminate these terrorists groups. But it would eliminate most of the profits that help fund terrorism, and it would free national armies and police to target insurgent or terrorist groups rather than worrying about drug traffickers. Plus, legalization would not generate the resentment against government, and sympathy for insurgent groups, that occurs when governments conduct counter-drug operations like crop eradication.

Respect for the law

All experience to date indicates that, even with draconian enforcement, prohibition fails to deter a great many persons from supplying and consuming drugs. This fact signals to users and non-users that laws are for suckers; prohibition therefore undermines the spirit of voluntary compliance that is essential to law enforcement in a free society.

Direct costs of enforcement

Beyond all these effects, prohibition entails substantial direct costs for enforcement in the form of police, prosecutors, judges, and prisons. To some degree the effects of prohibition described above "double count" the direct costs, since the indirect effects of enforcement are part and parcel of enforcement (e.g., the threat of arrest faced by drug users). To a substantial degree, however, these indirect effects are separate, in part because enforcement can have effects that are disproportionate to the expenditure, in part because many of the indirect effects are externalities from enforcement that harm those with no direct involvement in drug supply or drug use (e.g., reduced civil liberties, increased terrorism, increased crime, restrictions on medicinal uses of drugs, and so on).

Given this assessment of prohibition's effects on drug users, nonusers, and society generally, I now consider under what conditions legalization is preferable to prohibition. Most effects of prohibition are unambiguously undesirable. The one possible exception is the impact on reducing drug consumption. I therefore discuss the conditions under which policy-induced reductions in drug consumption should be regarded as a cost or benefit.

Under the rational model of drug consumption, people consume drugs because it makes them better off.[2] In this case any prohibition-induced reduction in drug use is a cost, not a benefit. Thus, if all drug consumption is rational, prohibition's effects are all negative. Existing evidence in no way suggests that all drug use should be considered rational. At the same time, some drug use appears to fit the rational model. Many people claim to enjoy the high associated with marijuana consumption; others value the pain relief or mental calm produced by

---

[2] I use the term rational to mean rational and time-consistent, as in Becker and Murphy (1988).

opiates; still others appreciate the stimulation of cocaine. And many drugs users, even heavy users of hard drugs, do little harm to themselves or others. A full evaluation of prohibition, therefore, should include as a cost any reduction in drug use by persons who would use drugs responsibly.

Even if drug consumption is rational, however, such consumption might harm innocent third parties – generate externalities – and thus be excessive from society's perspective. For example, drug consumption can impair one's ability to drive a car or operate heavy machinery; it can have negative health effects on a fetus or it can cause additional use of publicly funded health care. If externalities are significant, policy should attempt to reduce drug use. The ideal policy is unlikely to be one that drives drug use to zero, however. In particular, if some users generate externalities and others do not, then policy would ideally target only the externality-generating behavior (e.g., driving under the influence) rather than targeting all drug use.

An alternate model of drug consumption holds that some consumers are not rational; they harm themselves by abusing drugs because they fail to account for the negative consequences. This possibility is especially relevant to the extent drug use is addictive and some people are not forward looking or suffer from problems with self-control.[3] According to this view, policy-induced reductions in drug consumption benefit such persons by preventing them from harming themselves. Whether this kind of paternalism is an appropriate basis for policy intervention is subject to some dispute, but I include it here for completeness. Thus, if the increased drug use due to legalization is irrational drug use, then this is a cost of legalization.

Table 16.1 summarizes the discussion above by listing the consequences of prohibition in the left-hand column. Prohibition has a broad range of negative outcomes for drug users, non-users, and society generally. One aspect of these negative outcomes is the reduced welfare of drug users. Prohibition might also have beneficial effects by reducing externalities from drug use and by reducing irrational drug consumption. The remaining question is how do the benefits compare to the costs?

---

[3] I include here both irrational or otherwise myopic consumers as well as rational but time-inconsistent consumers. See Laibson (1997).

Table 16.1. *The benefits and costs of legalizing illicit drugs, United States*

Benefits	Benefit amount
1. Elimination of expenditure on enforcement	$35 billion
2. Reduced crime and corruption	$30 billion
3. Reduced spread of AIDS	$15 billion
4. Improved welfare for drug users	$6 billion
5. Miscellaneous	$3 billion
Increased respect for the law	
Fewer restrictions on civil liberties	
Elimination of redistributions to criminals	
Total benefits from legalization	$89 billion

Cost category	Cost amount
1. Increased externalities from drug use	$12 billion
2. Increased irrational drug use	$12 billion
Total costs from legalization	$24 billion
Net benefits from legalization, US	$65 billion
Net benefits from legalization, Rest of world	$65 billion
Net benefits from legalization, Total	$130 billion

Benefits:
[1] *Elimination of expenditure on enforcement:* See Miron (2004)
[2] *Reductions in violent crime, property crime, and corruption:* Based on the evidence summarized in Miron (2004), I assume legalization would reduce crime by at least 25% overall. Similarly, legalization would reduce corruption. I then assume a per capita willingness-to-pay (WTP) for this magnitude of crime reduction of $100 per person per annum; this is consistent with estimates of the WTP for crime reduction from the literature on crime and property values (Linden and Rockoff 2006). Assuming a population of 300 million implies benefits from crime reduction of $30 billion.
[3] *Reduced incidence of AIDS:* Approximately 5,000 AIDS deaths per year are persons who contracted HIV through needle-sharing (Center for Disease Control 2004). Some of those might have acquired HIV via another mechanism if needle sharing had not occurred, but some pass HIV on to those who transmit it via methods other than needling sharing. Thus, 5,000 deaths is a reasonable base case. Multiplying this number by $3 million per statistical life generates an estimate benefit of $15 billion.
[4] *Improved welfare for existing drug users:* The benefits of legalization to existing drugs users include reduced risk of arrest and less uncertainty about quality. Expenditure on illegal drugs in recent years has been in excess of $60 billion. I assume users would be willing to pay on average 10% extra to avoid the prohibition-induced risks of drug use. This implies a benefit of $6 billion per annum.
[5] *Miscellaneous:* I assume a WTP of $10 per person. Multiplying this by a population of 300 million gives $3 billion.

Table 16.1. (*cont.*)

Costs:

[1] *Externalities from drug use:* To provide a benchmark number, I utilize data on the externalities from cigarettes. Existing estimates (see Gruber and Koszegi (2002)) suggest that the externalities from smoking are roughly the same magnitude as the underlying private costs of production. As a reasonable bound, I therefore assume the externalities from drug use are the same magnitude as the private costs.

To estimate the private costs of drug production, I start with data from ONDCP (2001) on US spending on illicit drugs:

Cocaine	$36.1 billion
Heroin	$11.9 billion
Marijuana	$10.4 billion
Other	$4.5 billion
Total	$62.9 billion

These amounts represent both the private costs that would exist under legalization and the costs due to prohibition enforcement. I estimate the private costs as follows based on Miron (2003) and Miron (2006):

Cocaine	$12 billion
Heroin	$1 billion
Marijuana	$10 billion
Other	$1 billion
Total	$24 billion

Assuming externalities of the same magnitude as private costs, as suggested by the evidence on cigarettes, implies the external costs from drugs under current prohibition are roughly $24 billion.

The cost of drug user externalities due to legalization depends on the amount and nature of any increase in drug use under legalization. Consistent with the evidence discussed in Miron (2004), I take 50% as an upper bound on the increase in drug use, and I assume all of this increase generates externalities at the same rate as current use. This last assumption is plausibly too strong because those whose use would increase under legalization are probably not those generating large externalities.

The combination of these assumptions means the increase in externalities from drug use due to legalization would be $12 billion.

[2] *Increased irrational drug use*

I assume the costs due to increased irrational drug use would be the same magnitude as the externalities from increased drug use; this is consistent with calculations for cigarettes in Gruber and Koszegi (2002). This means an estimate of $12 billion.

Calculating the net benefit of legalization versus prohibition

Quantifying the elements in Table 16.1 is a daunting task. The conceptually clean way to measure many components is WTP data. These

Table 16.2. *PV of benefits, costs and net benefits from legalization under different discount rates*

	Discount factor 3%	Discount factor 6%
Benefits	$5,625 billion	$2,957 billion
Costs	$1,517 billion	$798 billion
Net benefits	$4,108 billion	$2,160 billion
Ratio, B/C	3.71	3.71

Note: The assumed time horizon is one hundred years.

are unavailable for most items, however, and WTP measures are untrustworthy in many instances. I nevertheless provide broad-brush estimates in Table 16.1. The assumptions that underlie these numbers are designed to bias downward the estimated benefits from legalization. Details are provided in the notes after Table 16.1.

I focus on data for the United States because US enforcement of drug prohibition is stronger than in most other countries. This means the benefits and costs from legalization in the rest of the world are plausibly an order of magnitude smaller on a per capita basis. However, aggregating across all countries other than the US, implies at least a similar magnitude of benefits and costs.

The overall implication of these assumptions, as shown in Table 16.1, is that legalization would produce net benefits to the world of $130 billion per year. This would require no increase in government expenditure, and it would produce tax revenue of at least tens of billions of dollars per year. This tax revenue is not by itself an additional benefit; it is a transfer from drug consumers and drug users to the general taxpayer. It is nevertheless a kind of transfer that most citizens would value.

The estimates included in Table 16.1 are an annual flow. The benefit, costs, and net benefits in present value terms depend on the discount rate and the time horizon.[4] Table 16.2 provides some plausible calculations based on two assumed discount rates, 3 percent and 6 percent, and a one-hundred-year time horizon. This table also shows the cost/benefit ratio for the legalization of drugs.

---

[4] The estimates do not depend on an assumed Disability Adjusted Life Year (DALY), so I do not include any tables addressing sensitivity to the DALY.

The bottom line is that legalization would generate a present value net benefit of $2.2 trillion under a 6 percent discount rate and $4.1 trillion under a 3 percent discount rate. The cost/benefit ratio is about 3.7.

Conclusions

The implications of the calculations in Table 16.1 are profound. For many policy interventions, the cost/benefit calculation involves a substantial expenditure of resources in order to obtain a benefit that is uncertain and which might never materialize. This does not mean such interventions are inadvisable, but the risk of spending a lot while getting little return is definitely present.

For the policy intervention proposed here, the situation is reversed. Repeal of prohibition generates a certain, immediate, and substantial reduction in government expenditure. The other potential benefits are uncertain and might not arise, so this aspect of the net benefit calculation involves speculation. At the same time, however, some of the potential costs (e.g., increased abuse of drugs) might also never materialize (if most abusive drug users are already using drugs). Thus, the risk of getting more harm than good is minimal; if anything, legalization might generate the benefits outlined above with few of the costs.

The other key feature of the policy proposed here is that it provides consistency across policies regarding alcohol, tobacco, and drugs. Most societies currently permit, and intend to continue permitting, legal production and consumption of alcohol and tobacco. Since from any reasonable perspective most illicit drugs are no more harmful, if not substantially less harmful, than these legal substances, consistency demands that drugs be legal as well.

References

Becker, Gary S. and Kevin M. Murphy (1988), "A Theory of Rational Addiction," *Journal of Political Economy*, 96, 675–700.
Becker, Gary, Michael Grossman, and Kevin Murphy (2004), "The Economic Theory of Illegal Goods: The Case of Drugs," NBER Working Paper No. 10976.
Center for Disease Control (2004), *HIV/AIDS Surveillance Report*, Vol. 16.
Gruber, Jonathan and Botond Koszegi (2002), "A Theory of Government Regulation of Addictive Bads: Optimal Tax Levels and Tax Incidence for Cigarette Excise Taxation," NBER Working Paper No. 8777.

Laibson, David I. (1997), "Golden Eggs and Hyperbolic Discounting," *Quarterly Journal of Economics*, **62**(May), 443–77.

Linden, Leigh L. and Jonah E. Rockoff (2006), "There Goes the Neighborhood? Estimates of the Impact of Crime Risk on Property Values from Megan's Law," NBER Working Paper No. 12253.

Miron, Jeffrey A. (1999), "Violence and the U.S. Prohibitions of Drugs and Alcohol," *American Law and Economics Review*, 1–2, 78–114

    (2003a), "A Critique of Estimates of the Economic Costs of Drug Abuse." *Report to the Open Society Institute,* August 2003.

    (2003b), "Do Prohibitions Raise Prices? Evidence from the Markets for Cocaine and Heroin," *Review of Economics and Statistics*, 85(3), 522–30.

    (2004), *Drug War Crimes: The Consequences of Prohibition,* Independent Institute, Oakland, CA, 2004.

    (2006), "The Budgetary Implications of Marijuana Prohibition." In *New Directions in Marijuana Policy,* Mitch Earleywine (ed.), Oxford: Oxford University Press.

Office of National Drug Control Policy (2001), *What America's Users Spend on Illegal Drugs*, Washington, DC: ONDCP.

17 | Disease Control

DEAN T. JAMISON*

This paper identifies priorities for disease control as an input into the Copenhagen Consensus 2008 (CC08). As such it updates the evidence and differs somewhat in its conclusions from the communicable disease paper (Mills and Shillcutt, 2004) prepared for Copenhagen Consensus 2004, which Lomborg (2006) summarizes.

The paper builds on the results of the Disease Control Priorities Project (DCPP).[1,2] The DCPP engaged over 350 authors and among its outputs were estimates of the cost-effectiveness of 315 interventions. These estimates vary a good deal in their thoroughness and in the extent to which they provide regionally specific estimates of both cost and effectiveness. Taken as a whole, however, they represent a comprehensive canvas of disease control opportunities. Some interventions are clearly low priority. Others are attractive and worth doing but

* Preparation of this paper was supported in part by the Fogarty International Center of the U.S. National Institutes of Health through Purchase Order 263-MK-610514. Conclusions and opinions in the paper do not necessarily reflect those of the sponsor. The author is T. & G. Angelopoulos Visiting Professor of Public Health and International Development, Kennedy School of Government and School of Public Health, Harvard University; and Professor, School of Medicine, University of California, San Francisco.

1 The DCPP was a joint effort, extending over four years, of the Fogarty International Center of the US National Institutes of Health, the World Bank, and the World Health Organization with financial support from the Bill & Melinda Gates Foundation. While the views and conclusions expressed in this paper draw principally on the DCPP, others might draw different broad conclusions. In particular, views expressed in this paper are not necessarily those of any of the sponsoring organizations.

2 The DCPP resulted in two main volumes, both of which Oxford University Press published in 2006. One is *The Global Burden of Disease and Risk Factors* (Lopez et al., 2006a). The other, *Disease Control Priorities in Developing Countries*, 2nd edition (Jamison et al., 2006a), discusses interventions to address diseases and risk factors and the health systems to deliver those interventions. A first edition was published by Oxford University Press for the World Bank in 1993. This paper will refer to these two volumes as *DCP1* and *DCP2*.

either address only a relatively small proportion of disease burden or are simply not quite as attractive as a few key interventions. This paper identifies those key priority interventions and discusses them in the context of a limited range of other possibilities. Separate papers for CC08 deal with malnutrition (Behrman, Alderman, and Hoddinott, this volume), and with water and sanitation (Hutton, this volume).

Section 1 of the paper documents the enormous success in much of the world in the past forty years in improving health in low- and middle-income countries. Its conclusion is that future investments will build on past successes – increasing confidence in the practical feasibility of major additional gains in disease control. Section 2 summarizes evidence that health gains have had major economic impact, and Section 3 uses this economic context to describe the methods used for the cost–benefit analyses reported. Sections 4, 5, and 6 discuss problems and opportunities in child health, HIV/AIDS and noncommunicable disease. Section 7 concludes by identifying the few most attractive options and presenting (very approximate) cost–benefit analyses for them. This paper emphasizes, although not exclusively, opportunities relevant to low-income countries in South Asia and sub-Saharan Africa.

1. Progress and challenges

Health conditions improved markedly throughout the world during most of the second half of the twentieth century and this section begins by highlighting those achievements. Nonetheless major problems remained at the beginning of the twenty-first century. Parts of the world had simply been left behind; declines in mortality and fertility had led to an increasing importance of noncommunicable disease; and the altogether new problems of HIV/AIDS had rapidly become prominent in many countries. Addressing these multiple problems within highly constrained budgets will require hard choices. This section concludes by reviewing these challenges.

1.1 Progress

Table 17.1 shows progress in life expectancy by World Bank region between 1960 and 2002. For the first three decades of this period, progress was remarkably fast – a gain of 6.3 years in life expectancy

Table 17.1. *Levels and changes in life expectancy, 1960–2002, by World Bank Region*

Region	Life expectancy (years)			Rate of change (years per decade)	
	1960	1990	2002	1960–90	1990–2002
Low- and middle-income countries	44	63	65	6.3	1.7
East Asia and the Pacific	39	67	70	9.3	2.5
(China)	(36)	(69)	(71)	(11)	(1.7)
Europe and Central Asia	—	69	69	—	0.0
Latin America and the Caribbean	56	68	71	4.0	2.5
Middle East and North Africa	47	64	69	5.7	4.2
South Asia	44	58	63	4.7	4.2
(India)	(44)	(59)	(64)	(5)	(4.6)
Sub-Saharan Africa	40	60	46	3.3	−3.3
High-income countries	69	76	78	2.3	1.7
World	50	65	67	5.0	1.7

Source: World Bank 2004 (CD-ROM version)
— = not available.
Note: Entries are the average of male and female life expectancies.

per decade on average, in the low- and middle-income countries, albeit with substantial regional variation. Progress continued between 1990 and 2002 but at a much slower pace. This slower pace is due, in great part, to mortality increases from HIV/AIDS. Sub-Saharan Africa actually lost more than four years of life expectancy (although as this chapter goes to press, the United Nations has revised upward its estimates of African life expectancy to suggest neither gain nor loss over the period). Eastern Europe and Central Asia realized no gains.

Since 1950, life expectancy in the median country has steadily converged toward the (steadily growing) maximum, and cross-country differences have decreased markedly (Oeppen and Vaupel, 2002). This reduction in inequality in health contrasts with long-term *increases* in income inequality between and within countries. Yet despite the magnitude of global improvements, many countries and populations have failed to share in the overall gains or have even fallen behind. Some countries – for example, Sierra Leone – remain far behind. China's interior provinces lag behind the more advantaged coastal regions. Indigenous people everywhere probably lead far less healthy lives than do others in their respective countries, although confirmatory data are scant.

Much of the variation in country outcomes appears to result from the very substantial cross-country variation in the rate of diffusion of appropriate health technologies (or "technical progress"). Countries range from having essentially no decline in infant mortality rate caused by technical progress to reductions of up to 5 percent per year (Jamison, Sandbu, and Wang, 2004). Cutler, Deaton, and Lleras-Muney (2006) provide a complementary and extended discussion of the importance of technological diffusion for improvements in health. Factors from outside the health sector also affect the pace of health improvement: education levels of populations appear most important; the level and growth rate of income appear much less so. The importance of technical progress and diffusion should be viewed in this larger context.

However technical progress or diffusion may be manifested, the large differences in its magnitude across countries suggest important effects of a country's health-related policies. This point bears reiterating in a slightly different way: income growth is neither necessary nor sufficient for sustained improvements in health. Today's tools for improving health are so powerful and inexpensive that health conditions can be reasonably good even in countries with low incomes.

Reasons for remaining health inequalities thus lie only partially in poverty or income inequality: the experiences of China, Costa Rica, Cuba, Sri Lanka, and Kerala state in India, among others, conclusively show that dramatic improvements in health can occur without high or rapidly growing incomes. The experiences of countries in Europe in the late nineteenth and early twentieth centuries similarly show that health conditions can improve without prior or concomitant increases in income (Easterlin, 1996). A recent review identified many specific examples of low-cost interventions leading to large and carefully documented health improvements (Levine and the What Works Working Group, 2007). The public sector initiated and financed virtually all of these interventions. The goal of this paper is to assist decision- makers – particularly those in the public sector – to identify the highest priority low-cost intervention to rapidly improve population health and welfare health where the needs are greatest.

1.2 Remaining challenges

Three central challenges for health policy ensue from the pace and unevenness of the progress just summarized and from the evolving nature of microbial threats to human health.

Unequal progress

The initial challenge results from continued high levels of inequality in health conditions across and within countries. Bourguignon and Morrisson (2002) have stressed that global inequalities are declining if one properly accounts for convergence across countries in health conditions, which more than compensates for income divergence. However, in far too many countries health conditions remain unacceptably – and unnecessarily – poor. This factor is a source of grief and misery, and it is a sharp brake on economic growth and poverty reduction. From 1990 to 2001, for example, the under-five mortality rate remained stagnant or increased in twenty-three countries. In another fifty-three countries (including China), the rate of decline in under-five mortality in this period was less than half of the 4.3 percent per year required to reach the fourth Millennium Development Goal (MDG-4). Meeting the MDG for under-five mortality reduction by 2015 is not remotely possible for these countries. (See Lopez, Begg, and Bos [2006] for country-specific estimates of child and adult mortality rates in 1990 and 2001 that were generated in a consistent way over time and across countries.) Yet the examples of many other countries, often quite poor, show that with the right policies dramatic reductions in mortality are possible. A major goal of this paper is to identify strategies for implementing interventions that are known to be highly cost-effective for dealing with the health problems of countries remaining behind – for example, treatment for diarrhea, pneumonia, TB, and malaria; immunization; and other preventive measures to reduce stillbirths and neonatal deaths. Much of the excess burden of disease in high-mortality countries occurs in children, particularly very young children and Table 17.2 summarizes what is known about the causes of deaths under the age of five, and under the age of twenty-eight days, in 2001. Figure 17.1 illustrates the large proportion that occurs under the age of twenty-eight days.

Table 17.2. *Causes of under-five mortality, worldwide in 2001, estimates from the GBD (in thousands)*

Cause	Total	Age 0 to 4	Neonatal (age 0–27 days)	Stillbirths
HIV/AIDS	340	340		
Diarrheal disease	1,600	1,600	116	
Measles	557	557		
Tetanus	187	187	187	
Malaria	1,087	1,087		
Respiratory infection (and sepsis)	1,945	1,945	1,013	
Low birth weight	1,301	1,301	1,098	
Birth asphyxia and birth trauma	739	739	739	
Congenital anomalies	439	439	321	
Injuries	310	310		
Other	5,375	2,101	446	3,274
TOTAL	13,874	10,600	3,900	3,274

Source: Mathers, Murray and Lopez (2006); Jamison (2006); Jamison et al. (2006).
Notes:
1. Of the estimated 13.9 million under-five deaths in 2001 only 0.9% occurred in high-income countries. Thus the cause distribution of deaths in this table is essentially that of low- and middle-income countries.
2. "Stillbirths" are defined as fetal loss in the third trimester of pregnancy. About 33% of stillbirths occur after labor has begun – so-called intrapartum stillbirths. No good estimates exist for stillbirths by cause, but some of the cause categories (e.g. birth asphyxia, birth trauma, congenital anomalies) are the same as for age 0 to 4 so part of what is categorized as "other" in the total row will be distributed among the other existing rows when estimates are available.

Epidemiological transition

A second challenge lies in noncommunicable disease and injury. The next two decades will see continuation of rising trends resulting from dramatic fertility declines (and consequent population aging) in recent decades. The key consequence is that the major noncommunicable diseases – circulatory system diseases, cancers, and major psychiatric disorders – are fast replacing (or adding to) the traditional scourges – particularly infectious diseases and under-nutrition in children. Additionally, injuries resulting from road traffic are replacing more

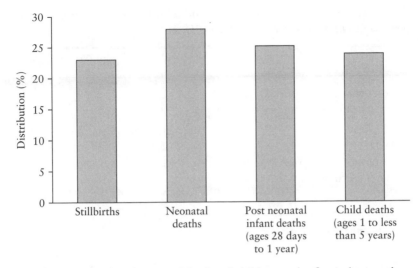

Figure 17.1. Age distribution of deaths of children under five in low- and middle-income countries, 2001

Source: Jamison et al. (2006).

traditional forms of injury. Responding to this epidemiological transition with sharply constrained resources is a key challenge. Table 17.3 provides cause-specific estimates of the number of deaths over age five due to major causes in low- and middle-income countries. This summary indicates that noncommunicable disease already accounts for two/three of all deaths over age five in these countries, although nearly 22 percent of deaths continue to be from infection, undernutrition and maternal conditions, creating a "dual burden" that Julio Frenk and colleagues have pointed to (Bobadilla et al., 1993).

HIV/AIDS epidemic
A third key challenge is the HIV/AIDS epidemic. Control efforts and successes have been very real but, with only a few exceptions, limited to upper-middle-income and high-income countries. Poorer countries remain in the epidemic's deadly path.

2. The economic benefits of better health

The dramatic health improvements globally during the twentieth century arguably contributed as much or more to improvements in

Table 17.3. *Causes of death in low- and middle-income countries, age 5 and older, estimates from the GBD, 2001*

	Deaths (in millions)	% of total
1. *Communicable, maternal, perinatal and nutritional conditions*		
TB	1.5 million	4.0%
AIDS	2.2	5.8
Respiratory infections	1.5	4.0
Maternal conditions	0.5	1.3
Other	2.5	6.6
Subtotal	8.2	21.7
2. *Noncommunicable disease*		
Cancers	4.9	13.0
Diabetes	0.7	1.9
Ischaemic and hypertensive heart disease	6.5	17.2
Stroke	4.6	12.2
Chronic obstructive pulmonary disease	2.4	6.3
Other	6.1	16.1
Subtotal	25.2	66.7
3. *Injuries*		
Road traffic accidents	1.0	2.6
Suicides	0.7	1.9
Other	2.7	7.1
Subtotal	4.4	11.6
TOTAL	37.8 million	100%

Source: Aggregated from Mathers, Murray and Lopez (2006, pp. 126–31).

overall well-being as did the equally dramatic innovation in and expansion of the availability of material goods and services. To the substantial extent that appropriate investments in health can contribute to continued reductions in morbidity and mortality, the economic welfare returns to health investments are likely to be exceptional and positive – with previously unrecognized implications for public sector resource allocation. The purpose of this section is to motivate the high values this paper places on mortality reduction in its cost–benefit analyses. Returns to better health go far beyond the contribution better health makes to per capita income, which itself appears substantial (see

Bloom, Canning, and Jamison, 2004; Lopez-Casasnovas, Rivera, and Currais, 2005). This section first summarizes the evidence concerning health's effect on per capita income and then turns to more recent literature concerning the effect of health changes on a broader measure of economic well-being than per capita income.

2.1 Health and income

How does health influence income per person? Healthy workers are more productive than workers who are similar but not healthy. Supporting evidence for this plausible observation comes from studies that link investments in health and nutrition of the young to adult wages (Strauss and Thomas, 1998). Better health also raises per capita income through a number of other channels. One involves altering decisions about expenditures and savings over the life cycle. The idea of planning for retirement occurs only when mortality rates become low enough for retirement to be a realistic prospect. Rising longevity in developing countries has opened a new incentive for the current generation to save – an incentive that can dramatically affect national saving rates. Although this saving boom lasts for only one generation and is offset by the needs of the elderly after population aging occurs, it can substantially boost investment and economic growth rates while it lasts.

Encouraging foreign direct investment is another channel: investors shun environments in which the labor force suffers a heavy disease burden. Endemic diseases can also deny humans access to land or other natural resources, as occurred in much of West Africa before the successful control of river blindness. Boosting education is yet another channel. Healthier children attend school and learn more while they are there.

Demographic channels also play an important role. Lower infant mortality initially creates a "baby-boom" cohort and leads to a subsequent reduction in the birth rates as families choose to have fewer children in the new low-mortality regime. A baby-boom cohort thereby affects the economy profoundly as its members enter the educational system, find employment, save for retirement, and finally leave the labor market. The cohorts before and after a baby boom are much smaller; hence, for a substantial transition period, this cohort creates a large labor force relative to overall population size and the potential for accelerated economic growth (Bloom and Canning, 2006).

If better health improves the productive potential of individuals, good health should accompany higher levels of national income in the long run. Countries that have high levels of health but low levels of income tend to experience relatively faster economic growth as their income adjusts. How big an overall contribution does better health make to economic growth? Evidence from cross-country growth regressions suggests the contribution is consistently substantial. Indeed, the initial health of a population has been identified as one of the most robust drivers of economic growth – among such well-established influences as the initial level of income per capita, geographic location, and institutional and economic policy environment. Bloom, Canning, and Sevilla (2004) found that one extra year of life expectancy raises GDP per person by about 4 percent in the long run. Jamison, Lau, and Wang (2005) estimated that reductions in adult mortality explain 10 to 15 percent of the economic growth that occurred from 1960 to 1990. Although attribution of causality is never unequivocal in analyses like these, household-level evidence also points consistently to a likely causal effect of health on income.

Health declines can precipitate downward spirals, setting off impoverishment and further ill health. For example, the effect of HIV/AIDS on per capita GDP could prove devastating in the long run. The International Monetary Fund (IMF) recently published a collection of important studies of the multiple mechanisms through which a major AIDS epidemic can be expected to affect national economies (Haacker, 2004).

2.2 Health and economic welfare

Judging countries' economic performance by GDP per person fails to differentiate between situations in which health conditions differ: a country whose citizens enjoy long and healthy lives clearly outperforms another with the same GDP per person but whose citizens suffer much illness and die sooner. Individual willingness to forgo income to work in safer environments and social willingness to pay for health-enhancing safety and environmental regulations provide measures, albeit approximate, of the value of differences in mortality rates.

Many such willingness-to-pay studies have been undertaken in recent decades, and their results are typically summarized as the *value of a statistical life* (VSL).

Although the national income and product accounts include the value of inputs into health care (such as drugs and physician time), standard procedures do not incorporate information on the value of changes in longevity. In a seminal paper, Usher (1973) first brought estimates of VSL into national income accounting. He did this by generating estimates of the growth in what Becker, Philipson, and Soares (2003) later called *full income* – a concept that captures the value of changes in life expectancy by including them in an assessment of economic welfare. Estimates of changes in full income are typically generated by adding the value of changes in annual mortality rates (calculated using VSL figures) to changes in annual GDP per person. These estimates of change in full income are conservative in that they incorporate only the value of mortality changes and do not account for the total value of changes in health status. This paper will later use a measure of "disability-adjusted life years" (DALY), that includes disability as well as premature mortality in a way that calibrates disability weight in terms of mortality changes. Valuation of changes in mortality, it should be noted, is only one element – albeit a quantitatively important one – of potentially feasible additions to national accounts to deal with nonmarket outcomes. The US National Academy of Sciences has recently proposed broad changes for the United States that would include but go beyond valuation of mortality change (Abraham and Mackie, 2005). Of specific relevance to this paper is the economic welfare value of reductions in financial risk potentially associated either with a health intervention – typically prevention or early treatment – or with a risk-pooled way of financing it.

For many years, little further work was done on the effects of mortality change on full income although, as Viscusi and Aldy (2003) document, the number of carefully constructed estimates of VSLs increased enormously. Bourguignon and Morrisson (2002) address the long-term evolution of inequality among world citizens, starting from the premise that a "comprehensive definition of economic well-being would consider individuals over their lifetime." Their conclusion is that rapid increases in life expectancy in poorer countries have resulted in declines in inequality (broadly defined) beginning sometime after 1950, even though income inequality had continued to rise. In another important paper, Nordhaus (2003) assessed the growth of full income per capita in the United States in the twentieth century. He concluded that more than half of the growth in full income in the first half of the century – and less than half in the second half of the century – had resulted from mortality decline. In this period, real income in the United States increased sixfold and life expectancy increased by more than twenty-five years.

Three lines of more recent work extend those methods to the interpretation of the economic performance of developing countries. All reach conclusions that differ substantially from analyses based on GDP alone. Two of those studies – one undertaken for the Commission on Macroeconomics and Health (CMH) of the World Health Organization (WHO) (Jamison, Sachs, and Wang, 2001) and the other at the International Monetary Fund (IMF) (Crafts and Haacker, 2004) – assessed the impact of the AIDS epidemic on full income. Both studies conclude that the AIDS epidemic in the 1990s had far more adverse economic consequences than previous estimates of effects on per person GDP growth would suggest. The benefit estimates used in this paper for successful interventions against HIV/AIDS are consistent with these findings from the CMH and IMF. Accounting for mortality decline in Africa before the 1990s, on the other hand, leads to estimates of much more favorable overall economic performance than does the trend in GDP per person. Figure 17.2 shows that in Kenya, for example, full income grew more rapidly in GDP per person before 1990 (and far more rapidly in the 1960s). After 1990 the mounting death toll from AIDS appears to have only a modest effect on GDP per person but a dramatically adverse impact on changes in full income. Becker, Philipson, and Soares (2003) confirmed and extended the earlier work of Bourguignon and Morrisson (2002) in finding strong absolute convergence in full income across countries over time, in contrast to the standard finding of continued divergence (increased inequality) of GDP per person. Finally, Jamison, Jamison, and Sachs (2003) have adapted standard cross-country growth regressions to model determinants of full income (rather than GDP per person). Like Becker, Philipson, and Soares (2003), they conclude that inequalities have been decreasing.

The dramatic mortality declines of the past 150 years – and their reversal in Africa by AIDS subsequent to 1990 – have had major economic consequences. The effect of health on GDP is substantial. The intrinsic value of mortality changes – measured in terms of VSL – is even more substantial. What are the implications of these findings for devel-

Annual change as percentage of initial year GDP per capita

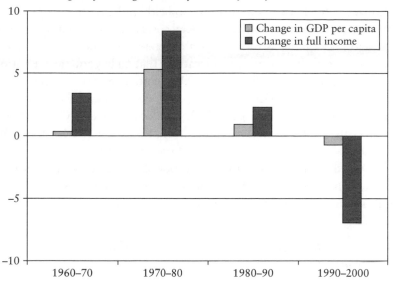

Figure 17.2. Changes in GDP and full income in Kenya, 1960–2000

Source: Jamison, Sachs, and Wang 2001.

opment strategy and for cost–benefit analyses of public sector investment options? Using full income in cost–benefit analyses of investments
in health (and in health-related sectors such as education, water supply
and sanitation, and targeted food transfers) would markedly increase
estimates of net benefits or rates of return. A careful, quantitative
reassessment of competing policies for improving a country's living
standards would probably conclude that development assistance and
budgetary allocations to health deserve greater relative priority.

3. Cost–benefit methodology

The basic approach to cost–benefit analysis used in this paper is to start
with the cost-effectiveness (CE) results from the extensive comparative
analyses reported in *DCP2* (Jamison et al., 2006a; Laxminarayan et
al., 2006). These results are expressed as the cost of buying a DALY, a
summary measure involving mortality change and a valuation of disability change that can be considered to have been generated by
calibration against mortality change.

Section 3.1 describes an idealized version of our approach to CE –
idealized in the sense that it seeks to explicitly call attention to the value
of financial protection and nonfinancial costs (e.g. use of limited system
capacity). The point is to serve as a reminder in drawing conclusions
of some specific important considerations that go beyond the CE ratios
reported. Section 3.2 discusses DALYs and explicitly argues for a
change in the way DALYs associated with deaths under the age of five
are calculated. This change, which is adopted in our CB analyses,
reduces the DALY cost of a typical death under age five by about 50
percent while leaving the construction of DALYs for older ages
unchanged. Section 3.3 draws on Section 2 to assign, very conserva-
tively, dollar values to DALYs for the subsequent CB assessment. It
then summarizes this paper's approach to costing.

3.1 Cost-effectiveness analysis broadly and narrowly construed

A starting point for cost-effectiveness analysis broadly construed is to
observe that health systems have two objectives: (a) to improve the
level and distribution of health outcomes in the population and (b) to
protect individuals from financial risks that are often very substantial
and that are frequent causes of poverty (WHO 1999, 2000). Financial
risk results from illness-related loss of income as well as expenditures
on care; the loss can be ameliorated by preventing illness or its progression and by using appropriate financial architecture for the system.

We can also consider two classes of resources to be available:
financial resources and health system capacity. To implement an intervention in a population, the system uses some of each resource. Just as
some interventions have higher dollar costs than others, some interventions are more demanding of system capacity than others. In
countries with limited health system capacity, it is clearly important to
select interventions that require relatively little of such capacity.
Human resource capacity constitutes a particularly important aspect
of system capacity, discussed in a recent report of the Joint Learning
Initiative (2004). Figure 17.3 illustrates this broadly construed vision
of CE and, in its shaded region, the more narrow (standard) approach
for which quantitative estimates are available.

Although in the very short run little tradeoff may exist between
dollars and human resources or system capacity more generally,

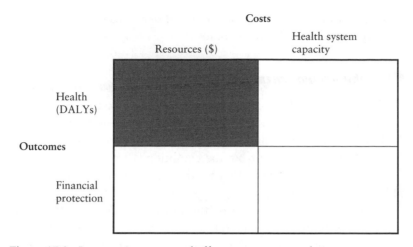

Figure 17.3. Intervention costs and effects: a more general view

Note: The shaded box represents the domain of traditional cost-effectiveness analysis.

investing in the development of such capacity can help make more of that resource available in the future. Mills, Rasheed, and Tollman (2006) discuss different types of health system capacity and intervention complexity and point to the potential for responding to low capacity by selecting interventions that are less demanding of capacity and by simplifying interventions. Mills, Rasheed, and Tollman also explore the extent to which financial resources can substitute for different aspects of system capacity (see also Gericke et al., 2003). An important mechanism for strengthening capacity, inherent in highly outcome-oriented programs, may simply be to use it successfully – learning by doing.

The literature on economic evaluation of health projects typically reports the cost per unit of achieving some measure of health outcome – quality-adjusted life years (QALYs) or DALYs or deaths averted – and at times addresses how that cost varies with the level of intervention and other factors. Pritchard (2004) provides a valuable introduction to this literature. *DCP1* reported such cost-effectiveness findings for about 70 interventions; *DCP2* does so as well, in the end providing evidence on about 315 interventions. *DCP2* authors were asked to use methods described in Jamison et al. (2003). Cost-effectiveness calculations provide important insights into the economic attractiveness of an intervention, but other considerations – such as consequences for financial protection and demands on health system capacity – need to be borne in mind.

3.2 Defining and redefining DALYs

The DALY family of indicators measures the disease burden from the age of onset of a condition by summing an indicator of years of life lost (YLL) due to the condition and an indicator of years of life lost due to disability (YLD) resulting from the condition. Disability-adjusted life years (DALYs) due to a condition are the sum of the relevant YLLs and YLDs.

DALYs generate a measure of the disease burden resulting from premature mortality by integrating a discounted, potentially age-weighted, disability-adjusted stream of life years from the age of incidence of the condition to infinity using a survival curve based on the otherwise expected age of death. The formulation within the family of DALYs previously used to assess empirically the global burden of disease specifies a constant discount rate of 3 percent per year and an age-weighting function that gives low weight to a year lived in early childhood and older ages and greater weight to middle ages. The current comprehensive volume on burden of disease reports global burden of disease estimates generated with the 3 percent discount rate but uniform age weights (Lopez et al., 2006a). Mathers, Murray, and Lopez (2006) provide an extensive exploration of the uncertainty and sensitivity inherent in disease burden assessment, including the results of differing assumptions about age weighting and discount rates.

To be clear about the particular form of DALY being used, the terminology from Mathers et al. is employed. DALYs(r,K) are DALYs constructed using a discount rate of r percent per year and an amount of age weighting indexed by a parameter K. DALYs(3,1) are DALYs generated with a discount rate of 3 percent per year and with full age weighting, that is, $K = 1$. DALYs(3,0) are DALYs generated with a discount rate of 3 percent per year and with no age weighting, that is, $K = 0$. Mathers, Lopez, and Murray (2006) present results concerning the burden of disease based on DALYs(3,0); Ezzati et al. (2006) present estimates of the burden of major risk factors. This paper is based on DALYs (3,0), but slightly generalized.

This paper uses an extension of the DALY family generated by modeling a concept of "acquisition of life potential" (ALP). The intuition behind the ALP concept is that an infant (or fetus) only gradually acquires the full life potential reflected in a stream of life years beginning at birth, that is, ALP can be gradual. Operationalizing this concept involves introducing a parameter, A, that indicates the speed of ALP (see Jamison et al., 2006a/b for precise definitions and assessments of the burden of disease that result). A is constructed so that for the fastest possible speed of ALP, namely, instantaneous ALP, $A = 1$. A is bounded below by 0. This chapter extends the notation DALYs(r,K) in two ways. First, it explicitly indicates the level of A by extending the DALY nomenclature to DALYs(r,K,A). Thus using this nomenclature, DALYs(3,0) become DALYs(3,0,1), because the standard DALY is the special case with instantaneous ALP. Second, when stillbirths are included in the range of events to be measured in the global burden of disease, this is explicitly noted in the DALY nomenclature as $DALYs_{SB}(r,K,A)$. Notation around YLL is similarly extended.

Explicit modeling of ALP permits three instrumentally useful improvements to the previous formulation of DALYs:

- The DALY loss from a death seconds before birth is, in the previous formulation, 0; it jumps to more than thirty years at birth. The ALP formulation allows, but does not require, this discontinuity to be avoided.
- The ALP formulation allows, but does not require, a positive DALY loss associated with stillbirths.
- The ratio of the DALY loss from a death at age twenty, say, to that at birth is close to 1 for any reasonable set of parameter values in the previous DALY formulation. Many people's ethical judgments would give this ratio a value substantially greater than 1. The ALP formulation allows, but does not require, these judgments.

Only a limited number of empirical studies have attempted to assess directly the views of individuals concerning deaths at different ages. In an important early study, Crawford, Salter, and Jang (1989) relate grief from a death to the concept of reproductive potential in population biology. They conclude that for several diverse human groups the relationship shows grief to be closely related to prehistoric reproductive value. An Institute of Medicine (1985) review of vaccine development priorities uses infant mortality equivalence in cost-effectiveness calculations. The committee members preparing the report collectively judged that the loss from a death at age twenty should be about two

Table 17.4. *Discounted YLL at different ages of death for several*
DALY formulations

Age group	Representative age of death (years)	YLL(3,1)	YLL(3,0)	YLL$_{SB}$ (3,0,1)	YLL$_{SB}$ (3,0,0.54)
Antepartum	−0.080	0	0	30.42	4.95
Intrapartum	−0.001	0	0	30.42	9.13
Neonatal	0.020	33.09	30.42	30.42	9.40
Infant	0.300	33.36	30.40	30.40	12.95
Postneonatal infant	0.500	33.56	30.39	30.39	15.42
Child	2.000	34.81	30.28	30.28	26.40

Source: Jamison, et al. (2006), table 6.6.
Note: YLL(3,1), YLL(3,0), and YLL$_{SB}$(3,0,1) assume instantaneous acquisition of life potential, ALP ($A = 1$). YLL(3,1) assumes full age weighting ($K = 1$); the other three formulations assume uniform age weights ($K = 0$). YLL$_{SB}$(3,0,.54) assumes gradual acquisition of life potential ($A = .54$). The subscript SB refers to formulations that do not give stillbirths zero weight.

times that from an infant death. However, some preliminary trade-off studies suggest a value closer to three or four times. All three lines of evidence point to gradual rather than instantaneous ALP. What is clear, however, is that no completely defensible estimate (or even range) is currently available, and hence the numbers used in Jamison et al. (2006a/b) should be viewed as only suggestive. Table 17.4 shows the YLLs associated with deaths at different young ages for alternative formulations of the DALY, including one with their preferred value of $A = .54$. This final column reports several estimates. (It is important to note the DALYs and YLLs for deaths above age five are unaffected by introduction of ALP.) *Weighting the YLLs at different ages by the relative frequency of deaths at those ages gives a DALY$_{SB}$ (3,0,0.54) loss of 16.4 DALYs for a typical under-five death, about half what is typically used. Our analyses use this figure.*

3.3 The value and cost of a DALY

The VSL estimates discussed in Section 2.2 yield a range of values for a statistical life – from around 100 to almost 200 times per capita income. Very approximately this can be translated to a value for a statistical life *year* in the range of two to four times per capita income. The emphasis in this paper is on low-income countries defined by the World Bank for 2001 as countries with per capita incomes of less than $745 (exchange rate). The World Bank's estimate of the average income of people living in low-income countries is $430 per year (World Bank, 2003, table 17.1). Choosing a value for a statistical life year near the low end of the range (a little above 2) would give a convenient value of $1,000, which is what this paper will use as the value of a DALY. (Note that for the reasons discussed in Section 3.2 the DALY loss from a death under age five – and hence the benefit from preventing it – would be about half that used in standard DALYs.)

The cost of buying a DALY with different interventions was calculated, in *DCP2*, based on construction of "typical" prices for a geographical region (Mulligan et al., 2003). For internationally traded inputs prices were the same for all regions. For local costs regional estimates were used. Intervention costs, therefore, are *not* expressed in PPP dollars. The reason for this is that local costs present decision-makers with the appropriate numbers for budgeting and for comparing interventions in the context where they are working. (Regional costs are taken to be a better approximation of local costs than global costs would be.) On this point the methods of this paper differ from those of its predecessor (Mills and Shillcutt, 2004).

4. Child health

A small number of conditions accounts for most of the (large) differences in health between the poor and the not so poor. Less than 1 percent of all deaths from AIDS, TB, and malaria, for example, occur in the high-income countries. Available technical options – exemplified by but going well beyond immunization – can address most of the conditions that affect children, and can do so with great efficacy and at modest cost. That short list of conditions, including undernutrition, relates directly to achieving the MDGs for health. Public expenditures to address those conditions have, in the past, benefited the relatively well off, albeit within poor countries (although global inequities have decreased because many poor countries have made much progress).

Table 17.5. *Health expenditures by country income level, public and total, 2001*

Country group	Health expenditure per capita (2001 US$)	Health expenditure (percentage of GDP)	Public sector expenditures (percentage of total health expenditures)
Low income	23	4.4	26.3
Middle income	118	6.0	51.1
High income	2,841	10.8	62.1
(Countries in the European Monetary Union)	(1,856)	(9.3)	(73.5)
World	500	9.8	59.2

Source: World Bank 2004, table 2.14.

4.1 Under-five health problems and intervention priorities

The Millennium Development Goal for under-five mortality (MDG-4) (reducing its level in 2015 by two-thirds relative to what it was in 1990) is highly ambitious. Yet its implication of an average 4.3 percent per year decline is well within recent experience. In the first half of the MDG period (1990–2002), forty-six countries achieved rates of decline in under-five mortality greater than 4.3 percent per year (Lopez, Begg, and Bos, 2006).

Basic knowledge about the cost-effectiveness of interventions to address maternal and child health has been available from the 1980s. *DCP2*'s work provides a reassessment with few surprises but some additions. It makes two important, relatively new points. The first results from noting that half of under-five deaths occur at ages less than twenty-eight days, when the substantial but usually neglected problem of stillbirth is considered. *DCP2* identifies some highly cost-effective approaches to intervention against stillbirth and neonatal death (Lawn et al., 2006). The second new point results from the rapid spread of resistance of the malaria parasite to chloroquine and to sulfadoxine-pyrimethamine (SP). These inexpensive, highly effective, widely available drugs provided an important partial check on the high levels of malaria mortality in Africa. Their loss is leading to a rise in malaria mortality and morbidity that could be substantial.

Under-five deaths per 1,000 births

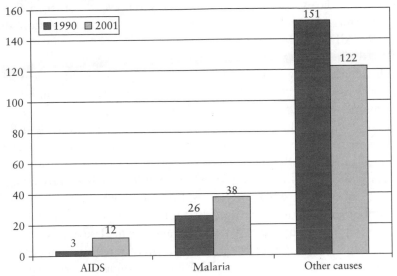

Figure 17.4. Under five deaths from AIDS, malaria, and other causes, per thousand births, 1990 and 2001, sub-Saharan Africa

Source: Lopez, Begg and Bos, 2006, table 17.2. 17.4

Figure 17.4 illustrates increases in malaria death rates in under-five children in sub-Saharan Africa in the period from 1990 to 2001. (This rate increase results in hundreds of thousands of deaths more than would otherwise have occurred.) The design of instruments for financing a rapid transition to effective new treatments – artemisinin combination therapies (ACTs) – is a high priority (Arrow, Gelband, and Jamison, 2005).

In addition to the above, other intervention priorities for addressing under-five mortality are for the most part familiar:

- Expand immunization coverage.
- Expand the use of the simple and low-cost but highly effective treatments for diarrhea and child pneumonia through integrated management of childhood illness or other mechanisms.
- Prevent transmission of and mortality from malaria by expanding coverage of insecticide-treated bed nets, by expanding use of intermittent preventive treatment for pregnant women; and by use of indoor residual spraying with DDT.

- Ensure widespread distribution of key micronutrients.
- Expand the use of a package of measures to prevent mother-to-child transmission of HIV (further discussed in the next section on HIV/AIDS).

In addition to interventions to reduce under-five mortality, one other priority is clear. The world's most prevalent infections are intestinal helminth (worm) infections, and children of all ages are among the most heavily affected. Hotez et al. (2006) discuss these infections, which a low-cost drug (albendazole), taken every six months to a year, can control effectively. Bundy et al. (2006)'s discussion of school health services points to both the importance to children's school progress of taking albendazole where needed and the potential efficacy of school health programs as a vehicle for delivery. In the long run, improved sanitation and water supplies will prevent transmission. Use of albendazole is only an interim solution, but it is one that may be required for decades if the experience of the currently high-income countries is relevant.

4.2 Delivering child health interventions

The list of potential interventions is far from exhaustive, and different regions, countries, and communities will face different mixes of the problems these interventions address. However, there can be little dispute that any short list of intervention priorities for under-five mortality in low- and middle-income countries would include many on the list in the preceding section. Why not, then, simply put money into scaling up these known interventions to a satisfactory level?

To greatly oversimplify – and these issues are discussed more substantially in Mills, Rasheed, and Tollman (2006) – two schools of thought exist. One line of thinking – often ascribed to macroeconomist Jeffrey Sachs and his work as chair of the WHO CMH – concludes that more money and focused effort *are* the solutions. Although acknowledging dual constraints – of money and of health system capacity – Sachs and his colleagues (WHO CMH, 2001) contend that money can buy (or develop, or both) relevant system capacity even over a period as short as five years. Major gains are affordable and health system capacity constraints can be overcome. Immunization provides an example of where, even in the short term, money can substitute for system capacity. Adding antigens for *Haemophilus influenzae* type B

(Hib) and hepatitis B (HepB) to the immunization schedule is costly (although still cost-effective). In some environments, however, it proves less demanding of system capacity than expanding coverage does. Money can be effectively spent by adding antigens at the same time as investing in the capacity to extend coverage.

A second school of thought acknowledges the need for more money but asserts that health system capacity is often a binding short- to medium-term constraint on substantial scaling up of interventions. Van der Gaag (2004) emphasized this point in his critique of an earlier Copenhagen Consensus paper on health. Critical priorities are, therefore, system reform and strengthening while ensuring that such reforms focus clearly on achieving improved health outcomes and financial protection.

This paper's perspective is closer to that of Sachs than of Van der Gaag while emphasizing the need (in Section 3.1) to be explicit about intervention costs that are nonfinancial. This points both to the need for considering how to relax these constraints and to selecting interventions in part on the extent to which they are less demanding of non financial inputs.

Mills, Rasheed, and Tollman (2006), as indicated, discussed these issues further in the context of all the problems facing a health system. From an individual country's perspective, however, if financial resources are available, the question is very much an empirical one: to what extent can those resources be effectively deployed in buying interventions, in buying out of prevailing system constraints, and in investing in relevant system capacity for the future? What needs to be constantly borne in mind throughout this continued controversy is that *something* works: under-five mortality rates have plunged by more than half since 1960 in the low- and middle-income countries.

5. HIV/AIDS

For dozens of countries around the world – including several of the most populous – the AIDS epidemic threatens every aspect of development. No other threat comes close, with the possible exceptions of use of nuclear weapons in densely populated areas or a devastating global pandemic similar to the 1917–18 influenza episode. Most governments of affected low- and middle-income countries and most providers of development assistance have only recently begun to respond more than minimally. Creation of the Global Fund to Fight AIDS, Tuberculosis, and Malaria can be viewed as an attempt of the world's top political leaders to improve on the records of existing institutions. The Global Fund's initial years have seen substantial success, but that success is potentially undermined by sharp constraints on resource availability (Bezanson, 2005).

In contrast to the initially slow programmatic movement of most national leaders and international institutions, the research and development community – public and private – has made rapid progress in developing tools to control the HIV/AIDS epidemic, although both a vaccine and a curative drug remain distant objectives. Sensitive, specific, and inexpensive diagnostics are available; means of prevention have been developed and tested; modes of transmission are well understood; and increasingly powerful drugs for controlling viral load allow radical slowing of disease progression. Tools for dealing with HIV/AIDS are thus available: Bertozzi et al. (2006) emphasized that a number of countries show by example that those tools can be put to effective use. Most of the high-income countries have done so, and Brazil and Mexico provide examples of upper-middle-income countries that have forestalled potentially serious epidemics. Mexico succeeded, for example, with a policy of responding both early and forcefully to the epidemic (Del Rio and Sepulveda, 2002). The major successes of Thailand and Uganda demonstrate that countries with fewer financial resources can also succeed – and succeed against more established epidemics that had already penetrated deeply into their populations.

This section first discusses prevention then antiretroviral therapy.

5.1 Prevention and management

Prevention underpins success. At the time the World Bank's *World Development Report: Investing in Health* (World Bank, 1993) was being written in 1992 and 1993, the only tool for dealing with the epidemic was prevention. In collaboration with the then Global Programme against AIDS at WHO, the *World Development Report* commissioned very approximate estimates of the consequence for the new infection rate of fully implementing available preventive measures (its optimistic case scenario) or of doing very little (worst case). Actual incidence numbers for 2000 fall very close to the worst-case projection.

Bertozzi et al. (2006) point out that even by 2003 fewer than one in five people at high risk of infection had access to the most basic preventive services. In much of the world, little has been spent on prevention, and little has been achieved. In addition, the current US administration may be partially responsible for discouraging condom use in some countries and in stigmatizing and alienating commercial sex workers who are particular priorities for prevention programs. Despite those problems, the potential for prevention is very real, and a number of successful countries have shown the possibility of using that potential well. Treatment of sexually transmitted infections (STIs) to prevent HIV transmission is one priority (Aral et al., 2006). Bertozzi et al. (2006) discuss a broad menu of preventive measures and experiences with their implementation. Among them, treatment of STIs may be of particular salience both because the diseases are well worth treating in their own right and because the absence of STIs greatly reduces transmission of HIV.

In addition to prevention, better management of patients with AIDS could avert much misery, both by treating opportunistic infections and by ameliorating the often excruciating pain associated with many AIDS deaths. Medically inappropriate restrictions on the use of inexpensive but powerful opiates for pain control continue to deny dignity and comfort to millions of patients with AIDS and cancer in their final months (Foley et al., 2006).

5.2 Antiretroviral treatment

Intensive research and development efforts have led in the past decade to the availability of well over a dozen antiretroviral drugs that can greatly reduce the quantity of HIV in an infected person. This reduction in viral load slows or halts progression of AIDS and can return individuals from serious illness to reasonable health. Available drugs leave a residual population of HIV in the body, however, and this population grows if the drugs are stopped. At present the drugs must be taken for life. Widespread use of these drugs in high-income (and some middle-income) countries has transformed the life prospects of HIV-infected individuals.

Early generation antiretroviral drugs suffered notable shortcomings: they were enormously costly; regimens for their use were complicated, making adherence difficult; their use generated unpleasant side effects;

and rapid evolution of HIV led to resistant mutants that undermined the efficacy of therapy. In a remarkably short time scientific advances have substantially attenuated those problems, making feasible, at least in principle, antiretroviral therapy in low-income settings. WHO's "3 by 5" program had as its objective, for example, to reach 3 million people in low- and middle-income countries with antiretroviral therapy by 2005. Although that goal was far from being met, the global effort to make treatment widely available is well under way. An important contributor has been the Clinton Foundation's effort to negotiate reductions in the prices of first-line drugs and, more recently, second-line drugs.

Despite the indicated progress against the problems with antiretroviral drugs, challenges to their effective use in low-income environments remain formidable. The complexity of patient management is very real. Management requires high levels of human resources and other capacities in many of the countries where those capacities need to be most carefully rationed. Perhaps in consequence, achieving effective implementation has been difficult on even a limited scale. Bertozzi et al. (2006) review those problems and how they might be addressed.

Three points concerning widespread antiretroviral drug use are particularly noteworthy:

- Poor implementation (low adherence, development of resistance, interruptions in drug supplies) is likely to lead to very limited health gains, even for individuals on therapy. (This outcome is unlike that of a weak immunization program in which health gains still exist in the fraction of the population that is immunized.) Poorly implemented antiretroviral drug delivery programs could divert substantial resources from prevention or from other high-payoff activities in the health sector. Even worse, they could lead to a false sense of complacency in affected populations: evidence from some countries suggests that treatment availability has led to riskier sexual behavior and increased HIV transmission. The injunction to "do no harm" holds particular salience.

- Unless systematic efforts are made to acquire hard knowledge about which approaches work and which do not, the likelihood exists that unsuccessful implementation efforts will be continued without the appropriate reallocation of resources to successful approaches. Learning what works will require major variations in approach and careful evaluation of effects. Failing to learn will lead to large numbers of needless deaths. Most efforts to scale up antiretroviral therapy unconscionably fail to commit the substantial resources required for evaluation of effects. Such evaluations are essential if ineffective programs are to be halted or effective ones are to receive more resources.

- Many programs rely exclusively on the cheapest possible drugs, thereby risking problems with toxicity, adherence, and drug resistance. From the outset a broader range of drug regimens needs to be tested.

Use of ARVs is likely to have a benefit–cost ratio greater than 1 in many circumstances. However if it competes with other highly attractive health investments in environments with limited human and financial resources, widespread adoption needs to be carefully sequenced.

6. Noncommunicable disease

At the same time that most low- and middle-income countries need to address health problems that are now effectively controlled in high-income countries, they are increasingly sharing the high-income countries' heavy burdens of cardiovascular system disease, cancers, psychiatric disorders, and automobile-related injuries. *DCP2* has chapters addressing each of these NCDs and others. The public health research and policy community has been surprisingly silent about these epidemics even though, for example, cardiovascular disease (CVD) in low- and middle-income countries killed over twice as many people in 2001 as did AIDS, malaria, and TB combined (see Table 17.3 for data on deaths over age five). An important early exception was Feachem et al. (1992), who indicated approaches to treatment and prevention of these conditions that can be adapted to the tighter budget constraints of developing countries. The World Health Organization provides a valuable and more up-to-date discussion that emphasizes prevention (WHO, 2005). In addition, low-cost but effective approaches to long-term management of chronic conditions need to be developed and implemented.

The remainder of this section briefly discusses, as examples, the prevention and management of cardiovascular diseases, and smoking as a risk factor for multiple NCDs.

6.1 Cardiovascular disease

Cardiovascular diseases in low- and middle-income countries result in about 13 million deaths each year, over a quarter of all deaths in those countries. Most cardiovascular deaths result from ischemic heart disease (5.7 million) or cerebrovascular disease (4.6 million). (A potentially substantial fraction of the heart disease deaths may result from congestive heart failure.) Because such deaths occur at older ages, they account for a substantially smaller fraction of total disease burden in disability-adjusted life years (DALYs) – 12.9 percent – than they do of deaths.

The main risk factors for CVD account for very large fractions of the deaths (and even more of the burden) from those diseases. For ischemic heart disease, they collectively account for 78 percent of deaths in low- and middle-income countries; for stroke, they account for 61 percent (Ezzati et al., 2006). Measures to reduce the levels of those risk factors – high blood pressure, high cholesterol, smoking, obesity, excessive alcohol use, physical inactivity, and low fruit and vegetable consumption – are the goals for prevention. Unlike the favorable experience with controlling tobacco use, attempts to change the behaviors leading to obesity, hypertension, high cholesterol, or physical activity appear to have had little success at a population level. However, as Willett et al. (2006) document, many promising approaches remain to be tried. Common sense suggests that they should be initiated even while more systematic efforts to develop and evaluate behavior-change packages are ramped up.

Pharmaceutical interventions to manage two major components of cardiovascular risk – hypertension and high cholesterol levels – are well established and are highly cost-effective for individuals at high risk of a stroke or heart attack. From at least the time of publication of *Disease Control Priorities in Developing Countries*, 1st edition (*DCP1*), researchers have recognized that the low cost and high effectiveness of drugs to prevent the reoccurrence of a cardiovascular event made their long-term use potentially cost-effective in low-income environments. Even if sustained behavior change proves difficult to achieve, medications have the potential to reduce CVD risks by 50 percent or more. Gaziano et al. (2006) and Rodgers et al. (2006) develop the current evidence on that point. A key problem, however, concerns the health care personnel and systems requirements associated with the need for lifelong medication use, a problem also faced with antiretroviral therapy for AIDS and the use of medications to target several major psychiatric disorders. (These problems illustrate the importance of the nonfinancial costs discussed in Sections 3 and 4 and related issues of health system development.) How to achieve effective long-term management of lifesaving drugs is a key delivery and research challenge for health system reformers.

In contrast to the lifelong requirement for drug use associated with CVD risk reduction in high-risk individuals, treatment of acute heart attacks with inexpensive drugs is both less demanding of system resources and highly cost-effective (Gaziano et al., 2006). Given the high incidence of these problems, system-wide efforts to achieve high rates of appropriate drug use in response to acute heart disease are a high priority.

6.2 Tobacco addiction

Growing tobacco use accounts for a substantial and avoidable fraction of CVD and of cancers. Reasonable projections show the number of tobacco-related deaths to be not only large but also growing, particularly in developing countries. In 2001, the number of tobacco-related deaths in developing countries was estimated to be 3.34 million or about 9 percent of deaths over age five in these countries (Lopez et al., 2006b). For those reasons, controlling smoking is a key element of any national strategy for preventing CVD or for promoting health more generally. Preventing the initiation of smoking is important because addiction to tobacco makes smoking cessation very difficult, even for the numerous individuals who would like to do so. However, helping people quit smoking is at least as important as preventing initiation. Figure 17.5 portrays estimates showing that far more lives could be saved between now and 2050 with successful efforts to help people stop smoking than with efforts to keep them from starting. Reducing smoking levels is well demonstrated to be within the control of public policy. The principal instrument is through taxation: complementary measures as discussed in Jha et al. (2006) are important as well.

7. Opportunities for disease control

The preceding three sections identified a range of attractive options for disease control based, for the most part, on the 315 interventions

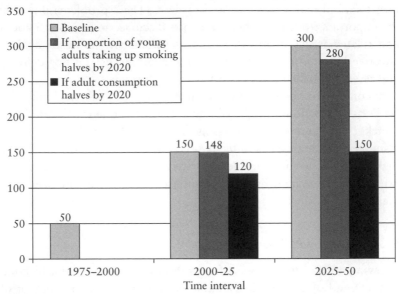

Tobacco deaths worldwide in the indicated quarter century (millions)

Figure 17.5. Increase in tobacco-related deaths as populations age

Source: Jha et. al., 2006.

that *DCP2* reviewed (Jamison et al., 2006a). Laxminarayan et al. (2006) summarized the main findings on cost-effectiveness which form the basis for the cost–benefit analyses reported here. Appendix Table 1 provides highlights of those findings for South Asia and sub-Saharan Africa. One thing that is clear in the summarization of the cost-effectiveness information is that there is a broad range of reasonable estimates for most interventions. This results partly from (often highly) incomplete information and uncertainty. It results also, and even more importantly, from the responsiveness of the cost-effectiveness function to variations in prices, in the scale of the intervention (and of its substitutes and complements), and in the epidemiological environment.

Given these often broad ranges in CE ratios, and hence in BC ratios, it makes little sense to conclude with precise estimates and extensive uncertainty analyses. Rather I have identified seven major opportunities for investment in interventions that address a large disease burden highly cost-effectively. Even valuing DALYs at a conservative $1,000 and, again conservatively, reducing by 50 percent the DALY loss associated with an under-five death (this affects the malaria and immunization numbers) the benefit–cost ratios associated with investing in these opportunities is enormously high.

This concluding section provides a summarizing table on these seven interventions. All but two of the seven interventions have been previously discussed. Number 1 on the list in Table 17.6 is case finding and treatment of tuberculosis (Dye and Floyd, 2006). The seventh intervention, strengthening and expanding surgical capacity at the district hospital level is broadly systemic and addresses multiple conditions (Debas et al., 2006). Although the list of conditions that district

Table 17.6. *Disease control: key investment priorities*

Priority area	Indicative benefit-cost ratio	Level of capacity required[a]	Financial risk protection provided[a]	Annual costs ($ billions)	Annual benefits[b]
1. Tuberculosis: appropriate case finding and treatment	30:1	M	H	1	1 million adult deaths averted or 30 million DALYs
2. Heart attacks (AMI): acute management with low-cost drugs	25:1	M	H	.2	300,000 heart attack deaths averted each year or 4.5 million DALYs
3. Malaria: prevention and ACT treatment package	20:1	M	L	.5	500,000 (mostly child) deaths averted or 7.5 million DALYs
4. Childhood diseases: expanded immunization coverage	20:1	L	L	1	1 million child deaths averted or 20 million DALYs

Table 17.6. (*cont.*)

Priority area	Indicative benefit–cost ratio	Level of capacity required	Financial risk protection provided	Annual costs	Annual benefits
5. Cancer, heart disease, other: tobacco taxation	20:1	H	H	1	1 million adult deaths averted or 20 million DALYs
6. HIV: prevention package	12:1	M	H	2.5	2 million HIV infections averted or 22 million DALYs
7. Injury, difficult childbirth, other: surgical capacity at the district hospital	10:1	H	H	3	30 million "surgical" DALYs averted or about 20% of DALYs

[a] Level of capacity required and extent of financial risk protection are judged by the author to be high (H), medium (M) or low (L).

[b] In the formulation of DALYs the benefits of averting a death in a given year all accure in that year and are calculated as the present value (at a 3% discount rate) of the future stream of life years that would have occured if the death had been prevented.

hospital surgeons address is long, the most important in terms of benefits are dealing with difficult childbirths and with injury.

Table 17.6 orders opportunities by benefit–cost ratio – from 30:1 for appropriate TB treatment to 10:1 for expansion of surgical capacity at district hospitals. Every opportunity in the table has not only a very high estimated B:C but, also, addresses major disease burden. The interventions that would address the most DALYs are TB treatment (#1) and district hospital surgery (#7). Each would provide relatively a high degree of financial protection to populations.

Experience with implementation of heart attack treatment and, to a lesser extent, tobacco taxation and surgery, is much more limited in low-income countries than is experience with the other four interventions on the list. There is a strong case for early, large-scale implementation trials in each of these three areas.

With the exception of surgery in the district hospital, the opportunities identified do not explicitly address the strengthening of health system capacity. It will be important to ensure that implementation includes related investments in manpower and institutions, with "related" broadly defined. One might consider there to be two broad approaches to strengthening health systems. One involves relatively non-specific investments in capacity and reforms of process. The second involves creating specific capacity to deliver priority services in volume and with high quality. In the second model, capacity strengthening spreads out from high-performing initial nodes. This paper is very much in the spirit of the latter approach.

In conclusion, TB treatment stands out as perhaps the most important investment on grounds of its high B:C, its high level of financial risk protection, its moderate systemic requirements and in the size of disease burden potentially averted. All the others in the table have advantages and disadvantages relative to each other and different individuals might well order them differently. The overwhelming general conclusion, however, is that even if all costs were increased by a factor of 2 or 3, there is a substantial and very specific list of major and highly attractive investment opportunities within the health sector.

Appendix Table 1 *Neglected low-cost opportunities and high-cost interventions in South Asia and sub-Saharan Africa*

	Cost per DALY averted ($)*	Thousands of DALYs averted* † per 20% increase in coverage	Burden of target diseases (millions of DALYs)*
Neglected low-cost opportunities in south Asia			
Childhood immunisation			
Increased coverage of traditional EPI programme	8	Not assessed	28.4
HIV/AIDS			
Voluntary counselling and testing	9–126	Not assessed	7.4
Peer-based programs for at-risk groups (eg, commercial sex workers) to disseminate information, services (clean needles and condoms), and teach specific skills			
School-based interventions to disseminate information			
Prevention of mother-to-child transmission with antiretroviral therapy			
Surgical services and emergency care	6–212	21.8	48.0–146.3
Surgical ward in district hospital, primarily for obstetrics, trauma, and injury			
Staffed community ambulance			

Training of lay first-responders and volunteer paramedics			
Tuberculosis			
Childhood vaccination against endemic disease	8–263	Not assessed	13.9
Directly observed short-course chemotherapy			
Isoniazid treatment of epidemic disease			
Management of drug resistance			
Lower acute respiratory illnesses of children younger than age 5 years			
Community-based or facility-based case management of non-severe cases	28–264	0.7–1.8	9.7–26.4
Case management package, including community-based and facility-based care for non-severe cases and hospital-based care for severe cases			
Cardiovascular diseases			
Management of acute myocardial infarction with aspirin and β blocker	9–304	20.1	25.9–39.1
Primary prevention of coronary artery disease with legislation, substituting 2% of trans fat with polyunsaturated fat, at $0.50 per adult			
Secondary prevention of congestive heart failure with ACE inhibitors and β blockers incremental to diuretics			
Secondary prevention of myocardial infarction and stroke with polypill, containing aspirin, β blocker, thiazide diuretic, ACE inhibitor, and statin			

Appendix Table 1 (*cont.*)

	Cost per DALY averted ($)*	Thousands of DALYs averted* † per 20% increase in coverage	Burden of target diseases (millions of DALYs)*
Tobacco use and addiction			
Tax policy to increase price of cigarettes by 33%	14–374	22.5	15.7
Advertising bans, health information dissemination, tobacco supply reductions, and smoking restrictions			
Nicotine replacement therapy			
Maternal and neonatal care			
Increased primary-care coverage	127–394	21.3	37.7–47.8
Improved quality of comprehensive emergency obstetric care			
Improved overall quality and coverage of care			
Neonatal packages targeted at families, communities, and clinics			
Neglected low-cost opportunities in sub-Saharan Africa			
Childhood immunisation			
Second opportunity measles vaccination‡	1–5	Not assessed	Not assessed
Increased coverage of traditional EPI programme			
Traffic accidents			
Increased speeding penalties, and media and law	2–12	Not assessed	6.4

Intervention			
enforcement			
Speed bumps at most dangerous traffic intersections			
Malaria			
Insecticide-treated bed nets‡	2–24	20.8–37.6	35.4
Residual household spraying‡			
Intermittent preventive treatment during pregnancy‡			
Surgical services and emergency care			
Surgical ward in a district hospital, primarily for obstetrics, trauma, and injury	7–215	1.6–21.2	25–134.2
Staffed community ambulance			
Training of lay first-responders and volunteer paramedics			
Childhood illnesses			
Integrated management of childhood illnesses‡	9–218	21.2	9.6–45.1
Case management of non-severe lower acute respiratory illnesses at community or facility level			
Case management package, including community-based or facility-based care for non-severe cases and hospital-based care for severe lower acute respiratory illnesses			
Breastfeeding to prevent malnutrition			
Cardiovascular disease			
Management of acute myocardial infarction with aspirin and β blocker	9–273	20.04	4.6
Primary prevention of coronary artery disease with legislation, substituting 2% of trans fat with			

Appendix Table 1 *(cont.)*

	Cost per DALY averted ($)*	Thousands of DALYs averted* † per 20% increase in coverage	Burden of target diseases (millions of DALYs)*
polyunsaturated fat, at $0.50 per adult			
Secondary prevention of congestive heart failure with ACE inhibitors and β blockers incremental to diuretics			
Secondary prevention of myocardial infarction and stroke with polypill, containing aspirin, β blocker, thiazide diuretic, ACE inhibitor, and statin			
HIV/AIDS			56.8
Peer-based programmes for at-risk groups (eg, commercial sex workers) to disseminate information and teach specific skills	6–377	Not assessed	
Voluntary counselling and testing			
Diagnosis and treatment of sexually-transmitted diseases‡			
Condom promotion and distribution‡			
Prevention and treatment of coinfection with Mycobacterium tuberculosis‡			
Blood and needle safety programs			
Prevention of mother-to-child transmission with antiretroviral therapy			

Maternal and neonatal care			
Increased primary-care coverage	82–409	22.8	29.8–37.7
Improved quality of comprehensive emergency obstetric care			
Improved overall quality and coverage of care			
Neonatal packages targeted at families, communities, and clinics			
High-cost interventions in south Asia			
Depression			
Episodic treatment with new antidepressant drug (SSRI)	1003–1449	0.4–0.8	14.6
Episodic or maintenance psychosocial treatment plus treatment with new antidepressant drug (SSRI)			
High blood pressure and cholesterol			
Primary prevention of stroke and ischaemic and hypertensive heart disease with aspirin, β blocker, and statin, incremental to policy-induced behaviour change, at 15% risk of cardiovascular disease event over 10 years	1120–1932	26.7	48.6
Primary prevention of stroke and ischaemic and hypertensive heart disease with a polypill, containing aspirin, β blocker, thiazide diuretic, ACE Inhibitor, and statin, at 15% risk of cardiovascular disease event over 10 years			
Lifestyle diseases			
Primary prevention of diabetes, ischaemic heart disease,	1325–1865	1.3–1.8	39.5

Appendix Table 1 (*cont.*)

	Cost per DALY averted ($)*	Thousands of DALYs averted* † per 20% increase in coverage	Burden of target diseases (millions of DALYs)*
and stroke through policy that replaces saturated fat with monounsaturated fat in manufactured foods, accompanied by a public education campaign			
Primary prevention of diabetes, ischaemic heart disease, and stroke through legislation that reduces salt content plus public education			
Stroke (ischaemic)			
Acute management with recombinant tissue plasminogen activator within 48 h of onset	1630–2967	0.03–0.4	2.2–9.2
Acute management with heparin within 48 h of onset			
Secondary prevention with carotid endarterectomy			
Diarrhoeal diseases			
Oral rehydration therapy if package cost is > $2.30 per child per episode	500–6390	0.02–2.5	22.3
Rotavirus or cholera immunisation			
Tuberculosis			
Isoniazid treatment for latent endemic disease in patients uninfected with HIV	5588–9189	Not assessed	13.9

Schizophrenia and biopolar disorder			
Antipsychotic medication and psychosocial treatment for schizophrenia	1743–17702	0.02–0.12	2.2–2.9
Valproate and psychosocial treatment for bipolar disorder			
Cardiovascular diseases			
Management of acute myocardial infarction with streptokinase or tissue plasminogen activator, incremental to aspirin and β blocker	638–≥4040	0.04–0.3	25.9
Secondary prevention of ischaemic heart disease with statin, incremental to aspirin, β blocker, and ACE Inhibitor			
Secondary prevention of ischaemic heart disease with coronary artery bypass graft			
High-cost interventions in sub-Saharan Africa			
Diarrhoeal diseases			
Oral rehydration therapy if cost per episode is > $2.80 per child	500–≥658	0.1–4.6	22
Rotavirus or cholera immunisation			
HIV/AIDS			
Home care treatment‡	673–1494	Not assessed	56.8
Antiretroviral therapy in populations with low adherence‡			
Traffic accidents			
Random driver breath tests	973–2146	20.05	6.2–6.4
Enforcement of seatbelt laws			
Child restraint promotion			

Appendix Table 1 (*cont.*)

	Cost per DALY averted ($)*	Thousands of DALYs averted* † per 20% increase in coverage	Burden of target diseases (millions of DALYs)*
High blood pressure and cholesterol			
Primary prevention of stroke and ischaemic and hypertensive heart disease with aspirin, β blocker, and statin, incremental to policy-induced behavior change, at 15% risk of cardiovascular disease event over 10 years	1920	Not assessed	10.6
Lifestyle diseases			
Primary prevention of diabetes, ischaemic heart disease, and stroke through policy that replaces saturated fat with monounsaturated fat in manufactured foods, accompanied by a public education campaign	1766–2356	1.4–1.8	9.6
Primary prevention of diabetes, ischaemic heart disease, and stroke through legislation that reduces salt content plus public education			
Stroke (ischaemic)			
Acute management with recombinant tissue plasminogen activator within 48h of onset	1284–2940	0.02–0.3	0.9–3.6
Acute management with heparin within 48h of onset			
Secondary prevention with carotid endarterectomy			

Tuberculosis			
Isoniazid treatment for latent endemic disease in patients uninfected with HIV	4129–5506	Not assessed	8.1
Cardiovascular diseases			
Management of acute myocardial infarction with streptokinase or tissue plasminogen activator, incremental to aspirin and β blocker	634–26813	0.03–0.2	4.6
Secondary prevention of ischaemic heart disease with statin, incremental to aspirin, β blocker, and ACE inhibitor			
Secondary prevention of ischaemic heart disease with coronary artery bypass graft			

* Ranges represent variation in point estimates of cost-effectiveness, DALYs averted, or burden of disease for different interventions. Point estimates of cost-effectiveness and DALYs averted obtained from DCP2[4] or calculated as midpoint of range estimates reported. Burden of disease estimates obtained from reference 7. †Avertable DALYs per 20% increase intreatment coverage in a hypothetical sample population of 1 million people. ‡Only assessed for sub-Saharan Africa.

Source: This table is based on chapters in *Disease Control Priorities in Developing Countries*, 2nd edition (Jamison et al., 2006a) as summarized in Laxminarayan et al. (2006), table 2.

References

Abraham, Katherine G., and Christopher Mackie, eds. 2005. *Beyond the Market: Designing Nonmarket Accounts for the United States.* Washington, DC: National Academy Press.

Aral, S. O., M. Over, L. Manhart, and K. K. Holmes. 2006. "Sexually Transmitted Infections." In *Disease Control Priorities in Developing Countries*, 2nd edition, ed. D. T. Jamison et al., 311–30.

Arrow, K. J., H. Gelband, and D. T. Jamison. 2005. "Making Antimalarial Agents Available in Africa." *New England Journal of Medicine* 353: 333–35.

Barr, N. 2001. *The Welfare State as Piggy Bank: Information, Risk, Uncertainty, and the Role of the State.* Oxford: Oxford University Press.

Becker, G. S., T. J. Philipson, and R. R. Soares. 2003. "The Quantity and Quality of Life and the Evolution of World Inequality." *American Economic Review* 95: 277–91.

Behrman, J. R., H. Alderman and J. Hoddinott. "Hunger and Malnutrition." This volume.

Bertozzi, S., N. S. Padian, J. Wegbreit, et al. 2006. "HIV/AIDS Prevention and Treatment." In *Disease Control Priorities in Developing Countries*, 2nd edition, ed. D. T. Jamison et al., 331–70.

Bezanson, D. 2005. "Replenishing the Global Fund: An Independent Assessment." www.theglobalfund.or/en/about/replenishment (accessed 4 May 2005).

Bloom, D. E., D. Canning, and D. T. Jamison. 2004. "Health, Wealth and Welfare." *Finance and Development* 41 (1): 10–15.

Bloom, D. E., D. Canning, and J. Sevilla. 2004. "The Effect of Health on Economic Growth: A Production Function approach." *World Development* 32 (January): 1–13.

Bloom, David E., and David Canning. 2006. "Booms, Busts and Echoes: How the Biggest Demographic Upheaval in History is Affecting Global Development." *Finance and Development* 43: 8–13.

Bobadilla, J. L., J. Frenk, R. Lozano, et al. 1993. "Cardiovascular Disease." In *Disease Control Priorities in Developing Countries*, ed. D. T. Jamison, W. H. Mosley, A. R. Measham, J. L. Bobadilla, 51–63. Oxford: Oxford University Press.

Bourguignon, F., and C. Morrisson. 2002. "Inequality among World Citizens: 1820–1992." *American Economic Review* 92: 727–44.

Breman, J. G., A. Mills, R. W. Snow, et al. 2006. "Conquering Malaria." In *Disease Control Priorities in Developing Countries*, 2nd edition, ed. D. T. Jamison et al., 413–32.

Brenzel, L., L. J. Wolfson, J. Fox-Rushby, M. Miller, and N. A. Halsey. 2006. "Vaccine-Preventable Diseases." In *Disease Control Priorities in Developing Countries*, 2nd edition, ed. D. T. Jamison et al., 389–412.

Bundy, D. A. P., S. Shaeffer, M. Jukes, et al. 2006. "School-Based Health and Nutrition Programs." In *Disease Control Priorities in Developing Countries*, 2nd edition, ed. D. T. Jamison et al., 1091–108.

Clemens, M., S. Radelet, and R. Bhavnani. 2004. "Counting Chickens When They Hatch: The Short-Term Effect of Aid on Growth." Working Paper 44, Center for Global Development, Washington, DC.

Crafts, N., and M. Haacker. 2004. "Welfare Implications of HIV/AIDS." In *The Macroeconomics of HIV/AIDS*, ed. M. Haacker, 182–97. Washington, DC: International Monetary Fund.

Crawford, C. B., B. E. Salter, and K. L. Jang. 1989. "Human Grief: Is Its Intensity Related to the Reproductive Value of the Deceased?" *Ethology and Sociobiology* 10 (4): 297–307.

Cutler, D., A. Deaton, and A. Lleras-Muney. 2006. "The Determinants of Mortality." *Journal of Economic Perspectives* 20 (3, summer): 97–120.

Davis, K. 1956. "The Amazing Decline of Mortality in Underdeveloped Areas." *American Economic Review* (Papers and Proceedings) 46 (2): 305–18.

de Savigny, D., H. Kasale, C. Mbuya, and G. Reid. 2004. *Fixing Health Systems*. Ottawa: International Development Research Centre.

Debas, H. T., R. Gosselin, C. McCord, and A. Thind. 2006. "Surgery." In *Disease Control Priorities in Developing Countries*, 2nd edition, ed. D. T. Jamison et al., 1245–60.

Del Rio, C. and J. Sepulveda. 2002. "AIDS in Mexico: Lessons Learned and Implications for Developing Countries." *AIDS* 16: 1445–57.

Dye, C., and K. Floyd. 2006. "Tuberculosis." In *Disease Control Priorities in Developing Countries*, 2nd edition, ed. D. T. Jamison et al., 289–310.

Easterlin, R. A. 1996. *Growth Triumphant: The Twenty-First Century in Historical Perspective*. Ann Arbor: University of Michigan Press.

Ezzati, M., S. Vander Hoorn, Alan D. Lopez, et al. 2006. "Comparative Quantification of Mortality and Burden of Disease Attributable to Selected Risk Factors." In *Global Burden of Disease and Risk Factors*, ed. A. D. Lopez et al., 241–68.

Feachem, R. G. A., T. Kjellstrom, C. J. L. Murray, M. Over, and M. Phillips (eds.). 1992. *Health of Adults in the Developing World*. New York: Oxford University Press.

Foley, K. M., J. L. Wagner, D. E. Joranson, and H. Gelband. 2006. "Pain Control for People with Cancer and AIDS." In *Disease Control Priorities in Developing Countries*, 2nd edition, ed. D. T. Jamison et al., 981–94.

Gaziano, T., K. S. Reddy, F. Paccaud, S. Horton, and V. Chaturvedi. 2006. "Cardiovascular Disease." In *Disease Control Priorities in Developing Countries*, 2nd edition, ed. D. T. Jamison et al., 645–62.

Gericke, C. A., C. Kurowski, M. K. Ranson, and A. Mills. 2003. "Feasibility of Scaling-up Interventions: The Role of Interventions Design." Working Paper 13, Disease Control Priorities Project, Bethesda, MD.

Graham, W. J., J. Cairns, S. Bhattacharya, C. H. W. Bullough, Z. Quayyum, and K. Rogo. 2006. "Maternal and Perinatal Conditions." In *Disease Control Priorities in Developing Countries*, 2nd edition, ed. D. T. Jamison et al., 499–530.

Haacker, M., ed. 2004. *The Macroeconomics of HIV/AIDS.* Washington, DC: International Monetary Fund.

Hotez, P. J., D. A. P. Bundy, K. Beagle, et al. 2006. "Helminth Infections: Soil-Transmitted Helminth Infections and Schistosomiasis." In *Disease Control Priorities in Developing Countries*, 2nd edition, ed. D. T. Jamison et al., 467–82.

Hutton, G. "Unsafe Water and Lack of Sanitation." This volume.

Institute of Medicine. 1985. *New Vaccine Development: Establishing Priorities.* Volume 1 of *Diseases of Importance in the United States.* Washington, DC: National Academies Press.

Jamison, D. T. 2002. "Cost-effectiveness Analysis: Concepts and Applications." In *Oxford Textbook of Public Health*, ed. R. Detels, J. McEwan, R. Beaglehole, and H. Tanaka, 903–19. Oxford: Oxford University Press.

Jamison, D. T. 2006a. "Investing in Health." In *Disease Control Priorities in Developing Countries*, 2nd edition, ed. D. T. Jamison et al., 3–34.

Jamison, D. T. 2006b. "The Neglected Problems of Stillbirths and Neonatal Deaths." Paper prepared for the Global Forum on Health Research, 10th Meeting, Cairo.

Jamison, D. T., J. Breman, A. R. Measham, G. Alleyne, M. Claeson, D. Evans, P. Jha, A. Mills, and P. Musgrove, eds. 2006a. *Disease Control Priorities in Developing Countries*, 2nd edition. Oxford and New York: Oxford University Press.

Jamison, D. T., E. A. Jamison, and J. D. Sachs. 2003. "Assessing the Determinants of Growth When Health Is Explicitly Included in the Measure of Economic Welfare." Paper presented at the 4th World Congress of the International Health Economics Association, San Francisco, June.

Jamison, D. T., L. J. Lau, and J. Wang. 2005. "Health's Contribution to Economic Growth in an Environment of Partially Endogenous Technical Progress." In *Health and Economic Growth: Findings and Policy* Implications, ed. G. Lopez-Casasnovas, B. Rivera, and L. Currais. Cambridge, MA: MIT Press.

Jamison, D. T., and S. Radelet. 2005. "Making Aid Smarter." *Finance and Development* 42 (2): 42–46.

Jamison, D. T., J. Sachs, and J. Wang. 2001. "The Effect of the AIDS Epidemic on Economic Welfare in Sub-Saharan Africa." CMH Working Paper WG1:13, Commission on Macroeconomics and Health, World Health Organization, Geneva.

Jamison, D. T., M. Sandbu, and J. Wang. 2004. "Why Has Infant Mortality Decreased at Such Different Rates in Different Countries?" Working Paper 21, Disease Control Priorities Project, Bethesda, MD.

Jamison, D. T., S. Shahid-Salles, J. S. Jamison, J. Lawn, and J. Zupan. 2006b. "Incorporating Deaths Near the Time of Birth into Estimates of the Global Burden of Disease." In *Global Burden of Disease and Risk Factors*, ed. A. D. Lopez et al., 427–62.

Jha, P., F. J. Chaloupka, J. Moore, et al. 2006. "Tobacco Addiction." In *Disease Control Priorities in Developing Countries*, 2nd edition, ed. D. T. Jamison et al., 869–86.

Joint Learning Initiative. 2000. *Human Resources for Health: Overcoming the Crisis*. Washington, DC: Communications Development.

Kanbur, R., and T. Sandler. 1999. *The Future of Development Assistance: Common Pools and International Public Goods*. Washington, DC: Overseas Development Council.

Keusch, G. T., O. Fontaine, A. Bhargava, et al. 2006. "Diarrheal Diseases." In *Disease Control Priorities in Developing Countries*, 2nd edition, ed. D. T. Jamison et al., 371–88.

Lawn, J. E., J. Zupan, G. Begkoyian, and R. Knippenberg. 2006. "Newborn Survival." In *Disease Control Priorities in Developing Countries*, 2nd edition, ed. D. T. Jamison et al., 531–50.

Laxminarayan, R., J. Chow, and S. A. Shahid-Salles. 2006. "Intervention Cost-Effectiveness: Overview of Main Messages." In *Disease Control Priorities in Developing Countries*, 2nd edition, ed. D. T. Jamison et al., 35–86.

Laxminarayan, R., A. J. Mills, J. G. Breman, et al. 2006. "Advancement of Global Health: Key Messages from the Disease Control Priorities Project." *Lancet* 367: 1193–208, April 8.

Levine, R. and the What Works Working Group. 2007. *Millions Saved: Proven Successes in Global Health*. Subbury, MA: Jones and Bartlett.

Lindert, P. H. 2004. *Growing Public: Social Spending and Economic Growth since the Eighteenth Century*. Vol. I. Cambridge: Cambridge University Press.

Lomborg, Bjørn, ed. 2004. *Global Crises, Global Solutions*. Cambridge: Cambridge University Press.

Lomborg, Bjørn, ed. 2006. *How to Spend $50 Billion to Make the World a Better Place*. Cambridge: Cambridge University Press.

Lopez, A. D., S. Begg, and E. Bos. 2006. "Demographic and Epidemiological Characteristics of Major Regions of the World, 1990 and 2001." In *Global Burden of Disease and Risk Factors*, ed. A. D. Lopez et al., 17–44.

Lopez, A. D., C. D. Mathers, M. Ezzati, D. T. Jamison, and C. J. L. Murray, eds. 2006a. *Global Burden of Disease and Risk Factors*. Oxford and New York: Oxford University Press.

Lopez, A. D., C. D. Mathers, M. Ezzati, D. T. Jamison, and C. J. L. Murray. 2006b. "Global and Regional Burden of Disease and Risk Factors, 2001: Systematic Analysis of Population Health Data." *Lancet* 367: 1747–57, May 27.

Lopez-Casasnovas, G., B. Rivera, and L. Currais, eds. 2005. *Health and Economic Growth: Findings and Policy Implications*. Cambridge, MA: MIT Press.

Mathers, C. D., C. J. L. Murray, and A.D. Lopez. 2006. "The Burden of Disease and Mortality by Condition: Data, Methods and Results for the Year 2001." In *Global Burden of Disease and Risk Factors*, ed. A. D. Lopez et al., 45–93.

Meltzer, D. 2006. "Economic Approaches to Valuing Global Health Research." In *Disease Control Priorities in Developing Countries*, 2nd edition. ed. D. T. Jamison et al., 157–64.

Mills, A., F. Rasheed, and S. Tollman. 2006, "Strengthening Health Systems." In *Disease Control Priorities in Developing Countries*, 2nd edition, ed. D. T. Jamison et al., 87–102.

Mills, A., and S. Shillcutt. 2004. "Communicable Diseases." In *Global Crises, Global Solutions*, ed. B. Lomborg, 62–114. Cambridge: Cambridge University Press.

Mulligan, J., J. A. Fox-Rushby, T. Adam, B. Johns, and A. Mills. 2003. "Unit Costs of Health Care Inputs in Low and Middle Income Regions." Disease Control Priorities Project Working Paper 9. Bethesda, MD: Fogarty International Center, National Institutes of Health.

Nordhaus, W. 2003. "The Health of Nations: The Contributions of Improved Health to Living Standards." In *Measuring the Gains from Health Research: An Economic Approach*, ed. K. M. Murphy and R. H. Topel, 9–40. Chicago: University of Chicago Press.

Oeppen, J., and J. W. Vaupel. 2002. "Demography, Broken Limits to Life Expectancy." *Science* 296 (5570): 1029–31.

Peabody, J. W., M. M. Taguiwalo, D. A. Robalino, and J. Frenk. 2006. "Improving the Quality of Care in Developing Countries." In *Disease Control Priorities in Developing Countries*, 2nd edition, ed. D. T. Jamison et al., 1293–308.

Preston, S. H. 1975. "The Changing Relation between Mortality and Level of Economic Development." *Population Studies* 29 (2): 231–48.

Preston, S. H. 1980. "Causes and Consequences of Mortality Declines in Less Developed Countries during the Twentieth Century." In *Population and Economic Change in Developing Countries*, ed. R. Easterlin, 289–360. Chicago: University of Chicago Press.

Pritchard, C. 2004. "Developments in Economic Evaluation in Health Care: A Review of HEED." OHE Briefing 40, Office of Health Economics, London, March.

Radelet, S. 2003. *Challenging Foreign Aid*. Washington, DC: Center for Global Development.

Rodgers, A., C. M. M. Lawes, T. A. Gaziano, and T. Vos. 2006. "The Growing Burden of Risk from High Blood Pressure, Cholesterol, and Bodyweight." In *Disease Control Priorities in Developing Countries*, 2nd edition, ed. D. T. Jamison et al., 851–68.

Simoes, E. A. F., T. Cherian, J. Chow, S. A. Shahid-Salles, R. Laxminarayan, and T. J. John. 2006. "Acute Respiratory Infections in Children." In *Disease Control Priorities in Developing Countries*, 2nd edition, ed. D. T. Jamison et al., 483–98.

Strauss, John, and Duncan Thomas. 1998. "Health, Nutrition, and Economic Development." *Journal of Economic Literature, American Economic Association* 36 (2): 766–817.

Usher, Dan. 1973. "The Measurement of Economic Growth." Working Paper 145, Queen's University, Department of Economics, Kingston, Ontario.

Van der Gaag, J. 2004. "Perspective Paper 2.2." In *Global Crises, Global Solutions*, ed. Bjørn Lomborg, 124–28. Cambridge: Cambridge University Press.

Viscusi, W. K., and J. E. Aldy. 2003. "The Value of a Statistical Life: A Critical Review of Market Estimates Throughout the World." Harvard Law and Economics Discussion Paper no. 392. Boston, MA: Harvard Law School.

WHO. 1999. *World Health Report 1999*. Geneva: World Health Organization.

WHO. 2000. *World Health Report 2000*. Geneva: World Health Organization.

WHO. 2005. *Preventing Chronic Diseases: A Vital Investment*. Geneva: World Health Organization.

WHO CMH. 2001. *Report of the Commission on Macroeconomics and Health*. Geneva: World Health Organization.

Willett, W. C., J. P. Koplan, Rachel Nugent, C. Dusenbury, P. Puska, and T. A. Gaziano. 2006. "Prevention of Chronic Disease by Means of Diet and Lifestyle Changes." In *Disease Control Priorities in Developing Countries*, 2nd edition, ed. D. T. Jamison et al., 833–50.

World Bank. 1993. *World Development Report: Investing in Health*. New York: Oxford University Press.

World Bank. 2003. *World Development Indicators*. Washington, DC: World Bank.

18 | Lack of People of Working Age

ROBERT E. WRIGHT
KATERINA LISENKOVA

Introduction

Population decline implies a decline in the size of the potential labour force. Assuming no changes in age-specific employment rates, a decline in the potential labour force will generate a decline in the number of people employed. Population ageing is an increase in the share of older people, and a decrease in the share of younger people, in the total population. It also implies ageing of the labour force. As a population ages, so will its labour force, with an increasing share of older workers and a decreasing share of younger workers. In this sense, population decline/labour force decline *and* population ageing/labour force ageing go hand-in-hand.

Problems

In most industrialised countries (taken here as North America, Europe, Russia, Japan, Australia and New Zealand), employment is concentrated in quite a narrow age range. For example, in Scotland, data from the 2001 Census indicates that of the total number of people employed (both part-time and full-time), about 95 percent of them are aged between 20 and 65. The situation is not much different in other industrialised nations. The problem of 'lack of people of working age' stems from the situation that if current demographic trends continue, the number of people in this key age group will plummet in most of these countries.

The scale of this change is illustrated in Figure 18.1, which shows the number of people aged 20–64 in industrialised countries in the period 1950–2050. The estimates for 2005 onwards are from the most recent round of United Nation population projections.[1] If these projections prove to be correct, the number of people in this age group will decline by around 80 million (or in percentage terms, by over 10%) in the next

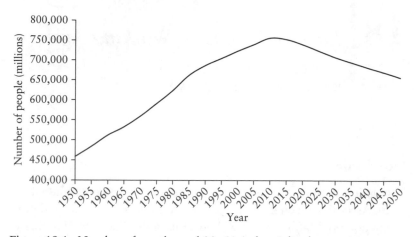

Figure 18.1. Number of people aged 20–64, industrialised countries, 1950–2050

Source: United Nations

four to five decades. The scale of this decline is further illustrated in Table 18.1, which shows the change in the number of people aged 20–64 in the 25 countries that currently make up the European Union. Significant decline is expected in most of these countries. It is hard to imagine that economic growth can be sustained in some of the 'new' EU countries, such as Latvia, Hungary, the Czech Republic, Slovenia and Lithuania, where the number of people of traditional labour force age is expected to decline by one-third by the middle of the century.[2]

Economics suggests that it is the interaction between labour demand (potential employers) and labour supply (potential employees) that determines the level of employment and wages paid. These population projections imply that the potential supply of labour will decrease substantially in industrialised countries. This will lead to increased competition in the labour market for workers, which will put upward pressure on wages.[3–6]

If producers of goods and services in industrialised countries are forced to pay higher wages because of demographically generated labour shortages, they will become less competitive in both domestic and international markets, which in turn will lead to lower rates of economic growth.[7,8] Lower rates of economic growth imply lower tax revenues. As tax revenues decline, governments will quickly find themselves without the necessary resources needed to provide the public services

Table 18.1. *Population Aged 20–64 EU Member and Candidate States, 2005 and 2050 (thousands)*

Country	2005	2050	Change	% Change
Italy	35,505	23,827	−11,678	−33%
Spain	27,557	20,022	−7,535	−27%
Austria	5,062	3,769	−1,293	−26%
Greece	6,895	5,541	−1,354	−20%
Germany	50,391	40,920	−9,471	−19%
Portugal	6,449	5,394	−1,055	−16%
Belgium	6,178	5,351	−827	−13%
Finland	3,187	2,810	−377	−12%
Netherlands	10,056	9,141	−915	−9%
France	35,763	33,515	−2,248	−6%
Denmark	3,285	3,195	−90	−3%
Sweden	5,315	5,404	89	−2%
UK	35,421	36,745	1,324	−4%
Ireland	2,568	3,092	524	+20%
Luxembourg	287	402	115	+40%
All EU 15	233,919	199,128	−34,791	−15%
EU-10: [1]				
Latvia	1,394	886	−508	−36%
Hungary	6,178	3,966	−2,212	−36%
Czech Republic	6,622	4,260	−2,362	−36%
Slovenia	1,265	820	−445	−35%
Lithuania	2,042	1,379	−663	−32%
Poland	24,321	17,255	−7,066	−29%
Estonia	800	601	−199	−25%
Slovakia	3,451	2,612	−839	−24%
Malta	247	225	−22	−9%
Cyprus	504	659	155	+31%
All EU-10	46,824	32,663	−14,161	−30%
All EU-25	280,743	231,791	−48,952	−17%

Notes: (1) Countries that joined in 2004

Source: United Nations

demanded by their ageing electorate. This will provide an incentive for governments to raise taxes. However, raising taxes will generate capital flights and the emigration of quality labour to lower tax regions, leading to even lower rates of economic growth.

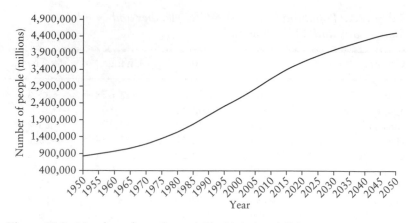

Figure 18.2. Number of people aged 20–64, industrialising countries, 1950–2050

Source: United Nations

It is important to note that the problem of a 'lack of people of working age' is a problem that industrialising countries are not going to have to face for some time to come. Consider Figure 18.2, which shows the number of people aged 20–64 in industrialising countries. In these countries, the number of people in this age group is expected to increase by over 1.5 billion (or by about 60%) in the period 2005–2050. This large expected increase suggests (as is discussed below) that one 'solution' to the problem of labour shortages in industrialised countries is the immigration from industrialising countries. That is, a transfer of people of working age from countries with 'excess supply' to countries with 'excess demand'.[9]

The United Nations population projections suggest that the number of people of 'traditional labour force age' will decline considerably in industrialised countries in the next four to five decades. However, as the *number* in this age group declines, its age *distribution* will also change, with an increasing proportion of the total concentrating in the older working age groups. An illustration of this labour force ageing pattern is shown in Figure 18.3. It shows the number of people aged 35–64 relative the number of people aged 20–34 in the European Union. Although not a perfect correspondence, this can be thought of as the ratio of 'older to younger' workers.

For the 25 EU countries taken as a group, this ratio will increase up until about 2030 and then it will decline. This implies that in the next

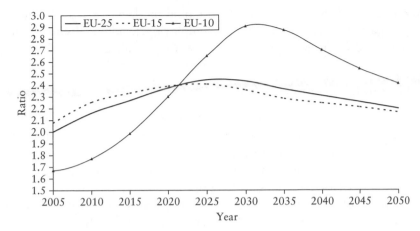

Figure 18.3. Ratio of population aged 35–64 to population aged 20–34, EU Member States, 2005–2050

Source: United Nations

two-and-a-half decades there will be a sharp increase in the potential supply of 'older workers' and a sharp decrease in the potential supply of 'younger workers'. In the ten countries that joined the EU in 2004 (EU-10), compared to the 'old' 15 EU countries, the ageing of the labour force is even more dramatic, with this ratio increasing from the current level of 1.6 to nearly 3.0 by 2030.

Why does the ageing of the labour force matter? The impact of population ageing can be thought of as an *increase* in the supply of older workers coupled with a *decrease* in the supply of younger workers. These supply shifts will generate several effects. First, assuming the labour market adjusts, the average wage of younger workers will increase while the average wage of older workers will decrease. Second, the number of younger workers employed will decrease, while the number of older workers employed will increase. In other words, the exogenous changes in labour supply generated by population ageing are absorbed by the relative wage of younger-to-older workers increase.[10-13] It is important to note that this new level of employment (i.e. fewer younger workers and more older workers) corresponds to the maximum level of output production, given a fixed stock of capital and constant technology. However, this new level of total employment may be higher or lower. In this sense, the impact of changes in the age structure of the labour force can be thought of as a 'trade-off' between earnings and employment effects. If labour markets don't adjust, then population ageing will generate unemployment, potentially for both older and younger people and even lower economic growth.[13-15]

Cost of labour force decline

The above discussion suggests that if the labour force is allowed to decline in industrialised countries then rates of economic growth will probably be lower in the future. Therefore one main 'cost' associated with this demographic change is the output or gross domestic product (GDP) loss caused by the shrinking of the potential labour force.

The most recent set of population projections carried out by the United Nations, suggests that the potential labour force, defined as individuals between the ages of 20 and 64, in the industrialised countries (as a group) will grow slowly until the end of this decade. However, after 2010, a steady and substantial decline will occur. The projections indicate that in 2010 there will be about 755 million people in this age group. However, by 2050, the number will be closer to 655 million. That is, in this 40-year period the potential labour force will shrink by about 100 million people, or in percentage terms, by more than 10 percent.

According to the World Bank, the combined GDP in these countries is almost $34 trillion ($34,000,000 million). Assuming moderate growth until the end of the decade, this total should reach about $US 341/4 trillion by 2010. It is worth noting that based on 2005 estimates these countries make up about 23 percent of the global population, but generate about 75 percent of global output.

In order to estimate the output loss associated with a declining potential labour force, quantitative information describing the relationship between labour and output is needed. Such information is generated in the standard production function interpretation of economic growth where capital, labour and technology are seen as the main determinants of economic growth. However, such estimates are usually derived using simple time-series econometric methods and have well-known weaknesses. Unfortunately, space does not allow for further elaboration on these difficulties.

The estimates used here to measure output loss are from the Computable Generated Equilibrium (CGE) model based at the University of Strathclyde.[16] This model is essentially a mathematical representation of the way in which the Scottish economy operates. It can be used to evaluate the impacts of a wide range of policies on key economic variables such as output, employment, inflation, etc. From this model, the elasticity of output (Y) with respect to the population age 20–64 is +0.56. That is, a 10 percent decrease in the size of this group is associated with a 5.6 percent lower level of output. Assuming this estimate is generalisable to other high-income industrialised countries, it can be used to generate an estimate an output loss associated with labour force decline.

More specifically, it is possible to calculate the GDP loss associated with the expected 100 million decline in the number of people aged 20–64 in the period 2010–2050. However, in order to do so, one needs a relevant baseline. The baseline that we use is the scenario where the number of people aged 20–64 remains fixed at the 2010 level of around 750 million. Likewise, the time horizon is 40 years (i.e. to the end of the population projection period). Under these assumptions, and discount rates set at 3 and 6 percent (as recommended), the present discounted value (PDV) of the output loss is $19 trillion and $8 trillion, respectively.

Solutions?

A possible policy response by governments in industrialised countries to population and labour force decline/ageing is to 'do nothing'. If they adopt this policy, populations and labour forces will start (continue) to decline in size and the ageing process of both will accelerate. As a consequence, economic growth will be lower and the standard of living will fall.

However, it is worth remembering that population ageing is a transitory phenomenon. Most industrialised countries have experienced below replacement level fertility for at least three decades and it seems unlikely that fertility is going to increase dramatically in the future (e.g. above the replacement level). Likewise, future improvements in mortality are expected to be modest, with life expectancy only increasing slowly in the coming decades. Without massive increases in net migration, the age structure of these populations will stabilise some time in this century – a point will be reached where the share of the population across the different age groups will be virtually constant. Therefore, the problem of population ageing is adjustment problems generated by a 'one-off' movement from a 'younger' to an 'older' age structure.

One view is simply to 'ride out the storm', since this situation of changing age structure (and its resulting socioeconomic challenges and problems) is a temporary phenomenon. It is often argued that once the age structure of a population stabilises, low rates of economic growth are needed to generate improvements in the standard of living. Such an approach will be costly in the adjustment period, and it would be a politically dangerous course to follow in countries with democratically elected governments. Not surprisingly it is a 'policy' not currently advocated by any government that I am aware of. What else can de done?

Increase the productivity of labour

Demographic change will generate a sizeable increase in the so-called 'economic dependency ratio', which is simply the ratio of 'people in work' relative to those 'not in work' (sometimes inaccurately proxied by the number of people aged 15–64 relative to the number of people aged 0–14 and aged 65+). In a pay-as-you-go welfare state (which is the norm in industrialised countries) the bottom line is that those that are 'in work' pay for those that are 'not in work'. If demographic trends continue it is likely that the number 'in work' will decline while the number 'not in work' (mainly retired) will increase. If the standard of living is not to fall, then those 'in work' will have to pay for an increasing number of those 'not in work'. This can only be achieved if labour productivity increases by a large enough amount. That is, with fewer workers, more must be produced per worker, or output will drop.[16]

Labour productivity can be increased by educational reforms that result in schooling and training systems that produce graduates that complement capital-intensive and skill-intensive domestic production. In most industrialised countries, between 4 and 6 percent of GDP is devoted to primary, secondary and tertiary schooling. A doubling of the amount spent would undoubtedly make younger workers more productive, but there is little hard and robust evidence on by 'how much'.

The decline in the size, coupled with the ageing of, the labour force suggests that investments in education and training will not have maximum benefit if exclusively focused on the young. This implies that in future, state-sponsored spending will need to be spread across the age range. This is consistent with the so-called 'life-long' learning approach to human capital investment.

Increase labour force participation

Policies that increase the potential supply of labour available to private sector employers, yet at the same time do not put upwards pressure on wages are desirable. For example, the rates of labour force participation and employment for women with children of pre-school and school age is still low in many industrialised countries. Survey evidence consistently demonstrates that a large number of mothers are prepared to enter the labour market, but the shortage of affordable day-care and other child-services makes it financially irrational for many of them to do so. Taxpayers' money should be spent on so-called 'family friendly' policies that make it easier for parents (particularly mothers) to combine child rearing and employment.

Such policies are most developed in the Scandinavian countries. Although there is considerable debate about whether or not such policies lead to higher fertility, there is no doubt that they lead to higher rates of female labour force participation, especially for women with pre-school age children. However, these policies are not cheap. Even though the majority of the costs are borne by the taxpayer, the cost to private sector is non zero. Therefore, in our view, for such policies to be successful in other countries, a considerable cultural shift will be required.

Higher levels of immigration

As briefly mentioned above, higher levels of immigration from industrialising to industrialised countries would increase the supply of workers in the latter countries.[16] This could be achieved by introducing or enhancing immigration systems that 'match people to jobs' such as the Canadian 'points system' or the German 'guest worker' programme (or some combination of the two). In a strict sense, such a policy would be 'cost free' in the sense that at the global level, the potential supply of immigrants is effectively inelastic. This is because the combined population size of the industrialising countries dwarfs that of the combined population size of the industrialised countries.

The success of increased immigration policies will depend on how effectively immigrants assimilate into host societies. It has been

Table 18.2. *Benefit/cost ratios of a per-head immigrant subsidy*

	Discount rate	
Subsidy	Low (3%)	High (6%)
$10,000	40.6	33.1
$20,000	20.3	16.5
$50,000	8.1	6.6
$100,000	4.1	3.3

Notes: In these calculations, the countries classified as being 'industrialised' are the United States, Canada, Japan, Australia, New Zealand, all the countries of Western Europe, as well as Belarus, Bulgaria, Croatia, Moldova, Romania, Russian Federation, Ukraine, Iceland, Norway, Albania, Bosnia and Herzegovina. This is the same group of countries included in the United Nations population projections.

suggested that subsidising immigration through a one-off payment to immigrants increases assimilation. In order to explore this idea further in a cost–benefit framework, we have assumed that each immigrant is given a payment. One result of such a payment could be zero (or significantly reduced) return migration.

Using the estimates of output loss presented above, Table 18.2 presents benefit–cost (B/C) ratios for various levels of one-off immigrant subsidies. The table begins with a payment of $10,000 (US) per migrant. As the table suggests, if such a policy 'works', it is extremely cost effective. These ratios of course fall if the payment is larger. However, even at what seems at first glance to be a very high subsidy of $100,000 (US) per head, the B/C ratios in all possible combinations are large.

Labour market reforms

Population ageing and decline will create pressure for change in the labour market. There will be a decrease of the potential supply of workers caused by the decline in the population in the 20–64 age group. Taken on its own, this will put upwards pressure on wages. At the same time there will be an increase in the potential supply of older workers and a decrease in the potential supply of younger workers. This age structure change will put downward pressure on the wages of older workers and upwards pressure on the wages of younger workers. Labour markets must be free to adjust to supply and demand pressures. In many industrialised countries, labour markets are regulated, and adjustment is at best slow and hampered. In such countries, reforms (regardless of their political unpopularity) aimed at 'freeing up' the labour market would be desirable.

Increase the age of retirement

With increasing life expectancy in industrialised countries, many argue that the age of retirement, usually around age 60 or 65, is too low. 'Age of retirement' is usually interpreted as the age at which one is entitled to a state pension or a private pension in those occupations where retirement is mandatory. By increasing the age of retirement, some people will be 'forced' to work to an older age, while others would welcome the opportunity to work longer for a variety of reasons. Increasing the age of retirement would increase the potential supply of labour by increasing the potential supply of older workers. Whether this supply increase would be translated into employment would depend on the wages that were on offer from employers. These wages, on average, would probably be lower (perhaps considerably lower) than what was on offer before the age of retirement was raised. This of course would have massive political ramifications.

Conclusions and caveats

Demographic change in industrialised countries will lead to an increase in the number of individuals of pension age and a decrease in the number of individuals of working age. This will lead to a large increase in the demand for state-supplied health care, residential services, housing, pensions and other services consumed by the elderly. Unfortunately, at the same time, the base expected to pay for this increase – essentially people of working age – will become progressively smaller, both in absolute numbers and in relative population share. That is, those 'demanding' will increase while those 'supplying' will decrease. It is not hard to imagine that such a situation of increasing imbalance is unsustainable, and some argue that cracks in 'pay-as-you-go' welfare systems of industrialised countries are already starting to show. It is clear that there is no single solution to this problem. Addressing the problem of a shrinking and ageing labour force will require action along a variety of fronts and will, no doubt, be very expensive. However, of the five 'solutions' outlined above, increasing immigration seems the most likely given it clearly has the lowest direct cost to taxpayers.

References

1. United Nations (2005), *World Population Prospects: The 2004 Revision Population Database*, New York: Department of Economics and Social Affairs, Population Division, (http://esa.un.org/unpp/).
2. Lisenkova, K. and R. E. Wright (2005), 'Demographic Change and the European Union Labour Market', *National Institute Economic Review*, No 194, 74–81.
3. Borsch-Supan, A. (2003), 'Labour Market Effects of Population Ageing', *Labour*, Vol. 17 (Special Issue), 5–44.
4. Dixon, S. (2003), 'Implications of Population Ageing for the Labour Market', *Labour Market Trends* (February), 67–76.
5. Ermisch, J. F. (1995), 'Demographic Developments and European Labour Market', *Scottish Journal of Political Economy*, Vol. 42, 331–46.
6. Zimmermann, K. (1991), 'Ageing and the Labor Market', *Journal of Population Economics*, Vol. 4, 77–200.
7. Weil, D. (1997), 'The Economics of Population Ageing'. In M. Rosenzweig and O. Stark (eds.), *Handbook of Population Economics*, Vol 1B, Amsterdam: North Holland.
8. Fertig, M. and C. Schmidt (2005), 'Gerontocracy in Motion? European Cross-Country Evidence on the Labor Market Consequences of Population Ageing'. In R.E. Wright (ed.), *Scotland's Demographic Challenge*, Stirling: Scottish Economic Policy Network.
9. Martin, P. (2004), *Population and Migration: Challenge Paper*, Copenhagen: Copenhagen Consensus Center.
10. Freeman, R. B. (1976), 'The Effects of Demographic Factors on Age-Earnings Profiles', *Journal of Human Resources*, Vol. 14, 289–318.
11. Klevmarken, A. (1993), Demographics and the Dynamics of Earnings. *Journal of Population Economics*, Vol. 6, 105–22.
12. Welch, F. (1979), 'Effects of Cohort Size on Earnings: The Baby Boom Babies Financial Bust', *Journal of Political Economy*, Vol. 87 (Supplement), S65–S97.
13. Wright, R. E. (1991), 'Cohort Size and Earnings in Great Britain', *Journal of Population Economics*, Vol. 4, No. 4, 295–306.
14. Nickell, S. (1997), 'Unemployment and Labor Market Rigidities: Europe versus North America', *Journal of Economic Perspectives*, Vol. 11, 55–74.

15. Schmidt, C. (1996), 'Cohort Sizes and Unemployment: Lessons for Poland'. In L. Hartmut and J. Wadsworth (eds.), *Labour Markets by Design? Labour Market Policies and Creative Use of Household Surveys in Transition Economics*, Munich: Eltforum-Verlag.

16. Lisenkova, K., P. McGregor, N. Pappas, K. Swales, K. Turner, and R. E. Wright (2007), *Macroeconomic Impacts of Demographic Change in Scotland*, IZA Discussion Paper No 2623, Bonn: Institute for the Study of Labour.

19 | Living Conditions of Children

HARRY ANTHONY PATRINOS*

1. Extent of the problem

Nearly half the people of the world today are under 25 years of age. Nine out of ten of these young people live in developing countries. More importantly, the majority of the developing world's poor is children and youth, defined either as being under the age of eighteen years (based on the 1989 United Nations Convention on the Rights of the Child) or up to fourteen years (based on the Millennium Development Goal (MDG) framework). Although significant progress has been made in reducing poverty worldwide, the fact remains that most of the MDG outcomes are not likely to be met unless greater attention is paid to the next generation (World Bank 2005). Children are the hardest hit by poverty. More than half a billion children (40%) in developing countries are living on less than $1 a day (UNICEF 2005).

There are 115 million primary-school-aged children not enrolled in school, the majority (76%) are in sub-Saharan Africa and South Asia (UNESCO 2005). Another 150 million children start primary school but drop out before they have completed four years of education. Nearly half of the children in the least developed countries of the world do not have access to primary education. More than 45 percent of children in west and central Africa are out of school. For south Asia, this figure is 42 million.

For every 100 boys out of school, 117 girls miss out on primary education. While the gender gap in primary education has been closing steadily, many countries had failed to meet the MDG target of gender parity in primary education by 2005. The regions with the highest gaps will have to make even greater gains if gender parity is to be achieved

* The views expressed here are those of the author and are not to be attributed to the World Bank Group. The assistance received from Husein Abdul-Hamid and Vicente Garcia-Moreno is gratefully appreciated.

as part of universal primary school completion by 2015. The exclusion of girls from education in comparison to boys, especially in South Asia, sub-Saharan Africa and the Middle East and North Africa, is one of the clearest indicators of gender discrimination (UNICEF 2005).

Of those children in developing countries that are in school, most are not learning adequately. The few participating countries in international achievement tests such as TIMSS, PIRLS and PISA usually score near the bottom, especially when compared to middle and high-income countries. Their levels of comprehension are minimal in important subjects such as math, science and reading. In fact, 54 percent of Peruvian fifteen-year-olds are at the lowest level of comprehension in reading according to the OECD's PISA assessment; 23 percent of youths in Argentina and Brazil, 31 percent in Indonesia, and 10 percent in Thailand are at this level. By contrast only 3 and 4 percent of youths in the United Kingdom and France score at this level.

While life expectancy has increased, more than 10 million children a year still die before their fifth birthday (UNICEF 2005), largely from preventable causes – malnutrition is a contributing factor in more than half of these. More than 50 percent of these children die at home due to poor access to health care. Acute respiratory infections are the biggest single killer (2 million every year), followed by diarrhoeal diseases, malaria, measles, pertussis, tuberculosis and neonatal tetanus. More than half-a-million children die of HIV/AIDS each year. Maternal mortality ratios have remained high in some parts of the world, at 1,100 deaths per 100,000 live births in sub-Saharan Africa and 440 in developing countries, compared to 12 for developed countries (Belli and Appaix 2003).

More than half the world's children still have no access to safe water and sanitation (UNICEF 2002). While an estimated 1 billion people gained access to improved drinking water in the 1990s and global coverage rose from 77 to 82 percent, some 1.1 billion people, mostly from the poorest countries, still lack access to safe water. Gains were registered in increasing access to sanitary facilities yet a staggering 2.4 billion people still lack such access. Four out of five of them are found in Asia. Lack of access to safe drinking water or inadequate hygiene and sanitation causes over 3 million child deaths a year in developing countries – about one in every four such deaths. Moreover, fetching water is a time-consuming activity that is shouldered almost exclusively by women and children (UNICEF 2000).

Violent conflicts, along with HIV/AIDS, are giving rise to a massive generation of orphans in sub-Saharan Africa. The region has 13 million orphans, most under the age of 15. In many countries, children and adolescents take part as soldiers. More than 300,000 children under 18 are fighting in armed conflicts in more than 30 countries worldwide. Over 300 million young people below the age of 25 live in countries affected by armed conflict (Rahim and Holland 2006). There are 26 countries in the world with at least a quarter of a million internally displaced persons and 15 countries and territories with 250,000 refugees (Sommers 2002). Two million children died as a direct result of armed conflict over the last decade. Six million children were seriously injured or permanently disabled (World Bank 2005).

Child labor persists in developing countries. More than 250 million children between the ages of 5 and 14 work. Most working children in rural areas were found in agriculture; urban children worked in trade and services, manufacturing, construction and domestic service. Great efforts have been made to reduce this problem, with some positive results. Hageman *et al.* (2006) show that while 23 percent of children aged 5 to 17 worked in 2000, only 20 percent did so in 2004. Estimates show that 11 percent of children worked in hazardous jobs in 2000, while only 8 percent did so in 2004 – a 26 percent decrease.

Many inequalities within countries are obscured (UNICEF 2005). Indigenous peoples and ethnic minorities are at greatest risk. Over the period 1995–2004, the International Decade of the World's Indigenous Peoples, Latin America's indigenous peoples made rapid progress in political representation, health and education. However, indigenous peoples still account for the highest poverty rates in the region (Hall and Patrinos 2006). While Mexico will clearly achieve the MDGs on average, its large indigenous population – 10 percent of the total population, or about 10 million people – is not making sufficient progress. However, this reality is masked by the fact that data used to measure MDG progress is not disaggregated.

2. Solutions

Although developing human capital is an easily agreed goal, finding cost-effective programs that lead to long-term increases is a challenge. Education represents both a human and social right for children everywhere, as well as a great investment. Monetary returns to schooling, through increased productivity and access to good jobs, and its contribution towards the elimination of poverty, make it a high priority investment everywhere. Despite the high proportions of resources allocated to education around the world, the challenge remains to find cost-effective ways to increase schooling among the poorest and to increase learning levels. There have been hundreds of empirical studies on the determinants of learning trying to estimate which factors affect school attainment and performance. Few have been based on randomized control experiments or used rigorous evaluation techniques. Nevertheless, there is little evidence to date that simply spending more money on schooling will improve outcomes. For example, a review of almost 100 studies estimating the effects of resources on education outcomes, only 55 percent produced significant effects, and not all were positive (Hanushek 1995). Solutions to the education problem require, therefore, a closer look at rigorous, or randomized, evaluations.

Schooling clearly is a priority investment for children. There is a need to enroll all children in primary school, as well as preschool. Getting children into school, and making sure that they complete their primary education, is effective for raising earnings in the future. Appropriate programs that address the supply and demand side can be very effective. Simply enforcing compulsory school legislation can be effective in raising school levels and increasing future earnings, as are programs designed to increase the supply of schooling, such as mass school construction programs; these findings have been verified by natural experiments. Duflo (2001) examined a large-scale school construction program in Indonesia by combining differences across regions in the number of schools constructed with differences across cohorts induced by the timing of the program. She showed that school construction led to overall increases in average schooling and wages. The returns to education range from 6 to 10 percent.

There is some evidence from India that spending, if well targeted, can improve outcomes. Banerjee *et al.* (2005) showed evidence in favor of building new non-formal schools in unserved areas as a cheap way of expanding enrollment. Case and Deaton (1999) showed that raising school resources increases years of completed schooling and enrollment rates for blacks, but not for whites, in South Africa. More evidence that spending can improve outcomes comes from the United States. Angrist and Guryan (2005) found that a $1,000 increase in per-pupil spending leads to a ⅓ to ½ of a standard deviation increase in average test scores.

Various school inputs can be effective. Kremer *et al.* (2002) found that providing uniforms and textbooks and building classrooms for seven schools randomly selected from a pool of 14 poorly performing schools led to a fall in dropout rates and after five years pupils in those schools had completed about 15 percent more years of schooling. In Chicago, Jacob and Lefgren (2004) found a small, but statistically significant, positive effect of summer school and grade retention on student reading skills at a cost of about $750 per student. This cost per student may be compared to other interventions, such as class size reduction, which have larger effects (more than three times as large) on student reading skills but cost more than $2,000 per student.

Providing scholarships and other investments are among the most effective investments for increasing school enrollment and attendance. Schultz (2004) found that Mexico's conditional cash transfer program, *Oportunidades*, increased the enrollment rate by 3.4 percent, on average. Fom Kenya, Kremer *et al.* (2004) showed that introducing secondary school merit scholarships could provide access to further education for the best performing disadvantaged students. While universal free secondary education funded for all children would cost 18 percent of Kenya's GDP, targeting bright children with scholarships might lead to improvements in average academic performance. Angrist and Lavy (20002) found that cash awards raised test performance among 500 high school students in Israel. Various experiments have been undertaken to improve test scores in Kenyan schools. While scholarships for girls, teacher incentives and textbooks are significant, the most effective and cost-effective are the scholarships.

School-based programs can be very effective. Mexico's compensatory program provides extra resources to primary schools in disadvantaged rural communities. One of the most important components of the program is the school-based management intervention (AGEs). The impact assessment of the AGEs, controlling for the presence of the conditional cash transfer (CCT) program, shows a significant effect on the reduction of failure and grade repetition, at a yearly cost of $6 per child (Gertler *et al.* 2006). Banerjee *et al.* (2004) conducted a randomized evaluation of a two- year remedial education program in India. On average, the program increased test scores by 0.14 standard deviations in the first year and 0.28 in the second year, at a yearly cost of $5 a child.

Schooling summary. Various attempts to improve schooling have been undertaken. The evidence on CCT-type programs and various incentives is strong and based on experimental data. Reducing demand-side constraints to school attendance and completion are a very cost-effective intervention. They help put children in school, thus making other investments more productive. At the same time, more needs to be done to improve the quality of those schools once the children are enrolled. Improving quality will remain a challenge, but incentive programs and school-based management is proving to be a worthwhile investment.

Scientific and economic work shows the benefits of investing in children (Heckman 2006). The labor market improves as more able people acquire more skills, and more skilled people become more able (Heckman 2004; Carneiro and Heckman 2003). The main mechanism through which early education affects labor force productivity and crime is through its effect on cognitive and non-cognitive skills (Heckman and Masterov 2004). Early childhood interventions are more effective than remedies that attempt to compensate later in life. Enriched pre-kindergarten programs, with home visitation, have a strong track record of promoting achievement for disadvantaged children, improving labor market outcomes and reducing crime (Heckman 2004). Quality early education is a key part of the solution to this problem.

The Perry Preschool program started in 1962 with 123 young African-American children assessed to be at risk of school failure in Ypsilanti, Michigan, and is used to follow beneficiaries over four decades. The beneficiaries attended roughly two years of preschool for 2.5 hours/day, and received home visits from a teacher once a week. Participants were compared to a control group that did not receive these services. Accumulated research shows significant returns (Barnett 2004; Currie and Thomas 1995). The greatest savings come from the reduction of crime and increases in earnings for participants (Barnett and Masse 2006).

From the developing world significant benefits are found. Berlinski *et al.* (2006) exploit variations introduced by the expansion of a preschool program in Argentina to identify the impacts of the program on child outcomes. One year of pre-primary increases third-grade test scores by 23 percent of the standard deviation of test score distribution. Armecin *et al.* (2006) evaluate an important early childhood initiative in the Philippines using longitudinal data collected over three years on a cohort of 6,693 children 0–4 years at baseline in two treatment regions and a control region. The authors found significant improvement in cognitive, social, motor and language development, and in short-term nutritional status.

Early interventions summary. Impact assessments of early interventions show significant short-term benefits for the child, including enhanced achievement, improved health, increased non-cognitive skills, and social competence. In the medium term, society benefits from greater school system efficiency; reduction in special education; reduction of grade repetition; higher learning; reduction in abuse and neglect; and lower reliance on public health care. In the long term, children benefit from higher likelihood of graduation and college enrollment; higher wages and employment; lower teen pregnancy; and less delinquency. Society benefits from sound education; increased tax revenues; lower welfare dependence and a reduction in delinquency and crime.

Getting children into school early and compensating for disadvantage is important. However, due to poverty and other factors, many children continue to work, even combining school and work (Basu 1999; Psacharopoulos 1997; Psacharopoulos and Patrinos 1997; Rosati and Rossi 2003; Cigno *et al.* 2002). How to prevent children from working is an ongoing challenge. CCT programs aim to reduce current income poverty. They might affect child work through the cash transfers contingent on the child attending school regularly by reducing the opportunity cost of schooling. The CCT programs are not tied to the cessation of child work (PETI in Brazil is the exception). *Oportunidades* shows an overall reduction in work for male youth with no impacts on work for female youth. PETI reduces all child work by 8 percent. In Bangladesh, Ravallion and Wodon (2000) showed evidence of significant negative effect on the labor force participation of children through subsidies in school and nutrition.

3. Costs and benefits of solutions

Various experiments have been undertaken to improve test scores in Kenyan schools (Table 19.1). While scholarships for girls, teacher incentives and textbooks are significant, the most effective and cost-effective are the scholarships. Glewwe (1999) showed that in terms of present discounted values of various school improvements, installing blackboards is the most cost-effective, followed by repairing leaking

Table 19.1. *Cost-effectiveness of various Kenya primary school interventions*

Project	Average test score gain, years 1–2	Cost/pupil	Cost/pupil per 0.1 s.d. gain	Cost/pupil per 0.1 s.d. adjust for deadweight loss	Cost/pupil per 0.1 s.d. gain, adjust for deadweight loss & transfers
Girls scholarship					
Busia & Teso districts	0.12 s.d.	$4.24	$3.53	$4.94	$1.41
Busia district	0.20 s.d.	$3.55	$1.77	$2.48	$0.71
Teacher incentives	0.07 s.d.	$2.39	$3.41	$4.77	$1.36
Textbook provision	0.04 s.d.	$1.50	$4.01	$5.61	$5.61
Deworming project	≈0	$1.46	∞	∞	∞
Flip chart provision	≈0	$1.25	∞	∞	∞

Source: Kremer *et al.* (2004); Glewwe *et al.* 2004, 2003, 1997; Miguel and Kremer 2004

Notes: Costs in nominal US$ at time of program (1996–2002); education budget cost effectiveness calculation yields upper bound on true social cost (column 4), while lower bound generated by treating entire payment as transfer (column 5) classrooms. Investments in textbooks are not shown to be cost-effective. Some interventions in health have been undertaken to improve education outcomes. The case of deworming in Kenya proved to have an impact not just in health, but also on schooling. The cost is approximately $5 per Disability Adjusted Life Year (DALY) averted and 649 DALYs were averted as a result of the program (Kremer *et al.* 2004).

For every dollar invested, Perry Preschool generates over $7 in benefits (Barnett 2004). Based on present value estimates, about 80 percent of the benefits go to the general public, yielding a 12 percent rate of return for society. The Abecedarian Project produced more favorable findings for children who participated in the program compared to children who did not, revealing a benefit of $3.78 for each dollar invested (Barnett and Masse 2006). Cost/benefit analyses may understate the true, long-term impact of early care and education because they do not measure the positive effects on children born to participant families after the study period (Temple and Reynolds 2006).

In Brazil, a benefit–cost ratio for preschool is 2 and the rate of return is 12–15 percent. Most benefit–cost ratios for industrial and agricultural projects are less than 2 (World Bank 2001). In Egypt, focusing on costs and benefits due only to increased enrollment in basic education and decreased repetition, a simulation shows a benefit–cost ratio of 2.3:1. Researches have estimated benefit–cost ratios of 2.4–3.2 for Bolivia (Van der Gaag and Tan 1998) and 3.0 for the Philippines (Glewwe *et al.* 2000; Table 19.2).

Evidence of cost-effectiveness available for CCT comes from a study by Coady and Parker (2002), in which they compared the cost-effectiveness of cash transfer with the school building program. They showed that in comparison with the building program, subsidies are around eleven times more cost-effective in expanding enrollments.

The returns to schooling are high, and the savings associated with less schooling may be significant. The simulated costs (school supply, transfer, intervention, opportunity cost) and benefits (education and health) of eliminating child labor have been estimated, with a benefit–cost ratio of 5.4 (IPEC 2004). The question, however, is *how* to reduce child labor. CCT programs appear highly effective, given their short-term goal of poverty alleviation and incentives to promote human capital development over the long run. The insistence on school enrollment helps to keep children enrolled, and rigorous evaluations

Table 19.2. *Benefits of various early intervention programs*

	Perry (US)	Abecedarian (US)	Child-parent centers (US)	Brazil	Egypt	Bolivia	Philippines
Program cost	$15,386	$63,476	$7,738	$178	$83		
Benefits							
Child care	919	27,612	1,916				
Compensation	79,743	37,531	32,099				
K-12 schooling	8556	8836	5,634				
College/adult ed	−1309	−8128	−644				
Crime	173,959	0	15,329				
Welfare	774	196	546				
Compensation future gen.		5722	4,894				
Abuse/neglect			344				
Maternal compensation		68,728					
Health/smoking		17,781					
Total benefits	$262,642	$158,278	$60,117				
NPV	$247,256	$94,802	52,380				
Benefit–cost ratio	9:1	2.5:1	7.8:1	2:1	2.3:1	3:1	3:1

Sources: Heckman 2004, 2006; Barnett and Masse 2006; World Bank 2001, 2002; Temple and Reynolds 2006; Van der Gaag and Tan 1998; Glewwe *et al.* 2001

Notes: US programs use 3% discount rate, 2004 $; other studies use figures from the year of study; Philippines 3% discount, benefits measured are wage increases; Bolivia, Brazil, Egypt benefits are labor market earnings; 7% discount rate for Bolivia accrue in that year and are calculated as the present value (at a 3% discount rate) of the future stream of life years that would have occurred if the death had been prevented.

have shown highly effective programs, especially on schooling, and on child labor reduction (Table 19.3).

Overview

Our crude simulations of various options appear in Table 19.4. The lack of data in general, and more importantly, the scarcity of rigorous research makes it difficult to go beyond the theoretical stage. Nevertheless, the evidence is sufficient to draw a few broad conclusions. Studies of the effects of pre-school education and other interventions on later performance have provided fairly conclusive evidence that *quality* early intervention programs can increase children's educational potential, and will likely have long-lasting effects. Other interventions produce, in comparison, small benefits relative to cost. We present different scenarios to highlight these differences. These include improved school indicators: 5–16 percent reduction in grade repetition; 18–21 percent reduction in high school dropout rate; 14–26 percent reduction in special education placement; higher grade completion rates in second, third and fourth grades; higher scores on achievement tests; higher attendance; and less age-grade distortion. They include significant effects on economic potential: significantly higher monthly earnings; higher rates of home ownership; higher rates of school completion; and an 18 percent chance of employment at age 19 (Filp 1983; Feijo 1984; Pontieri *et al.* 1981; Barnett 1995; Kagitcibasi *et al.* 1987). In order to make meaningful comparisons we build on this and use a Mincerian model for age-earning profile to make benefit–cost scenarios. In all these scenarios the benefits are based on minimum estimates, as there are many other side benefits that we did not attempt to estimate.

Scenario I: Preschool program. We look at an early childhood development intervention program that is based on preschool education and use the above success indicators, and assume the cost per child is $1,000. Since the returns to schooling are different across countries and among countries, we looked at different levels (within the ranges in Psacharopoulos and Patrinos 2004): 5 percent return to a year of schooling in industrial countries, and 10–30 percent in very poor countries. We assume a discount rate of 10 percent.

Scenario II: Preschool plus nutrition and health. This scenario assumes the settings of scenario I and adds health and nutrition interventions before and during preschool years. Benefit–cost calculations were

Table 19.3. *Effectiveness of CCT programs*

Program (country)	Type of evaluation	Age	School enrollment increase (percentage points)	Child work reduction (percentage points) Finding	Stipend (annual)	Public education expenditure (% GDP pc)
Red de Protección Social (Nicaragua)	DID	7–13	18.0	4.9	$21	9.1
		10–13		9.0		
Oportunidades (Mexico)	Random	8–11 boys	1.1–1.8	1.3		
		12–17 boys	3.2–5.8	3.2–4.7		
		8–11 girls	–	–	$109–$218	14.4
		12–17 girls	7.5–9.5	1.1–2.3		
PETI (Brazil)	DID	10–14	–	8.3		11.4
		7–14	–	N.S.	$173	
		6–12	–	N.S.	$60	
Programa de Asignación Escolar (Honduras)						
Bangladesh's Food for Education		5–16	16.0–17.0	4.2	$35	7.2
Familias en Acción (Colombia)	DID	10–13 rural	1.5	10.3–14.1[a]	$96	16.7
		14–17 rural	5.0	N.S.	$192	
		10–13 urban	7.0	Decrease		
		14–17 urban	2.5	Decrease		

Sources: Raju 2005; Maluccio & Flores 2004; Pianto & Soares 2004; Attanasio et al. 2006a; Glewwe & Olinto 2004
Note: Public expenditure data: Nicaragua 2004, Mexico 2004, Brazil 2000, Honduras, Bangladesh 2004, Colombia 2004
N.S. Not significant.
[a] = all ages

Table 19.4. *Cost–benefit analysis of ECD interventions in comparison to other options*

	Economic status				
	Poorest	2nd level	Average	4th level	Richest
Rate of return for a year of schooling	30	20	15	10	5
	Cost–benefit ratio for intervention				
Scenario I: Early childhood development program (focus on preschool)	3.50	2.70	2.30	2.10	1.80
Scenario II: Early childhood development program (preschool plus nutrition and health interventions)	4.10	3.35	2.93	2.45	1.92
Scenario III: As in scenario II, but with additional intervention in first two grades	4.50	4.03	3.20	2.70	2.30
Other interventions:					
Reduce class size (50%) (assume increased performance, future attainment by 5%)	1.10	1.20	1.30	1.50	1.70
Reduce class size (50%) with building cost (assume increased performance, future attainmentby 5%)	0.90	1.00	1.10	1.20	1.30
Raise teacher salary (50%) (assume increased efficiency, student achievement, college entry by 5%)	1.70	1.50	1.20	1.20	1.20
Incentives to students ($200/year/child) (assume increased enrollment in 1st grade by 5%)	2.00	1.80	1.00	0.50	0.30
Computers (assume improved learning, increased employability, productivity by 5%)	1.00	1.10	1.20	1.30	1.30

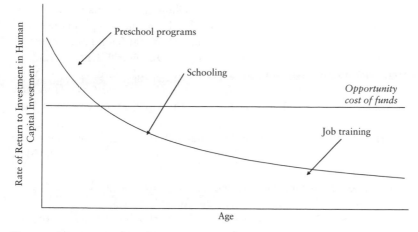

Figure 19.1. Rates of return to human capital investment

Source: Carneiro and Heckman 2003

conducted based on international studies of the effects of providing nutritional supplements and health interventions on survival, enrollment and achievement rates, and reducing dropout rates. We assume the cost increases to $2,000 a child.

Scenario III: Preschool, nutrition, health and classroom interventions in first two grades. This scenario assumes the settings of scenario II and adds more interventions (teacher training, additional material, breakfast, health). We assume a cost of $3,000 a child.

In addition to these scenarios Table 19.4 includes similar benefit–cost calculations based on different comparable interventions. It is clear that the ECD interventions surpass other investments. A review of the literature suggests that early interventions are very cost-effective. Early interventions have the best payoff (Carneiro and Heckman 2003; Figure 19.1).

References

Angrist, J. and V. Lavy. 2002. "The Effect of High Schooling: Some Lessons for the Economics of Education." *Journal of Economic Literature* 40: 1167–1201.

Angrist, J. D. and J. Guryan. 2005. "Does Teacher Testing Raise Teacher Quality? Evidence from State Certification Requirements." IZA Discussion Paper 1500.

Armecin, G., J. R. Behrman, P. Duazo, S. Ghuman, S. Gultiano, E.M. King and N. Lee. 2006. "Early childhood development through an integrated program: evidence from the Philippines." World Bank Policy Research Working Paper, Series 3922. Washington DC: World Bank.

Attanasio, O., E. Battistin, E. Fitzsimons, A. Mesnard and M. Vera-Hernandez. 2006a. "How Effective are Conditional Cash Transfers? Evidence from Colombia." Institute for Fiscal Studies Briefing Note No. 54.

Banerjee, A., S. Cole, E. Duflo and L. Linden. 2004. "Remedying Education: Evidence from two randomized experiments in India." MIT. Unpublished paper.

Banerjee A., S. Jacob, M. Kremer, J. Lanjouw and P. Lanjouw. 2005 "Moving to Universal Primary Education!" Processed.

Barnett, W. S. 1995. "Long-term effects of early childhood programs on cognitive and school outcomes." *The Future of Children* 5: 25–50.

Barnett, W. S. 2004. "Does Head Start have lasting cognitive effects? The myth of fade-out." In E. Zigler and S. Styfco (eds.), *The Head Start Debates*. Baltimore, MD: Paul H. Brookes Publishing Co.

Barnett, W. S and L. N. Masse. 2006. "Comparative Benefit-Cost Analysis of the Abecedarian Program and Its Policy Implications." *Economics of Education Review* (forthcoming).

Basu, K. 1999. "Child Labor: Cause, Consequence and Cure, with Remarks on International Labor Standards." *Journal of Economic Literature* 37(3) 1083–1119.

Belli, P. C. and O. Appaix. 2003. "The Economic Benefits of Investing in Child Health." World Bank, Health, Nutrition and Population Discussion Paper. Washington DC: World Bank.

Berlinski, S., S. Galiani and P. Gertler. 2006. 'The Effect of Pre-Primary Education on Primary School Performance." University College London. Unpublished draft paper.

Carneiro, P. and J. Heckman. 2003. "Human Capital Policy," in J. Heckman and A. Krueger (eds.), *Inequality in America: What Role for Human Capital Policy*. Cambridge: MIT Press.

Case, A. and A. Deaton. 1999. "School Inputs and Educational Outcomes in South Africa." *Quarterly Journal of Economics* 114(3): 1047–84.

Cigno, A., F. C. Rosati and L. Guarcello. 2002. "Does Globalization Increase Child Labor?" *World Development* 30(9): 1579–89.

Coady, D. P. and S. W. Parker. 2002. "A cost-effectiveness analysis of demand- and supply-side education interventions." FCND Discussion Paper No. 127, International Food Policy Research Institute.

Currie, J. and D. Thomas. 1995. "Does Head Start Make a Difference?" *American Economic Review* 85(3): 341–64.

Duflo, E. 2001. "Schooling and Labor Market Consequences of School Construction in Indonesia: Evidence from an Unusual Policy Experiment." *American Economic Review* 91(4): 795–813.

Feijo, M. 1984. "Early Childhood Education Programs and Children's Subsequent Learning: A Brazilian Case." Unpublished Ph.D. Dissertation, Stanford University.

Filp, J., C. Cardemil, E. Donoso, E. Schiefelbein, J. Torres. 1983. "Relationship between Pre-School and Grade One Education in Public Schools in Chile," in IDRC, *Preventing School Failure*. Ottawa: IDRC.

Gertler, P., H. Patrinos and M. Rubio-Codina. 2006. "Empowering Parents to Improve Education: Evidence from Rural Mexico." World Bank Policy Research Working Paper Series 3935. Washington DC: World Bank.

Glewwe, P. 1997. "A Test of the Normality Assumption in the Ordered Probit Model." *Econometric Review* 16(1): 1–19.

Glewwe, P. 1999. *The Economics of School Quality Investments in Developing Countries : An Empirical Study of Ghana*. New York: St. Martin's Press.

Glewwe P., M. Kremer, S. Moulin and E. Zitzewitz. 2000. "Retrospective vs. Prospective Analyses of School Inputs: The Case of Flip Charts in Kenya." NBER Working Paper 8018, National Bureau of Economic Research, Inc.

Glewwe, P., H. G. Jacoby and E. M. King. 2001. "Early Childhood Nutrition and Academic Achievement: A Longitudinal Analysis." *Journal of Public Economics* 81: 345–68.

Glewwe, P., N. Ilias and M. Kremer. 2003. "Teacher Incentives." National Bureau of Economic Research.

Glewwe P. and P. Olinto. 2004. "Evaluating of the Impact of Conditional Cash Transfers on Schooling: An Experimental Analysis of Honduras' PRAF Program." USAID.

Glewwe, P., M. Kremer, S. Moulin and E. Zitzewitz. 2004. "Retrospective vs. Prospective Analyses of School Inputs: The Case of Flip Charts in Kenya." *Journal of Development Economics* 74(1): 251–68.

Hageman F., Y. Diallo, A. Etienne and F. Mehran. 2006. *Global Child Labour Trends*. International Labour Office, SIMPOC.

Hall, G. and H. A. Patrinos (eds.). 2006. *Indigenous Peoples, Poverty and Human Development in Latin America*. London: Palgrave Macmillan.

Hanushek, E. 1995. "Interpreting Recent Research on Schooling in Developing Countries." *World Bank Research Observer* 10: 247–54.

Heckman, J. J. 2004. "Lessons from the Technology of Skill Formation." *Annals of the New York Academy of Sciences* 1038: 179–200.

Heckman, J. J. 2006. "Skill Formation and the Economics of Investing in Disadvantaged Children." *Science* 312: 1900–02.

Heckman, J. J. and D. V. Masterov. 2004. "The Productivity Argument for Investing in Young Children." Invest in Kids Working Paper No. 5. Washington DC: Committee for Economic Development.

International Programme on the Elimination of Child Labour (IPEC). 2004. *Investing in Every Child, an Economic Study of the Costs and Benefits of Eliminating Child Labour*. Geneva: International Labour Office.

Jacob, B. and L. Lefgren. 2004. "Remedial Education and Student Achievement: A Regression-Discontinuity Analysis." *Review of Economics and Statistics* 86(1): 226–44.

Kagitcibasi, C., D. Sunar and S. Bekman. 1987. "Comprehensive Preschool Education Project: Final Report." Istanbul, Bogazici University.

Kremer M., E. Miguel and R. Thornton. 2004. "Incentives to Learn." Harvard University: The Brookings Institution. Draft.

Kremer M., S. Moulin and R. Namunyu. 2002. "The Political Economy of School Finance in Kenya." Washington, DC: World Bank.

Maluccio, J. A. and R. Flores. 2004. "Impact Evaluation of A Conditional Cash Transfer Program: The Nicaraguan Red de Protección Social." IFPRI FCND Discussion Paper No 184.

Miguel, E. and M. Kremer. 2004. "Worms: Identifying Impacts on Education and Health in the Presence of Treatment Externalities." *Econometrica* 72(1): 159–217.

Pianto, D. M. and S. Soares. 2004. "Use of Survey Design for the Evaluation of Social Programs: The PNAD and PETI." Unpublished draft paper.

Pontieri, M. J., M. L. Ferrari Cavalcanti, and Y.R. Gandra. 1981. "Avaliação do Aproveitamento Escolar de Pre-Escolares do Programa Centro de Educação e Alimentação do Pre-escolar." *Revista de Saude Publica* 15: 148–58.

Psacharopoulos, G. 1997. "Child labor versus educational attainment. Some evidence from Latin America." *Journal of Population Economics* 10(4): 377–86.

Psacharopoulos, G. and H. A. Patrinos. 1997. "Family size, schooling and child labor in Peru: An empirical analysis." *Journal of Population Economics* 10(4): 387–405.

Psacharopoulos, G. and H. A. Patrinos. 2004. "Returns to investment in education: a further update." *Education Economics* 12(2): 111–34.

Rahim, A. and P. Holland. 2006. "Facilitating Transitions for Children and Youth: Lessons from Four Post-Conflict Fund Projects." Social Development Papers No. 34, Washington, DC: World Bank.

Raju, D. 2005. "The effects of conditional cash transfer programs on child work: A critical review and analysis of the evidence." Washington, DC: World Bank.

Ravallion, M. and Q. Wodon. 2000. "Does Child Labour Displace Schooling? Evidence on Behavioural Responses to an Enrollment Subsidy." *Economic Journal* 110(462): 158–75.

Rosati, F. C. and M. Rossi. 2003. "Children's Working Hours and School Enrollment: Evidence from Pakistan and Nicaragua." *World Bank Economic Review* 17(2): 283–95.

Schultz, T. P. 2004. "School Subsidies for the Poor: Evaluating the Mexican PROGRESA Poverty Program." *Journal of Development Economics* 74(1): 199–250.

Sommers, M. 2002. "Children, Education and War: Reaching Education For All (EFA) Objectives in Countries Affected by Conflict." Working Papers Conflict Prevention and Reconstruction Unit Paper No. 1, Education Team, Human Development Network, Washington, DC: World Bank.

Temple, J. A. and A. J. Reynolds. 2007. "Benefits and Costs of Investments in Preschool Education: Evidence from the Child-Parent Centers and Related Programs. *Economics of Education Review* Vol. 26, 126–44.

UNESCO 2005. *Children out of School: Measuring Exclusion From Primary Education*. Montreal: UNESCO Institute of Statistics.

UNICEF. 2000. *Poverty Reduction Begins with Children*. New York: UNICEF.

UNICEF 2002. *Addressing the Affordability Gap: Framing Child Care as Economic Development. Finance Development: Invest in Children*. New York: UNICEF.

UNICEF 2005. *The State of the World's Children 2006*. New York: UNICEF.

Van der Gaag, J. and J.-P. Tan. 1998. "The Benefits of Early Child Development Programs: An Economic Analysis." Washington DC: World Bank.

World Bank. 2001. *Brazil: Early Child Development: A Focus on the Impact of Preschools* (Report No. 22841-BR). Washington, DC: World Bank.

World Bank. 2002. *Arab Republic of Egypt: Strategic Options for Early Childhood Education* (Report No. 24772-EGT). Washington, DC: World Bank.

World Bank. 2005. *Reshaping the Future: Education and Postconflict Reconstruction*. Washington, DC: World Bank.

20 | *Living Conditions of Women*

BRINDA VISWANATHAN*

The challenge to improve the living conditions of women

Compared to men, women have benefited less during the course of economic development. This has resulted in a lowered status for women within the house, in the workplace and in the community.[1] It is well established by now that the unequal status between men and women is not due to their biological or physiological differences, but a socially created difference, connoted as gender inequality. Consequently, from time to time, social reformers have attempted to remedy the deeply entrenched notions about women's position in society.

In order to alleviate the living conditions of women in this broader context, financial resources are necessary but not sufficient and changes in social and cultural attitudes play a very important role. The suggestions for positive outcomes on improving women's living conditions are drawn from various country-level experiences, where the use of economic instruments is fewer and the emphasis is more often on creating social and legal institutions. Under these circumstances, it may not always be possible to measure the costs and benefits of these initiatives in monetary units alone. However, an attempt is made to illustrate the likely benefits to the countries when an opportunity to reduce the gender gap is put into practice, and the costs of implementation. Two examples are given here that would improve the living conditions for women:

* The author would like to thank Kavi Kumar for useful discussions while preparing this chapter and the participants of the seminar "Bill Gates for a day" held at Copenhagen Business School, March 2007. The responsibility for any errors rests solely with the author.
[1] Boserup (1990) traces the status of women during the course of economic development and indicates how women seem to have benefited in only a few instances, while in most other situations their status continued to remain subordinate to men.

(1) Reduce the gap between male and female education, particularly at primary level.
(2) Provide childcare facilities to allow more women to participate more effectively in the labour market.

Reduce the gap between male and female education

Gaps in education between men and women are rather glaring in many parts of the world. Table 20.1 shows the gaps that exist at primary and secondary school level among some of the very poor regions of the world. In the new millennium, in the least-developed countries, for every 100 men only 71 women are educated, while further regional classification shows even worse gaps in South Asia (SA) and West and Central Africa. The gap at the primary school net attendance ratio is less than one, but this has improved in the past decade. Much needs to be done at secondary school level, wherein the boys are also disadvantaged compared to their counterparts in other developed countries.

More importantly, tertiary education reflects the level of human capital formation resulting in higher returns to education, thereby also to high rates of economic growth. The poorer regions of the world form a very small percentage of those enrolled for tertiary education and not surprisingly, university graduation ratios are the highest in North America and Western Europe (NAWE) at 33.1% followed by Central and Eastern Europe (CEE) at 29.3%, and some countries in the East Asia and Pacific (EAP) region in 2004 (UIS, 2006). However, women from NAWE and EAP account for 30% each and in CEE about 18%, indicating gender gaps in regions with generally higher educational attainment. Focussing on these countries one further notices huge gaps in the type of tertiary education attained. As shown in Figure 20.1, women are heavily enrolled among the non-science courses like education, social sciences, business and law and health and services which account for about 95% for the total of all countries. The field of study at the tertiary education is driven by preferences in labour demand, which in turn is influenced by the cultural and social understanding about gender-specific jobs.

Education in itself has other benefits. For instance, in Zimbabwe among girls aged 15–18, secondary school dropouts reported six times higher HIV positive instances compared to those enrolled in schools.

Table 20.1. *Summary of selected education indicators across regions of the world*

| | Adult Literacy Rates[a] 2000–2004 Female as % of male | Net attendance ratio:[b] 1996–2005 | | | | | |
| | | Primary school | | | Secondary school | | |
		Male	Female	GPI[c]	Male	Female	GPI[c]
Sub-Saharan Africa	76	63	59	0.94	21	20	0.95
Eastern and Southern Africa	85	66	66	1.00	16	17	1.06
West and Central Africa	63	59	52	0.88	26	22	0.85
Middle East and North Africa	77	83	77	0.93	50	44	0.88
South Asia	64	81	75	0.93	54	48	0.89
East Asia and Pacific	92	–	–	–	53	55	1.04
Latin America and Caribbean	99	89	89	1.00	44	51	1.16
Central and Eastern Europe	97	91	89	0.98	–	–	–
Developing countries	85	78	75	0.96	46	43	0.93
Least-developed countries	71	64	59	0.92	22	20	0.91

Notes:

[a] Adult literacy rate: Percentage of persons aged 15 and over who can read and write.

[b] The net primary/secondary school attendance ratio is defined as the percentage of children in the age group that officially corresponds to primary/secondary schooling eligibility who attend primary/secondary school or higher.

[c] GPI: Gender Parity Index is calculated as the ratio of female enrolment ratio to male enrolment ratio and was calculated by the author.

Source: UNICEF (2006).

Secondary education (supplemented with good school education programmes) made them better equipped to recognize the dangers involved in risky behaviour and use refusal tactics effectively in difficult sexual situations (UN Millennium Project, 2005).

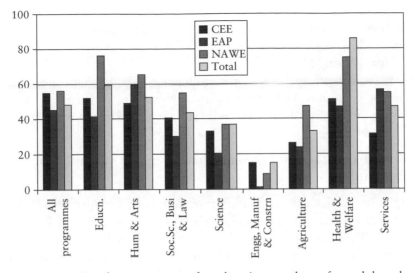

Figure 20.1. Females as a percent of total tertiary enrolment for each broad field of tertiary education, 2004 (%)

Notes:

(1) CEE: Central and Eastern Europe; EAP: East Asia and Pacific; NAWE: North America and Western Europe.

(2) The countries included within these regions are as per UNESCO (2006).

Source: Author's calculations based on UIS (2006), Table 15: Enrolments by broad field of education in tertiary education.

It is well known that educated women are healthier, less likely to be exploited sexually, participate effectively in household decisions as well as in the public sphere, have better access to employment opportunities and are less likely to be discriminated against in the workplace. In addition, they contribute to the well-being of the household in terms of improved nutrition and health status of children and also in eliminating discrimination between girls and boys within the household. These micro-level benefits can further enhance macro-level growth and reduce inter-country inequality. Gender inequality in education accounts for a sizable portion of the empirically observed growth differences between countries and regions (Blackden *et al.*, 2006 and Klasen and Lamanna, 2003). A higher level of human capital formation in society impacts positively on economic performance as does a lower fertility rate among educated women since it raises the per capita resources available. The evidence for this lies in high growth performance among the East Asian economies and continued low performance among several countries in sub-Saharan Africa (Klasen, 2005).

Based on these issues, the following section illustrates the benefit–cost ratio (BCR) of reducing gender gaps, keeping East Asia Pacific which has reduced the gender gap very quickly, as a benchmark.

Benefit–cost ratios for reducing gender gap in education: an illustration

The intervention costs from the Bangladesh Food for Education (FFE) programme are used to calculate the cost (UN Millennium Project, 2005). These estimates are for the year 2000 and the latest values available for such an intervention. FFE in Bangladesh improved primary enrolment by 48% for girls compared to 25% for boys. The annual cost per child is $36 for Bangladesh and the same figures are used for South Asia and also for sub-Saharan Africa due to lack of similar cost figures for these regions as a whole. Total annual cost of intervention for the year 2000 is calculated using existing Gender Parity Index (UIS, 2006), the number of girls of primary school age (UIS, 2006) and the cost of intervention per child. For the benefits, the estimates of additional GDP growth due to the reduction in gender gap for both South Asia and sub-Saharan Africa from Klasen and Lamanna (2003) are used. The additional GDP growth rates are with reference to the EAP region where the gender gap is much lower than that observed in South Asia (SA) and sub-Saharan Africa (SSA). Since the benefits are due to interventions at the primary level of education, two additional cost scenarios – with 50% and 100% cost escalations compared to the base value of $36 – are also considered for benefit–cost calculations. These scenarios are assumed to capture the higher cost of intervention required for secondary and tertiary levels of education.

The benefit of intervention in the year 2000 is assumed to manifest after a gap of 15 fifteen years (when the child attains twenty years of age). Furthermore, the benefits are considered for a ten-year and a forty-year stream in two separate scenarios. Two discount rates – 3% and 6% – are used to calculate the present value of benefits. Table 20.2 reports the benefits, costs and the benefit–cost ratios for South Asia and sub-Saharan Africa.

Table 20.2. *Benefit/cost ratios for education intervention for South Asia and sub-Saharan Africa, 2000*

Region: South Asia

	Benefits accrue up to											
	10 years						40 years					
Discount Rates	3%			6%			3%			6%		
Cost/child/year	Benefits	Cost	BCR	Benefits	Cost	BCR	Benefits	Cost	BCR	Benefits	Cost	BCR
36	106,768	1,328	80.4	61,632	1,328	46.4	289,316	1,328	217.9	125,994	1,328	94.9
54	106,768	1,992	53.6	61,632	1,992	30.9	289,316	1,992	145.2	125,994	1,992	63.3
72	106,768	2,656	40.2	61,632	2,656	23.2	289,316	2,656	108.9	125,994	2,656	47.4

Table 20.2. (*cont.*)

Region: sub-Saharan Africa

Benefits accrue up to

	10 years						40 years					
	3%			6%			3%			6%		
Discount Rates	Benefits	Cost	BCR	Benefits	Cost	BCR	Benefits	Cost	BCR	Benefits	Cost	BCR
Cost/child/year												
36	56,747	840	67.6	32,757	840	39.0	153,771	840	183.1	66,966	840	79.7
54	56,747	1,260	45.1	32,757	1,260	26.0	153,771	1,260	122.1	66,966	1,260	53.2
72	56,747	1,679	33.8	32,757	1,679	19.5	153,771	1,679	91.6	66,966	1,679	39.9

Note: The benefits and costs are all in USD for the year 2000.

Source: Author's own calculations based on a combination of information on cost and population from the UN Millennium Project (2005) and benefits from Klasen and Lamanna (2003).

The benefit–cost ratios may seem high for an education intervention. Here, the benefits are not in terms of the private returns to education, but to the increased GDP growth rate in each of these regions. Since improvements in female education has an economy-wide benefit as discussed earlier, so high BCR could be justified. The estimates of the benefit–cost ratios decline with discount rates and increase in the cost of education as expected. It also increases with the extent of benefit stream, that is, a smaller period of accrual results in lower benefit–cost ratios. Since SSA has a fewer number of children, this results in its lower cost but the gender imparity is also higher which brings down the benefit. Further, the growth rate in SSA is not that strongly affected by education variables and other variables have a larger weight, which naturally brings down the benefit of reducing the gender imparity, compared to SA.

The limitations of these calculations lie in several assumptions that have been made to arrive at them and can at best serve as an illustration. Though this example's main focus was on primary education the preferred option would be to improve tertiary education for all without any gender bias. With an assumed cost of tertiary education at $72 in 2000 per child per year, the choice of 6% as discount rate and benefits accruing up to forty years, the BCR would amount to 47 for South Asia and 40 for sub-Saharan Africa.

Improve access and affordability to childcare facilities to enhance higher rate of female participation in the labour force

Female education does result in better status and empowerment but not all of this translates into a woman's ability to make decisions and one of these is the choice to participate in the labour market and also whether it is full time or part time. Not all countries provide reliable labour force data and where this is available, it may often not be comparable across regions. Across OECD countries there is wide variation in participation rates (age 15–64) ranging from 27% in Turkey, 42% in Mexico and 76% each in Denmark and Sweden, while there are significantly lower gaps in male–female participation among the high female participation rate countries (OECD, 2005). Similarly, the Middle East and South Asian countries are among the lower end, while East Asian countries have the highest participation rates in Asia (UNHDR, 2005).

Table 20.3. *FPLF and pre-school enrolment in the Republic of Korea and Argentina*

	Republic of Korea (1996–1998)	Argentina (1991–1995)
Average level of education (years)	11.8	9.4
FPLF rates for elementary education and under (%)	47.0	54.1
FPLF rates for college and higher education (%)	65.0	87.7
Pre-school enrolment ratio (%)	30.0	53.0
Private schools' share of total enrolment (%)	78.0	26.0

Note: FPLF: Female Participation in Labour Force

Source: Lee and Cho (2005)

While it is acknowledged that higher education enables higher participation rates Lee and Cho (2005) in a comparative study between Argentina and the Republic of Korea show that higher average years of education among the Korean women did not translate into higher work participation rates (Lee and Cho, 2005). In the Republic of Korea, a large proportion of pre-school enrolment is in private schools and the overall pre-school enrolment is relatively lower compared to Argentina (see Table 20.3). The authors infer that this is primarily due to lack of childcare facilities provided by the state in Korea. This consequently results in an M-shaped curve in rates for Korea across age groups with a dip in participation observed at the age of 20–24 continuing up to 30–39. For Argentina, it is an inverted U-shaped.

That there are socio-cultural differences in participation rates is further illustrated in the case of Switzerland, which has three cultural regions: French, Germanic and Italian (Losa and Origoni, 2005). The labour market participation rates are likely to be the least among married women with young children and among such women, the French speaking regions showed higher participation rates compared to the Italian and German speaking regions. This study highlights that the emphasis on the role of woman as a homemaker in the Italian speaking region. This appeared to influence the fact that there is a lower provision of public childcare facilities compared to the French speaking region which affected the participation of women in the labour market in the Italian region.

Childcare provision not only enables women to join the labour market but it also reduces absenteeism, improves their chances of retaining their jobs and allows them to opt for full-time rather than part-time jobs (Gelbach (2002), Blau and Tekin (2003), Jaumotte (2003), Lokshin and Fong (2006)). China has very high participation rates – about 80% in 2000 compared to the world total of about 60%. This has been possible due to universal childcare policies and ensuring that wage gap between male and female is minimised thereby encouraging more women to work (Jiang *et al.*, 2004).

This challenge concerns many developed nations as well. While this policy is undergoing major restructuring to improve access, affordability, awareness and quality of service in developed countries it is in the initial stages in several developing nations. For this opportunity benefit–cost ratios could not be calculated due to inadequate information on intervention costs and potential benefits. However, an attempt has been made to present the available evidence on benefits and costs separately.

Benefits

- Meyers, *et al.* (2002) show that when the probability of subsidy receipt increases from 0.0 to 0.5 in USA, employment probability rises from 0.21 to 0.73 (controlling for other regressors).
- Similarly, for the USA, Gelbach (2002) finds that the probability of receiving assistance has positive effects on hours of work per week, weeks worked per year, and wage/salary income.
- A fall in childcare costs helps mothers (single or low-income in particular) to move away from welfare dependence. This results in sustained remuneration for the household, thereby improving the well being of its members (Jaumotte, 2003).
- Improving economic self-sufficiency, access to gainful employment and reducing child poverty are among the reasons cited for introducing childcare particularly for single mothers in the USA (Adams, *et al.* 2006) and the UK (Viitanen, 2002).

- Countries with low fertility rates (like Italy) find that providing child-care improves the fertility rate (Del Boca, 2002). Higher subsidies in a progressive manner are provided to families with more children in Sweden (Government of Sweden, 2000).
- In developing countries, childcare facilities also serve as protection measure for problems like child labour, school drop-outs, child prostitution, outreach for medical and health programmes and female literacy (GOI, 2005).
- Early childcare, in particular after the age of two, seems to have a beneficial impact on child growth and development. Hence policy interest is evinced in developing countries.

Costs

Childcare, being part of social policy, is quite often provided largely by the state as in Sweden where the parents share at most 20% of the cost or 1–3% of the total family income (Government of Sweden, 2000). On the other hand countries like the USA and the UK provide child-care subsidy for lower income families, particularly for single mothers, at a subsidized rate, while others have to pay a much higher price. Given that efficiency in targeting is low in several developing countries, and with limited resources available for social spending, for implementing most social policies a mix of private and public expenditure is the likely option.

- Depending on the framework of the political economy of the country, the cost-sharing between the state and the household is rather disproportionate. The average cost of childcare in the USA (market-oriented policies) in several states was higher than that of public college tuition fees, ranging from $2,000 to $4,000 per year in 2002–2003. The high cost meant that the services were being underutilized. A case study in Ohio showed that a reduction in co-payments as well as increasing the income cut-off to allow participation in the programme had positive impacts on access (Honeck and Lovell, 2004).
- Due to stricter regulations in the supply of childcare arising out of quality concerns, excess demand for this service is noted in both the UK and Germany, where the supply of childcare did not meet the demand (Chevalier and Viitanen, 2002; Wrohlich, 2004).

- In the USA, many women did not participate in the subsidized childcare programme due to lack of awareness about it (Blau and Tekin, 2003).
- The providers of childcare are usually women from the informal sector (as in Canada and USA). However, denying access to social security benefits or an indexation of wages not only adversely affects such women, but also reduces the childcare provision.

While it may not be feasible to calculate benefit–cost ratios, the benefits as stated above could clearly outweigh the costs as the latter are significantly influenced by political will and the participation of the civil society.

Conclusion

Spending more money to improve female education levels and childcare provision are two examples of intervention mechanisms that can bring about much needed improvements in the living conditions of women. Improvements in other areas such as a reduction in sex trafficking, domestic violence and improved access to reproductive health care are all very important for the betterment of women's lives in the developing countries. A clear demarcation in sex roles and the substantially larger proportion of time spent by men on leisure activities would need urgent changes in the attitudes of both men *and* women which applies to almost all parts of the world. For several of these, the quantitative cost–benefit calculations may not be easily calculated or even be feasible. Even among those welfare states that are trying to reduce the exclusion of women from the process of development, women with similar educational attainment are often paid less than men and fail to occupy important positions in both politics and business, emphasising the deep-rooted gender biases in society.

The approach which would cost nothing monetarily would entail a total change in society's attitudes towards women. The benefit–cost ratios of this cannot necessarily be measured in monetary units, so alternative methods like the capabilities approach could be attempted. To conclude, education improves womens' ability to bargain and participate more effectively in the decision-making process that affects their own lives. This would enable women to make their own choices while improving their own lives and the lives of those around them.

References:

Adams, Gina, Robin Koralek, Karin Martinson, (2006), 'Child Care Subsidy and Leaving Welfare: Policy Issues and Strategies.' Washington D.C.: Study Report of the Urban Institute, www.urban.org/UploadedPDF/311304_policy_issues.pdf

Blackden, Mark, S. Canagarajah, S. Klasen and D. Lawson, (2006), 'Gender and Growth in Sub-Saharan Africa', WIDER Research Paper. www.csae.ox.ac.uk/conferences/2006-EOI-RPI/papers/gprg/Klasen.pdf

Blau, D and E. Tekin, (2003), 'The Determinants And Consequences Of Child Care Subsidies For Single Mothers', NBER Working Paper No. 9665, Cambridge: MA. www.nber.org/papers/w9665

Boserup, E. (1990), 'Economic Changes and the Role of Women.' In I. Tinker (ed.), *Persistent Inequalities*. New York: Oxford University Press, pp. 14–26.

Chevalier, Arnaud and Tarja K. Viitanen (2002), 'The Causality Between Female Labour Force Participation and The Availability of Childcare', *Applied Economics Letters* 9, 915–18.

Del Boca, Daniela (2002). 'The Effect of Child Care and Part Time Opportunities on Participation and Fertility Decisions in Italy', IZA Discussion Paper Series, 427.

Gelbach, Jonah, (2002). 'Public Schooling for Young Children and Maternal Labor Supply', *American Economic Review*, 92 (1): 307–22. (downloaded from JSTOR).

Honeck, Jon, and Vicky Lovell, (2004), 'Staying Employed: Trends in Medicaid, Child Care, and Head Start in Ohio'. Washington D.C: IWPR Publication B246.

Jaumotte, F. (2003), 'Female Labor Force Participation: Past Trends and Main Determinants in OECD countries.' OECD Economics Department Working Paper No. 376. www.olis.oecd.org/olis/2003doc.nsf/ 43bb6130 e5e86e5fc12569fa005d004c/b7c9b45202b081b1c1256e0000317f04/$ FILE/JT00155820.pdf

Jiang, Lin, Erkang Gao, and Huang, Lujin, (2004), 'The Situation of Female Employment in China.' Working Paper of the Research Group of Shanghai Urban Women Unemployment and Re-Employment Project. Napier: Employment Research Institute. http://www.napier.ac.uk/depts/eri/Downloads/ChinaWP1.pdf

Klasen S., (2005), 'Pro Poor Growth and Gender: What can we learn from the Literature, and the OPPG Case Studies?' Final Draft of the Discussion Paper to the Operationalizing Pro-Poor Growth (OPPG) Working Group of AFD, DFID, BMZ (GTZ/KfW) and the World Bank. http://siteresources.worldbank.org/INTPGI/Resources/342674–11150 51862644/GenderFinal22_04.pdf

Klasen S and F. Lamanna, (2003), 'The Impact of Gender Inequality in Education and Employment on Economic Growth in the Middle East and North Africa.' University of Munich Working Paper. www.iai.wiwi. uni-goettingen.de/klasen/klasenlamanna.pdf

Lee Kye Woo and Kisuk Cho (2005), 'Female Labour Force Participation During Economic Crises in Argentina and the Republic of Korea', *International Labour Review*, 144 (4), 423–49.

Lokshin, M and M. Fong, (2006), 'Women's Labour Force Participation and Child Care in Romania' *Journal of Development Studies*, Vol. 42, No. 1, 90–109.

Losa, Fabi B and Pau Origoni (2005), 'The Socio-cultural Dimension of Women's Labour Force Participation Choices in Switzerland', *International Labour Review*, 144 (4), 473–94.

Meyers, Marcia (2002), 'Child Care Subsidies and the Employment of Welfare Recipients', *Demography* 39 (1), 165–79.

OECD (Organization for Economic Cooperation and Development), (2005), 'OECD Employment Outlook: Statistical Annex', www.oecd. org/dataoecd/36/30/35024561.pdf

United Nations, (2005), 'The Millennium Development Goals Report: 2005', www.un.org/millenniumgoals

UIS (2006), 'Comparing Global Education Statistics across the World', *Global Education Digest*. Montreal: UNESCO Institute for Statistics (UIS).

UNDP (United Nations Development Program), (2006), 'Human Development Report 2006: Human Development Indicators', http://hdr.undp.org/hdr2006/

UNICEF (2006), 'Women and Children: The Double Dividend of Gender Equality', State of the World's Children 2007, New York: United Nations Children's Fund (UNICEF).

UN Millennium Project (2005), 'Taking Action: Achieving Gender Equality and Empowering Women', Task Force on Education and Gender Equality: New York. www.unmillenniumproject.org/reports/tf_gender.htm.

Viitanen Tarja K. (2002), 'Cost of Childcare and Female Employment in the UK', *Labour*, 19 (Special Issue) 149–70.

Wrohlich, Katharina (2004), 'The Excess Demand for Subsidized Child Care in Germany', IZA, Discussion Paper No. 1515, March 2005 http://opus.zbw-kiel.de/volltexte/2005/3274/pdf/dp1515.pdf

21 | *Hunger and Malnutrition*

JERE R. BEHRMAN, HAROLD ALDERMAN
AND JOHN HODDINOTT[*]

Describing the problem: hunger and malnutrition

Severe hunger episodes, such as famines, receive considerable press coverage and attract public attention. But chronic hunger and malnutrition are considerably more prevalent. At least 12 million low-birth-weight (LBW) births occur per year and around 162 million pre-school children and almost a billion people of all ages are malnourished. In poorly nourished populations, reductions in hunger and improved nutrition convey considerable productivity gains and save resources that otherwise would be used for the care of malnourished people who are more susceptible to infectious diseases and premature mortality. It is these potential gains in productivity and reductions in economic costs that provide the focus of this chapter.

Hunger

This is the "condition, in which people lack the basic food intake to provide them with the energy and nutrients for fully productive lives" (Hunger Task Force, 2004, p. 33). It is measured in terms of calories relative to requirements that vary by age, sex and activities. The most widely cited data on hunger come from the Food and Agriculture Organization (FAO). FAO (2003) estimates that over the last decade, the number of people undernourished in the developing world declined slightly from 816 to 798 million, or from 20 to 17% of the population. Two regions, Asia and the Pacific and sub-Saharan Africa account for nearly 90% of the world's hungry. However, in Asia, both the number (505 million) and prevalence of undernourishment fell during the 1990s in contrast to increases in Africa (198 million). The Hunger Task

---

[*] This chapter builds extensively on Behrman, Alderman and Hoddinott (2004), which provides considerable details and references that are precluded here due to lack of space.

Force (2003, p. 27) suggests that on a *global* basis: 50% of the hungry are in farm households, mainly in higher-risk production environments; 22% are the rural landless, mainly in higher-potential agricultural regions; 20% are urban and 8% are directly resource-dependent (i.e., pastoralists, fishers, forest-based).

Malnutrition

Nutrients provided by food combine with other factors, including the health state of the consumer, to produce "nutritional status."[1] Many poor nutritional outcomes begin *in utero*. Significant determinants of intrauterine growth retardation (IUGR) and therefore LBW include: mother's long-run nutritional status, her weight and micro-nutrient status prior to conception, and her weight gain during pregnancy. Infections and parasites may lead to IUGR; where endemic, malaria is a major determinant. LBW is especially prevalent in South Asia where prevalences up to 30% are reported (ACC/SCN, 2004). The cumulative impact of events affecting nutritional status results in stunting: 162 million children – about one child in three – are stunted (ACC/SCN, 2004). While stunting rates are highest in South Asia and sub-Saharan Africa, in South Asia numbers and prevalence have been declining since 1990 whereas in sub-Saharan Africa, prevalence has remained largely unchanged and numbers have increased. Multiple factors contribute to poor child nutritional status: LBW, limited periods of exclusive breast-feeding, poor diets and infections (primarily gastrointestinal). Most malnutrition occurs in the first two years of life (Shrimpton *et al.* 2001) and often leads to deficits in cognitive development.

Micro-nutrient deficiencies

This is a further dimension of malnutrition. Particularly important are deficiencies in iron, iodine, and Vitamin A. Iodine deficiency adversely

---

[1] More food can relieve hunger through providing macro-nutrients such as calories and proteins and provide nutrients that lessen some, but not all, forms of malnutrition. Some forms of malnourishment are relieved by reducing calories (e.g., obesity), others by reducing debilitating health stresses such as parasites. Undernutrition with regard to macro and micro-nutrients historically has been, and continues to be, the dominant nutritional problem in developing countries but other forms of malnutrition – in particular those that lead to obesity and diets heavy in fats – are an increasing concern.

affects development of the central nervous system and individuals with an iodine deficiency have, on average, IQs that are 13.5 points lower than comparison groups (Grantham-McGregor, Fernald and Sethuraman 1999). ACC/SCN (2004) reports that globally, approximately 2 billion people are affected by iodine deficiency including 285 million children aged six to twelve years. Adequate iron intake is also necessary for brain development as well as for work capacity at all ages. More than 40% of children ages 0–4 in developing countries suffer from anemia (ACC/SCN 2000); further anemia in school-age children may also affect schooling whether or not there had been earlier impaired brain development. Vitamin A deficiencies, which are estimated to affect 140 million pre-school children, are associated with increased risk of infant and child mortality.

Describing solutions: opportunities related to hunger and malnutrition

Some considerations for estimating the benefits from these solutions

Reduced hunger and improved nutrition can have positive effects through averting early mortality, saving resources that otherwise would be used for sick individuals (since better nourished individuals are less susceptible to diseases) and increasing productivity. For any individual, these effects may be spread out over a number of years. For example, Behrman, Alderman and Hoddinott (2004) (hereafter, BAH) identify seven effects of reducing LBW:

- Reduced infant mortality;
- Reduced neonatal care;
- Reduced costs of infant/child illness;
- Productivity gain from reduced stunting through adulthood;
- Productivity gain from increased ability through adulthood;
- Reduction in the costs of chronic diseases; and
- Benefits for future generations of better maternal nutrition.

This list of effects reducing LBW points to at least four important considerations in assessing the benefits from an intervention.

First, the impacts of many interventions – and most of those considered in this chapter – occur over time, so there is the question of how

Table 21.1. *PDV of $1,000 received with various lags at alternative discount rates*

Discount rate	3.00%	6.00%	10.00%
Lag in years			
10	$744	$558	$386
40	$307	$97	$22
60	$170	$30	$3
100	$109	$13	$1

best to combine effects at different points in time. Gains in the future are discounted because a gain of $1,000 decades in the future is worth less than a gain of $1,000 now, which can be reinvested. For this reason all of the Copenhagen Consensus 2008 (CC08) papers, are using "low" (3%) and "high" (6%) discount rates. The first three columns of Table 21.1 give the present discounted value (PDV) for discount rates of 3% and 6% for $1,000 received with various lags: 10 years (from the perspective of a new-born infant, about the middle of the schooling years), 40 years (about the middle of the adult work years for points 4 and 5 above), 60 years (about the middle of the life period that might be affected by the chronic diseases in point 6 above) and 100 years (the time period that CC08 suggests be considered). For comparison, the third column also gives the PDV for a discount rate of 10%, a rate often recommended for use in developing countries by international organizations and used by a number of governments.[2] For interventions that have effects after many years, such as the reduction in the costs of chronic diseases, it is clear that the discount rate has a big effect. A $1,000 impact after 60 years, for example, has a PDV of $170 for a discount rate of 3%, $30 for a discount rate of 6% and $3 for a discount rate of 10%. The higher the discount rate, obviously, the more important are effects earlier in the life cycles (i.e., points 1–3 above relative to points 4–7 above). Effects of $1,000 with a lag of 100 years have PDVs that are fairly small even for the low 3% discount ($109) and much smaller yet for the 6% rate ($13) or the 10% rate ($1).

[2] For example, Belli *et al.* (1998) and Adhikari, Gertler and Lagman (1999) suggest that discount rates of 10–12% are appropriate for the World Bank and the Asian Development Bank.

Table 21.2. *PDV of $1,000 received with various lags at alternative discount rates, adjusted for survival probabilities*

Discount rate	3.00%	6.00%	10.00%	Survival prob
Lag in years				
10	$675	$506	$350	0.9067
40	$252	$80	$18	0.8232
60	$112	$20	$2	0.6615
100	$2	$0	$0	0.0157

Survival probabilities based on life tables for India.

Second, the solutions in this chapter and some of the others (e.g., on education, infectious illnesses), primarily affect individuals. This means that in addition to the question of adjusting future benefits for their lags by discounting, there is a need to incorporate individual survival probabilities. Column 4 in Table 21.2 gives survival probabilities based on Indian life tables. These indicate, for example, that on average, two-thirds of Indians survive to age 60. The first three columns of Table 21.2 give the PDVs of $1,000 received with the same lags as in Table 21.1, but with adjustment for the survival probabilities since the direct effects of investing in a person (points 1–6 above) depend on the person surviving to the age when the effects occur. The survival probabilityadjusted PDVs in Table 21.2, of course, are lower than the unadjusted PDVs in Table 21.1 – about a third lower for benefits received at age 60 and virtually nil for benefits received at age 100. However in addition to these direct effects on individuals, there may be intergenerational effects (point 7) for which a mixture of survival probabilities for the individuals directly affected and for their children, etc. are relevant.

Third, because of the multiple effects over long periods of time, there are not likely to be many systematic studies that follow a single cohort over long periods to assess the magnitudes of each of the different effects over the life cycle of each of the possible solutions. Indeed, to piece together these effects for a stereotypical low-income country as for this chapter requires careful evaluation of many studies from many different contexts. Presenting this evaluation is far beyond the scope of this chapter, but BAH gives the basic details.

Fourth, to combine the multiple effects of a solution into one measure and to compare those benefits with the costs, it is necessary to translate the effects (and the costs) into one common unit, such as dollars ($). For some of the effects (e.g., points 2 and 3 on resources saved, points 4 and 5 on productivity effects) such a translation is not too difficult using prices, in this case, from low-income countries. Even for these effects and costs, however, identifying the appropriate prices is not completely trivial because what is desired are the real resource prices, not prices that are distorted by governmental policies such as price ceilings or subsidies and taxes. And for other effects, the appropriate procedures for "pricing" are much less clear. The leading example for this and at least some of the other chapters is the value ("price") of averting early mortality. The CC08 has proposed some consistency on this particular price by using a value per DALY (Disability Adjusted Life Years) of $1,000 ("low") and $5,000 ("high"). We use these values in this chapter. But we also note that they are fairly high in comparison with average incomes in low-income countries. The PDV of averting an infant mortality at a DALY of $1,000 per year adjusted for average Indian survival probabilities, for example, is $25,600 (or over 51 times average earnings of $500 per year for low-income target populations) for a discount rate of 3% and $14,700 (or over 29 work years at $500 per year) for a discount rate of 6%. The PDV of averting an infant mortality at a DALY of $5,000 per year adjusted for average Indian survival probabilities, likewise, is $128,300 (or over 256 work years at $500 per year) for a discount rate of 3% and $73,300 (or over 146 work years at $500 per year) for a discount rate of 6%. This implies what may be viewed as very high values on infant mortality averted in terms of adult productivities and incomes in low-income societies. Therefore in BAH we followed Summers (1992, 1994) and used instead of DALYs at such levels, the alternative resource cost that these societies had chosen to allocate to avert an infant mortality, which was estimated to be $1,250 in PDV terms (from inoculations) – a much lower value than implied by DALYs of $1,000 or $5,000. While we present estimates of benefits and costs and benefit–cost ratios using the CC08 "high" and "low" DALYS of $1,000 and $5,000 for our basic estimates in Tables 21.3 and 21.4 below, for comparison we also present estimates of the benefit–cost ratios in Table 21.5 that are parallel to those in BAH by using $1,250 for the resource cost of an infant mortality adverted and

Table 21.3. *Overview table of costs and benefits for solutions given discount rates and DALYs*

		Discount rate			
		3%		6%	
Solutions	DALY	Benefit	Cost	Benefit	Cost
1. Reducing LBW for pregnancies with high probabilities of LBW (particularly in S. Asia)					
1a. Treatments for women with asymptomatic bacterial infections	$1,000 $5,000	$3,023 $12,475	$1,100 $1,100	$1,538 $6,455	$1,100 $1,100
1b. Treatment for women with presumptive STD	$1,000 $5,000	$3,023 $12,475	$276 $276	$1,538 $6,455	$276 $276
1c. Drugs for pregnant women with poor obstetric history	$1,000 $5,000	$3,023 $12,475	$154 $154	$1,538 $6,455	$154 $154
2. Improving infant and child nutrition in populations with high prevalence of child malnutrition (fairly widespread in poor populations in developing countries)					
2a. Breastfeeding promotion in hospitals in which norm was promotion of infant formula	$1,000 $5,000	$38,128 $159,401	$599 $599	$19,176 $82,288	$599 $599
2b. Integrated child care programs (adding improved home child care practices)	$1,000 $5,000	$555 $555	$40 $40	$256 $256	$40 $40
3. Reducing micro-nutrient deficiencies in populations in which they are prevalent					

Table 21.3. (*cont.*)

		3%		6%	
Solutions	DALY	Benefit	Cost	Benefit	Cost
3a. Iodine (per woman of	$1,000	$1,793	$3	$834	$3
childbearing age)	$5,000	$6,316	$3	$2,936	$3
3b. Vitamin A (per child	$1,000	$652	$6	$371	$6
under six years)	$5,000	$3,219	$6	$1,837	$6
3c. Iron (pregnant women	$1,000	$3,369	$19	$1,685	$16
and then over life cycle	$5,000	$12,821	$19	$6,602	$16
of children)					

Benefits are calculated as described in Behrman, Alderman and Hoddinott (2004), but with the discount rates and DALYs indicated at the column head of this table and with the survival probabilities implied by life tables from India. Costs are the mid points of costs from Behrman, Alderman and Hoddinott (2004, Table 6). For iron the costs are the mid-point for pregnant women initially with the per capita costs in subsequent years.

ten years of income at an average of $500 per year for the gain from adverting chronic diseases with impact centered around age 60.

Some considerations for estimating the costs of these solutions

In addition to assessing the benefits, of course, in order to obtain benefit–cost ratios for possible solutions it is necessary to assess the costs. Comments parallel to the first three above for benefits also apply for costs. The first two probably are less important for costs because for most of the interventions considered the costs are one-time initial costs, so discounting and survival probabilities are not relevant. The third comment about the difficulties and the complexities of obtaining good estimates, however, applies very much for costs. In part this is the case because what is wanted is the public and the private resource cost, including any distortion costs (e.g., from raising governmental revenues) – not governmental budgetary financial costs. Once again, BAH provides extensive discussion of the information available and assumptions

Table 21.4. *Overview table for benefit–cost ratios*

Discount rate	3%		6%	
DALY	$1,000	$5,000	$1,000	$5,000
1. Reducing LBW for pregnancies with high probabilities LBW (particularly in S. Asia)				
1a. Treatments for women with asymptomatic bacterial infections	2.7	11.3	1.4	5.9
1b. Treatment for women with presumptive STD	11.0	45.2	5.6	23.4
1c. Drugs for pregnant women with poor obstetric history	19.6	81.0	10.0	41.9
2. Improving infant and child nutrition in populations with high prevalence of child malnutrition (fairly widespread in poor populations in developing countries)				
2a. Breastfeeding promotion in hospitals in which norm was promotion of infant formula	63.7	266.3	32.0	137.5
2b. Integrated child care programs (adding improved home child care practices)	13.9	13.9	6.4	6.4
3. Reducing micro-nutrient deficiencies in populations in which they are prevalent				
3a. Iodine (per woman of childbearing age)	683.0	2,406.0	317.8	1,118.7
3b Vitamin A (per child under six years)	118.6	585.3	67.5	334.1
3c. Iron (pregnant women and then over life cycle of children)	181.4	690.1	107.1	419.7

Table 21.5. *Overview table for benefit–cost ratios under alternative assumptions*

	Alternative value of adverting mortality		Alternative Discount Rate	
Discount rate	3%	6%	10%	10%
DALYS			$1,000	$5,000
Cost of adverting mortality $1250	X	X		
1. Reducing LBW for pregnancies with high probabilities of LBW (particularly in S. Asia)				
1a. Treatments for women with asymptomatic bacterial infections	0.8	0.4	0.8	3.5
1b. Treatment for women with presumptive STD	3.1	1.6	3.2	13.8
1c. Drugs for pregnant women with poor obstetric history	5.6	2.8	5.7	24.7
2. Improving infant and child nutrition in populations with high prevalence of child malnutrition (fairly widespread in poor populations in developing countries)				
2a. Breastfeeding promotion in hospitals in which norm was promotion of infant formula	14.0	7.0	18.2	80.7
2b. Integrated child care programs (adding improved home child care practices)	13.9	6.4	3	3
3. Reducing micro nutrient deficiencies in populations in which they are prevalent				
3a. Iodine (per woman of childbearing age)	307.5	140.7	170.9	616.5
3b. Vitamin A (per child under six years)	7.8	6.6	41.6	206.8
3c. Iron (pregnant women and then over life cycle of children)	65.3	36.7	66.3	271.7

necessary to make the costs estimates on which the tables above are based.

Three solutions or opportunities for reducing hunger and malnutrition

Taking into account the above considerations related to estimating the benefits and costs, we now set out three opportunities for reducing hunger and malnutrition. Table 21.3 gives estimates of benefits and costs and Table 21.4 gives benefit–cost ratios for "low" (3%) and "high" (6%) discount rates and for "low" ($1,000) and "high" ($5,000) DALYs.

Reducing the prevalence of LBW

Many of the 12 million LBW infants born each year die at young ages, contributing significantly to neonatal mortality, which makes up the largest proportion of infant mortality in many developing countries. Unfortunately, rates of LBW have remained relatively static in recent decades. Because LBW infants are 40% more likely to die in the neonatal period than their normal weight counterparts, addressing LBW is essential to achieve reductions in infant mortality. Moreover, many of the LBW children who survive infancy suffer cognitive and neurological impairment and are stunted as adolescents and adults. Thus, in addition to contributing to excess mortality, LBW is associated with lower productivity in a range of economic activities. LBW may also be important in light of new evidence that shows that LBW infants may have an increased risk of cardiovascular disease, diabetes and hypertension later in life. LBW may also be an intergenerational problem because LBW girls who survive tend to be undernourished when pregnant, with relatively high incidence of LBW children.

The benefits from reducing LBW encompass the PDV of the six impacts over the life cycle and the one across generations that are summarized above. Under the assumptions for this chapter, the dominant effect is from adverting mortality (effect 1 in the list above), accounting for 66–89% of the total benefit. Second in importance and the only other effect that accounts for more than 10% of the total are the productivity effects (4 and 5 in the list above) if DALY = $1,000, in which case they account for 17% (with a discount rate of 3%) or 14% (with a discount rate of 6%) of the total. Tables 21.3 and 21.4 summarize the benefits and costs for three interventions to reduce LBW. The benefit–cost ratios range from 1.4–81.0 – with higher values for the "low" (3%) discount rate, the "high" DALY ($5,000) and the intervention of providing drugs for pregnant women with poor obstetric histories.

Improving infant and child nutrition

The nutritional literature emphasizes that undernutrition is most common and severe during two periods of greatest vulnerability, the *in utero* period covered above and the first two years or so of life (Martorell 1997; UNICEF 1998). Young children have high nutritional requirements, in part because they are growing so fast. Unfortunately, the diets commonly offered to young children in developing countries to complement breast milk are of low quality (i.e., with low energy and nutrient density), and as a result, multiple nutrient deficiencies are common. Young children are also very susceptible to infections because their immune systems are both developmentally immature and compromised by poor nutrition. In poor countries, foods and liquids are often contaminated and are thus key sources of frequent infections that both reduce appetite and increase metabolic demands. The second solution/opportunity that we emphasize is directed towards improving the nutrition of infants and young children. This solution/opportunity has effects at most points of the life cycle in the list of seven above (except 2 – Reduced neonatal care and 6 – Reduced costs of chronic diseases associated with LBW). Tables 21.3 and 21.4 summarize the costs and benefits for two interventions to reduce LBW. The benefit–cost ratios range from 6.4–266.3 – with higher values for the "low" (3%) discount rate, the "high" DALY ($5,000) and the intervention of breastfeeding promotion in hospitals.

Reducing the prevalence of iron, iodine and Vitamin A deficiencies

Deficiencies in iron, iodine, and Vitamin A all have both immediate and long-term consequences. Iodine deficiency adversely affects development of the central nervous system and individuals with an iodine deficiency have, on average, lower IQs. Adequate iron intake is also necessary for brain development. More than 40% of children aged 0–4 in developing countries suffer from anemia; further anemia in school-age children may also affect schooling whether or not there had been earlier impaired brain development. Vitamin A deficiencies, which are estimated to affect 140 million pre-school children, are associated with increased risk of infant and child mortality. The third solution/opportunity that we emphasize is directed towards lessening these micronutrient deficiencies, which has effects at most points of the life cycle in the list of seven above. Tables 21.3 and 21.4 summarize the costs and benefits for three such interventions. The benefit–cost ratios range from 67.5 to 2406 – with higher values for the "low" (3%) discount rate, the "high" DALY ($5,000) and the provision of iodine.

Conclusions and caveats

Reducing hunger and malnutrition, endemic in many parts of developing world, is intrinsically important. Our focus here has been on the *economic* case for investing in activities that reduce hunger and malnutrition. We have focused on three solutions or opportunities: (1) Reducing the prevalence of low birth weight; (2) Improving infant and child nutrition; and (3) Reducing the prevalence of iron deficiency anemia and Vitamin A and iodine deficiencies. Under the assumptions outlined above, all of these solutions are promising in the sense that they have benefit–cost ratios that are greater than one and in some cases, particularly for reducing micronutrient deficiencies, the estimated benefit–cost ratios far exceed one.

But some caveats are in order. Firstly, these estimates are based on many assumptions needed to integrate many studies to obtain both the estimated effects and the estimated costs, as is elaborated in BAH. Secondly, the CC08 rightly identified the discount rates and the DALYS as critical parameters and indeed for the possible solutions/ opportunities considered in the chapter, the estimates are fairly sensitive to the choices between the "low" and "high" values for both the discount rates and the DALYS. Moreover, the estimates are very sensitive to alternative values of both of these parameters that arguably may be more appropriate – e.g., a discount rate of 10% as is advocated by some international agencies and valuing averting mortality at the resource cost of the cheapest way of doing so, which BAH argue may be a preferred way to deal with this difficult question. Table 21.5 presents estimated benefit–cost ratios for these alternatives; they are appreciably smaller than those presented in Table 21.4. Nevertheless as illustrated here and in BAH, a number of interventions still give high benefit–cost ratios even with low assumed values for reducing mortality; often the productivity gains alone support favorable benefit–cost ratios. Thirdly, as discussed in the conclusion to BAH, some of the solutions considered in other problem papers are likely to have positive effects on health and nutrition as well as other effects (e.g., improving women's education and status; addressing infectious diseases such as malaria and HIV/AIDS; improving infrastructure to reduce possibilities of famine or chronic hunger; improving water and sanitation; reducing international trade barriers; lessening conflicts and improving governance). In addition, there may be other possibilities that are fairly directed towards alleviating hunger and malnutrition, such as improving agricultural technology for developing countries and lessening zinc deficiencies (discussed in BAH), that have considerable potential, but for which information is not available for an evaluation under the assumptions and constraints of this chapter. Fourthly, all in all the estimated benefit-to-cost ratios for the three solutions/opportunities to directly address hunger and malnutrition that we present in this chapter suggest attractive opportunities. Indeed, the high estimated benefit–cost ratios raise important questions as to why such opportunities have not been seized. Are there upward biases in the estimated impacts? Would induced price and policy changes counter the benefits? Are the discount rates used by governments much higher than those in our illustrations? Do the beneficiaries – primarily infants and children in poor households – have too little voice to be weighed sufficiently heavily in the welfare functions that are dictating intrahousehold allocations and policies? Do marginal costs rapidly increase if interventions are scaled up? Do important market failures preclude private exploitation of sufficient gains? Investigating such questions should be given very high priority.

References

ACC/SCN (Administrative Committee on Coordination/Sub-Committee on Nutrition), 2000: *Fourth Report on the World Nutrition Situation*. New York: United Nations (in collaboration with the International Food Policy Research Institute, Washington DC).

ACC/SCN (Administrative Committee on Coordination/Sub-Committee on Nutrition), 2004: *Fifth Report on the World Nutrition Situation: Nutrition for Improved Development Outcomes*, New York: United Nations.

Adhikari, Ramesh, Paul Gertler and Anneli Lagman, 1999, "Economic Analysis of Health Sector Projects–A Review of Issues, Methods, and Approaches," Manila: Asian Development Bank (March).

Behrman, Jere R., Harold Alderman and John Hoddinott (BAH), 2004, "Hunger and Malnutrition." In Bjorn Lomborg (ed.), *Global Crises, Global Solutions*, Cambridge, UK: Cambridge University Press, 363–420.

Belli, Pedro, J. Anderson, H. Barnum, J. Dixon and J.P. Tan, 1998, *Handbook on Economic Analysis of Investment Operations*, Washington, DC: The World Bank (January).

FAO (United Nations Food and Agriculture Organization), 2003: *The State of Food Insecurity in the World, 2003*, Rome: FAO.

Grantham-McGregor, S., L. Fernald and K. Sethuraman. 1999. "Effects of Health and Nutrition on Cognitive and Behavioural Development in Children in the First Three Years of Life. Part 2. Infections and Micronutrient Deficiencies: Iodine, Iron and Zinc," *Food and Nutrition Bulletin*, 20(1): 76–99.

Hunger Task Force, 2004: *Interim Report*, Millennium Project, New York: UNDP.

Martorell R., 1997: "Undernutrition during Pregnancy and Early Childhood and its Consequences for Cognitive and Behavioral Development." In M.E. Young (ed.), *Early Child Development: Investing in Our Children's Future* , Amsterdam: Elsevier.

Shrimpton R., C. Victora, M. de Onis, R. Costa Lima, M. Blössner and G. Clugston. 2001. "Worldwide Timing of Growth Faltering: Implications for Nutritional Interventions," *Pediatrics*, 107(5): 75–81.

Summers, L. H., 1992: Investing in All the People, *Pakistan Development Review*, 31(4): 367–406.

1994: Investing in All the People: Educating Women in Developing Countries, World Bank, Economic Development Institute Seminar Paper No. 45, Washington, DC: The World Bank.

United Nations Children's Fund (UNICEF). 1998: *The State of The World's Children 1998*. New York: Oxford University Press.

22 | Unsafe Water and Lack of Sanitation

GUY HUTTON

The problem

In the year 2002, it was reported that 1.1 billion people lacked access to improved drinking water sources and 2.6 billion people lacked access to improved sanitation [1]. In some less developed world regions, the proportion of the population lacking access to improved water supply and sanitation (WS&S) was disturbingly high, especially for improved sanitation access. In terms of overall numbers, more than 90% of the world's population lacking access live in Asia and Africa. In fact, around 70% of the 1.1 billion lacking access to improved drinking water sources and around 78% of the 2.6 billion lacking access to improved sanitation access are located in just 11 countries[1] [2].

Unsafe and inaccessible water and sanitation is a human problem for many reasons, covering personal hygiene and dignity, disease risk[2] [3], environmental impact, as well as overall developmental impact related to health status, time use and production decisions. Furthermore, coverage of improved water and sanitation is strongly related to household income and dwelling location, thus indicating severe inequalities in society such as between the rich and the poor, and between rural and urban populations [1].

The real size of the water and sanitation problem is worse than past statistics suggest. The ramifications for humans of unsafe water and lack of sanitation are expected to become worse over time due to unsustainable water consumption, increasing contamination of water

---

[1] These countries are: India, China, Indonesia, Nigeria, Bangladesh, Pakistan, Ethiopia, Vietnam, Brazil, Democratic Republic of Congo, and Afghanistan.

[2] Inadequate water, sanitation and hygiene are a major cause of diarrheal disease, which annually causes 2.2 million deaths and 82 million Disability Adjusted Life Years (DALYs), and helminthes which causes an additional 5.9 million DALYs and 26,000 deaths. In addition to these microbial pathogens, unsafe drinking water can result in exposure to chemical contaminants (arsenic, lead, solvents) and vector-borne diseases such as malaria, dengue, trypanosomiasis, and schistosomiasis.

sources, changing rainfall patterns, population movements, increased water demands from agriculture, and decaying infrastructure which has not been adequately maintained. These problems are critical in many developing regions due to the special geographical and meteorological features which make them more vulnerable to these predicted changes, as well as their lack of economic resources to tackle the problems.

The importance of unsafe water and lack of sanitation is underlined in their connection to several of the Millennium Development Goals (MDGs) [4]. As well as its "own" MDG target (goal 7) of improving water access and providing adequate sanitation, water and sanitation are connected closely to health and nutrition targets (goals 1, 4, 5 and 6), environmental sustainability (goal 7), gender equality (goal 3), primary school attendance (goal 2), and overall poverty rates (goal 1). Partly in recognition of the central importance of water for supporting life on the planet, the UN has declared 2005–2015 the International Decade for Action – Water for Life.

The solution

The solution to the problem is, essentially, to give considerably greater attention to ensuring basic access to *improved* water and sanitation for the world's unserved population. The MDG target for water and sanitation is one response to the current crisis: to halve, by 2015,[3] the proportion of people without sustainable access to safe drinking water and basic sanitation. If the MDG target is achieved, important steps will have been made to improve global sustainable development. However, such a target should be part of a broader long-term vision to increase coverage to universal access. The MDG target has been criticized for its emphasis on physical, as opposed to quality access. For example, the sanitation indicator focuses on access to improved services such as flush toilets, VIP latrines and simple pit latrines, but does not directly consider whether sewage is treated or properly disposed of, which clearly has environmental as well as human health implications [2]. Likewise, the water indicator focuses on time access to water sources with adequate water quantity and the type of source or technology used, but does not involve measurement of actual water quality [5].

---

[3] Base year for comparison is 1990.

These concerns aside, it is clear that there are a number of "basic" improvements to water supply and sanitation which can be achieved at relatively low cost and in a short space of time, and that they can have substantial impacts on the quality of life of underserved populations. For example, evidence shows that having adequate water *quantity* is key for preventing water-washed disease transmission such as scabies or trachoma [5]. However, good water *quality* is key for the prevention of waterborne diseases such as diarrhea, dysentery, or typhoid fever. Cairncross and Valdmanis distinguish four intervention categories:[4]

- Hygiene (hand washing; education).
- Sanitation (sanitary pit latrine; septic tank; household sewer connection).
- Water supply (new water supply or improved distribution in community; piped household water supply).
- Water quality (treatment at community source; treatment at water plant for household piped water supply; treatment at point of use using chemical, pasteurization, filter, boiling, or solar disinfection techniques – all combined with safe water storage).

In the 1992 Rio-Dublin Principles which form the basis of subsequent efforts to define Integrated Water Resources Management, water is recognized as an economic good: "water has an economic value in all its competing uses". Hence cost–benefit analysis is a relevant tool for choosing between alternative options for water (and sanitation) improvement, as it provides key information on the relative economic efficiency of these options.

However, given the lack of published cost–benefit studies on water and sanitation options, this current chapter is limited to presenting the results of a global study [6, 7]. This study presented the costs, benefits, and benefit–cost ratios of a range of interventions with a focus on the water and sanitation MDG targets and low-cost improvements, as well as access to advanced or high cost options. In order to reflect as fully as possible the four main intervention categories above, three scenarios are presented in this current chapter: (1) water supply alone; (2) water supply and sanitation combined; and (3) water supply and sanitation

---

[4] A typology of water supply and sanitation technologies is provided in the UN Millennium Project Taskforce Assessment.

combined, plus a low-cost and simple intervention to improve drinking water quality. Education on hygiene is implicitly included within these three interventions.

It is important to note that these interventions are all preventive in nature, with a focus on achieving MDG targets and on point-of-use interventions that potentially yield large health gains for limited cost. Other options may be considered, but are excluded from this current chapter. One set of options includes "curative" options, such as disease treatment, which are appropriate for the mitigation of some of the negative side effects of the overall problem described earlier. However, in the context of water supply and sanitation interventions, such curative approaches only focus on one part of the problem (i.e. disease) at the cost of other problems that are more comprehensively addressed by the preventive options (time use, dignity, etc.). A second set of options address some of the underlying issues in water resource management, such as international agreements over water supply and water pollution, or power generation (e.g. hydroelectric dams), which are often not addressed in dealing with "basic" access issues. In terms of this larger picture, the Millennium Taskforce concentrates on four major factors to address in water management: institutional, political, financial, and technological [4]. However, these concerns are not the subject of this chapter, and are addressed in separate chapters.

Cost–benefit analysis

Global cost–benefit assessments of any development intervention risk being over-generalized, non-specific in nature and therefore difficult to interpret for any country-specific decision-making context. In order to understand more fully the cost–benefit results presented in this chapter, the sources and nature of different costs and benefits are presented separately, before the overall cost–benefit results.

Intervention costs

For a micro-economic evaluation, costs per capita that accurately reflect the full annual cost per capita of the interventions assessed are needed. A number of studies have been conducted to cost the MDG Target 10 on water supply and sanitation, reviewed by the World

Table 22.1. *Estimates of per capita costs from various sources (US$, year 2000)*

	Region	Construction costs per capita (US$) [9]	Annual total costs per capita (US$) [6, 10]
Water supply			
Basic improvement[1]	Asia	17–64	1.26–4.95
	Africa	21–49	1.55–3.62
	LA&C	36–55	3.17–4.07
Household connection[2]	Asia	92	4.78–9.95
	Africa	102	5.30–12.75
	LA&C	144	7.48–15.29
Sanitation			
Basic improvement[3]	Asia	26–50	3.92–5.70
	Africa	3–91	4.88–6.21
	LA&C	52–60	5.84–6.44
Septic tank	Asia	104	9.10
	Africa	115	9.75
	LA&C	160	12.39
Household connection[4]	Asia	154	8.99–11.95
	Africa	120	7.01–10.03
	LA&C	160	9.34–13.38

[1] Borehole, stand post, dug well, rainwater harvesting
[2] Lower estimate: piped water, not regulated; higher estimate: piped water connection, regulated
[3] VIP, small pit latrine, and pour flush
[4] Lower estimate: sewer connection; higher estimate: sewer connection, with partial treatment

Water Council [8]. Thus various cost estimates are available, ranging from country-specific, to region-specific, to multi-region. While many sources are available for the unit and global costs of improving WS&S, a single estimate is needed for cost–benefit analysis. One reliable and globally comprehensive cost data source is the evidence on *intervention costs* available from the WHO and UNICEF Joint Monitoring Program (JMP) for Water Supply and Sanitation. The latest cost data from the program were presented in the Assessment Report from the year 2000 [9]. Investment cost per capita in United States dollars (year 2000) were provided by countries, and aggregated for three developing regions (see Table 22.1). Given that large variations were observed in cost per capita between countries of similar geographical and economic conditions, regional averages were presented in the JMP report and used in the subsequent cost–benefit analysis [6, 7]. Ranges in costs in Table 22.1 reflect the variation in the cost of different improvement options (see table footnotes). Total costs were calculated by assuming that similar proportions of the population receive different improvement options.

For *water*, four types of basic improved water source were considered: borehole, stand post, dug well, and rainwater harvesting. These varied in construction cost from US$17 to US$55 per capita. Household piped water supply was considerably more expensive per capita (US$102 in Africa, US$92 in Asia, and US$144 in LA&C) due to the increased hardware and the water production costs. In order to estimate the cost–benefit of improved water access, Hutton and Haller make several assumptions about likely recurrent costs and length of life of the different technologies to estimate total annual equivalent costs, presented in the final column of Table 22.1 [6, 10]. When the costs were annualized, the intervention cost per person reached varies between US$1.26 and US$4.95 for Asia, US$1.55–US$3.62 for Africa, and US$3.17–US$4.07 for LA&C, depending on intervention choice.

For *sanitation*, improvement options vary from the relatively simple such as a VIP and small pit latrine, to those options requiring greater availability of water supply such as pour flush, to more advanced options with partial treatment such as septic tank and sewer connection. The construction cost per capita of these options varies considerably in developing regions, from US$26 to US$91 for basic improvements; US$104–US$160 for septic tank; and US$120–US$160 for sewer connection [9]. The cost differences between basic and advanced sanitation options becomes smaller when annual per capita costs are calculated, due to the longer assumed length of life of septic tank and sewer connection.

While these figures presented by JMP are strongly indicative of the levels of cost per capita expected in these settings, the actual unit costs in specific locations may vary considerably. As pointed out by Cairncross and Valdmanis, the local conditions such as size of community to be served and presence of suitable aquifers, can cause tremendous variations in the unit cost of water supply [5]. This is particularly true for household water and sewerage connections, where most investment in major works is made before house connections can be offered, so the marginal cost of each additional connection is only a fraction of the total cost. Thus unit cost is strongly correlated with the percentage of capacity use of a given facility (returns to size). Furthermore, cost assessments would ideally distinguish between urban and rural areas, given the different population densities and access to resources, and hence unit costs of extending services to additional households.

Intervention benefits

While there is at least some clarity and methodological agreement on which costs should be included and how they are valued, on the *intervention benefit* side there is considerably less clarity and agreement. From a Ministry of Health perspective, the World Health Organization recommends cost-effectiveness analysis, which in practice means comparing the costs of the intervention with health effects, measured in terms of incidence and mortality averted, and preferably converted to an index comparable across disease states and health interventions such as DALYs or healthy life-years (HLY) [11]. The WHO also recognizes that health cost savings due to fewer people seeking treatment should be taken into account, and thus recommends deducting these savings from intervention costs to give a net health sector cost. The WHO's CEA results for water and sanitation interventions were presented in the World Health Report 2002, and more comprehensively presented in Haller et al. [10].

However, as recognized in a WHO discussion paper in 2000, many development interventions that have an impact on health also impact outside the health sector, so should be included in an analysis [12]. Thus either CEA can be broadened to include productivity effects attributable to the intervention [13], or a full social cost–benefit analysis (SCBA) can be conducted. Since the 1960s, SCBA has been conducted as a matter of routine in many large development projects in developing countries, especially those funded by external donors [14, 15]. However, despite large strides in methodological refinement and application, SCBA has been practiced less and less according to fundamental principles, although it is still a part of development bank project appraisals [16]. Furthermore, there is considerable variation in the SCBA methodologies applied, such as which benefits to include and how to value benefits in monetary terms. These days, a dominant approach in development project appraisal is to measure welfare gain for water projects by multiplying the expected price of water by the quantity of water supplied. While this simply aggregates the market value of water traded, it risks omitting some important benefits.

A large range of benefits result from water and sanitation interventions, with differences as well as similarities between the two. Benefits common to both are health benefits and the related economic benefits and household time saving. Water interventions bring potential gains to households through changing production technology (e.g. small home businesses), the private sector (water supply as an input to production), as well as agriculture (irrigation). Sanitation interventions likewise can change the development pathway of households, as well as providing raw materials for agriculture (fertiliser). The economic peer-reviewed and project literature has been presented previously, revealing very few studies, but a wide range of economic methodologies [17]. For example, Suarez estimates the costs associated with the cholera epidemic in Peru in 1989–1990, including health care cost savings, productivity savings, value of saved lives (VOSL), tourism and domestic production impact [18]. To estimate the household economic impact of improved water supply in various settings, Whittington and colleagues estimate willingness to pay using contingent valuation and observed wage rates [19–22]. North and Griffin attempt to value the economic impact of improved water source by measuring its influence on house prices [23].

Cost–benefit analysis

To date, there has been one single attempt, a WHO report in 2004, to measure the social cost–benefit of a range of options for improving water supply and sanitation globally [6]. This was published in 2007 [7], and was recently adapted for a background paper for the UNDP Human Development Report 2006[5] [24]. The results reported have

---

[5] This new study estimates the cost–benefit of achieving the MDG targets compared to the predicted coverage in 2015 based on coverage increase trend line since 1990. Hence this new analysis focuses on the countries that are off-target to meet the MDGs.

been variously used, including the United Nations Commission on Sustainable Development [25, 26], a report for DFID [27], and the Water Challenge paper in the first Copenhagen Consensus in 2004 [28]. This current chapter presents a selection of results from the most recent version of this analysis, including a one-way sensitivity analysis on four of the most key determinants of benefit–cost [7]. The key study aims and methods are reported below.

The aim of this global benefit–cost analysis was to estimate the equivalent annual costs and benefits – from the base year 2000 to the target year 2015 – associated with improving water supply and sanitation in order to meet, separately and together, the water supply and sanitation MDGs and to achieve universal access. Estimates of costs and benefits were made for each developing country separately and aggregated to eleven developing world sub-regions based on WHO classification.[6] Populations with unimproved WS&S were moved to "improved" coverage, assuming equal proportions of the unserved population moving to a range of intervention options. For example, in the case of water supply, populations to be served received in equal proportions the following interventions: borehole, stand post, dug well, harvested rainwater and household piped water supply. Costs were estimated accordingly, and included both investment and recurrent costs, as reported in Table 22.1. Benefits included those that were most widespread globally, measurable, and significant, and included averted health care costs due to diarrheal disease, productivity and welfare implications of less diarrheal disease, averted deaths associated with lower diarrheal incidence, and time savings of more conveniently located water supply or sanitation facility or less waiting time associated with an improved water supply or sanitation facility. Future costs and benefits were discounted at 3%, a rate that reflects international consensus [11, 29, 30] and provided by the Copenhagen Consensus Center in order to increase comparability of interventions across different sectors. For the purpose of this chapter for the Copenhagen Consensus 2008, benefit–cost ratios were also estimated based on each DALY averted being worth US$1,000 (lower bound) and US$5,000 (higher bound), and in these calculations the valuation of health effects (welfare associated with less morbidity and less mortality) were excluded to avoid

---

[6] http://www.who.int/choice/demography/regions/en/index.html

Table 22.2. *Global results for three intervention scenarios (all figures in millions)*

Variable	Water supply MDG alone	Water supply and sanitation MDG combined	WS&S universal access + disinfection at point of use
Disaggregated costs and benefits			
Costs (US$)	1,748	11,047	26,225
DALYs averted (DALY)	1.544	4.923	27.638
Health cost savings (US$)	546	1,870	9,735
Productivity (morbidity) (US$)	1,148	3,880	24,098
VOSL (mortality) (US$)	677	2,461	13,487
Time savings (US$)	12,958	121,060	242,120
Benefit–cost ratios			
DALY valued at US$1,000	8.6	11.6	10.7
DALY valued at US$5,000	12.1	13.4	14.9
Health valued using human capital	8.8	11.7	11.0

double-counting. DALYs averted by WHO sub-regions are available from Haller *et al.* [10].

Table 22.2 presents a summary of the results at the global level, while Table 22.3 presents results for the eleven WHO developing country sub-regions separately. All costs and benefits are presented as annual values and in units of millions, while the benefit–cost ratio reflects the expected social welfare return in United States dollars for every US$1 spent.

The results show that, for the eleven developing sub-regions, an annual US$1.75 billion needs to be spent between the year 2000 and 2015 in order to meet the water supply MDG, increasing to US$11.05 billion for the combined WS&S MDG. To calculate the total cost of meeting the MDGs, it is not appropriate to multiply these annual figures by 15 years, given that the increase in coverage will not all be achieved at once. Assuming a linear increase in coverage from the base year (2000) to the target year (2015), the water MDG alone would cost US$13 billion, the sanitation MDG alone US$70 billion and the combined WS&S MDG a total of US$83 billion. These figures are different to the ranges referred to in the UN Millennium Project Taskforce on Water and Sanitation [4], where the water MDG target costs between US$51 and US$102 billion; and sanitation MDG target costs between US$24 and US$42 billion.

For universal WS&S access plus disinfection using chlorination technique at the point-of-use, the annual cost is US$26.2 billion. While the actual annual costs required may vary considerably for each sub-region, as presented in Table 22.3, this global estimate represents a ballpark figure. However, it is evident that the sub-region requiring the largest increases in resource allocations is Western Pacific (WPR-B), followed by South and South-East Asia, and Africa.

In terms of economic value of intervention benefits, it is clear from the results that convenience time savings are the greatest contributor to overall benefits, accounting for US$12.96 billion for achieving the water supply MDG, compared with US$546 million for health cost savings, US$1.15 billion for morbidity savings and US$677 million for VOSL.

Using these economic benefit values, the benefit–cost ratio for eleven developing country sub-regions is 8.8, ranging from 4.4 (AFR-D) to 31.6 (AMR-D). When health-related time gains are valued at US$1,000 per DALY instead of GNI per capita, the benefit–cost ratio is little changed at 8.6, ranging from 5.1 (AFR-D) to 28.5 (AMR-D). At the higher DALY value of US$5,000, the benefit–cost ratio increases to a global average of 12.1, ranging from 8.5 (WPR-B) to 29.8 (AMR-D). Under the DALY valuation scenario, it is interesting to note the increase in benefit–cost ratio in low-income countries, especially AFR and SEAR-D, compared to higher income regions where the GNI per capita is closer to the US$1,000 value. However, the standardization of the DALY value across sub-regions does not greatly narrow the differences between regions with high GNI per capita (e.g. AMR) and low GNI per capita (e.g. AFR). This is because the major differences in economic benefit are from the different time valuations between regions, which are directly based on the GNI per capita.

In terms of the benefit–cost results for the other interventions presented in Tables 22.2 and 22.3, it is important to note the increase in the economic attractiveness when sanitation is added, signified by a rising benefit–cost ratio (BCR). Globally the BCR jumps from 8.8 for water supply alone to 11.0 for WS&S combined, ranging from 5.5 (AFR-D) to 45.5 (AMR-B). By including disinfection at the point of use (POU) does not greatly change the BCR, at 11.0 globally, given that the contribution of the increased health gains to overall economic benefit is still relatively small. Note, however, the dramatic increase in health-related economic gains when POU treatment is included. For example, when POU treatment is added to universal WS&S, the number of DALYs averted increases from 10 million to 27.6 million annually, and the combined productivity and VOSL gain from US$10.5 billion to US$37.5 billion annually.

Sensitivity analysis

Due to the high level of uncertainty in the costs as well as the benefits in such a global study, sensitivity analysis was conducted to give an indication of how much the base case cost–benefit results are affected by changes in the values taken by some key parameters. Table 22.4 presents the results of a one-way sensitivity analysis, with the effects of uncertainty in each parameter assessed independently of the others. The extreme values in Table 22.4 are therefore not unrealistic for some settings within the sub-regions, and furthermore the values may be even higher or lower than these values when combining more than one type of uncertainty:

- In SA1, based on different assumptions about the calculation of recurrent costs and hardware length of life, unit cost inputs varied quite considerably and therefore had a considerable effect on the benefit–cost ratios, more than halving it in the pessimistic scenario and more than doubling it in the optimistic scenario.
- In SA2, when time savings were valued at 30% of GNI per capita instead of 100%, the impact was even greater – reducing BCR from 6.0 to 2.0 in AFR-E.
- In SA3, when convenience time savings were given realistic upper and lower values [5, 31], the impact was also considerable – reducing the BCR from 6.0 to 3.5 in AFR-E.

Table 22.3. *Results of global cost–benefit analysis: costs, benefits and benefit–cost ratio by developing world sub-regions*

Interventions and variables	Africa		The Americas		E Mediterran		Europe		S 1 SE Asia		W Pacific	Developing
	AFR-D	AFR-E	AMR-B	AMR-D	EMR-B	EMR-D	EUR-B	EUR-C	SEAR-B	SEAR-D	WPR-B	World
Total population in 2015 (million)	487	481	531	93	184	189	238	223	473	1,689	1,488	6,076
Diarrhea cases (million)	620	619	459	93	133	153	87	43	304	1,491	1,317	5,319
1. Water supply MDG alone (all figures annually in millions)												
1.1 Costs (US$)	222	268	133	38	24	33	52	8	121	282	566	1,748
1.2 DALYs averted ('000 DALY)	0.388	0.328	0.042	0.027	0.004	0.101	0.010	0.000	0.027	0.447	0.170	1.544
1.3 Health cost savings	78	77	82	29	7	24	6	1	22	76	145	546
1.4 Productivity (morbidity) (US$)	172	146	67	21	11	49	14	1	103	238	638	1,459
1.5 VOSL (mortality) (US$)	148	174	74	16	22	33	9	0	15	153	33	677
1.6 Time savings (US$)	671	952	3,680	320	442	305	743	77	957	1,023	3,789	12,958
1.7 BCR1 (DALY at US$1,000)	5.1	5.1	28.5	9.8	18.6	13.1	14.4	10.2	8.3	5.5	7.3	8.6
1.8 BCR2 (DALY at US$5,000)	12.1	9.9	29.8	12.7	19.2	25.5	15.2	10.4	9.2	11.8	8.5	12.1

Table 22.3 (cont.)

Interventions and variables	Africa		The Americas		E Mediterran		Europe		S + SE Asia		W Pacific	Developing World
	AFR-D	AFR-E	AMR-B	AMR-D	EMR-B	EMR-D	EUR-B	EUR-C	SEAR-B	SEAR-D	WPR-B	World
1.9 BCR3 (Productivity & VOSL)	4.4	4.9	31.6	10.6	20.1	12.1	14.7	10.4	8.6	4.8	7.6	8.8
2. Water supply and sanitation MDG combined (all figures annually in millions)												
2.1 Costs (US$)	947	1,074	631	157	100	163	186	71	466	3,628	3,621	11,047
2.2 DALYs averted ('000 DALY)	0.816	0.789	0.104	0.057	0.023	0.223	0.024	0.002	0.062	2.305	0.517	4.923
2.3 Health cost savings (US$)	231	237	249	83	30	70	20	3	64	405	477	1,870
2.4 Productivity (morbidity) (US$)	269	340	1,137	118	69	95	48	9	162	574	1,059	3,880
2.5 VOSL (mortality) (US$)	460	528	225	47	71	95	33	1	44	846	111	2,461
2.6 Time savings (US$)	4,271	5,341	27,124	2,023	2,463	2,132	3,596	1,457	5,054	22,408	45,191	121,060
2.7 BCR1 (DALY at US$1,000)	5.6	5.9	43.5	13.7	25.1	14.9	19.5	20.5	11.1	6.9	12.8	11.6
2.8 BCR2 (DALY at US$5,000)	9.1	8.9	44.2	15.2	26.0	20.4	20.1	20.6	11.6	9.5	13.3	13.4

2.9 BCR3 (Productivity & VOSL)	5.5	6.0	45.5	14.4	26.3	14.7	19.8	20.6	11.4	6.7	12.9	11.7

3. WS&S universal access + disinfection at point of use (all figures annually in millions)

3.1 Costs (US$)	2,216	2,466	1,613	376	322	450	530	290	1,245	8,371	8,347	26,225
3.2 DALYs averted ('000 DALY)	4.307	4.313	0.896	0.348	0.406	2.067	0.301	0.069	0.509	11.948	2.475	27.638
3.3 Health cost savings (US$)	840	853	1,791	387	402	490	200	93	385	2,078	2,216	9,735
3.4 Productivity (morbidity) (US$)	1,168	1,577	8,023	591	1,317	773	552	303	1,495	2,938	5,361	24,098
3.5 VOSL 503 (mortality) (US$)	2,011	2,419	1,596	262	852	831	355	47	342	4,271	502	13,487
3.6 Time savings (US$)	8,542	10,682	54,248	4,047	4,925	4,265	7,192	2,913	10,107	44,817	90,382	242,120
3.7 BCR1 (DALY at US$1,000)	6.2	6.4	35.3	12.7	17.8	15.2	14.5	10.6	8.8	7.0	11.4	10.7
3.8 BCR2 (DALY at US$5,000)	14.0	13.4	37.5	16.4	22.8	33.6	16.8	11.6	10.5	12.7	12.6	14.9
3.9 BCR3 (Productivity & VOSL)	5.7	6.3	40.7	14.1	23.3	14.1	15.7	11.6	9.9	6.5	11.8	11.0

BCR: benefit–cost ratio; VOSL: value of a saved life; DALY: disability adjusted life year

Table 22.4. *Sensitivity of benefit–cost ratios to model assumptions in five selected developing regions (WS&S MDG targets)*

Parameter	Scenario	AFR-E	AMR-D	EMR-D	SEAR-D	WPR-B
SA1: Intervention	Pessimistic	2.7	6.4	6.7	3.2	6.0
costs	*Base*	*6.0*	*14.4*	*14.7*	*6.7*	*12.9*
	Optimistic	14.7	35.5	36.0	16.3	31.6
SA2: Time value	Pessimistic	2.0	4.7	4.7	2.1	4.0
	Base	*6.0*	*14.4*	*14.7*	*6.7*	*12.9*
	Optimistic	10.8	9.6	32.8	7.3	6.6
SA3: Time savings	Pessimistic	3.5	7.9	8.0	3.6	6.6
	Base	*6.0*	*14.4*	*14.7*	*6.7*	*12.9*
	Optimistic	9.4	23.0	23.3	10.1	20.3
SA4: Diarrheal	Pessimistic	5.5	13.6	13.9	6.4	12.7
disease	*Base*	*6.0*	*14.4*	*14.7*	*6.7*	*12.9*
incidence rate	Optimistic	6.5	15.2	15.5	6.9	13.2

- In SA4, the effect of changes in starting values for diarrheal disease incidence had less impact on the BCR due to the relatively less important contribution of health benefits compared to non-health benefits. The effect would be larger for interventions that specifically address the health outcomes, such as point of use treatment.

The impact of changes in the discount rate from the base case value of 3% was not assessed quantitatively in terms of impact on BCR. The main implication of changing the discount rate is to affect the VOSL and the annual cost per capita of the interventions. For example, when a discount rate of 6% was applied to the cost of capital, the annual cost per person covered increased by 30%, 42%, and 54% depending on length of life assumed of 20, 30 and 40 years, respectively. Hence, a considerably higher discount rate than 3% could have a large impact on the BCR. For the value of future years of work lost calculation for VOSL, the greater impact is for the younger age group (0–4 years) who are still many years from entering the labor force, with a decline in value of 54%. For children (5–14 years) the reduction is 41% while for adults (15+) the reduction is 20%. Hence the overall impact on the BCR is likely to be large considering that the majority (>75% in all sub-regions) of deaths averted are in the 0–4 year age group.

Implications and outlook

Cost–benefit analysis not only indicates likely returns on investment, but also can contribute to identifying ways of financing interventions through an understanding of the beneficiaries of the interventions. At household level, families with "unimproved" water sources already pay for some services, whether it is paying a water vendor, purchasing bottled water, or buying materials and energy for water purification; households also pay for water sources in-kind through their time for water collection and waiting. In some instances, this is also true of unimproved sanitation, where households pay for sewage to be removed or in-kind through travel and waiting time. Hence, by switching to an alternative and improved water source or sanitation choice, households can save on some costs that contribute to meeting the cost of the improved source. In some contexts, it is even possible that the new source is cheaper in financial terms than the old source, as it has been widely documented that households can pay high prices to access adequate water supply from vendors.

However, several barriers exist to accessing the improved water and sanitation options. A major barrier is the financial constraint of paying the up-front costs of improved WS&S options. Interventions requiring large investments, such as household connection to water or sewerage systems are one such financial barrier as households may not be able to pay these costs, and bank loans may not be an attractive or available option. Recurrent costs such as paying bills to piped water providers may also be high; especially as water use may increase substantially after a piped water connection is made. Hence, when examining the financial requirements for household connections, some households may be dissuaded from improving their water supply or sanitation. Cost–benefit analysis can, however, be used as a source of information which helps advocate for improved water and sanitation, as it takes into account not only financial implications but also the probable impact on quality of life (e.g. health) and the economic situation, through time savings and household production opportunities.

In addition to financing issues, there remain questions over the feasibility of expanding access to improved water and sanitation, especially in resource-constrained settings, covering not only financial resources but also water resources. As noted earlier, a large proportion of those targeted to meet the water and sanitation MDG target are

living in eleven countries, which either have very low income per capita
and government spending (e.g. Bangladesh, Pakistan, Ethiopia) and/or
have very weak institutions to oversee the expansion of water supply
(e.g. Nigeria, Democratic Republic of Congo, Afghanistan). These
eleven countries also tend to be countries with large populations,
where it is questionable that governments have the willingness and
capacity to substantially improve the situation in a time period of less
than ten years (e.g. India, Indonesia, or Brazil).

However, as well as promoting the routine business of drilling wells,
constructing dams and infrastructure, there are also some quick wins
and innovative ways of working to hasten the coverage of the more vulnerable populations and to target certain impacts that can be achieved
at low cost. These options include the mobilization of the health sector
to improve household water purification at the point of use or in the
community; hygiene education in the community; health promotion
and latrine building in schools and health centres and extending micro-
credit to households to allow them to invest in water and sanitation
improvement. Furthermore, improved advocacy of the benefits of water
and sanitation could be supported by country-level and sub-national
studies that help convince government departments, as well as the population, that water and sanitation are worth investing in.

References

1. WHO/UNICEF/JMP (2004). Meeting the MDG Drinking Water and
   Sanitation target: A mid-term assessment of the progress. Geneva and
   New York: World Health Organization and United Nations Children's
   Fund Joint Monitoring Program. www.wssinfo.org/pdf/JMP_04_
   text.pdf
2. Rheingans R, Dreibelbis R and Freeman M (2006). Beyond the
   Millennium Development Goals: Public health challenges in water and
   sanitation. *Global Public Health*, 1(1) 31–48.
3. Prüss A, Kay D, Fewtrell L and Bartram J (2002). Estimating the global
   burden of disease from water, sanitation, and hygiene at the global level.
   Environmental Health Perspectives, 110(5) 537–42.
4. Lenton R, Wright A and Lewis K (2005). *Health dignity and development: What will it take?* 2005, UN Millennium Project, Task Force on
   Water and Sanitation, London and Sterling Va: Earthscan.
5. Cairncross S and Valdmanis V (2006). Water supply, sanitation and
   hygiene promotion. In *Disease Control Priorities in Developing
   Countries*, Jamison D, Breman J, Measham A, Alleyne G, Claeson M,

Evans D, Jha P, Mills A and Musgrove P (eds.). 2nd edn. New York: Oxford University Press.

6. Hutton G and Haller L (2004). Evaluation of the non-health costs and benefits of water and sanitation improvements at global level. World Health Organization. WHO/SDE/WSH/04.04.

7. Hutton G, Haller L and Bartram J (2007). Global cost–benefit analysis of water supply and sanitation interventions. *Journal of Water and Health*, 5(4).

8. World Water Council (2005). Costing MDG Target 10 on Water Supply and Sanitation. http://www.worldwatercouncil.org/fileadmin/wwc/ Library/Publications_and_reports/FicheMDG_UK_final.pdf.

9. WHO/UNICEF/JMP (2000). Global Water Supply and Sanitation Assessment 2000 Report. Geneva and New York: World Health Organization, United Nations Children's Fund, Water Supply and Sanitation Collaborative Council.

10. Haller L, Hutton G and Bartram J (2007). Estimating the costs and health benefits of water and sanitation improvements at global level. *Journal of Water and Health*, 5(4).

11. Tan-Torres Edejer T, Baltussen R, Adam T, Hutubessy R, Acharya A, Evans D and Murray C (2003). *Making choices in health. WHO guide to cost-effectiveness analysis*. Geneva: World Health Organization.

12. Hutton G (2000). Considerations in Evaluating the Cost-effectiveness of Environmental Health Interventions. Sustainable Development and Healthy Environments Cluster. Geneva: World Health Organization. WHO/SDE/WSH/00.10.

13. Borghi J, Guinness L, Ouedraogo J and Curtis V (2002). Is hygiene promotion cost-effective? A case study in Burkina Faso. *Tropical Medicine and International Health*, 7(11) 960–9.

14. Little I and Mirrlees J (1969). *Manual of Industrial Project Analysis in Developing Countries, Vol. 2: Social Cost Benefit Analysis*. Paris: OECD.

15. United Nations Industrial Development Organization (1972). *Guidelines for project evaluation*. New York: United Nations.

16. Asian Development Bank (1999). *Handbook for the economic analysis of water supply projects*. ADB, Manila: Economics and Development Resource Center.

17. Hutton G (2001). Economic evaluation and priority setting in water and sanitation interventions. In Fewtrell L and Bartram J (eds.) *Water quality: Guidelines, standards and health. Risk assessment and management for water-related infectious disease*. London: IWA Publishing.

18. Suarez R and Bradford B (1993). The economic impact of the cholera epidemic in Peru: An application of the cost-if-illness methodology. Water and Sanitation for Health Project; WASH Field Report No. 415.

19. Whittington D, Mu X and Roche R (1990). Calculating the value of time spent collecting water: Some estimates for Ukunda, Kenya. *World Development*, 18 (2).

20. Whittington D, Lauria DT and Mu X (1991). A study of water vending and willingness to pay for water in Onitsha, Nigeria. *World Development*, 19(2/3) 179–98.

21. Whittington D, Lauria DT, Wright AM, Choe K, Hughes JA and Swarna V (1993). Household demand for improved sanitation services in Kamasi, Ghana: A contingent valuation study. *Water Resources Research*, 29(6) 1539–60.

22. Whittington D, Briscoe J, Mu X and Barron W (1990). Estimating the willingness to pay for water services in developing countries: A case study of the use of contingent valuation surveys in Southern Haiti. *Economic Development and Cultural Change*, 293–311.

23. North J and Griffin C (1993). Water source as a housing characteristic: Hedonic property valuation and willingness to pay for water. *Water Resources Research*, 29(7) 1923–29.

24. Hutton G, Haller L and Bartram J (2006). Economic and health effects of increasing coverage of low cost water and sanitation interventions. Geneva and new York: World Health Organization and United Nations Development Program.

25. Sanctuary M, Tropp H and Haller L (2005). *Making water a part of economic development*. Stockholm: International Water Institute.

26. Evans B, Hutton G and Haller L (2004). Closing the sanitation gap – the case for better public funding of sanitation and hygiene. Background paper for the OECD Round Table on Sustainable Development Meeting on Water and Sanitation, March 2004. SG/SD/RT(2004)2.

27. Environmental Resources Management (2005). Meeting the water and sanitation Millennium Development Goal. Report to the UK Department for International Development.

28. Rijsberman F (2004). The Water Challenge. Copenhagen Consensus Challenge Paper, 2004.

29. Drummond MF, O'Brien B, Stoddart GL and Torrance GW (1997). *Methods for the economic evaluation of health care programmes*. Oxford: Oxford University Press, 2nd edn.

30. Gold MR, Siegel JE, Russell LB and Weinstein MC (1996). *Cost-effectiveness in health and medicine*. Oxford: Oxford University Press.

31. Dutta S (2005). Energy as a key variable in eradicating extreme poverty and hunger: A gender and energy perspective on empirical evidence on MDG No1. DFID/ENERGIA project on *Gender as a Key Variable in Energy Interventions*. Draft version, September 2005.

23 | *Population: Migration*

MICHAEL J. GREENWOOD

Introduction

International migration appears at the present time to be at or near historically high levels (Organization for Economic Co-operation and Development [OECD], 2005), but the illegal component is the most perplexing to receiving nations and the component that probably has increased most in recent years. Much illegal migration is from less- to more-developed countries and presents serious challenges in migrant-receiving nations. The first problem is that whereas the illegals may be known to be present, in some cases in large numbers, even approximate estimates of their actual numbers are difficult to obtain (Espenshade, 1995; Bean *et al.*, 1998; Tapinos, 1999; Hanson, 2006). Thus, the discussion of their effects and what to do about them is not grounded in substantive data.

Where illegal migrants and/or their children qualify for social benefits or education, social programs and educational systems may be stressed as transfers occur from indigenous residents to migrants. Ethnic tensions may rise as cultures clash. Those migrants who do not speak the receiving country's primary language often have difficulty assimilating, and some of these problems may spill over into the educational system through higher costs of bi-lingual education and in other ways. In many cases, citizenship may not be available or may be possible only after a long wait, which leaves a potentially large group disenfranchised.

Figure 23.1 reports the percentages of population that were foreign-born *circa* 1993 and *circa* 2002 in selected OECD countries. For 75% of these countries, the most recent annual observation shows 10% or more of the population as foreign-born, and these figures do not include all of the illegals. For every country for which two observations are available, this percentage increased from the early or mid-1990s to the early twenty-first century. Thus, for many countries immigration

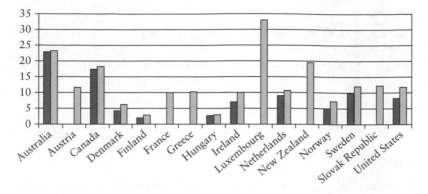

Figure 23.1. Percentages of foreign-born population in selected OECD countries, circa 1993 and circa 2002

Note: Australia 1993 &2002; Canada, 1996 & 2001; Finland, 1995 & 2002; France, 1999; Greece, 2001; Hungary, 1995 & 2002; Ireland, 1996 & 2002; Luxembourg, 2001; Netherlands, 1993 & 2002; New Zealand, 2001; Norway, 1993 & 2002; Slovak Republic, 2001; Sweden, 1993 & 2002; United States, 1994 & 2002.

has become the most important source of population growth. Due to their ageing populations, many industrialized countries view migration as beneficial. The migrants tend to be young adults in their prime years of labor-force participation.

Because the migrants tend to come from less-developed countries, they tend to be less educated than the average national or native. The OECD (2005, p. 65, Table I.12) documents such differences. For example, for Austria 42.9% of the foreigners aged between 25 and 64 had less than an upper secondary education, compared to 19.3% of the nationals.[1] Comparable figures for other countries are as follows: Belgium – 52.3% versus 37.8%; France – 63.9% versus 33.5%; Germany – 47.1% versus 13.6%; Luxembourg – 43.8% versus 27.5%; Switzerland – 31.4% versus 8.1%; United Kingdom – 30.9% versus 17.4%; and United States – 30.5% versus 9.0%. Canada has much more comparable percentages – 16.7% versus 16.6%.[2] Bustamante *et al.* (1998) show that, during the mid-1990s, 83% of Mexican illegal

---

[1] "Upper secondary" refers to completed year 12. The figures refer to 2002–2003 averages.
[2] The Canadian figures refer to 2001–2002 averages, and US and Canadian figures refer to natives rather than nationals.

immigrants in the USA were male with an average 4.2 years of education. Clearly, many nations are finding it necessary to absorb immigrants with relatively low levels of educational attainment. Because the migrants tend to be poor, less-educated, young, and less-skilled, they tend to the extent that they find employment to compete with and displace the lowest-income indigenous residents while putting downward pressure on the wages of those who remain employed.

Identifying the redistributions inherent in migration

Although some studies have attempted to estimate the international transfer inherent in migration (Martin, 2004; Rosenzweig, 2004), no effort has been made to measure comprehensively the benefits and costs of internal or international migration. However, economic theory allows for qualitative assessments of the redistributions inherent in migration (Greenwood and McDowell, 1986). Any labor migration results in three types of redistributions: (1) from origin to destination; (2) within the destination; and (3) within the origin. Most quantitative attention has focused on the first type of redistribution, as reflected in the earlier work of Martin (2004) and Rosenzweig (2004). The major focus here is on the second redistribution. The three redistributions are qualitatively the same whether they refer to legal or illegal international migrants or to internal migrants.

The redistribution from origin to destination involves a productive human being (i.e., one with a positive marginal product) now working in the destination rather than the origin. Because the individual typically has a higher marginal product in the destination, which is reflected in a higher wage there, he has a potential incentive to move and his movement improves the global distribution of labor resources. The magnitude of this redistribution depends upon several factors, including the individual's personal characteristics (e.g., sex, age, education, skills) that help determine his labor force participation, marginal product, and wage. The positive transfer from the origin to the destination that is implicit in most economic analyses of migration assumes a productive individual whose contributions raise the Gross Domestic Product (GDP) of the destination country (Rosenzweig, 2004). Where this positive productivity is lacking, the benefits in the destination are much less clear, but still may exist through family reunification and other linkages.

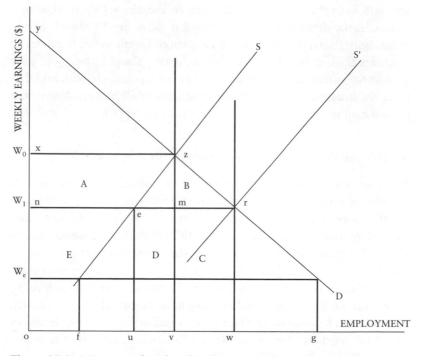

Figure 23.2. Migrant-Induced Redistributions in the country of destination

The second type of transfer involves redistributions in the destination. In a simple model with homogeneous labor, if migration does not cause a shift of labor demand in the destination, the wage rate will fall and the return to other factors of production will rise. This situation is shown in Figure 23.2, where immigration causes a shift of (perfectly inelastic) labor supply from vz to wr. The destination country has imposed a quota of mr and its wage falls from W_0 to W_1. The return to factors of production other than labor (capital, land) rises from xyz in the absence of immigration to nyr in the presence of mr immigration.

Now suppose that the supply curve has a positive slope and shifts from S to S′ due to migration. Whereas mr legal migrants and em illegal migrants are employed at a wage rate of W_1, em native workers (and perhaps former immigrants) withdraw from the labor force. Consequently, immigrant labor has displaced native labor and reduced the wage of continuing native workers. These are the potential economic outcomes that have driven the international migration debate for over 200 years. If no immigration controls were imposed, the destination country's wage rate would fall to W_e, as *fg* immigrants from the perfectly elastic world labor supply find work in the destination at the expense of *fv* native workers.

With *er* migrants, GDP rises from Oyzv to Oyrw. This is the first type of transfer noted above. The area *mzr* (or area B) is an additional return to the non-labor factors of production and is due to the additional workers. The area *nxzm* (area A) demonstrates the position of owners of capital and land regarding immigrants. They favor migration because the return on their assets rises. The diagram indicates that, whereas some groups benefit from migration, others lose, and it reflects the tremendous ambiguity about immigration.

"Economic migrants" presumably gain from migration or they would not voluntarily choose to bear the cost of moving – a cost that involves not only travel expenses, but also separation from family and friends. For those with less than twelve years of schooling, Rosenzweig (2004) reports post-immigration mean US annual earnings of $18,885 compared to pre-immigration, origin-country annual earnings of $11,322 – an annual return almost 60% higher in the USA. Returns to economic migration are shown in Figure 23.2 as *vmrw* (or area C) (less foregone earnings in the origin). Returns to migration from less-developed to more-developed countries are frequently tremendous, as implicitly noted by Rosenzweig.

In Figure 23.2, elasticities of labor demand and of native labor supply are critical in any assessment of the economic consequence of immigration. If labor demand is more elastic, a given increase in immigrant labor supply will cause a smaller decrease in the wage, and less displacement, of native labor. If native labor supply is more elastic, a given increase in immigrant labor supply will cause the wage to fall less, but displacement of native labor would be greater.

Quantifying the redistributions

Much work has been done on labor demand (Hammermesh, 1993) and supply (Killingsworth, 1983) relationships. For the United States, Table 23.1 illustrates the potential magnitudes of some of the possible consequences of immigration. These measures are not presented as exact or even approximate, but only to provide an idea of possible magnitudes. The table uses a range of labor demand and supply elasticities that is realistic in terms of numerous empirical studies of these types of relationships. Because the service sector typically provides nontraded goods and immigrants are known to account for a significant fraction of the jobs in this sector, the service sector is used for illustrative purposes (OECD, 2005, p. 66). Four alternative elasticities of native labor supply are assumed (0.0, 0.5, 1.0, 1.5), along with three elasticities of the wage with respect to an exogenous change in employment (0.5, 1.0, 2.0). These latter elasticities are equivalent to the inverse of the typical labor demand elasticity (respectively, 2.0, 1.0, 0.5). The calculations in Table 23.1 assume a 1% increase in employment due to immigration, although this increase can be greater if immigrants displace natives. Point elasticities are utilized at a starting level of US service employment of 40.457 million (natives and perhaps prior immigrants) and initial average weekly earnings of $455.51 (Jacobs, 2003, pp. 158, 175). These are actual figures for 2000. All values are annualized by assuming a 52-week work year, which inflates the figures, but average hours worked per week in the service sector (32.7) are taken into account.

With perfectly inelastic domestic labor supply, Table 23.1 shows that a 1% increase in employment due to immigration (404,570 jobs) that reduces the weekly wage rate by $2.28 results in a $4.8b transfer from workers to other factors of production (area A in Figure 23.2), which amounts to about 0.5% of original labor income. This transfer increases in proportion to the wage reduction ($9.6b for a 1% reduction of $4.56 per week and $19.2b for a 2% reduction of $9.11 per week). Because domestic labor is supplied perfectly inelastically, no reduction occurs in domestic employment, but domestic workers lose the entire amount of the transfer to the other factors of production.

At the new, lower wage, the migrants earn $9.5b, or 1.0% of labor income. This amount changes little if the wage rate falls by 1% ($9.5b) or by 2% ($9.4b). The triangle labeled B is an efficiency gain that goes to other factors of production. This gain amounts to $24.0m with a wage reduction of $2.28 per week, to $48.0m for a reduction of $4.56, and to $95.8m for a reduction of $9.11. The output due to the immigrants is (B+C) in Figure 23.2, and B as a fraction of (B+C) is 0.25%, 0.5%, and 1.0%, respectively, depending upon the magnitude of the wage reduction.

With a domestic supply elasticity of 0.5, employment of the original workers falls by 101,143, and they lose $2.4b in earnings. These jobs and earnings are assumed go to additional (illegal) migrants, who stand

Table 23.1. *Possible transfers inherent in migration: the US service sector, 2000*

		Elasticity of the wage with respect to the quantity of labor demanded					
		0.5		1.0		2.0	
≈	Area	Dollar Magnitude	Fraction of Original Total	Dollar Magnitude	Fraction of Original Total	Dollar Magnitude	Fraction of Original Total
0	A (1)	$4.797b	0.0050	$9.593b	0.010	$19.165b	0.020
	B (2)	23.983m	0.0025	47.966m	0.005	95.826m	1.010
	C (3)	9.535b	0.0100	9.487b	1.010	9.391b	0.010
	D (4)	—	0.0000	—	0.000	—	0.000
0.5	A (1)	4.797b	0.0050	9.593b	0.010	19.165b	0.020
	B (2)	23.983m	0.0025	47.966m	0.005	95.826m	0.010
	C (3)	9.535b	0.0100	9.487b	0.010	9.391b	0.010
	D (4)	2.384b	0.0025	4.767b	0.005	9.534b	0.010
1.0	A (1)	4.797b	0.0050	9.593b	0.010	19.165b	0.020
	B (2)	23.983m	0.0025	47.966m	0.005	95.826m	0.010
	C (3)	9.535b	0.0100	9.487b	0.010	9.391b	0.010
	D (4)	4.797b	0.0050	9.487b	0.010	18.782b	0.020
1.5	A (1)	4.797b	0.0050	9.593b	0.010	19.165b	0.020
	B (2)	23.983m	0.0025	47.966m	0.005	95.826m	0.010
	C (3)	9.535b	0.0100	9.487b	0.010	9.391b	0.010
	D (4)	7.151b	0.0075	14.230b	0.015	28.174b	0.030

Elasticity of native labor supply

Areas A,B,C, and D refer to Figure 23.2.
1. A/(A+E+D) Transfer from labor to other factors as a fraction of initial labor income.
2. B/(B+C) Efficiency gain to other factors as a fraction of nonreplacement immigrant income.
3. C/(E+D+C) Immigrant income as a fraction of labor income.
4. D/(A+E+D) Lost native income as a fraction of initial labor income.

ready to fill the jobs at any wage. This second group of migrants accounts for 0.25% of labor earnings. With a unitary elastic domestic supply, this wage reduction results in the loss of twice as many jobs (202,285) and twice the earnings ($4.7b). Correspondingly, a 1% reduction in the weekly wage ($4.56) and a unitary elastic domestic supply results in 404,570 jobs lost by domestic workers and $9.5b in lost earnings, which go to the second group of migrants, amounting to 1.0% of labor earnings.

The absolute numbers are substantial. Given that immigrants account for far more than 1% of the US work force and that of many other destination countries, and that wage reductions may correspondingly be much greater than those assumed in Table 23.1, the actual effects of immigrants on natives may be somewhat greater than the illustration suggests. Martin (2004), for example, assumes an overall 3% wage reduction due to immigration. Moreover, in 2000, service employment accounted for 30.7% of total US employment.

The migrants clearly benefit. In Table 23.1, in the case of perfectly inelastic domestic labor supply and a 0.5% decrease in the wage due to a 1% increase in employment due in turn to migration, the migrants enjoy a $9.5b increase in their income. Domestic workers lose $4.8b, but this loss is a transfer to the non-labor factors of production, so domestically the net transfer amounts to nothing. If the migrants own no capital, or if they do and leave it behind, the owners of the non-labor factors of production gain $24.0m that is a net gain to the original residents of the destination country. Although redistributions occur, on net the original residents of the country are better-off.

The above conclusions change dramatically if the supply schedule of the original residents has a positive slope. In the case of a supply elasticity of 0.5, the original workers who remain employed lose 99.75% of the transfer to the non-labor factors of production, plus $2.4b in income that now goes to the illegal migrants. If the migrant gains (now $11.9b = $9.5b + $2.4b) are not taken into account, the original residents are losers because the losses to workers ($2.4b) are far greater than the $24.0m net gain enjoyed by the non-labor factors of production. Only a slight supply response by the original residents is required to offset the net gain of $24.0m that goes to the non-labor factors of production. However, the gains to the illegal migrants and the losses to the original residents exactly offset one another.

The construction sector is another important sector in which illegals participate, at least in the USA. In 2000, the construction sector in the USA had 6.653m jobs and average weekly earnings of $702.68. Many illegal migrants are in agriculture, where wages are somewhat lower. By some estimates, one-half the US agricultural labor force is illegal migrants (Johnson, 2006).

Cost–benefit analysis

A major issue with respect to any cost-benefit analysis of migration regards who enjoys the benefits and who suffers the losses. We have seen that the migrants themselves, along with their employers, benefit from migration. Native workers (and prior migrants) experience losses. Some of the losses borne by native workers are transfers to other factors of production (owners of capital and land, or, generally, employers of the migrants), whereas other losses go to the migrants as native workers suffer job displacement and lower wages. Table 23.2, which is derived from Table 23.1, provides two cost-benefit ratios: (i) areas B and C in Figure 23.2 (gains to the economy as a whole) relative to the losses suffered by native workers (A + D); and (ii) areas D and C (gains to migrant workers) relative to areas A and D (losses to native workers). The first entry in each cell shows for each pair of elasticities the ratio of the net benefit to the economy as a whole to the net cost to native workers. The second entry shows the benefit to migrant labor relative to the cost to native labor. If we assume that wages grow at the same rate as the discount rate (say 3%), there is no need to calculate present values. The figures in Table 23.1 are annual figures, so if future wage increases of 3% were discounted at 3%, the table for future years would be the same in real terms. Higher discount rates would yield lower figures.

The first question is: under what circumstances do the gains to the economy as a whole outweigh the losses to native workers? According to Table 23.2, if labor demand is highly elastic (i.e., 2.0, which yields an elasticity of the wage with respect to the quantity of labor demanded of 0.5) and the elasticity of native labor supply is between zero and unitary elastic, the gains to migrant workers and the owners of the other factors of production outweigh the losses to native labor. The same is true for unitary elastic labor demand and perfectly inelastic labor supply. For all other combinations, the losses to native labor outweigh the gains to the economy as a whole.

Table 23.2. *Possible cost-benefit ratios for gainers (migrant workers and owners of other factors of production) and losers (native workers) due to immigration*

			Elasticity of the wage with respect to the quantity of labor demanded		
		Measure	0.5	1.0	2.0
Elasticity of native labor supply	0	i	2.04	1.04	0.53
		ii	1.99	0.99	0.49
	0.5	i	1.36	0.69	0.36
		ii	1.66	0.99	0.66
	1.0	i	1.02	0.52	0.27
		ii	1.50	0.99	0.74
	1.5	i	0.82	0.42	0.22
		ii	1.40	1.00	0.79

Values in this table are calculated from figures in Table 23.1 and refer to the following ratios from Figure 23.2: i.(B+C)/(A+D); ii.(C+D)/(A+D).

When we look at workers only, the gains to the migrants exceed the losses to native labor (row [ii]) when demand is elastic (an elasticity of labor demand of 2.0, which yields an elasticity of the wage with respect to the quantity of labor demanded of 0.5, as in the first column of Table 23.2). This result is due to the modest decrease in native wages due to the influx of migrants. When labor demand is unitary elastic, the gains to migrants almost exactly offset the losses to native workers. Only when demand is inelastic, and migrant labor therefore results in more significant wage losses to natives, does the migrant gain fail to offset the native loss.

Where does the cost-benefit treatment of Table 23.2 leave us? Under some circumstances the gains to the economy as a whole more than compensate for the losses to native workers, so in theory compensatory payments could be made to the losers by some method of taxing the migrants and making transfers to the native losers. Such taxes on the migrants would reduce their incentive to come and thus reduce the benefits, as well as the costs, of their migration. However, I suggest below a possible payment for a visa and/or the posting of a bond that would have much the same effect as taxing the migrants. Under other circumstances (inelastic labor demand and elastic native labor supply), native workers lose more, often substantially more, than the economy as a whole gains. Under such circumstances, native workers ought to be wary of migrants.

When the analysis focuses on workers only, the cost-benefit ratios suggest that inelastic labor demand (in Table 23.2, the third column of ratios where the elasticity of the wage with respect to the quantity of labor demanded is 2.0) leads to migrant gains that are considerably less than the losses to native workers. Again native workers ought to be wary of migrants.

Caveats and conclusions

The above discussion provides a baseline for thinking about the potential monetary benefits from illegal US migration. However, one of the most troublesome assumptions in Figure 23.2 is that labor is homogeneous (Greenwood and McDowell, 1986). This assumption rules out issues associated with immigration's differing impact on various members of the indigenous labor force. If world-wide international migration is becoming more oriented toward less-educated and less-skilled individuals, the most directly relevant labor demand and labor supply elasticities are those in the low-wage labor market. Thus, the assumption of two or more labor groups makes great sense. Low-skilled migrants may now have the greatest effects on low-skilled indigenous workers for whom they are good labor-market substitutes, but through various channels they could have positive impacts on more-skilled domestic workers.

The production theory channel of immigrant influence discussed above is the most common theoretical approach to studying the economic consequences of immigration, but production theory is only one of many potentially important channels through which immigrant workers affect the wages and employment of native and prior-immigrant workers. Many, but not all, of these channels may offset, at least in part, some of the negative effects of migrants on indigenous workers (Greenwood and Hunt, 1995).

Perhaps the major issue relating to contemporary international migration is border control, or more generally, control of illegal migration. Poverty, unemployment, and risk of non-survival are genuine in many parts of the world, so millions have an incentive to circumvent entry restrictions in developed countries. Information about prospects elsewhere has never been less costly to acquire. Migration flows, once begun, have a self-sustaining character due to information and family and community ties embodied in earlier migrants (Greenwood, 1969; Massey *et al.*, 1993). Thus, millions have strong incentives to move and accept the risks of illegal entry and clandestine living in high-income destinations.

In reality, labor is not homogeneous. In destination countries, less-skilled and less-educated migrants tend to compete for jobs with other less-skilled and less-educated individuals, both natives and prior migrants, for whom they are good labor-market substitutes. Other labor groups, such as those who manage the new workers, those who teach their children, higher-income individuals who employ their services, and generally those who are complements in the labor market, may benefit from the migration. This point is a further illustration that migration involves gainers and losers in the destination. One question involves how society weights the returns to and costs of the gainers and losers. If the gainers were taxed and the losers were compensated, then exchange medium would provide the weights. However, such redistribution never occurs. Taxing relatively poor migrants (the most obvious big winners) is not popular. Employers may pay some additional taxes on their gains. Thus, the issue becomes one of how to weight the losers and the gainers. If the gainers have higher incomes, then they might receive lower weights than those who bear the costs (presumably lower-income persons who are good labor-market substitutes).

In terms of attempting to assess the costs and returns involving illegal migrants, at least two major problems are evident. (1) Do the gains enjoyed by the migrants count? The global distribution of labor resources improves due to the migration, but in terms of winners and losers in the destination, should one of the biggest and most obvious winners – the migrants themselves – be counted? (2) Most analyses of international migration are essentially partial equilibrium exercises.

However, no study accounts for very many of the complex general equilibrium aspects of immigration. Consequently, even if the first issue were resolved, the second prevents an accurate assessment of the true benefits and costs of immigration.

At the time of this writing, the US Congress was considering policies to control illegal migration, as well as methods for dealing with those illegal aliens presently in the USA. Congress appeared to be using an estimate of 12 million illegals currently in the USA, but it also appears to have had little idea of the overall economic impact of this many individuals working in the country. Although the characteristics of the flow of illegal aliens have changed over time, it still remains largely young, less-educated, less-skilled, and in search of work. Suppose that 75% of illegals are employed at the minimum wage (then $5.15 per hour) and that they worked on average thirty-seven hours per week (Bustamante *et al.*, 1998) and fifty weeks per year. These seemingly conservative assumptions yield an estimate of $85.75b per year in labor earnings. Rosenzweig (2004) provides an estimate of the fraction of US earnings that is remitted (0.04), which yields an estimate of $3.43b in remittances, leaving well over $80b circulating in the US economy. Nine million workers would be almost 7% of the 2000 US work force, and $85.75b in earnings would be almost 2.5% of total compensation of employees in 2000. Of course, the numbers connected to illegal workers may have been lower in 2000.

Apart from the fact that one group enters legally whereas the other enters illegally, which is an important distinction in a country that generally adheres to laws, an important distinguishing feature of legal entrants compared to illegal entrants is that the former group is willing to wait for a visa number whereas the latter group demands immediate entry and is willing to consider circumventing the entry requirements of the receiving country. Few efforts have ever been made to consider the "market" for permits to enter a country. Obviously, demand for legal entry to high-income countries exists. The countries themselves control the supply of entry permits (i.e., immigrant visas). However, no "market-clearing" price has ever been established, so it is not surprising that demand exceeds supply at a price that is essentially zero (except for the waiting time for one's visa number to come up).

Entry into the USA and other developed countries is clearly valuable for many individuals from the less-developed parts of the world. According to reports in the popular press, Mexican illegal migrants pay considerable sums to "coyotes" to help them by-pass border control. Estimates run as high as $3,000 to $4,000 per migrant. Presumably, the potential migrants have the funds to pay the coyotes (or expect to earn them in the USA and pay later). Both the US and Canadian governments currently allow individual "investors" to "buy" their way into the countries. One possibility would be for the US government to allow individuals from some Western Hemisphere countries and perhaps elsewhere to "buy" their way in. If each of the presumed 12 million illegal aliens in the USA were to have paid $1,000 each to gain legal entry, $12b would have been received by the US Treasury, some fraction of which would otherwise have gone to the coyotes. Given labor turnover, many more migrants would have come, paid their entry fee, and returned, thus providing significantly more revenues. The other clear gainer from migration (employers) could provide part or all of a one-time, or perhaps an annual, fee for specific migrants they wished to hire. Presumably, the USA would also enjoy significant cost savings by not requiring such intense border control. Might we determine some equilibrium price for such a permit that would equate the demand for low-wage workers with the supply of such workers? Such a program would provide a more market-oriented approach to immigration. A further refinement of this idea would be to have the migrants post a substantial bond on entering the USA. If they depart at a specified time, the bond would be returned in full. If not, they would forfeit the bond (possibly as a rising percentage related to time overdue).

References

Bean, F. D., R. Corona, R. Tuiran, and K. A. Woodrow-Lafield, 1998. The quantification of migration between Mexico and the United States, in *Migration between Mexico and the United States*, Volume I, US Commission on Immigration Reform, Austin: Morgan Printing, 1–89.

Bustamante, J. A., G. Jasso, J. E. Taylor, and P. T. Legarreta, 1998. Characteristics of migrants: Mexicans in the United States, in *Migration between Mexico and the United States*, Volume I, US Commission on Immigration Reform, Austin: Morgan Printing, 91–162.

Espenshade, T. J., 1995. Unauthorized immigration to the United States, *Annual Review of Sociology*, 21, 196–216.

Greenwood, M. J., 1969. An analysis of the determinants of geographic labor mobility in the United States, *Review of Economics and Statistics*, 51 (2), 189–194.

1994. Potential channels of immigrant influence on the economy of the receiving country, *Papers in Regional Science*, **73** (3), 211–240.

Greenwood, M. J. and J. M. McDowell, 1986. The factor market consequences of U.S. immigration, *Journal of Economic Literature*, **24** (4), 1738–1772.

Greenwood, M. J. and G. L. Hunt, 1995. Economic effects of immigrants on native and foreign-born workers: complementarity, substitutability, and other channels of influence, *Southern Economic Journal*, **61** (4), 1076–1097.

Hammermesh, D. S., 1993. *Labor demand*, Princeton: Princeton University Press.

Hanson, G. H., 2006. Illegal migration from Mexico to the United States, *Journal of Economic Literature*, **46** (4), 869–924.

Jacobs, E. E., 2003. *Handbook of U.S. labor statistics*, Lanham: Bernan.

Johnson, H. P., 2006. *Illegal immigration*, Public Policy Institute of California.

Killingsworth, M. R., 1983. *Labor supply*, Cambridge: Cambridge University Press.

Martin, P., 2004. Migration, in B. Lomborg (ed.), *Global crises, global solutions*, Cambridge: Cambridge University Press, 443–477

Massey, D. S., J. Arango, G. Hugo, A. Kouraouci, A. Pellegrino, and J. E. Taylor, 1993. Theories of international migration: a review and appraisal, *Population and Development Review*, **19** (3), 431–466.

Organization for Economic Co-operation and Development, 2005. *Trends in international migration: annual report, 2004 edition*, Paris: OECD.

Rosenzweig, M. R., 2004. Perspectives paper 8.1, in B. Lomborg (ed.), *Global crises, global solutions*, Cambridge: Cambridge University Press, 478–488.

Tapinos, G., 1999. Clandestine immigration: economic issues and political issues, in Organization for Economic Co-operation and Development, *Trends in international migration, Sopemi, 1999 edition*, Paris: OECD, 229–251.

Conclusion: Making Your Own Prioritization

BJØRN LOMBORG

This book has brought together analyses of twenty-three global problems, and proposals for their solution or mitigation. The authors have used economic cost–benefit analysis to provide a coherent framework for evaluation. This approach has been criticized by some people, especially by those who argue that climate change policy should have a higher priority. This is hardly surprising because, when you ask what you should do first, you also have to work out what should have a lower priority, and this inevitably means displeasing some people.

But we have to make choices. Not prioritizing explicitly means we still make choices, we just don't talk as clearly about them. We believe that putting prices on the world's solutions make our decisions better informed. They are still hard, but perhaps we have a sounder basis to get them right. This is not a perfect approach. But, like Winston Churchill's description of democracy, we believe that this is the least bad option. In particular, it gives a common framework of reference for comparing programs which might otherwise seem so far apart that comparison was not possible.

The other big plus of cost–benefit analysis is that it enables you, the reader, to make your own comparisons and judgments. There is no one right answer. Our aim is to encourage debate and to get people to think in a different way about the world's biggest problems. The challenges covered by our contributors have been with us for a long time. In an increasingly prosperous world, we can surely make a difference. Although some of the problems are seemingly still intractable, we now know better what we can do and what we cannot do. The next step is to decide what we should do first.

On the Copenhagen Consensus website, we provide you with the tools to make your own prioritization.

The problems covered in this book come in many guises. Under the general heading of economics, we have financial instability, lack of intellectual property rights, money laundering and subsidies and trade

440

barriers. Many readers may wonder why we should be dealing with such matters when there are other more directly humanitarian challenges. But the authors of these chapters argue we should tackle these problems to provide a productive environment for further development.

Environmental problems – air pollution, climate change, deforestation, land degradation, loss of biodiversity and vulnerability to natural disasters – are challenges many people instinctively regard as high priority. Enormous strides have been made in improving the environment in the developed world, but there are major issues outstanding. Since some degradation may be essentially irreversible – species extinction most certainly is – these problems certainly demand careful consideration.

Arms proliferation, conflict, corruption, lack of education and terrorism are a mixed bag which we have grouped together as governance issues. Arms proliferation, conflict and terrorism cause untold misery for people on a daily basis. Corruption and lack of education hold back societies from reaching their full potential. Solving them could bring great benefits to millions of people, but should they have higher priority than other issues?

Health and population issues form the final subset of problems. These cover illegal drugs, the continuing burden of disease, changing demographics in the industrialized world reducing the working population, the living conditions of women and children, malnutrition and hunger, unsafe water and lack of sanitation and population migration. Some of these – malnutrition and lack of access to safe water supplies, for example – have major impacts on the health of populations, and all of them have a large economic cost. Both these and humanitarian considerations suggest that some or all of these challenges should have a high priority.

As you will have realized while reading this book, no problem is truly a stand-alone one. Many are directly related, and solutions proposed for one may have beneficial effects in other areas. Poor water supplies and air pollution inevitably increase rates of disease, while corruption and money laundering take funds out of normal circulation and weaken efforts to address a whole range of problems. Other connections are less obvious. Lack of access to water reduces the participation of women and children in education and the workforce because they spend many hours a day fetching and carrying.

Now, it's over to you. You have access to the same information as the panel of experts who will choose the ten problems to be thoroughly analyzed in the 2008 Copenhagen Consensus. You are equally capable of making your own choices about the most deserving solutions for our attention. We invite you to visit the website (www.copenhagenconsensus. com) to make your own prioritization of all the twenty-three problems and their solutions, and to tell us what you think.

You may find that you agree with other readers, and you may not. Whatever the outcome, we hope that participating in this process will help you to think about why you have reached a particular decision. There is no single set of "right" answers, but the more viewpoints that we can gather, the better our chances of using our limited resources in the most effective way.